Steamboat
Entertains

Winning Recipes From
Ski Town USA

presented by
The Steamboat Springs
Winter Sports Club

Steamboat Entertains

The Steamboat Springs Winter Sports Club will use proceeds from the sale of
Steamboat Entertains to support ski training programs for Olympic hopefuls.

For additional copies, use the order forms at the back of the book or write:
Steamboat Entertains Cookbook
2155 Resort Drive, Suite 207
Steamboat Springs, CO 80487
Price is $17.95 plus $3.00 shipping per book,
and $1.50 handling per order.
Colorado residents add $.54 sales tax.

ISBN 0-9631010-2-1

printed in the U.S.A. by Eastwood Printing
Denver, Colorado

Graphic Design and Typesetting
Square One
Kathy Keel and Jo Lauter
Steamboat Springs, Colorado

...the winning recipe

Once you experience the beauty and peace of the Yampa Valley, you'll know the truth of the ancient Ute Indian legend that visitors inevitably lose their hearts to this splendid piece of the earth and are never again able to stay away.

Some have called this phenomenon a curse, but to those of us who have the great fortune to live here, it's a blessing...and a most wonderful way of life. Whether it's in the sparkling champagne powder of a winter morning, or the soft alpenglow of a relaxing summer's eve, the magic of Steamboat pervades and prevails.

Every day we feel the "magic" throughout Steamboat's active, family-oriented community. And it's in this spirit that we've tried to share a bit of the Steamboat state-of-mind in the *Steamboat Entertains Cookbook*.

The recipes included were collected from famous ski champions, renowned local chefs, true gourmands, and infamous local cooks. We looked for delicious and imaginative recipes with fresh, quality ingredients ... recipes that would require minimal preparation time to accommodate active, healthy lifestyles. We made sure that those which didn't meet our criteria for relatively quick preparation would be well worth the effort. As we put the final touches to this project, we feel comfortable in saying that these are indeed ... "Winning Recipes from Ski Town U. S. A."

Scattered throughout these pages you'll also find tidbits of local history, whimsical artwork and sketches of Steamboat landmarks to give you a pinch of Western heritage and the aroma of wholesome Rocky Mountain living. All of this combined makes *Steamboat Entertains* a truly unique experience in cooking and collecting.

Sales of this cookbook will benefit the Steamboat Springs Winter Sports Club which offers competitive training programs in Alpine, Nordic and Freestyle skiing. More Olympic athletes have been trained by the Steamboat Springs Winter Sports Club than by any other organization in the United States. And that's how Steamboat earned the title "Ski Town U. S. A."

Steamboat Entertains combines the area's adventurous pioneer spirit and winning tradition of ski champions with the legendary magic of the Yampa River Valley. Join us as we savor the results of this undeniably winning recipe.

Thank You

To The Artists

Carol Perricone

is a corporate and private art consultant who lives with her husband in Denver. She has two grown children and four grandchildren, two of whom are team members of the Winter Sports Club in Steamboat Springs. Carol has been involved with art since the age of 5, and for the past 23 years has worked as a docent at the Denver Art Museum, specializing in children's tours. She is also a council member for the Cultural Facilities District serving metro Denver.

Don Bertrand

immigrated from the bayous of southern Louisiana to Steamboat Springs in 1986. Don has been interested in and involved with cooking since his early childhood. Residents of Steamboat know Don for his involvement with the annual Sizzlin' Chefs Classic, his monthly food column in the *Steamboat Review* and as founder of the Steamboat Culinary Association. And, most have, no doubt, tasted some of his creations in cooking classes or local restaurants. Don presently lends his culinary talents to the In-Season Bakery, Deli & Cafe where he also operates a specialty catering operation "The Guest Chef."

Don's experiences as a chef along with his desire to create art has evolved naturally to food illustration. Don has garnered awards in local art shows and continues to work in mixed media and prisma color, in addition to his varied styles of pen and ink. His art education includes the University of Southwestern Louisiana, University of Colorado at Boulder, and continues with classes at Colorado Mountain College here in Steamboat Springs.

W. C. Matthews, Jr.

is a nationally acclaimed watercolorist whose love of color and understanding of his subject brings the American West to life. Among his many accolades, Matthews has been honored as the featured artist in the prestigious *Southwest Art* magazine.

Born in Manhattan, Matthews was inspired by his grandfather who had an advertising agency in New York City. He studied art at the San Francisco Art Institute and traveled extensively throughout Europe and North America before returning to Colorado where he continues to paint, design and illustrate.

In the early '70s, Matthews lived in Steamboat Springs and forged a bond with the Yampa Valley and its people. His original watercolors of Mt. Werner and Howelsen Hill, which grace the covers of *Steamboat Entertains*, are intimate expressions of life in Steamboat, painted from the heart.

To purchase your copy of one of these prints contact
W. C. Matthews Gallery • 26907 Cold Spring Gulch • Golden, CO 80401 • (303) 526-1696

Thank You

To The Cookbook Committee

Tamara Adams, Co-Chairperson
Mary Kurtz, Co-Chairperson

Chapter Chairpersons

Tamara Adams   Nancy Perricone
Sue Beauregard   Sarah Pruett
Janet Borden   Marne Roberts
Diane DeGroff   Monica Verploeg
Mary Kurtz   Lindsay Yates
Linda Malone

Publicity and Marketing

Diane DeGroff, Marketing
Beverly Glenn, Marketing
Allison Powell, Marketing
Barbi Wither, Special Events

Accounting

Lindsay Yates, Chairperson

Special Thanks to

Robin Allen   Reba Dobell
Meg Bentley   Gael Fetcher
Janet Borden   Becky Little
Robi Chalmers   Doris MacFarland

Special Thanks to

Marilyn Simons   Sue Stambaugh
Diane Newell   Sureva Towler
Leslie Ponrick   Terry VandeVelde
Marne Roberts   Tread of Pioneers Museum
Lisa Saddler   June Buntain, Proofreader

Vicki Wadlington and Richard Anderson of Wimmer Brothers for steering us in the right directions and patiently answering our million and one questions.

W. C. Matthews, Carol Perricone, and Don Bertrand for their beautiful artistic contributions.

1st National Land Company for their donation of office space.

Laura Dirks and the ladies of the Junior League of Denver for their advice and help.

RAC Transport for their donation and for getting the cookbooks over the mountains in rain, sleet, and snow.

Our families who tasted and evaluated endless recipes and donated so much of their family time to this project. Thanks for all of your support and advice ... you are wonderful.

All of the incredible cooks who have donated recipes; we wish we could have used them all. We thank everyone who took the time to share their favorites. You have made this cookbook outstanding.

And finally, we are forever grateful to Kathy Keel and Jo Lauter of Square One for their artistic talent, computer expertise, support and never-ending humor. What a pleasure to work with such wonderful women. Our heartfelt thanks.

Steamboat

a glimpse into the past ...

In Northwestern Colorado, not far from the Continental Divide, the Yampa River Valley and the town of Steamboat Springs lie in peaceful splendor at the foot of the peak once known as Storm Mountain.

The area's first seasonal inhabitants were the nomadic Ute Indians who followed summer and winter game trails through the valley as early as the fourteenth century. Four hundred years later, men like Jim Bridger and Kit Carson found their way into this paradise where they were assisted by friendly Ute and Arapahoe Indians in their explorations of what is now Routt County.

In 1866 Joseph Hahn and two companions found gold in Routt County and in 1870 the county's first settlement was established near their claim. By 1874 mines were operating at International Camp, nicknamed "Bug Town," or Poverty Bar and later named Hahns Peak.

Steamboat Springs' founding father and first permanent settler was James Harvey Crawford who heard about the wonders of the Yampa Valley while on a hunting trip along the Gore Trail in the fall of 1874. The following July, Crawford brought his family to Steamboat Springs and built the first cabin on the banks of Soda Creek.

Stories about the area spread and by the fall of 1875, five other families had built cabins around the springs. But transportation problems and fear of local Indians kept growth slow; and when James Crawford opened Steamboat's first post office in 1879, the town was still the home of less than a dozen families.

With his wife, Margaret, the Missouri-born Crawford carved out a home in the big valley at the bend in the river. During the town's early years, the Crawford cabin hosted everything from a polling place for Presidential elections to Routt County's first school. Homesteaders found hospitality at the cabin where the Crawfords' oldest daughter, Lulie, kept a diary noting their visits and chronicling the day-to-day life of her pioneer family. Quotes from that diary are sprinkled throughout the pages of this cookbook.

Though the Crawfords and their neighbors had a few cattle, the first significant herds were brought into Routt County in 1871 by George Baggs. From 1880 to 1920 cattle were the mainstay of Routt County's economy. But "war" between cattle and sheep men broke out in 1899 and eventually this dissension combined with other economic factors to destroy the big cattle outfits that had once prevailed. Smaller ranches have since replaced the vast holdings and today the cattle industry remains an integral part of the county's economy. Cattle still graze the mountain meadows in summer and, in winter, thrive on hay raised in the rich Yampa and Elk River Valleys.

Today, although Steamboat's principal industry is tourism, the ranching and mining that have carried this town through the years are still its backbone. And the friendly, hometown atmosphere for which Steamboat is so well known is based upon the solid and enduring values of a long established community.

Steamboat

... and the town's skiing history

The ski was Steamboat's earliest form of individual winter transportation. Early day skis, which measured three to four inches wide and eight to twelve feet long, were usually homemade from hickory, white pine or spruce boards. The boards were secured by a toe and sometimes a heel strap. A single pole was used as a brace, a rudder, and to drag between the legs to reduce speed.

Until the late 1880's, when a horse-drawn sled began providing mail service, mail carriers skied to a cabin on Morrison Creek to meet their counterparts who came from Rock Creek. Among the first of Routt County's mail carriers were George Wren, Elmer Brooks, Sr. and a fellow by the name of "Old Man Moon" for whom Moon Hill was named. (Be sure to look for the adventures of "Mr. Moon" in the pages ahead.)

In her diary, Lulie Crawford gives us a glimpse of the perils faced by those early day mailmen: Saturday, January 1, 1881: *"It has been snowing all day, but now the stars are shining. Dave came in with the mail. He brought bad news. One of the mail carriers is lost and hasn't been seen or heard of since last Tuesday. Was lost in that dreadful hard storm. Poor fellow!"*

Tuesday, January 4, 1881: *"Good news, yes, just splendid. The mail carrier is found (or rather found himself) and came in to Rock Creek cabin but is now at the Middle Station (on Morrison Creek). His feet are badly frozen, so Dave says, who has come from there with the mail today and got in here real early, too. I am so glad that man is found. They are going to try to bring him down to George's or here."*

In the early 1900s, the same hardy settlers who battled severe winters just to survive, turned the hills of Routt County into a winter playground. Carl Howelsen, winner of 13 medals in Norway by the time he was 26, arrived in Steamboat

Springs in 1912. Within a year after the young Norwegian stonemason began ski jumping off a wooden platform in Strawberry Park, skiing had become a popular sport.

Local youngsters, challenged as they watched Howelsen jump, started building small jumps on every hill in town. Beginning in the winter of 1913, high school students were excused from classes to participate in the jumping lessons given by Howelsen on Woodchuck Hill (present site of CMC). In 1914, the first Winter Carnival and jumping competitions were organized.

The Steamboat Springs Winter Sports Club was founded in 1915. The first official ski club west of the Mississippi, this organization was established expressly to promote the annual Winter Carnival. During the 1917 Winter Carnival, the town honored the man who brought recreational skiing to the area by naming Steamboat's first official ski slope Howelsen Hill.

It didn't take long for adventurous downhillers to try their wings on hills other than Howelsen. As soon as Rabbit Ears Pass Road opened to winter traffic, skiers began to make runs down the back slopes of the pass to its base. Devil's Hangover, a favorite ski trail, was cut by WPA crews in the early 1930s. It provided a downhill course from the gentle slopes of the west summit to a steep drop near the Valley View Lodge, now the Timbers. During the mid 1930s several Winter Carnival races were held on this run.

Development of a second official ski area at the base of the 10,600 foot Storm Mountain was spearheaded in 1955 by Jim Temple, son of an early ranching family. Engineered and largely constructed by John R. Fetcher, the new hill opened in 1962. The mountain was renamed Mt. Werner in 1965 in honor of Steamboat's Buddy Werner, who was killed in an avalanche in Switzerland while filming a ski movie.

Thank You to our Contributors

John Adams
Tammy Adams
Eileen Allen
Susie Allen
Kirsten Ames
Robert Ames
Diane Anderson
Robin Anderson
Tommy Anno
Carolyn Arithson
Patti Asbury
Suzanne Ascher
Tracy Barnett
Allie Barr
Jim Moose Barrows
Maurine Barrows
Elva Basden
Shirley Beal
Millie Beall
John Beaupre
Sue Beauregard
Karen Beauvais
Susan Behler
Vikki Behrens
Jane Bennett
Sue Bennett
Meg Bentley
Evlyn Berge
Maren Berge
Moran Berge
Peggy Berglund
Don Bertrand
Marguerite Bieber
Madge Bishop
Eleanor Bliss
Cherie Blomquist
Janet Borden
Marie Bowes
Clara Bradley
Olive Brollier
Mary Burman
Jean-Marie Button
Adele Carlson
Paula Cooper-Black
Linda Corkadel
Priscilla Craig
Marv Crawford
Morris Darling
William Davis
Barbara Day
Annie DeGroff
Diane DeGroff
Edward DeGroff
Joanie De La Garza
Barbara DeVries

Reba Dobell
Patty Duke
Patty Early
Raeanna Ellis
Kitty Ellison
Kay Erley
Kathy Evans
Peggy Fancler
Bridget Ferguson
Clarissa Fetcher
Gael Fetcher
Shirlee Finney
Tim Fisher
Penny Fletcher
Michael Fragola
Kjersten Fulton
Sara Gagen
Kathy Gayer
Suzanne Golub
Bettina Grandey
Virginia Grillo
Diane Halvorson
Susan Hansen-Buccino
Rebecca Hicks
Bill Hill
Ellen Hill
Dara Hoffman
Morton Hoj
Suzy Holloran
JoAnne Hough
Liese Hottenroth
Sandra Iamartino
Sandy Jenny
Karen Jimmerson
Kimberly Jones
Mitzi Kaminski
Betty Kaplan
Hank Kashiwa
Jacquelyn Kaster
Kerry Kaster
Nancy Kern
Billy Kidd
Joel Kunkle
Antonia Klohr
Kathleen Knaus
Nancy Kramer
Peggy Kuntz
Alma Kurtz
Mary Kurtz
Melrose Kuusinen
Terry Lawler Usry
Gail Lefors
Alice Lewis
Janet Liefer
Dale Link

Lynne Litzau
Jeanne Lodwick
Betty Lorenz
Jackie Loughridge
Marylen Lyons
Sue MacCarthy
Bonnie Madderom
Cindy Maddox
Linda Malone
Winnie Marcum
Nanny Marno
Marian Marti
Kimberly Martinez
Marilyn McCaulley
Lora McGinn
Cheryl McKenzie
Marilyn Menten
Ruth Ann Mewborn
Marybeth Bradfield
Mac Moore
Mabel Mortensen
Nancy Mucklow
Dina Murray
Clyde Nelson
David Nelson
Diane Newell
Rebecca Nickle
Mary Beth Norris
Monica Olson
Geoff Pay
Roberta Pay
Rosemary Pearson
Marit Perkins
Carol Perricone
Nancy Perricone
Anne Pielstick
Roy Powell
Sarah Pruett
Roger Reynolds
Paula Rhoadarmer
Joe Rife
John Ritter
Marne Roberts
Jeanne Rohrbaugh
Jane Romberg Pollack
Robin Romick
Ann Root
Barb Ross
Gail Schisler
Anne Severson
Vicki Sharp
Terry Sherrill
Norma Shettle
Elizabeth Skinner
Charles Smith

Ranene Smith
Tammie Smith
Mike Smith
Barb Smith
Dixie Soots
Nancy Spillane
Susan Stearns
Dona Steele
Sheri Stephens
Arianthé Stettner
Ilene Stevenson
Tomas Stone
Anne Taylor
Kathleen Thayer
Marybeth Thompson
Jerry Thornton
Karen Thurber
Terry Tifft
Sheri Townes
Judy Travis
Betty Usilton
Ruth Valdick
Don Valentine
Terry VandeVelde
Monica Verploeg
Doak Walker
Skeeter Werner Walker
Cameron L. Warkentin
Imogene Waugh
Karyl Webb
Hazie Werner
Loris Werner
Laurie Weston
Sue Whallon
Betsy White
Esther Whittemore
Linda Alyce Whittle
Pat Whittle
Paul Wegeman
Cathy Wiedemer
Stacey Wiese
Sven Wiik
Barb Williams
Holly Williams
Molly Beaudin Wilson
Ellen Winchell
Annabel Wither
Barbi Wither
Candy Wither
Frances Wither
Trish Woodruff
Lorene Workman
Gordon Wren
Eliza Yeager
Diana Yeager
Andy Zuercher

A sincere thank you to all who have donated recipes. We apologize to anyone who was inadvertently omitted due to the big paper shuffle. We truly appreciate your time, creativity and effort.

and Testers

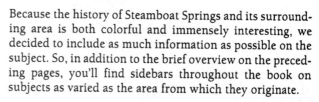

And By the Way about those Sidebars

Tamara Adams
Susie Allen
Suzanne Ascher
Allie Barr
Tracy Barnett
Sue Beauregard
Cherie Blomquist
Janet Borden
Jean-Marie Button
Dee Chedister
Diane DeGroff
Gael Fetcher
Michael Fragola
Beverly Glenn
Christine Kadlub
Antonia Klohr
Mary Kurtz
Janet Liefer
Lynne Litzau
Bonnie Madderom
Linda Malone
Laura McGinn
Nancy Perricone
Dan Phelan

Judy Phelan
Anne Pielstick
Allison Powell
Sarah Pruett
Roger Reynolds
Marne Roberts
Michael Roberts
Barb Ross
Anne Severson
Mike & Barb Smith
Tomas Stone
Kathy Thayer
Karen Thurbe
Terry Tifft
Terry VandeVelde
Monica Verploeg
Julie Walsh
Barbi Wither
Cindy Wither
Trish Woodruff
Susan Wykstra
Lindsay Yates
Eliza Yeager
Diana Yeager

Because the history of Steamboat Springs and its surrounding area is both colorful and immensely interesting, we decided to include as much information as possible on the subject. So, in addition to the brief overview on the preceding pages, you'll find sidebars throughout the book on subjects as varied as the area from which they originate.

We've inserted short pieces on everything from pioneer life to Olympic ski competition, from landmarks to historic events. These references are in no particular order, so you'll just have to browse. And no matter what your particular area of interest, we think you'll enjoy this glimpse into Steamboat's past.

Among those segments that were the most enjoyable to compile were the quotes from *The Diary of Lulie Margie Crawford, A Little Girl's View of Life in the Old West 1880-1881.* Edited by Lulie's daughter, Lulita Crawford Pritchett, *The Diary* offers wonderful insight into the joys and the hardships of Steamboat's pioneer days. We hope you have as much fun with this part of the book as we did.

We would like to thank the Tread of Pioneers Museum for sharing the historical information and allowing us to use it throughout this book. Should the sidebars whet your appetite and make you anxious for more information, the books we used are all available at the Museum. They are: *The Diary of Lulie Margie Crawford* and *The Historical Guide to Routt County.*

The background on Olympians was gathered from Sureva Towler's *The History of Skiing at Steamboat Springs;* we thank her for her expert contributions.

Thanks for joining us! All proceeds from the sale of *Steamboat Entertains* will help Steamboat Springs Winter Sports Club athletes go for the gold!

...and those Symbols

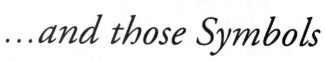

"Quick" Clock
A recipe that can be made very quickly.

"Healthy" Skier
A recipe with healthy ingredients.

"Make-Ahead" Jar
A recipe that can easily be made ahead of time.

Table of Contents

*A*ppetizers

Appetizers

Alligator Eye	13	15	Hot Lobster Dip
Antipasta	25	24	Italiano Pickled Garden
Arianthé's Greek Appetizer	20	20	Lox Cheesecake
Artichoke Stuffed Mushrooms	28	18	Marinated Mozzarella Bites
Asparagus Rolls	28	14	Mexicana Chip Dip
Authentic Mexican Salsa	15	23	Mexicana Tartare
Baba Ghanouj	14	21	Mushroom and Liver Pâté
Baked Brie with Lingonberries	19	13	Negro Frijole Dip
Beach House Oysters	32	14	Oriental Creamy Dip
Caponata	18	29	Pagoda Dumplings
Catamount Caviar	15	29	Pheasant Kabob Appetizers
Ceviche	23	17	Picadillo Dip
Char Su Ribs	30	22	Rainbow Trout Pâté
Chili Con Queso	17	30	Red Park Spareribs
Chili Con Queso Dip	17	31	Sand Mountain Stuffed Puffs
Christie Chicken Pâté	21	24	Sesame Marinated Shrimp
Country Cheese Ring	19	31	Shrimp Puffs
Crab Cream Cheese Spread	16	22	Snake River Salmon Pâté
Crab Rangoons	32	26	Spanakopeta
Crab Stuffed Mushrooms	29	16	Spicy Shrimp and Artichoke Dip
East Indian Cheese Ball	19	26	Summer Pizza
Green Chile Canapés	24	27	Sun Dried Tomato Tartlets
Hahns Peak Salmon Spread	15	22	Tuna Tartare
Herbed Stuffed Snow Peas	25	13	Under the Sea Dip
Hot Artichoke Dip	16	30	Valentine's Brajoles
Hot Chili Mushrooms	25	32	Wrapped Shrimp Appetizer

Alligator Eye

2 large tomatoes, chopped
1 bunch green onions, chopped
13 oz. can chopped black olives
7 oz. can chopped green chilies
½ - ¾ cup medium hot salsa
3 Tbsp. salad oil
2 Tbsp. apple cider vinegar

Combine all ingredients and mix well. Chill for at least 6 hours before serving. A great alternative to salsa. A must for olive lovers!

Negro Frijole Dip

15 oz. can black beans
1 large tomato, quartered
½ red bell pepper, quartered
½ red onion, quartered
1 clove elephant garlic, minced
1-2 jalapeño peppers, seeded and quartered
1 tomatillo, husked and washed
2 Tbsp. cilantro, minced
⅛-¼ tsp. cumin
⅛-¼ tsp. cayenne pepper
salt to taste

Process all ingredients in a food processor until smooth. Garnish with more chopped red onion and minced cilantro. Serve with tortilla chips, black bean chips, sunflower seeds, jicama sticks or assorted fresh vegetables.

The first settler in Steamboat Springs was a Missourian named James H. Crawford, who arrived in 1875.

Excerpts from the diary of his daughter Lulie—who was just 9 years old when the family moved to Steamboat—appear throughout this book.

Under the Sea Dip

2 - 8 oz. cans crabmeat
½ lb. shrimp
2 - 8 oz. pkgs. cream cheese
1 cup mayonnaise
1 white onion, minced
2 tsp. minced parsley
scallion slices (garnish)

Blend together cream cheese and mayonnaise. Add remaining ingredients. Mix well and chill. Garnish with scallion slices. Serve with crackers or Stoned Wheat Thins. Best if prepared a day ahead to enhance flavor.

Oriental Creamy Dip

10 oz. soft tofu
2 Tbsp. red miso
1 ½ tsp. peanut butter
1 Tbsp. tahini
1 tsp. sesame chile oil
6 cloves garlic, minced
2 Tbsp. fresh grated ginger
2 dashes cayenne pepper
1 Tbsp. white vinegar
2 Tbsp. lemon juice
3 Tbsp. soy sauce

Blend all ingredients together in blender or food processor. Serve with fresh vegetables. Yields 1 cup dip.

Hahns Peak was once a booming gold town and the county seat. It was named after Joseph Hahn, a German, who led a party of prospectors to the area.

Baba Ghanouj

This is high in protein and nutritious.

1 medium eggplant, baked and peeled
3 Tbsp. sesame oil
juice of 2 lemons
2 cloves garlic, chopped
1 tsp. salt
water

Blend all ingredients in blender, adding enough water to reach desired consistency. Serve with favorite crackers or pita bread. Garnish with parsley and lemon slices.

Mexicana Chip Dip

An easy, colorful dip

16 oz. can refried beans with green chilies
1 cup sour cream
1 pkg. taco mix
2 avocados, mashed
¼ cup minced cilantro
1 cup sliced black olives
1 cup grated Cheddar cheese
1 cup sliced green onions

Layer ingredients as listed in a shallow oval dish, with beans on the bottom and top with green onions. Serve with tortilla chips.

Authentic Mexican Salsa

4 tomatoes, diced
1 medium onion, finely diced
3 - 4 jalapeño peppers, finely diced
garlic salt, to taste

Mix all ingredients well and chill until use.
*Minced cilantro or lime juice may be added for a variation.

Hahns Peak Salmon Spread

1 15 oz. can salmon, drained and cleaned
8 oz. pkg. cream cheese
½ cup sliced black olives
4-6 green onions, sliced

In a food processor, purée the salmon and cream cheese until fluffy.
Fold in black olives and green onions. Serve with vegetables and/or
crackers.

Catamount Caviar

12 hard boiled eggs, chopped
1 cup mayonnaise
1 pint sour cream
1 red onion, finely chopped
2 jars small black caviar

Mix together eggs and mayonnaise, add more mayonnaise if needed to
hold together well. Form into a dome; cover with sour cream. Sprinkle
onions over the sour cream and caviar over the onions. Serve with
melba toast.

Hot Lobster Dip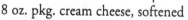

8 oz. pkg. cream cheese, softened
¼ cup mayonnaise
1 clove garlic, minced
2 tsp. onion, grated
1 tsp. prepared mustard
1 tsp. sugar
⅛ tsp. white pepper
1 cup lobster, flaked
3 Tbsp. Sauterne or dry white wine

*Hahns Peak was
the county seat
from 1879 to
1915, at which
time it was moved
to Steamboat
Springs.*

Mix together first 7 ingredients in a large saucepan. Stir in lobster and
Sauterne. Heat thoroughly. Serve with melba toast or crackers.

Spicy Shrimp & Artichoke Dip

This is a great combination of flavors!

14 oz. can artichoke hearts
6 oz. pkg. tiny frozen shrimp, thawed, cooked and squeezed dry
3 oz. pkg. cream cheese, softened
½ cup mayonnaise
½ cup salsa
⅓ cup grated Parmesan cheese
red pepper, cut into julienne strips
green onion tops, thinly sliced

Drain, rinse and chop artichoke hearts and place in a large mixing bowl. Add shrimp, cream cheese, mayonnaise, salsa and Parmesan cheese. Mix well. Spoon into a 9" pie plate or shallow baking dish. Bake at 350° for 20 minutes. Garnish with red peppers and green onion. Serve with tortilla chips or vegetable dippers.

Hot Artichoke Dip

A perfect dip for "last-minute" entertaining.

2 cups artichoke hearts
1 cup mayonnaise
1 cup grated Parmesan cheese
dash garlic salt
dash Worcestershire sauce

Drain artichoke hearts. Blend all ingredients well. Pour into a casserole dish, cover, and bake at 350° for 15 minutes or until bubbly. Serve with Bremer Wafers or Stoned Wheat Thins.

Crab Cream Cheese Spread

Make the night before and cook before serving.

2 - 8 oz. pkgs. cream cheese, softened
2 tsp. horseradish (or more to taste)
1 Tbsp. milk
6 oz. pkg. frozen crabmeat, thawed
¼ cup grated onion
sliced almonds

Blend cream cheese, horseradish and milk together. Add crabmeat and onion. Mix well. Pour into a 1 quart casserole dish. Garnish with sliced almonds. Bake at 350° for 20 minutes or until bubbly. Serve warm with crackers. Serves 10-12.

Picadillo Dip
An unusual blend of flavors.

1 lb. ground beef
1 small onion, chopped
¾ cup pimiento
4 oz. chopped black olives
1 cup golden raisins
10 oz. tomato and green chilies
1 lb. Velveeta cheese
2 -3 cloves garlic
¾ tsp. oregano
¾ cup slivered almonds, toasted

Brown beef in a large skillet, drain. Add remaining ingredients and simmer, stirring frequently, for ½ hour or more. Serve hot in a chafing dish with tortilla chips.

Chili Con Queso Dip
A great warm-up dip for après skil

1 Tbsp. olive oil
½ lb. lean pork, cubed in bite size pieces
2 large cloves garlic, pressed
1 large onion, chopped
2 - 15 oz. cans Mexican stewed tomatoes
2 Tbsp. flour
¼ cup evaporated milk, undiluted
2-3 - 7 oz. cans chopped green chilies
1 lb. Monterey Jack cheese, coarsely grated
½-1 tsp. chili pepper (opt.)

Sauté pork in oil until brown and remove from fat. Leave enough fat to sauté garlic and onion. Add tomatoes and simmer until liquid is slightly reduced and mixture is thickened. Make paste of flour and milk and stir into tomato mixture. Add chopped green chilies and pork. Add cheese shortly before serving. Keep warm in a chafing dish. Serve with tortilla chips or crackers.

Chili Con Queso
Also a great sauce for vegetables.

½ qt. half and half
¼ lb. American cheese, cubed
¾ cup salsa

Heat half and half in double boiler. Add cheese until mixture thickens. Add salsa. Serves 6-8.

Caponata

An outstanding Italian dish--wonderful with good wine and toasted baguette slices.

1 large eggplant, cut in ½" cubes
½ cup olive oil
2 medium onions, diced
1 cup diced celery
1 lb. Italian tomatoes, chopped
⅓ cup wine vinegar
1 Tbsp. sugar
2 tsp. salt
¼ tsp. pepper
3 dashes cayenne
1 clove garlic, minced
1 - 4 oz. can sliced black olives
1 Tbsp. capers and 1 tsp. caper juice
2 Tbsp. pine nuts
juice of 1 lemon
Toasted baguette slices or melba toast

Sauté eggplant in ¼ cup oil until it changes color slightly. In remaining oil, sauté onions, celery and tomatoes; simmer 15 minutes until sauce is reduced and thickened. Stir in vinegar, sugar, salt, pepper, cayenne, garlic and eggplant. Cook, covered, for 10 minutes. Add olives, capers and juice, and nuts; cook, uncovered, 10 minutes. Add lemon juice and chill. Best if made 1 day ahead. May store in refrigerator 2 weeks or freeze.

Marinated Mozzarella Bites

A creative, multi-use dish... keeps well in the fridge.

3 cloves garlic, minced
2 cups olive oil
2 Tbsp. red wine vinegar
2 tsp. dried basil
¼ tsp. crushed red pepper
2 Tbsp. capers, drained (opt.)
10 oz. pkg. string cheese, cut into ¾" chunks
1 small green pepper, cut into ½" pieces
½ medium onion, thinly sliced

Combine garlic, olive oil, vinegar, basil, red pepper and capers and mix well. In a quart jar, layer the cheese, pepper and onion. Pour the oil and spice mixture over. Screw top down and refrigerate. This should be prepared 1-2 weeks ahead of time. Serve alone as an appetizer or lunch dish by topping French bread with the cheese, some vegetables and oil mixture. Broil and serve. It can also be served as an addition to mixed greens for a salad. Keeps refrigerated up to 1 month.

Baked Brie with Lingonberries

1 4-5" round of Brie
1 ½ - 2 Tbsp. confectioners sugar
½ cup sliced almonds
¾ cup Lingonberry Sauce

Place Brie on an ovenproof serving dish. Top with powdered sugar and almonds. Bake at 400° until Brie is warm and soft, but not runny. Remove from the oven and top with the Lingonberry Sauce. Return to the oven for a couple of minutes to warm the sauce. Serve with Carrs Water Crackers.

Country Cheese Ring

16 ozs. sharp Cheddar cheese, grated
1 cup chopped pecans
¾ cup mayonnaise
1 medium onion, grated
1 clove garlic, pressed
½ tsp. Tabasco sauce
1 cup strawberry preserves

Combine all ingredients except preserves; mix well. Pour into ring mold and chill until firm. Remove and fill center with preserves. Serve with favorite crackers.

Only after the railroad arrived in Wolcott in 1888 were stage and freight lines established from Steamboat Springs over Yellow Jacket Pass to Yampa, Toponas and McCoy and finally into Wolcott. Until the railroad reached Steamboat almost 20 years later, this was the major access to Routt County.

East Indian Cheese Ball

A unique and tantalizing combination of flavors.

11 ozs. cream cheese, softened
½ cup cottage cheese
½ cup finely chopped green onions, tops only
½ cup peanuts
½ cup raisins
½ cup coconut
½ tsp. curry powder
chutney

In a medium bowl, combine all ingredients except chutney; mix well. Form into 2 balls and wrap in waxed paper. Chill. To serve, place on a platter, cover with chutney and surround with crackers.

Arianthé's Greek Appetizer

So easy and so good!

1 block Feta cheese
olive oil
Greek oregano
Greek peppers
Greek olives
pita bread, sliced into triangles

Place the cheese on a serving dish. Drizzle oil generously over the cheese. Sprinkle with oregano. Serve with peppers, olives and pita bread slices. Serves 6.

"I packed my diary in the trunks and they didn't come on here so I have to write back. Had a dreadful time coming. A car broke down and delayed us in Louisville a long time and our baggage won't come until tomorrow noon.

The stagecoach was so crowded that we didn't go today and have to wait until Thurs. Pa got me a pair of boy's shoes. Won't I have fine times fishing! Our trunks came. Mr. Yates has decided to go with us."

From the diary of
Lulie Margie Crawford
August 17, 1880

Lox Cheesecake

Earned rave reviews at a tasting party!

1 lb. cream cheese, softened
2 eggs
several dashes red pepper sauce
1 Tbsp. capers
1 Tbsp. grated or finely minced red onion
fresh dill to taste
1 ½ tsp. grated lemon rind
½ lb. smoked salmon or Gravlax
1 cup sour cream
1 Tbsp. sugar
2-3 dashes red pepper sauce
mustard dill sauce (recipe follows)

Mix cream cheese and spices; add 1 egg at a time. In layers, spread ⅓ of mixture in bottom of 7" springform pan sprayed with non-stick vegetable spray. Layer salmon on top. Repeat 1 more time and finish with cream cheese mixture on top. Bake at 325° for 35-40 minutes or until center is puffed and firm to the touch. Remove from oven; let center settle. Mix sour cream, sugar and red pepper sauce on top. Bake at 375° for 5 minutes. Serve with mustard dill sauce, extra capers and red onions. Best if refrigerated 1-2 days before serving. Serves 15 - 20.

Mustard Dill Sauce
½ cup brown sugar
½ cup Guldens mustard
¼ cup fresh dill or 2 tsp. dried dill

Blend well over low heat. May be served chilled or hot.

Christie Chicken Pâté

¼ cup butter
1 medium onion, sliced
3 whole chicken breasts, boned, skinned and cut into small pieces
1 cup tawny port wine
3 oz. pkg. cream cheese, softened
2 Tbsp. heavy cream
1 ¼ tsp. crumbled tarragon
1 tsp. salt or to taste
¼ tsp. pepper
2 ¾ ozs. slivered almonds, toasted
paprika
assorted crackers

Melt butter. Add onion and chicken. Sauté over moderate heat, about 8 minutes. Add ½ cup of the wine. Bring to a boil. Cook over medium heat, until liquid is reduced to about half. Purée mixture in a blender or food processor. Break cheese in small pieces. Add cheese, cream, tarragon, salt, pepper and remaining wine. Mix until smooth. Add almonds, reserving some for garnish. Firmly pack pâté into decorative crock. Refrigerate, covered, 1-2 days before serving. Garnish with reserved almonds and paprika. Serve on crackers.

Mushroom and Liver Pâté

1 Tbsp. unflavored gelatin
¼ lb. chicken livers
cognac
3 slices uncooked bacon, chopped
3 Tbsp. unsalted butter
½ lb. mushrooms, coarsely chopped
⅓ cup onion, coarsely chopped
¼ lb cream cheese, softened

Cover chicken livers in cognac and soak for 30 minutes. Meanwhile, dissolve gelatin in 2 Tbsp. cognac. Sauté bacon until crisp, remove, drain and discard fat. Add butter to pan and sauté drained chicken livers, mushrooms and onions until livers are no longer pink. Blend liver mixture in food processor, add bacon pieces. Cream the cheese and gelatin, blend until smooth and add to food processor. Pour in mold and refrigerate overnight. To serve, bring to room temperature and invert onto a platter. Serve with crackers or bread rounds.

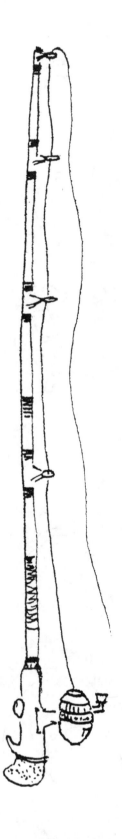

Rainbow Trout Pâté

1 rainbow trout, cleaned, leaving the head and tail intact
½ cup dry white wine
¼ cup plus 2 Tbsp. unsalted butter, softened
1 Tbsp. fresh lemon juice, or to taste
¼ cup heavy cream
melba toast

Put the trout and the wine in a buttered heavy skillet. Bring the wine to a simmer, covered, and cook the trout at a bare simmer, for 10 minutes, or until it just flakes when tested. Let the trout cool in the liquid, uncovered. Transfer to a cutting board, reserving the liquid in the skillet, and discard the skin and bones. Reduce the liquid in the skillet over moderately high heat to about 1 Tbsp. In a bowl with an electric mixer, cream ¼ cup of butter. Beat in the reduced fish liquid and the trout, a little at a time. Beat in the lemon juice, add the cream in a stream, beating the mixture until it is light and fluffy. Season with salt and pepper. Transfer to a 2 cup terrine or bowl, and smooth the top. In a small saucepan, melt the remaining 2 Tbsp. butter, pour it over the pâté, and chill for at least 2 hours, or until the butter is hard. The pâté keeps, chilled, for up to 1 week. Serve the pâté with melba toast. Makes about 2 cups.

Snake River Salmon Pâté

½ lb. fresh salmon fillet
1 ½ tsp. olive oil
1 Tbsp. lemon juice
1 Tbsp. shallots, chopped
1 Tbsp. basil or other fresh herb
2 Tbsp. sour cream
½ tsp. salt

Poach the salmon fillet and cool. In a food processor, combine all the ingredients. Process until light and well blended. Serve with thin slices of cocktail rye bread. Serves 4-6.

Tuna Tartare

1 lb. fresh tuna
4 shallots, finely chopped
2-3 jalapeños, finely chopped
2 serrano chiles, finally chopped
1 bunch cilantro, chopped
2 egg yolks
1 Tbsp. extra virgin olive oil
2 Tbsp. lime juice
2-3 Tbsp. capers, drained
salt and pepper to taste

Chop tuna by hand or in a food processor, being careful not to over process. Fold in all remaining ingredients. Serve with tortilla chips or melba toast.

Mexicana Tartare

6 dried red chilies
¼ red onion, finely minced
1 ½ cups fresh lime juice
1 lb. very fresh beef tenderloin, trimmed and finely minced
⅓ cup extra virgin olive oil
½ cup loosely packed fresh cilantro leaves
½ red pepper
2 medium tomatoes, finely diced
1 jalapeño pepper
½ tsp. salt
8 Romaine lettuce leaves, trimmed and thickly sliced
25 - 2 ½" round crisp corn tortilla chips
fresh cilantro leaves (garnish)

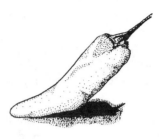

Place chilies in large shallow bowl. Cover with boiling water.
Weight chilies with plate to keep submerged. Let soak 30 minutes.
Drain chilies well; stem. Purée chilies with lime juice until smooth.
Place meat in large shallow glass dish. Pour chili mixture over
meat, adding more lime juice if necessary to cover completely. Stir
in minced onion. Cover dish with plastic, pressing plastic directly
onto surface of meat. Refrigerate until meat is no longer pink,
about 4 hours. Combine olive oil and cilantro in work bowl and
process until cilantro is minced. Drain meat in fine sieve, pressing
lightly to remove excess lime juice. Return meat to dish. Stir in
cilantro mixture, tomatoes and salt. Adjust seasoning. Line large
platter with lettuce. Using slotted spoon, mound some of ceviche
onto each tortilla chip. Arrange chips atop lettuce. Garnish with
cilantro. Serve immediately.

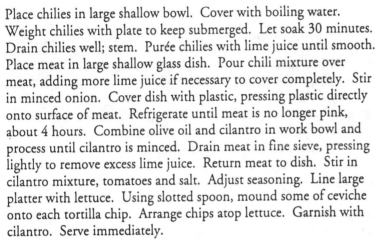

Ceviche

Looks great in a bowl lined with red leaf lettuce.

1 lb. bay scallops or shrimp
¾ cup fresh lime juice
⅓ cup freshly diced yellow pepper
⅓ cup finely diced sweet red pepper
⅓ cup chopped green onions
2 avocados, peeled and diced
1-2 fresh jalapeños, minced
¼ cup chopped cilantro leaves
1 Tbsp. extra virgin olive oil
salt to taste

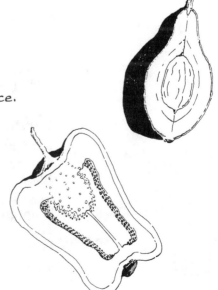

Marinate scallops in lime juice 3-4 hours. Drain and toss with
remaining ingredients. Serve with tortilla chips.

Sesame Marinated Shrimp

½ cup extra virgin olive oil
2 Tbsp. sesame oil
2 cloves garlic, minced
1 tsp. soy sauce
1 lb. medium size shrimp (30-32 ct.), shelled and deveined
1 Tbsp. parsley, finely minced

Combine oils, garlic and soy sauce in a zip lock bag or a shallow dish. Add shrimp, toss to coat with marinade. Seal tightly and refrigerate at least 4 hours, or up to 24 hours. Place shrimp in shallow baking dish and sprinkle with parsley. Bake, uncovered, at 375° for 10 minutes or until shrimp turn pink. Serve hot with wooden toothpicks.

Italiano Pickled Garden

Often found on traditional Italian antipasto plates.

½ small head cauliflower, cut into small flowerets
2 carrots, quartered and cut into 2" pieces
2 celery stalks, cut into 1" strips
1 red or yellow bell pepper, seeded and cut into 2" strips
1 green pepper, seeded and cut into 2" strips
3 oz. jar stuffed pitted green olives with oil
¾ cup olive or salad oil
2 Tbsp. sugar
1 tsp. salt
1 tsp. oregano
½ tsp. pepper
1 tsp. basil
¼ cup water

Combine all ingredients in a 3-4 quart saucepan. Bring to a boil and simmer, covered, for 5 minutes. Refrigerate until well chilled. Serve cold. This keeps for several weeks when refrigerated.

Green Chile Canapés

2 ½ cups butter or margarine
4 oz. can diced green chilies
1 lb. Monterey Jack or Cheddar cheese, grated
1 cup mayonnaise
½ tsp. garlic salt
dash hot pepper sauce
French bread
paprika

In a blender, combine butter, chilies, cheese, mayonnaise, garlic salt and pepper sauce and blend well. Spread on thin slices of French bread. Sprinkle with paprika. Place under broiler until lightly toasted.

Herbed Stuffed Snow Peas
A beautiful presentation!

1 lb. snow peas
2 pkgs. boursin herbed garlic cheese
2 Tbsp. cream

Break ends off of snow peas and pull string from straight side of peas. Blanch peas in boiling water for 1 minute. Remove from water immediately and pour peas into a bowl of ice water. Mix cream with boursin cheese and put mixture in a pastry bag. Slit the straight side of peas to open and pipe cheese mixture into peas. Arrange on a plate and serve well chilled.

Hot Chili Mushrooms

1 lb. fresh mushrooms, small to medium in size
½ cup olive oil
⅓ cup red wine vinegar
3 cloves garlic, minced
1 tsp. salt
1 tsp. oregano
½ tsp. dried hot red chilies, crushed

Wash and trim mushrooms. Place in a saucepan of boiling water. Turn off heat and let stand 15 minutes. Drain and place in cold water. In a medium bowl, combine remaining ingredients. Drain mushrooms and add to marinade. Let stand at least 1 hour before serving. Best if made a day ahead.

Antipasta
Makes a great hostess gift at Christmas time.

6 oz. can tomato paste
8 oz. can tomato sauce
7 ozs. ketchup
Tabasco to taste
⅛ cup vinegar
9 oz. can chunk light tuna, drained
1-2 oz. can anchovies
15 oz. can sliced black olives, drained
8 oz. can mushrooms with juice, sliced or stems and pieces
½ cup cocktail onions
4 ½ oz. can tiny shrimp

Combine tomato paste, tomato sauce, ketchup, vinegar and Tabasco in a saucepan. Boil until thick. Remove from heat and add remaining ingredients. Pour into quart jars and refrigerate. When serving, pour into a small bowl and spoon onto saltine crackers. Can be stored in refrigerator up to 2 weeks.

In the summer of 1876 Jeannie Bennett opened the town's first school in the Crawford family living room for Lulie and Roger Crawford. The Steamboat Springs School District, organized on August 25, 1883, built a one-room log cabin in Soda Creek next to the Crawford house. Lulie Crawford was the first teacher—she was 16 years old.

Spanakopeta
Always a crowd pleaser.

¼ cup butter or margarine
½ cup finely chopped onions
½ cup chopped mushrooms (opt.)
2 lbs. spinach, cooked and drained
½ lb. crumbled Feta cheese or cottage cheese
2-3 eggs
¼ cup chopped parsley
2 Tbsp. chopped fresh dill
1 tsp. salt (opt.)
pepper
½ cup butter or margarine
1 lb. phyllo dough

Sauté onions and mushrooms in butter until golden. Add spinach and stir. Remove from heat. In a separate bowl, mix next 6 ingredients and add to spinach and onion mixture. Mix well. Brush a 13" x 9" baking pan lightly with melted butter. Lay 8 pastry sheets in bottom, brushing top of each with butter. Spread spinach mixture evenly over phyllo. Cover with 8 more sheets, again brushing each with butter. Pour remaining butter over top. Bake at 350° for 30-35 minutes or until top is golden brown. Serve warm.

George Baggs brought the first cattle, Texas Longhorns, into Routt County in 1871. By the late 1870s and early 1880s, large cattle companies began running thousands of head of cattle into Northwestern Colorado.

Summer Pizza
Use your imagination with this one!

2 pkgs. crescent rolls
2-8 oz. pkgs. cream cheese, room temperature
⅔ cup mayonnaise
1 tsp. cayenne pepper or Tabasco to taste
1 tsp. onion salt
1 tsp. garlic salt
¾ tsp. dill
¼ cup chives, finely chopped
toppings (see variations below)
Monterey Jack or Cheddar cheese (opt.)

Unroll crescent rolls and lay in a 13"x 9" baking dish with flat sides touching. Bake at 350° for 18-20 minutes or until golden. Combine cream cheese, mayonnaise, spices and chives. Spread onto cooled crescent rolls. Top with desired toppings; top with cheese, if desired. Cut into 2" x 2" squares and serve.

Topping variations: raw vegetables such as chopped broccoli, cauliflower, mushrooms, green pepper, etc.; small canned shrimp; sliced black olives; cocktail onions; sliced cherry tomatoes.

Sun Dried Tomato Tartlets

An excellent appetizer--worth the preparation time.

Filling:
¼ cup vegetable oil
2 ½ cups onions, thinly sliced
2 cloves garlic, minced
12 oil cured sun dried tomatoes, drained and thinly sliced
12 oil cured olives, pitted and finely chopped
¼ cup pine nuts, lightly toasted
½ tsp. dried oregano
½ tsp. dried basil
pinch of cayenne pepper
freshly ground pepper to taste
freshly grated Parmesan cheese

Tartlet Shells:
2 cups all purpose flour
1 tsp. salt
¼ cup cold water
⅔ cup vegetable shortening

Preheat oven to 300°. In a heavy large frying pan, heat oil over medium low heat. Sauté onions and garlic slowly for 40 minutes. Add remaining ingredients except Parmesan cheese. Mix thoroughly and set aside. *May be made ahead to this point and refrigerated.

Bring this mixture to room temperature before baking. To make shells, preheat oven to 400°. In a large bowl, sift flour with salt. Take ⅓ cup of this mixture and place in a small bowl. Stir water into it to form a paste. Cut the shortening into the dry mixture until it is the size of peas. Stir the flour paste into the dough. Work with your hands until dough can be gathered into a ball. Roll on a floured surface. Using a 2" fluted cookie cutter, cut out rounds. Transfer to tartlet tins measuring 1" across base. Pierce bottom with a fork.

Bake 12-15 minutes. Fill tartlet with 1 tsp. filling, sprinkle with Parmesan cheese and bake at 300° for 5 minutes. Serve at once.

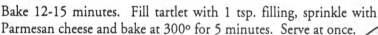

Artichoke Stuffed Mushrooms

24 medium mushrooms
2 Tbsp. butter
2 Tbsp. olive oil
5 cloves garlic, minced
Tabasco
¼ cup sherry
½ tsp. salt
1 tsp. black pepper
2 Tbsp. chopped parsley
¼ tsp. paprika
1 Tbsp. basil
5 artichoke hearts
2 cups breadcrumbs
1 ¼ cups grated Parmesan cheese

Remove stems from mushrooms and chop stems fine. Melt butter and oil and sauté stems until tender. Add garlic, Tabasco; simmer 1 minute. Add sherry, pouring around edges to deglaze. Add next 6 ingredients. Pour over breadcrumbs, add Parmesan, and if needed to shape mixture, more melted butter. Fill caps so that stuffing mounds slightly. Brush outside with olive oil. Dip in Parmesan for topping. Put sherry in bottom of baking dish, about ¼" deep. Place mushrooms in dish. Bake at 375° for 10 minutes, or until cheese topping melts and mushrooms are golden brown. Remove and serve with tomato wedges and sprigs of parsley.

Asparagus Rolls

1 bunch fresh asparagus
1 lb. puff pastry
½ cup sharp mustard
3 ozs. cream cheese, room temperature
1-2 Tbsp. heavy cream
1 egg, well beaten with 1 Tbsp. cold water

Use medium size asparagus, which are easier to wrap than the very thin ones. Trim asparagus and drop in a pot of rapidly boiling water for 2-4 minutes, until they are tender crisp. Immediately immerse the blanched asparagus in ice water to cool them, drain and refrigerate until ready to wrap. Roll the pastry ⅛-¼" thick on a floured board. Trim to the length of the asparagus. Combine the mustard and cream cheese, adding enough cream to make a spreadable consistency. Spread a thin layer of mixture on the dough. Lay asparagus spears on the edge and roll up the dough to completely wrap the asparagus with a slight overlap to keep it from unrolling during cooking. Cut rolls into bite-size pieces (about 1"). Place about 1" apart on a baking sheet. *Can be frozen at this point on the baking sheet and placed in an airtight container after freezing. Brush rolls lightly with the beaten egg mixture, being careful not to get glaze on edge of pastry. Bake at 400° for 10 minutes or until puffed and lightly golden. Makes 4-5 dozen.

Crab Stuffed Mushrooms

⅓ cup lump crabmeat
½ cup unsalted butter
⅓ cup green pepper, minced
⅓ cup red bell pepper, minced
¼ cup onion, minced
⅛ tsp. cayenne pepper
1 egg, beaten
¼ cup freshly grated Parmesan cheese
2 cloves garlic, minced
½ cup breadcrumbs
24 firm white mushrooms

Sauté peppers, onion and garlic in ¼ cup butter until soft. Remove from heat and add egg, cheese, crabmeat and breadcrumbs. Remove stems from mushroom caps. Melt remaining ¼ cup of butter and dip each cap in melted butter. Stuff with crabmeat stuffing. At this point, can be refrigerated up to 3 days. Bake at 400° until lightly browned on top. Serve immediately. Makes 2 dozen.

As a result of abundant snow, skis have played an important part in area history. Skis were first used in Routt County in the 1880s to carry mail.

Pagoda Dumplings

½ lb. ground veal or chicken
¼ lb. shrimp, chopped
4 water chestnuts, finely chopped
2 Tbsp. scallions, finely chopped
1 Tbsp. soy sauce
1 ½ Tbsp. cornstarch
½ tsp. sesame oil
⅛ tsp. dried or 1 slice fresh ginger, finely chopped
Won-Ton wrappers
soy sauce

Mix together meat, shrimp, water chestnuts and scallions. Add soy sauce, cornstarch, sesame oil and ginger. Add a touch of water if necessary to make mixture the consistency of meatballs. Fill Won-Ton wrappers with 1 tsp. of mixture and press sides up to enclose (the top will be open). Steam in a wok for 20-25 minutes and serve warm with extra soy sauce in a small bowl for dipping.

Pheasant Kabob Appetizers

1 whole pheasant, cut into ¾ " pieces
teriyaki sauce
red, green and yellow bell peppers, cut into 1" squares
10 wooden skewers

Marinate light meat 30 minutes, dark meat 50 minutes in teriyaki sauce. Steam or blanch peppers for 5 minutes so they slide on the skewers easily without cracking. Alternate meat and peppers on skewers. Leave 4" on the end. Cook on grill or broiler 5 minutes on each side.

Red Park Spareribs

4 lbs. spareribs
4 Tbsp. dry sherry
6 Tbsp. red wine vinegar
6 Tbsp. sugar
10 Tbsp. soy sauce
12 Tbsp. water

Ask your butcher to cut the ribs into 1-1 ½" pieces. Trim the fat and skin from ribs. Place ribs in a cooking pot and cover with water. Boil 1-2 minutes; drain. Rinse pot and place ribs and remaining ingredients in pot and bring to a boil. Cook, covered, over medium to medium high heat for 10 minutes. Turn heat on low and cook, uncovered, for 20 minutes. Sauce will reduce enough to form a glaze. Serves 12-14.

Char Su Ribs

4 lbs. baby back pork ribs
½ cup brown sugar
½ cup shoyu sauce
1 Tbsp. Chinese five spice
1 Tbsp. soy bean curd
½ cup oyster sauce
1 tsp. salt
1 tsp. pepper
1 cup honey
1 cup vegetable oil

"Rush to the Rockies" miners discovered gold at Hahns Peak and in 1866 the first miners established a mining district there. By 1874, mines were operating on an extensive scale and two major camps flourished: International Camp, "Bug Town," and Poverty Bar, later called Hahns Peak.

Mix brown sugar, shoyu sauce, five spice, soy bean curd, oyster sauce, salt and pepper in a large roasting pan. Add ribs and brush with sauce. Marinate in refrigerator overnight. Place ribs on wire rack with pan of water underneath. Bake at 350° for 35-45 minutes. Brush with honey and oil sauce during last 5 minutes of baking.

Valentine's Brajoles

An old time Steamboat favorite!

elk or venison, thinly sliced into 3"x 3" slices
garlic salt
pepper
chili powder
olive oil
minced dry parsley
bacon, uncooked, cut into 3" long thin strips

Lay meat slices on a cookie sheet. Sprinkle to taste with garlic salt, pepper, chili powder. Sprinkle with 6 large drops of olive oil and top with parsley. Roll each piece of meat into a tight roll and wrap one strip of bacon around it, secure with a toothpick. Broil, turning once, until bacon looks done, not crisp. Do not overcook.

Sand Mountain Stuffed Puffs

½ cup water
¼ cup butter or margarine
½ tsp. curry powder (opt.)
⅛ tsp. salt
½ cup all-purpose flour
2 eggs
½ cup Muenster or Swiss cheese, grated
2 cups shrimp, crab, chicken or tuna salad

Preheat oven to 400°. In a 2 quart saucepan, bring the water, butter, curry powder and salt to a boil. Add flour, stirring vigorously. Cook and stir until mixture forms a ball that doesn't separate. Remove from heat and cool for 10 minutes. Add eggs, 1 at a time, beating 1 minute after each addition or until smooth. Stir in cheese. Using 1 rounded tsp. dough for each puff, drop dough onto greased baking sheet. Bake for 20 minutes or until puffed. Remove from oven; cut or pinch off tops and reserve. Remove any soft dough. Cool puffs on a wire rack. Stuff with salad of your choice and replace tops. Makes 28 puffs.

Shrimp Puffs

Puffs:
½ cup butter
3 ozs. cream cheese
1 cup flour

Filling:
1 cup diced cooked shrimp
¼ cup celery, finely chopped
1 tsp. lemon juice
1 Tbsp. minced parsley
¼-½ tsp. cayenne pepper
dash Worcestershire sauce
2 Tbsp. mayonnaise
pepper

Blend butter and cream cheese together. Slowly blend in flour. Form into a ball and refrigerate for 1 hour. Roll out dough to about ⅛" and cut into rounds with a cookie cutter. Mix all filling ingredients together. Spread ½ of each round with 1 tsp. of shrimp filling. Fold each round in half and press edges with fork tines to seal all around edges. Bake at 400° for 10 minutes on an ungreased cookie sheet. Serve immediately.

*Jace Romick began ski-
ing with the Winter
Sports Club when he
was 5 years old. He
went on to compete on
the U.S. Ski Team
from 1981 to 1985.
He placed 8th in the
World Championship
Downhill in 1982 and
was the number one
U.S. Downhiller of
that year.*

Wrapped Shrimp Appetizer

1 lb. jumbo shrimp, peeled and deveined
bacon, enough for ½ slice per shrimp
horseradish
Worcestershire sauce

Fry bacon until cooked, but still soft. Split the backs of the shrimp,
fill with horseradish and wrap with the bacon. Secure with toothpicks
and put in a baking dish. Sprinkle generously with the Worcestershire
sauce. Cook on a hot grill for 5-7 minutes, turning once. *Can also
be cooked under a broiler.

Crab Rangoons

½ lb. crabmeat
8 ozs. cream cheese, softened
2 drops sesame oil
¼ cup thinly sliced green onions
pinch garlic powder
Won-Ton skins
peanut oil

Mix cream cheese and crab together. Blend in sesame oil, green onions
and garlic powder. Place a generous teaspoon of crab mixture in the
middle of each won-ton skin and fold as directed. Heat oil to 370°.
Fry rangoons for 3 minutes each. Drain on paper towels and serve
while hot with duck sauce.

Beach House Oysters

*A fiesta of flavors and colors makes these oysters
extra-special!*

2 dozen oysters on the half shell
½ cup bell pepper, minced
½ cup yellow onions, minced
½ cup celery, minced
¼ lb. pepper cheese, sliced thin
Tabasco sauce

If oysters on the half shell are not available, place oysters on a baking
sheet or in ramikens. Top each oyster with equal amount of each
vegetable. Sprinkle each oyster with a drop or two of Tabasco sauce.
Top each oyster with a slice of pepper cheese. Oysters can be either a)
baked at 450° until cheese is soft and lightly browned; b) placed under
the broiler until cheese is soft and lightly browned; or c) placed on the
grill until cheese is soft and lightly browned. Oysters should be hot,
but not cooked through.

Bread & Breakfast

Bread & Breakfast

Apple Bran Muffins	54	52	Morning Glory Muffins
Aunt Hannah's Sweet Bread	59	39	Oat Bran Banana Pancakes
Banana Muffins	53	36	Out On the Town Eggs
Bismarck	42	38	Pain Perdu (Lost Bread)
Blender Hollandaise	50	46	Pasta Pie
Blueberry Pecan Coffeecake	61	51	Picnic Basket Bread
Brioche Pecan Bread	58	36	Powder Morning Eggs
Buddy's Run Tea Bread	60	61	Powdered Sugar Icing
Buttermilk Pancakes	41	48	Quiche Montrachet
Carrot Bran Muffins	55	47	Rainbow Pepper Quiche
Cheese Fondue Veveysan Suisse	38	55	Raisin Bran Muffins
Cowboy Coffeecake	61	36	Ranch House Eggs
Crab Strata	45	41	Routt County Raised Waffles
Cranberry Muffins	54	37	Sleeping Giant Omelette
Dutch Babies	43	62	Sopapilla Pastry Dough
Dutch Hustle Cake	62	53	Sour Cream Peach Muffins
Eggs in a Hatch	37	40	Sourdough Pancakes
Emerald Mountain Eggs Picante	35	45	Southwest Brunch Rellenos
Fresh Tomato Quiche	48	56	Speedy Cinnamon Rolls
Gallery Apple Muffins	53	50	Spinach Crêpes with
Gore Pass Granola	44		White Wine Sauce
Grandma's Waffles	42	46	Spinach Parmesan Pie
Greek Spinach Quiche	47	56	Sticky Buns
Healthy Start Pancakes	39	49	Sunrise Crêpes
High Noon Rancheros	35	57	Swedish Tea Rings
Log Cabin Cake	61	52	Sweet Potato Muffins
Mexican Muffins	38	42	Ten (10)K Waffles
Mom's Ever-Ready Mix	41	40	Thin German Pancakes
Monkey Rice	44	43	Winona's Granola
Moon Hill Muffin Mix	51	40	Yahoo Yogurt Pancakes

High Noon Rancheros

½ red bell pepper, finely chopped
½ yellow or green bell pepper, finely chopped
½ onion or green onion, finely chopped
¼ cup butter
15 oz. can refried beans and green chilies
4 flour tortillas
4-8 eggs
½ lb. chorizo, cooked and crumbled (opt.)
1 jar salsa
¼ cup cilantro, minced
1 cup thinly sliced or grated Cheddar cheese

Sauté peppers and onions in ⅛ cup melted butter until onion is translucent. Remove from pan. Heat refried beans and chilies. Preheat broiler. Warm tortillas carefully in a pan on the stove or in the broiler, turning just as they start to brown. Heat remaining butter and fry eggs without turning until the whites are set. While eggs are frying, cover tortillas with refried beans to ¼" from edges. Place 1 or 2 fried eggs on each tortilla. Divide cooked chorizo equally on each tortilla if desired. Divide peppers and onion mixture equally on top of eggs. Put 2-3 Tbsp. salsa on eggs. Cover eggs and tortilla with cheese. Put under broiler until cheese is melted. Top with minced cilantro and serve with remaining salsa and a dollop of sour cream. Serves 4.

Emerald Mountain Eggs Picante

12 eggs
½ cup plain yogurt
½ cup and 2 Tbsp. medium-hot salsa
1 lb. bulk pork sausage
1 medium onion, chopped
6 oz. jar mushrooms, sliced
1 cup grated Cheddar cheese
1 cup grated mozzarella or jack cheese

Blend eggs and yogurt together with a wire whisk. Pour into a greased 13"x 9" baking pan. Bake at 350° for 15 minutes or until eggs are set. Remove and cool slightly. Brown sausage well, drain, add onion and mushrooms and sauté until limp. Drizzle salsa over eggs. Spoon sausage mixture over eggs. Top with cheeses and bake 25-30 minutes, until bubbly. Can be made 1 day ahead and final baking done the next day. Serves 8-10.

Emerald Mountain, once known as Quarry Mountain, was named for the verdant vegetation which gives the area a rich emerald hue in summer.

Early settlers built some of the first permanent buildings in Steamboat Springs with native stone from this quarry.

In 1947, the lift to the top of Emerald Mountain was one of the longest in the United States.

Out On the Town Eggs

8 slices firm white bread
2 - 8 oz. pkgs. light cream cheese
12 eggs
2 cups milk
1 tsp. salt

Stack bread, cut off crusts and cube. Sprinkle ½ of bread cubes into a buttered 8-10 cup casserole dish. Cut cream cheese into cubes and add to casserole. Add remaining bread cubes. Beat eggs, milk and salt together. Pour over bread. Cover with plastic wrap and refrigerate overnight. Remove the next morning and bake at 375° for 45 minutes. Serve with butter, maple syrup, fruit or kielbasa sausage. Serves 8.

Powder Morning Eggs

Can easily be doubled or tripled for large crowds.

6 eggs
¼ cup milk
⅓ cup sliced green onions
2 ozs. cream cheese, softened
2 Tbsp. butter

"One of our hens laid an egg yesterday and one today, and one of Aunt Nannie's laid an egg today; so we have 3."

From the diary of
Lulie Margie
Crawford
March 1, 1881

Melt butter in frying pan. Scramble eggs until light with wire whisk. Blend in milk. Sauté onions in butter over low heat for 5 minutes. Pour eggs into hot pan and gently stir, scrambling eggs. When eggs are just beginning to set, add cream cheese in chunks. Gently stir until eggs are hot. Serve while hot. Serves 4.

Ranch House Eggs

18 eggs
1 cup milk
2 Tbsp. butter
¼ tsp. garlic salt
salt and pepper to taste
1 ½ cups diced ham
½ cups grated or cubed Cheddar cheese

Beat eggs and milk with a wire whisk until eggs are yellow and frothy. Melt butter in a large frying pan and add eggs. Add garlic salt, salt, pepper and ham. Cook, occasionally scraping bottom of the frying pan, scrambling the eggs. When eggs are scrambled but still loose, add cheese and continue to stir gently, until eggs are firm but not brown. Serve with salsa or green chilies, if desired. Serves 8.

Eggs in a Hatch

Sauce:
½ cup buttermilk
½ cup mayonnaise
1 Tbsp. lemon juice
½ tsp. dry mustard
salt and pepper
¼ cup butter

6 frozen puff pastry shells
6 eggs, poached
½ lb. sliced ham
1 ½ cups sliced mushrooms
1 garlic clove, minced
fresh parsley, minced

Bake puff pastry shells according to directions. Combine buttermilk, mayonnaise, lemon juice, mustard and seasonings in a medium saucepan. Cook, stirring frequently, about 10 minutes. Do not boil. Add butter, stirring until melted. Melt remaining butter in a small sauté pan. Add garlic, sauté 3 minutes and add ham. Lightly brown ham and remove from pan. Add mushrooms and sauté 8-10 minutes. Poach eggs. Remove lids from pastry shells. Divide ham and mushrooms equally on the bottom of each shell. Place one egg in each shell. Top each shell with sauce. Serve garnished with minced parsley. Serves 6.

Sleeping Giant Omelette

This recipe easily doubles and is great for a hostess with a houseful of guests.

5 slices white bread
¾ lb. Longhorn Cheddar cheese, grated
4 eggs
2 cups milk
½ tsp. salt
½ tsp. dry mustard
dash of cayenne pepper

Sleeping Giant, called Elk Mountain by early pioneers, was named when residents noticed its shape resembled a man lying face up, head to the west and feet to the east. Locals still refer to the mountain by both names.

Cut crusts from bread and cut bread into 1 inch cubes. Put into a greased 9" x 9" pan. Cover bread with grated cheese. Whip remaining ingredients together and pour over bread and cheese. Refrigerate covered overnight. Bake covered at 350° for 1 hour until set, uncover the last 5 minutes. Serves 8.

Mexican Muffins

2 English muffins
guacamole
Monterey Jack cheese, grated
Cheddar cheese, grated
4 eggs, scrambled

Toast the English muffin halves and butter lightly. Keep warm. On each half, put a scoop of guacamole and approximately 1 scrambled egg. Top with grated cheeses; broil. Serve with fresh salsa. Serves 4.

Cheese Fondue Veveysan Suisse

1 clove garlic, halved
2 cups dry white wine
¼ lb. Gruyère cheese, grated*
¼ lb. Emmentaler cheese, grated*
½ lb. Fontina soft cheese, grated*
2 tsp. cornstarch
3 Tbsp. Kirsch
1 loaf crusty French bread, diced

Rub entire interior of chafing dish with garlic. Warm wine slightly, then pour into chafing dish. Add a little garlic. Add cheese, bring mixture almost to a boil, then reduce heat and stir constantly over low flame until cheese melts. Blend cornstarch with Kirsch, and pour into cheese mixture while stirring. Bring to boiling point, then reduce flame to keep warm. This fondue may be started over medium heat on burner of range and then transferred to chafing dish cooker.

Serve the fondue with diced French bread. Guests are to pierce the bread chunks with forks and dip them into the cheese mixture. Move forks in a figure 8 pattern, not around the edge of the dish—the fondue is better stirred this way.

*Other cheeses may be substituted, provided they are half hard and half soft. Do not substitute processed cheeses.

Pain Perdu (Lost Bread)

3 eggs, well beaten
1 ½ cups milk or 5 oz. can evaporated milk
½ cup sugar
½ tsp. vanilla
8 slices of French bread
½ cup butter
powdered sugar or syrup

Mix eggs, milk, sugar and vanilla. Dip each piece of bread in mixture to coat well. Fry each piece in about 1 Tbsp. melted butter. Top with powdered sugar or syrup. Serves 4.

Oat Bran Banana Pancakes

1 cup oat bran
1 cup all purpose flour
2 tsp. baking soda
1 Tbsp. sugar
1 extremely ripe banana, medium sized, mashed
2 tsp. vanilla extract
1 ½ cups plain low fat yogurt
4 egg whites
2 Tbsp. melted unsalted butter or margarine
warm maple syrup
fresh blueberries (opt.)

In a medium bowl, toss together oat bran, flour, baking soda and sugar. Using a wooden spoon, stir in banana and vanilla until well blended. Add yogurt; mix well. Heat a large skillet, preferably cast iron, over moderate heat. In a separate bowl, beat egg whites with an electric mixer until soft peaks form. Beat ⅓ egg whites into batter to lighten. Fold in remaining egg whites with a rubber spatula. Fold in melted butter. Ladle a few ¼ cup scoops of batter into heated skillet, spreading batter into 3 ½"-4" circles. Cook until bubbles appear on the surface. Flip and cook until bottoms are well browned, about 1 minute. Serve with maple syrup and blueberries. Serves 4.

Healthy Start Pancakes

A great, hearty pancake to start an active day!

1 ¼ cups whole wheat pastry flour
1 cup oats, old fashioned
¼ cup wheat germ
3 tsp. baking powder
1 Tbsp. sugar
¼ tsp. baking soda
1 ½ tsp. cinnamon
1 cup 2% milk
¾ cup lowfat buttermilk
2 eggs
1 Tbsp. safflower oil
1 banana, mashed
1 tsp. vanilla extract
3 Tbsp. sunflower seeds (opt.)

Combine all dry ingredients. In a separate bowl, whip eggs until light, add milk, buttermilk and oil. Stir in banana and vanilla. Add dry ingredients. Fry in light oil until dough bubbles, flip and fry until golden. Serve with syrup or honey butter. Serves 4.

Yahoo Yogurt Pancakes

2 cups whole wheat flour
1 tsp. baking powder
1 tsp. baking soda
3 eggs, separated
2 Tbsp. honey
2 cups yogurt, plain or flavored
¼ cup 2% milk
1 tsp. vanilla
nuts (opt.)

Sift together flour, baking powder and soda. In a small bowl, beat egg yolks. Add honey, yogurt, milk and vanilla. Mix well. Gradually add to flour mixture. In a separate bowl, beat egg whites until stiff and fold into batter. Add nuts. Pour onto hot, oiled griddle and cook until golden on both sides. Serves 4.

Yahoo Mountain (Little Snake/Slater area) was named by a cowboy who kept calling "yahoo-yahoo," to attract attention when he was lost in a snowstorm there.

Thin German Pancakes

⅔ cup flour
2 Tbsp. sugar
¼ tsp. salt
3 eggs
⅛ tsp. vanilla
1 ¾ cups milk
vegetable oil or shortening as needed

Mix first 5 ingredients. Add milk and stir until batter is smooth. In a hot, greased crêpe or frying pan, pour a thin layer of batter. Cook until set. Turn and cook until lightly browned. Sprinkle with powdered sugar, cinnamon and sugar or your favorite jelly. Serves 4.

Sourdough Pancakes

2 cups sourdough starter (see recipe in Bread Chapter)
1 cup flour
1 cup milk
1 egg, well beaten
½ Tbsp. baking soda
3 Tbsp. sugar
½ Tbsp. salt
2 Tbsp. melted butter

Add flour and milk to the starter. Mix well in a bowl, cover lightly and place in a warm place overnight. Next morning, stir in the egg, sugar, soda, salt and butter. Do not beat, just mix. If the batter is too thick or thin, add either more milk or flour. Allow batter to stand a few minutes. Spoon on a hot griddle and cook. Serves 4-6.

Buttermilk Pancakes

2 eggs
¾ cup buttermilk
2 Tbsp. butter, melted
1 cup flour
1 Tbsp. sugar
1 ½ tsp. baking soda
dash of salt

Beat eggs well, add buttermilk and butter. Add flour, sugar, baking
soda and salt and mix well. Fry in pan or griddle that is lightly oiled.
Flip when batter starts to slightly bubble. Should be golden brown.
Serves 4.

Mom's Ever-Ready Mix

9 cups flour, half whole wheat, half unbleached high altitude
(may substitute ½-1 cup wheat germ and/or oat bran)
3 Tbsp. baking powder
1 Tbsp. salt
2 cups shortening

Combine dry ingredients. Cut in shortening (an electric mixer works
well for this large amount). Store on shelf, tightly covered.

Variations:
Pancakes: combine 1 cup mix and 1 cup milk
Waffles: combine 1 cup mix, 1 cup milk and 1 egg
Shortcakes: combine 1¼ cups mix, ¼ cup sugar, 1 egg, 2 Tbsp. oil,
              ⅓ cup milk. Bake in 9" square pan at 400° for 15 min.

Routt County Raised Waffles

½ cup warm water
1 pkg. dry yeast
2 cups warm milk
½ cup butter, melted
1 tsp. salt
1 tsp. sugar
2 cups flour
2 eggs
¼ tsp. baking soda

Use a large bowl as batter will rise. Pour water in bowl, sprinkle in
yeast. Let stand to dissolve 5 minutes. Add milk, butter, salt, sugar,
and flour. Blend until smooth. Cover with plastic wrap and let stand
at room temperature overnight. Just before cooking in waffle iron,
beat in eggs and baking soda. These are extremely light and flavorful
waffles. Makes 8 waffles.

Grandma's Waffles

2 cups flour
1 Tbsp. sugar (opt.)
3 tsp. baking powder
½ tsp. salt
3 eggs, well beaten
2 cups milk
½ cup butter or margarine, melted

Sift dry ingredients together. Combine eggs and milk and slowly add to dry ingredients. Add butter; stir until just blended. Pour onto lightly oiled, hot waffle griddle and cook until golden. Serves 6-8.

10K Waffles

½ cup safflower oil margarine, melted
3 eggs, beaten or egg substitute
2 cups 2% milk
1 cup whole wheat pastry flour
½ cup unbleached flour
½ cup oatmeal
¼ cup wheat germ
1 Tbsp. baking powder
½ tsp. salt
1 tsp. vanilla
vegetable oil cooking spray

Blend margarine, eggs and milk in a medium bowl. Add remaining ingredients mixing until just blended. Pour batter into preheated waffle iron lightly sprayed with cooking spray. Cook until golden and serve immediately with fruits or syrup. Serves 4-6.

The history of Routt County's residents has always been strongly influenced by climate and topography. Its borders embrace 1,427,820 diverse acres in northwestern Colorado just west of the Continental Divide.

Bismarck

3 Tbsp. butter or margarine
½ cup flour
½ cup milk
2 eggs

Put butter in iron skillet or round, oven-proof baking dish. Turn oven to 450° and preheat skillet with margarine until bubbly. Mix flour, milk and eggs just until blended. Pour into hot skillet, and reduce heat to 350°. Bake for 12 minutes. Serve with any of the following: maple syrup, powdered sugar, jelly, melted cheese, or picante sauce. Great breakfast or light dinner, especially for kids. Serves 2.

Dutch Babies

½ cup butter
5 eggs
1 ½ cups milk
1 ½ cups flour
dash of cinnamon

Melt butter in 9" x 13" casserole dish in a 425° oven. In a blender, mix remaining ingredients. Pour into dish when butter is bubbly. Bake 20 minutes. Serve with fresh raspberries, a sprinkle of lemon juice, and top with powdered sugar, or serve with apple filling. (Recipe follows). Serves 6.

Apple Filling:
6 cups sliced apples
¼ cup butter or margarine
¼ cup brown sugar or honey
½ tsp. cinnamon (or to taste)

Sauté apples in butter 5 minutes. Add brown sugar or honey and cinnamon. Continue sautéing until tender. Keep warm. Serves 4-6.

Winona's Granola

½ cup finely packed brown sugar
¼ cup unsulfured molasses
¼ cup honey
¼ cup cold water
3 Tbsp. vegetable oil
2 tsp. cinnamon
3 cups old fashioned rolled oats (not instant)
½ cup diced walnuts
½ cup diced pecans
½ cup sliced almonds
½ cup shredded coconut
½ cup bran
¼ cup sunflower seeds
dried fruits: raisins, dried apricots, dates, etc.

Combine first 6 ingredients in a heavy saucepan. Bring to a boil over low heat, stirring constantly. Preheat oven to 325°. Combine next 7 ingredients. Drizzle syrup over top and stir thoroughly. Place on cookie sheet and bake for 40 minutes, stirring every 10 minutes. Cool and add dried fruits. Serve with milk, yogurt, ice cream, etc. Makes 2 quarts.

As Governor Routt traveled over Gore Pass, he was so inspired by the beauty of the valley below that he named the area "Egeria," which is derived from Greek mythology, meaning "beautiful woman." The name was changed to Yampa when Moffat and his men moved up with the railroad.

Gore Pass Granola

4 cups rolled oats*
½ cup sunflower seeds
¼ cup sesame seeds
½ cup sliced almonds
1 Tbsp. cinnamon
1 cup honey
1 cup vegetable oil
1 pkg. dried apricots, chopped
1 cup raisins

Stir grains together, preferably in a roasting pan to make stirring easier. Mix honey, oil and cinnamon together. Pour over grain mixture and stir well. This mixture will be very dry. Bake uncovered at 350° for 60 minutes, stirring well at 20 minute intervals. Grains should be a light golden brown. Remove from oven and stir in dried fruit; cool. Store in small quantities in a tightly sealed jar. Store the rest in plastic bags in the freezer until needed. Makes 2½ quarts.

*You may use any combination of rolled oats; wheat; rye; rice; or other rolled grain. Uses: morning cereal with juice or milk • snack food by the small cupful • topping for yogurt or ice cream • replacing the oatmeal in your oatmeal cookies or fruit crisp crusts.

Monkey Rice

Makes a great warm breakfast or nutritious snack!

1 cup long grain brown rice, uncooked
2 ½ cups cold water
1-3 bananas
skim milk
cinnamon to taste

Cook brown rice according to directions. Place in refrigerator until ready to use. When ready to serve, place a serving of rice in a bowl. Heat in the microwave for 30-40 seconds to warm. Thinly slice approximately ½ banana per serving and sprinkle on top. Pour a little skim milk over and sprinkle with cinnamon to taste. Add some raisins for a real sweet treat. Serves 3-4.

Southwest Brunch Rellenos

2 - 7 oz. cans whole green chilies, drained
9 large eggs
2 cups milk
½ cup flour
¼ tsp. garlic salt
¼ cup grated Parmesan cheese
3.5 oz. can sliced black olives, drained
4 oz. can chopped green chilies
1-2 Tbsp. chopped jalapeño peppers
¼ cup sliced green onions
¼ cup chopped fresh cilantro
8 oz. pkg. cream cheese, room temperature
¼ tsp. coarse ground pepper
2 tsp. dried sage (opt.)

Grease a 13"x 9" baking dish. Place whole green chilies, smooth side down, across bottom of pan. In large bowl, combine eggs, milk and flour and mix until frothy. Add remaining ingredients, blend well and pour over chilies. Bake at 375º for 45 minutes. Serve with a side of salsa. Serves 10-12.

Crab Strata

7 slices white bread
½ lb. mushrooms, sliced
¼ cup sliced green onions
1 Tbsp. butter or oil
6 eggs
3 cups milk
½ tsp. salt
¼ tsp. cayenne pepper
1 tsp. dry mustard
2 Tbsp. cooking sherry
8 ozs. crabmeat or imitation crab
10 ozs. grated Cheddar cheese

Trim crusts from bread and cube. Grease a 7 ½" x 12" pan. Sauté mushrooms and onions in oil until soft. Beat eggs, milk and spices. Add sherry. Spread bread cubes on bottom of greased pan. Spoon mushrooms and onions over top of bread. Crumble crabmeat over mushrooms. Pour egg mixture over crab. Sprinkle cheese evenly over the top. Cover with aluminum foil and refrigerate overnight. Remove foil and bake at 350º for 50-55 minutes. The crabmeat may be substituted with ham, shrimp, crumbled bacon or combinations for variations. Serves 6.

Pasta Pie

20 ozs. tortellini (spinach and plain)
1 ½ cups whipping cream
1 cup freshly grated Parmesan cheese
½ cup chopped parsley
1 pkg. puff pastry
egg, sugar and water (for glaze)

Cook tortellini; drain well. Add whipping cream, cheese and parsley to pasta and toss well. Roll puff pastry to ⅛" thickness. Line a 9-10" springform pan with pastry, leaving remainder rolled for the top. Put tortellini in puff pastry shell. Top with puff pastry top. Brush with egg glaze consisting of egg, sugar and water. Bake at 375º for 30 minutes. Reduce heat to 350º and continue baking approximately 30-45 minutes longer or until pastry is browned and puffed. Cover edges with foil if it looks like it is browning too much. Serves 6-8.

Spinach Parmesan Pie

Pastry:
3 eggs
½ cup butter, melted
1 Tbsp. oil
¼ cup dry skim milk solids
2 cups flour
1 tsp. baking powder
1 tsp. salt
½ tsp. nutmeg

Filling:
10 oz. fresh spinach, cooked and chopped
3 eggs, beaten
1 cup heavy cream
1 ⅔ cups grated Parmesan cheese
6 oz. can sliced black olives, drained
½ Bermuda onion, sliced
½ tsp. nutmeg
watercress (garnish)

To prepare pastry: Beat eggs until thick and pale yellow in color. Slowly add butter and oil. Gradually add remaining ingredients in order listed. Turn dough onto a pastry board. Knead until a uniform dough is reached, about 5 minutes. Roll out to fit into a 9" buttered pie plate.

To prepare filling: Preheat oven to 350º. Beat eggs and cream until frothy. Combine remaining ingredients and mix well. Pour filling into pastry shell. Bake for 30 minutes. Garnish with watercress and additional sliced olives. Serves 6-8.

Greek Spinach Quiche

9 inch pastry shell
3 eggs
1 ½ cups half and half
10 oz. pkg frozen spinach, thawed
3 Tbsp. butter
½ Bermuda onion, sliced
2 garlic cloves, minced
3 ½ cups sliced mushrooms
1 tsp. lemon juice
4-6 ozs. Feta cheese
¼-½ tsp. nutmeg
salt, pepper

Prepare pastry dough. Roll out to ⅛ inch thickness and line a 9"-10" quiche pan. Melt butter in medium sauté pan. Sauté onion and garlic for 5 minutes. Add mushrooms and lemon juice, sauté 8-10 minutes. Squeeze dry spinach until all excess liquid is gone. Add spinach and seasonings to sauté pan. Whisk eggs and half and half together. Drain spinach mixture and add to pastry shell. Crumble Feta cheese into pastry shell, pour egg mixture into pastry shell. Bake in preheated oven at 375° for 35 to 45 minutes. Quiche may easily be made a day ahead and re-warmed in a 350° oven until hot. Serves 6-8.

Corky and Ray Heid, Steamboat natives, began skiing as toddlers at Howelsen Hill. Both brothers became jumpers of world class caliber. Corky was named an alternate to the Cortina Olympics in 1956, and Ray for the Squaw Valley Olympics in 1960.

Rainbow Pepper Quiche

9 inch pastry shell
3 eggs
1 ½ cups half and half
1 Tbsp. olive oil
½ red bell pepper, sliced
½ yellow bell pepper, sliced
½ red onion, sliced
2 cloves garlic, minced
3.8 ozs. sliced black olives
6 ozs. grated Monterey Jack pepper cheese
⅓ cup cilantro, minced
½ tsp. cumin
¼ tsp. cayenne pepper
salt, pepper

Line quiche pan with pastry dough. Heat olive oil in a small sauté pan. Add red and yellow peppers and sauté 5 minutes. Add onions and garlic and sauté 5 more minutes. Add seasonings.   Pour vegetable mixture into pastry shell. Add drained black olives and cheese. Pour egg mixture over vegetables and bake in a 375° oven for 35 to 45 minutes. Serves 6-8.

Fresh Tomato Quiche

10 inch pie shell
2 Tbsp. olive oil
½ cup chopped onion
½ cup chopped green pepper
1 clove garlic, minced
2 lbs. firm, ripe, red tomatoes
½ tsp. each basil, oregano, salt
3 Tbsp. chopped, fresh parsley
⅛ tsp. pepper
3 eggs
¾ cup heavy cream
¾ cup plain yogurt
½-¾ cup grated Swiss cheese
⅓ cup grated Parmesan cheese

Sauté onion, green pepper and garlic in oil. Add tomatoes, spices and parsley. Cover and cook over low heat for 5 minutes. Remove cover and cook to allow water to evaporate, making sure not to scorch. Blend eggs, cream and yogurt; add Swiss cheese. Add to tomato mixture. Pour into partially baked pie crust and sprinkle with Parmesan cheese. Bake at 375° for about 30 minutes, or until set. Serves 6-8.

Mt. Werner was originally named Storm Mountain by beaver trappers who described the landmark to James Crawford prior to his homestead journey in 1875.

Quiche Montrachet

2 shallots, diced
4 eggs
1 cup heavy cream
7 oz. Montrachet or chèvre cheese
1 ½ tsp. fresh dill or basil
5 sun dried tomatoes, drained
freshly ground pepper
1 pie crust shell

Slice tomatoes into thin strips. Beat the eggs and cream together, mixing well. Add dill and pepper to taste. Put tomatoes and shallots in the bottom of pie shell. Crumble the cheese on top. Pour egg mixture into pie crust and bake in a 400° oven for 12 minutes; reduce heat to 300° and bake for 40 minutes. Serve while hot or at room temperature, garnish with fresh dill or basil. Serves 6-8.

Sunrise Crêpes

Crêpe Batter:
2 eggs
2 cups Wondra Instant Flour
2 cups water

Filling:
6-8 eggs, beaten
1 Tbsp. milk
salt and pepper to taste
2 Tbsp. butter
⅓ cup chopped green onion
½ lb. Canadian bacon, bacon, sausage or ham
Hollandaise Sauce (see recipe below)

To prepare batter: blend all ingredients in a food processor or blender for 1 minute. Let rest for 30 minutes. Cook and set aside.

To prepare filling: blend eggs and milk; season to taste. Sauté green onion in butter; add eggs and meat of your choice. Cook slowly until done.

To assemble, add a spoonful of filling in center of crêpe. Make a pouch by folding and tie with a green onion stem, which has been soaked in water briefly. Serve with Hollandaise Sauce. Serves 4-6.

For Mexican crêpes, add grated Cheddar cheese to eggs. Serve with warmed salsa or chile sauce.

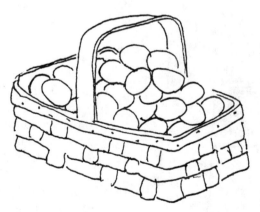

Blender Hollandaise

3 egg yolks
2 tsp. lemon juice
¼ tsp. salt
2 shakes Tabasco sauce, or dash of cayenne pepper or white pepper
½ cup unsalted butter, melted

In blender mix yolks, lemon juice, salt and Tabasco. Blend until light yellow. Slowly drizzle butter into blender while blending on low speed. Serve immediately.

Spinach Crêpes
with White Wine Sauce

Batter:
2 eggs
2 cups flour
2 cups water
1 Tbsp. vanilla extract
1 ½ Tbsp. honey (opt.)

Spinach Filling:
1 Tbsp. minced shallots
1 clove garlic, minced
4 mushrooms, chopped
butter
2 Tbsp. flour
10 oz. pkg. chopped frozen spinach, thawed and drained
1 cup cream
¼ cup grated, natural sharp Cheddar cheese
2 Tbsp. grated Parmesan cheese
salt, pepper and thyme to taste

White Wine Sauce:
2 Tbsp. butter
3 Tbsp. flour
1 cup half and half
1 cup chicken stock
3 Tbsp. white wine
salt, pepper and nutmeg to taste
1 Tbsp. grated Parmesan cheese

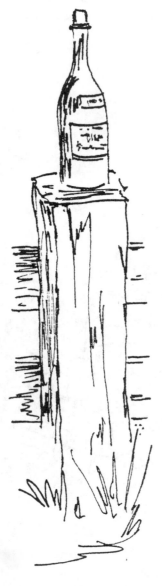

To prepare crêpe batter: blend ingredients in a food processor or blender for 1 minute. Let sit at room temperature for 30 minutes before cooking.

To prepare spinach filling: sauté shallots, garlic and mushrooms in butter. Stir in flour; cook 2 minutes. Stir in well-drained spinach, cream, cheese and spices.

To prepare white wine sauce: melt butter and stir in flour; cook 2 minutes, stirring. Add liquids and stir until sauce boils. Boil 1 minute; add seasonings and Parmesan cheese.

To serve: fill 8" cooked crêpes with spinach filling and cover with white wine sauce. Crêpes can also be served as a hot hors d'oeuvre without the sauce. Serves 4.

Picnic Basket Bread

A great make ahead and take along meal!

1 pkg. active dry yeast
1 cup warm water
2 ½-3 cups all-purpose flour
1 Tbsp. sugar
1 ¼ tsp. salt
2 cups chicken, cooked, deboned and chopped
1 ½ cups grated cheese (Swiss, Cheddar or Provolone)
10 oz. pkg. frozen chopped spinach, thawed and well drained
¼ cup grated Parmesan cheese
¼ cup finely chopped onion
1 egg white, beaten
2 Tbsp. sesame seeds

In a large mixing bowl, dissolve yeast in warm water. Add 1 cup of the flour, sugar and 1 tsp. salt. Beat on low 30 seconds, scraping bowl constantly. Beat on high for 3 minutes. Stir in as much remaining flour to bring to a dough-like consistency. Turn out onto a lightly floured surface. Knead in enough flour to make a moderately soft dough that is smooth and elastic (about 3-5 minutes). Cover and set aside. Combine chicken, cheese, spinach, Parmesan, onion and ¼ tsp. salt and mix well. Roll dough on a lightly floured surface and shape into a 16"x 10" rectangle. Spread filling lengthwise down the center ⅓ of the dough. Bring long edges together and seal. Seal ends. Place seam side down on a lightly greased baking sheet. Brush with mixture of beaten egg white and 1 Tbsp. water. Sprinkle with sesame seeds. Bake at 375° for 40 minutes or until loaf sounds hollow when tapped. May be necessary to cover with foil during last 10 minutes to prevent over-browning. Serve warm or chilled. Serves 4-6.

Moon Hill Muffin Mix

7 cups flour
2 cups sugar
3 Tbsp. + 1 tsp. baking powder
1 Tbsp. salt

Combine all ingredients and store in a tightly covered container until ready to use. To prepare muffins, combine 2 ¼ cups of the muffin mix, 1 egg, ¾-1 cup milk and ⅓ cup oil. Mix to create batter. Stir in desired fruit or flavorings as shown below. Bake at 375° for 20 minutes. Makes 1 dozen.

Variations: ½ cup blueberries • ½ cup applesauce, 1 tsp. cinnamon and ½ tsp. cloves • ½ cup pumpkin, ½ tsp. each cinnamon and nutmeg, ¼ tsp. ground cloves and ¼ cup raisins • ½ cup chopped cranberries, 1 tsp. orange zest, 3 extra Tbsp. sugar • 1 Tbsp. poppy seeds.

Mr. Moon was generally referred to as "Old Man Moon." Moon Hill, where he had a shanty, is named for him. He was described as not very big, bald, dark complected, stooped, and with a squeaky voice. "Jack Robinson" was his by-word. More about him later.

Morning Glory Muffins

1 cup golden raisins
2 cups unbleached flour
1 cup sugar
2 tsp. baking soda
2 tsp. cinnamon
½ tsp. salt
2 cups grated carrots
1 tart green apple, chopped
½ cup sliced almonds
½ cup shredded coconut
3 eggs
⅔ cup melted butter
2 tsp. vanilla

Cover raisins with hot water and soak for 30 minutes. Drain well. Preheat oven to 350°. Prepare muffin tin by greasing very well or lining with muffin papers. In a large bowl, mix flour, sugar, baking soda, cinnamon, and salt. Stir in raisins, carrots, apple, almonds, and coconut. In a separate bowl, mix together eggs, oil, and vanilla. Add to flour mixture and stir just well enough to blend all the ingredients together. Spoon into muffin cups and bake about 20-25 minutes. Let cool in pan a couple of minutes. Remove from pan and serve. Makes 12-18 muffins.

The Crawford home served as a fort for Hayden and Yampa River settlers during Indian scares in September and October of 1879 following the Meeker Massacre.

Sweet Potato Muffins

Excellent with holiday meals—easy to freeze.

½ cup butter
1 ¼ cups sugar
2 eggs
16 oz. can mashed sweet potatoes
1 ½ cups all purpose flour
2 tsp. baking powder
¼ tsp. salt
1 tsp. cinnamon
¼ tsp. nutmeg
1 cup milk
¼ cup chopped pecans or walnuts
½ cup raisins

Preheat oven to 400°. Grease muffin tins. Cream butter and sugar; add eggs and mix well. Blend in sweet potatoes. Sift flour with baking powder, salt, cinnamon and nutmeg. Add to sweet potato mixture, alternating with milk. Do not over mix. Fold in the nuts and raisins. Fill muffin tins ⅔ full and bake for 25 minutes. Makes 2 dozen large muffins or 6 dozen 1 ½" muffins.

Sour Cream Peach Muffins

1 ½ cups brown sugar, firmly packed
⅔ cup light vegetable oil
1 egg
1 cup sour cream
1 tsp. baking soda
1 tsp. vanilla extract
1 tsp. salt
2 ¼ cups flour
1 ½ cups peaches, fresh or canned
½ cup chopped nuts

Combine sugar, oil, and egg in a mixing bowl. In another bowl, mix sour cream, salt, vanilla, and soda. Add the sour cream mixture to the sugar mixture and slowly blend in the flour. Do not overmix. Fold in peaches and nuts. Pour into muffin cups and sprinkle top with sugar or cinnamon sugar mixture. Put a bit of butter on top of each. Bake at 325° for 30 minutes. Makes 12-15. Moist and yummy!

Banana Muffins

1 cup flour + 1 Tbsp.
2 tsp. baking powder
¼ tsp. baking soda
¾ tsp. salt
⅓ cup sugar
1 egg, well beaten
⅓ cup shortening, melted and cooled
1 cup mashed bananas

Sift first 4 ingredients. Mix remaining ingredients; add to dry ingredients. Pour into muffin tins. Bake at 375° for 20 minutes or until golden brown. Makes 10-12 muffins.

Gallery Apple Muffins

1 ½ cups brown sugar
⅔ cup vegetable oil
1 egg
1 cup sour cream
1 tsp. salt
1 tsp. vanilla
1 tsp. baking soda
2 ½ cups flour
1 ½ cups diced apples
½ cup chopped pecans

Combine sugar, oil, and egg in one bowl. In a second bowl, combine sour cream, salt, vanilla, and baking soda. Add sour cream mixture to sugar mixture and slowly blend in flour. Do not overmix. Fold in apples and pecans. Pour into greased muffin cups and bake at 350° for 30 minutes. Makes 12-15 muffins.

Cranberry Muffins

1-2 oranges
2 cups all purpose flour
1 Tbsp. baking powder
⅔ cup + 1 tsp. sugar
1 cup coarsely chopped cranberries
1 cup chopped walnuts
⅓ cup melted butter or safflower oil
1 egg

John Steele will forever be remembered as Steamboat's first Olympian. After moving to Steamboat from Minneapolis in 1918, he came under the influence of Carl Howelsen. In 1932, he was named to the four-man U.S. Olympic team and placed 7th in jumping at Lake Placid.

Preheat oven to 400°. Grease muffin pan. Remove the zest from oranges, mince and measure out 1 Tbsp. and 1 tsp. Squeeze the juice and reserve ⅔ cup. In a large bowl, toss together flour, baking powder, and ⅔ cup sugar. In medium bowl, toss together cranberries, nuts and orange zest. In another medium bowl, combine orange juice, melted butter and egg. Whisk until blended. Pour the liquid over the flour mixture and stir lightly, 3-4 times to combine. Add cranberry nut mixture and combine using as few strokes as possible (batter should be lumpy). Pour into muffin cups. Sprinkle a pinch of remaining sugar over top of each muffin. Bake in the middle of oven for 25 minutes or until golden. Let cool on wire rack for 15-20 minutes. Makes 12-15 muffins.

Apple Bran Muffins

2 cups flour (1 cup wheat, 1 cup white)
1 ½ cups bran
½ tsp. salt
1 ¼ tsp. baking soda
½ tsp. nutmeg
1 Tbsp. orange rind
½ cup chopped apple
½ cup raisins
½ cup sunflower seeds
2 cups buttermilk
juice of 1 orange
1 egg
½ cup molasses
2 Tbsp. oil

Mix together all dry ingredients; set aside. Mix together wet ingredients. Stir together the two. Stir in apple, raisins and sunflower seeds. Do not overmix. Fill muffin pan ¾ full and bake at 350° for 10-15 minutes. Makes 12-15 muffins.

Raisin Bran Muffins

Fresh muffins on hand whenever you like!

7 cups Raisin Bran
3 cups sugar
5 cups flour
5 tsp. baking soda
2 tsp. salt
4 eggs, well beaten
1 cup oil
1 quart buttermilk

Mix together Raisin Bran, sugar, flour, soda, and salt. Add eggs, oil and buttermilk. Mix well. Allow to sit 30-45 minutes before baking. Fill greased muffin pans half full and bake at 375° for 20-25 minutes. Keep extra batter in the refrigerator up to 6 weeks, covered tightly. These are moist and popular muffins. Makes 4 dozen muffins.

Carrot Bran Muffins

1 cup bran flakes
2 cups finely grated carrots
¼ cup golden raisins
¾ cup skim milk or orange juice
1 cup whole wheat flour
2 Tbsp. brown sugar
2 Tbsp. vegetable oil
1 Tbsp. lemon juice
1 tsp. baking powder
1 tsp. baking soda
½ tsp. cinnamon
¼ tsp. salt
1 egg, slightly beaten

Combine bran, carrots, raisins and milk or orange juice. Let stand for 5 minutes. Add remaining ingredients, stirring until all particles are moistened. Be careful not to over mix. Line muffin tin with paper liners. Fill half-full with batter. Bake at 400° for 15 minutes. Let cool. Makes 12-14 muffins.

Sticky Buns

2 pkgs. yeast
½ cup warm water
2 cups milk
½ cup butter
½ cup sugar
1 tsp. salt
6 ½ cups flour
¼ cup butter, softened
cinnamon and sugar

1 cup brown sugar
½ cup water
¼ cup butter
1-2 cups pecans

Mix yeast and warm water together. Let proof for 5 minutes. Heat milk and butter until very hot. Allow to cool. Add sugar and salt to milk and mix well. Add 2 cups flour to milk and beat until smooth. Add yeast mixture and mix. Gradually add remaining flour until the dough is workable but soft. Knead until smooth, turn into an oiled bowl, cover and let rise until doubled. Punch dough down and roll to ¼" thick rectangle. Spread dough with softened butter and sprinkle well with cinnamon and sugar mixture. Roll dough up lengthwise and cut into 1" thick slices. Grease an 11" x 14" glass pan and an 8" x 10" pan. Sprinkle pecans over pan. Mix brown sugar, water and butter in a medium saucepan. Bring to a boil and boil for 5 minutes. Pour into baking pans. Layer rolls on top of mixture in pans, cover and let rise until double. Bake at 375° for 25 minutes. Invert pan onto plate immediately. This recipe can be halved for smaller groups. Quick-rise yeast will work also. Makes one 11" x 14" pan and one 8" x 10" pan.

Speedy Cinnamon Rolls

4 cakes yeast
1 quart warm water
1 cup sugar
½ cup oil
1 cup dry milk
2 Tbsp. salt
2 eggs, well beaten
5 lbs. flour

Dissolve yeast in water. Add oil, sugar, dry milk and salt. Add eggs. Add enough flour to make dough light and spongy. Knead 5 minutes and let sit to rise. Punch down and roll out into cigar shapes. Roll in melted butter, then in cinnamon and sugar. Twist around fingers and twist into a knot. Set in pans and put in refrigerator to hold overnight. Bake slowly or let rise again and bake at 300° for 20 minutes. Top with powdered sugar. Makes 6-8 dozen rolls.

Swedish Tea Rings

2 pkgs. quick rise dry yeast
1 tsp. sugar
½ cup warm water
2 cups lukewarm milk, scalded and cooled
½ cup sugar
2 tsp. salt
2 eggs, slightly beaten
½ cup melted shortening
7 cups flour
raisins, chopped apples, maraschino cherries, chopped nuts
Powdered Sugar Icing (recipe follows)

Mix together yeast, sugar and warm water. Let stand until yeast is bubbly. Add milk, sugar and salt. Stir in eggs and shortening. Add flour in 2 additions. Flour hands to facilitate handling. Knead thoroughly. Place in oiled bowl. Cover, let rise in warm place until doubled in bulk. Punch down and turn over in bowl. Cover again and let rise, about 20 minutes, until doubled. Divide dough into 2 equal parts. Roll out each half on counter into a rectangle, ½" thick (about 6" x 18"). Brush with melted butter (approximately 4-6 Tbsp.) and spread with brown sugar and sprinkle with lots of cinnamon. Can use raisins, chopped apples or nuts. Roll up from long side sealing edge firmly. Shape into ring and place on pizza pan or cookie sheet, sealing the ends together. With scissors, cut through ring almost to the center; slices about 1" thick. Turn each slice slightly on side. Brush with melted butter. Bake at 350º for 18-20 minutes. When cool, ice and sprinkle with chopped nuts and halved maraschino cherries. Makes 2 rings.

Powdered Sugar Icing:
2 lbs. powdered sugar
1 tsp. vanilla
1/4 tsp. almond extract
2 tsp. liquid margarine
hot water

Combine ingredients for a glaze. Before icing dries, place maraschino cherries and nuts on rings.

"13 wagons passed here before breakfast."

"I baked light bread and it ran all over the stove."

From the diary of
Lulie Margie Crawford
April 25, 1881

The weeks after the Meeker Massacre (1879) were frightening. Men, women and children from Hayden and Elk River fled their homes to come to the Crawford Cabin. They never were attacked, but remained under great anxiety for several weeks.

Brioche Pecan Bread
A particularly nice bread for holiday breakfasts.

½ cup warm water
1 pkg. dry yeast
¼ cup sugar
1 tsp. salt
2 tsp. lemon extract
1 cup butter, softened
6 eggs or equivalent egg substitute
4 ½ cups all-purpose flour

Filling:
3 Tbsp. butter, softened
⅔ cup brown sugar, packed
2 egg yolks
2 Tbsp. milk
½ tsp. vanilla
2 cups ground pecans
3 Tbsp. butter, melted
powdered sugar

Prepare dough a day ahead. In a large mixing bowl, sprinkle yeast over warm water and allow to dissolve. Add sugar, salt, lemon extract, 1 cup butter, eggs, and 3 cups flour. Beat on medium speed 5 minutes. Add the rest of the flour and beat at low speed until smooth. Cover bowl with plastic wrap and let rise in a warm place until doubled, about 1-1 ½ hours. Punch down and refrigerate well-covered overnight. The next day, prepare filling. Combine butter, brown sugar, and egg yolks. Stir in the milk and vanilla. Add nuts. Remove brioche dough from the refrigerator. Lightly grease two 9" x 5" bread pans. Stir down dough and turn out onto lightly floured board. Divide in half. Roll each half into a 9" x 14" rectangle. Brush with 1 Tbsp. butter. Spread with half the filling to within 1" of the edges. Roll each lengthwise side into the center, jelly roll fashion, meeting in the center. Turn loaf over and place in prepared pan. Cover with plastic wrap. Repeat with the remaining half of dough. Let rise in a warm place until doubled, about 1 ½ hours. Preheat oven to 350º. Brush loaf tops with remaining melted butter. Bake 35 minutes or until golden brown. Remove from pan and cool on rack. Sprinkle tops with powdered sugar. Best served warm. Makes 2 loaves.

Aunt Hannah's Sweet Foundation Bread

2 pkgs. dry yeast
1 Tbsp. sugar
1 cup warm water
1 cup warm milk
6 Tbsp. margarine
½ cup sugar
1 tsp. salt
3 eggs
7 cups flour

Filling for Cinnamon Rolls or Tea Ring:
1 ½ cups brown sugar
1 ¼ tsp. cinnamon
½ tsp. nutmeg
1 ½ cups raisins or walnuts
5 Tbsp. butter, melted

Combine yeast, sugar, and water; allow to dissolve. In a large bowl, add yeast mixture, milk, margarine, sugar, salt, eggs, and 2 cups flour. Beat. Gradually add enough flour to make a soft dough. Knead lightly. Place in a greased bowl; cover and let rise. Punch down. When light, shape into rolls, tea ring, or cinnamon rolls. To shape for cinnamon rolls, divide dough into half. Roll each half out into a 12" x 9" rectangle. Brush with butter. Prepare filling by combining the first 3 ingredients. Sprinkle dough with half of the filling mixture and half the raisins or walnuts. Starting on the long side, roll up tightly. Pinch edges to seal. Cut into 12 slices. Place in a greased 9" x 12" pan. Cover and let rise until doubled; about 30 minutes. For rolls, bake at 375° for 20-25 minutes. For tea ring, bake at 350° for 20-25 minutes. When cool, top with a powdered sugar glaze (see recipe with Blueberry Pecan Coffeecake in this chapter). Makes 2 dozen rolls or 2 large tea rings.

Buddy's Run Tea Bread

A healthy loaf that freezes well!

1 cup unsalted butter
1 cup sugar
4 eggs, separated
½ cup cooked cream of wheat
1 small tart apple, peeled and grated
1 carrot, peeled and grated
½ cup raisins
½ cup chopped apricots
2 cups flour
2 tsp. baking powder
1 tsp. cinnamon
¼ tsp. nutmeg
¼ tsp. salt

Preheat oven to 350°. Grease and flour a 9" x 5" x 3" loaf pan. Beat together butter and sugar until light and fluffy. Beat in egg yolks, 1 at a time. Stir in cream of wheat, apple, carrot, raisins and apricots. Blend in flour, baking powder, cinnamon, nutmeg and salt. Beat egg whites until stiff peaks form; gently fold into batter. Turn into prepared pan. Bake for 1 hour 20 minutes or until toothpick comes out clean. Cool bread completely before removing from pans. This bread is best served the next day. Makes 1 loaf.

Blueberry Pecan Coffeecake

2 cups fresh or frozen blueberries
1 tsp. cinnamon
1 ¼ cups less 2 Tbsp. sugar
3 cups flour
6 Tbsp. cultured buttermilk powder
¾ tsp. baking powder
¾ tsp. baking soda
¾ tsp. salt
½ cup plus 2 Tbsp. butter or margarine, softened
1 ½ cups water
3 eggs
¼ cup brown sugar, firmly packed
½ cup chopped pecans
Powdered Sugar Icing (recipe follows)

Mix blueberries and cinnamon and add ¼ cup sugar. In a large bowl, mix flour, remaining sugar, buttermilk powder, baking powder, baking soda, salt, ½ cup butter, water and eggs. Beat on low for 2 minutes. Pour half of the batter (about 2 cups) into a greased 13" x 9" pan. Spoon half the blueberries (about 1 cup) over the batter. Repeat with remaining batter and blueberries. Sprinkle brown sugar and pecans over the top. Drizzle with remaining butter. Bake at 375° for about 45 minutes. Drizzle with Powdered Sugar Icing. Serves 12-16.

Powdered Sugar Icing

¾ cup confectioners sugar
⅛ tsp. vanilla
2-3 tsp. water
Mix together and drizzle over Blueberry Pecan Coffeecake.

Cowboy Coffeecake

2 ½ cups flour
2 cups brown sugar
½ tsp. salt
⅔ cup shortening
2 tsp. baking powder
½ tsp. baking soda
½ tsp. cinnamon
½ tsp. nutmeg
1 cup buttermilk
2 eggs, beaten

In a large mixing bowl, combine flour, sugar, salt and shortening. Mix until crumbly in texture. Set aside ½ cup of mixture. To remaining mixture, add baking powder, baking soda, cinnamon and nutmeg. Add milk and eggs and mix well. Pour into 2 greased and floured 8" round cake pans or a 13" x 9" baking pan. Top with reserved crumbs. Bake at 375° for 25-30 minutes. Serves 10-15. Recipe easily halved.

Log Cabin Cake

1 ¼ cups boiling water
1 cup regular oats
½ cup margarine
1 cup white sugar
1 cup brown sugar
2 eggs
1 ⅓ cups flour
1 tsp. baking soda
½ tsp. nutmeg
1 tsp. cinnamon
dash of salt

Topping:
6 Tbsp. margarine
½ cup cream
½ cup brown sugar
½ tsp. vanilla
1 cup chopped nuts
1 cup shredded coconut

Mix water, oats and margarine together and let stand for 20 minutes. Add remaining ingredients; mix well. Pour into an 8" x 12" baking pan and bake at 375° for 25-30 minutes. Prepare topping by combining all ingredients. Spread topping on warm cake and place under broiler until lightly toasted. Serves 8-10.

The first log cabins had a thick covering of dirt on their roofs which made excellent insulation, but leaked in wet weather. The roof was a convenient place to plant the earliest seeds––these were called "roof gardens."

Dutch Hustle Cake

2 Tbsp. brown sugar
¼ tsp. cinnamon
¼ tsp. nutmeg
1 ½ cups flour
¼ cup sugar
1 pkg. dry yeast
2 Tbsp. margarine, softened
¼ cup very hot water
1 egg, room temperature
1 ½ cups apple slices, blanched, drained and peeled
2 Tbsp. margarine
Powdered Sugar Icing (see recipe with Blueberry Pecan Coffeecake)

In a small bowl combine brown sugar, cinnamon and nutmeg and set aside. In a large bowl mix ½ cup flour, sugar and yeast. Add softened margarine. Gradually add hot water and beat 2 minutes at medium speed. Add egg and ½ cup flour or enough to make a soft batter. Beat at high speed 2 minutes scraping bowl occasionally. Stir in enough remaining flour to make a stiff, but not dry, batter. Spread batter in a 9" square or round baking pan. Arrange apple slices on top. Sprinkle with brown sugar mixture. Dot with remaining 2 Tbsp. margarine. Cover and let rise until doubled, about 1 hour. Bake at 400° about 25 minutes. Let stand 10 minutes before removing from pan. Drizzle icing over top. Serve warm.

Sopapilla Pastry Dough

4 cups flour
1 ½ tsp. salt
1 tsp. baking powder
1 Tbsp. yeast
¼ cup warm water
1 Tbsp. soy oil
1 ¼ cups milk
vegetable oil or shortening for frying

Combine flour, salt and baking powder; set aside. Dissolve yeast in warm water; set aside. Scald milk and add soy oil; let cool to room temperature. When milk is cooled, add to yeast and water; then add to flour mixture. Mix well. Dough should be moist, not wet. Let dough rise under wet towel or plastic wrap placed in a warm spot.

Punch down and roll dough into a rectangle ⅛ inch thick. Cut into triangles or any other fun cookie-cutter shape. Heat about 1 inch of oil in a large frying pan to 375°. Fry sopapillas until golden brown on both sides, turning once. Drain on paper towels and serve at once with honey.

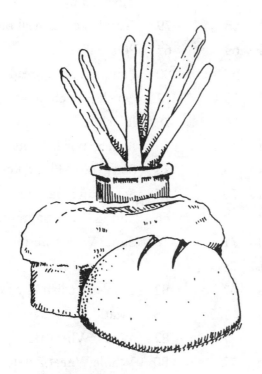

Breads

Breads

Easy Cheesy Bread Sticks

A hit with kids and adults alike.

⅓ cup butter
2 ½ cups flour
1 Tbsp. sugar
3 ½ tsp. baking powder
1 ½ tsp. salt
1 cup grated Cheddar cheese
1 cup milk
sesame seeds
garlic salt

Preheat oven to 450°. As oven is preheating, heat butter in a 13"x 9" baking dish. When butter is melted, remove from oven. In a large bowl, combine flour, sugar, baking powder, salt, and cheese; add milk. When well combined, turn out onto well floured surface. Knead gently 10 times. Roll dough into 12" x 8" rectangle. With a sharp knife, cut dough lengthwise and then across into 16 strips. Dip both sides of sticks in melted butter. Lay in rows in baking dish. Sprinkle with sesame seeds and garlic salt. Bake at 400° for 15 minutes. Yields 32.

Potato Biscuits

Heavenly!

2 medium size baking potatoes
1 Tbsp. dry yeast
1 ½ Tbsp. warm water
2 cups bread flour
1 tsp. salt
1 cup cold, unsalted butter
1 egg yolk, beaten with 1 Tbsp. cold water

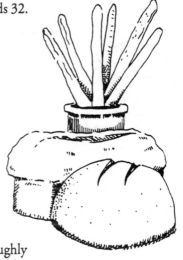

One day ahead, boil potatoes in water to cover until thoroughly cooked. Drain and cool completely. Dissolve yeast in water and let sit for 10 minutes. Combine the flour and salt in food processor. Cut in butter by pulsing. Peel and roughly chop the potatoes, add to the processor. Process briefly until you have a soft dough. Remove dough to floured work surface and pat out and shape into an 8" x 12" rectangle. Fold in thirds, cover loosely and chill 2 hours. Remove from refrigerator and roll out again into 8" x 12" rectangle. Fold and chill 24 hours.

Next day, remove from refrigerator and do 1 more turn. Chill 2 hours. Finally, roll out into 9" x 15" rectangle (½" to ⅝" thickness). With a sharp knife, cut dough into 45 1" x 3" rectangles. Place on lightly greased baking sheet. Let rise 20-25 minutes. Brush with egg wash and bake at 400° for 16-18 minutes. Yields 45 biscuits.

Spring Creek Sourdough Starter

3 cups warm potato water
3 cups flour
1 pkg. dry yeast
1 ½ Tbsp. sugar
½ tsp. salt

This recipe is from Mrs. Ward Wren, an ancestor to Gordy Wren. Mrs. Wren arrived in Steamboat Springs in 1894.

Boil 2 large potatoes, diced and cleaned. Drain 3 cups of water into a bowl. Dissolve the yeast in warm water. Blend in flour sifted with sugar and salt. Cover with a towel and let stand in a warm area for several days. When the starter is smelly and bubbly, 3-4 days, store in the refrigerator, covered. Before using, remove from the cool place and put back in a warm place to "work". It may help to get dough functioning again if a cup each of flour and warm water is added. Should be used once a week or the enzymes may die. Always add an equal amount of flour and warm water after using.

NOTE: Always use wood, plastic and glass utensils and dishes for the sourdough starter.

Ranch Style Biscuits

2 cups all-purpose flour
4 tsp. baking powder
2 tsp. sugar
½ tsp. salt
½ tsp. cream of tartar
½ cup vegetable shortening
⅔ cup milk
1 large egg, slightly beaten

Gordy Wren, Steamboat born and bred, is acknowledged to be "the greatest all-round American skier of all time." He is the only American ever to qualify for all of the original four Olympic skiing events, which he did in 1948, for the Olympics in St. Moritz.

Sift together dry ingredients. Cut in shortening until mixture resembles coarse crumbs. Combine egg and milk; add to flour mixture all at once. Stir until dough follows fork around bowl surface; knead gently with heel of hand, about 20 strokes. Roll dough to ¾" thickness. Dip 2" biscuit cutter in flour; cut straight down through dough, do not twist. Place on ungreased baking sheet. If desired, chill 1-3 hours. Bake at 450° for 10-14 minutes or until golden brown. Makes 2 dozen.

Sourdough Biscuits

½ cup sourdough starter
½ cup flour
½ cup milk
extra flour
½ tsp. baking soda
½ tsp. salt
1 Tbsp. melted butter

Several hours before preparing, remove the starter from the refrigerator and mix with flour and milk. Just before baking, add salt, soda, butter and enough flour to form a stiff dough. Lightly knead, pat out on a floured board and using a biscuit cutter, make biscuits ½" thick. Place on a baking sheet, brush with butter, bake at 450° for about 10 minutes. Serve. Makes 10-12 biscuits.

Cliff Dwellers Fry Bread

2 cups flour
3 tsp. baking powder
½ tsp. salt
2 Tbsp. sugar
⅔ cup milk or more, if needed

Mix dry ingredients; add milk and mix well. Divide into 6 pieces. Shape into balls and roll each out into a 5" circle. Punch a hole in the center for a traditional appearance. Fry in ½" oil until golden brown; drain on paper towels.

This bread is eaten with green chili dishes or served warm with honey or dusted with powdered sugar. It can also be covered with beans or stews. Yields six 5" breads.

The hole in the center of Cliff Dwellers Fry Bread is a reminder of the sticks used long ago to dip the bread in and out of the hot oil.

High Altitude Popovers

6 large eggs
2 cups milk
6 Tbsp. butter, melted
2 cups all-purpose flour
1 tsp. salt

Beat eggs in a large bowl. Stir in milk and butter; mix well. Add flour and salt. Stir vigorously, 3-4 minutes. Divide batter evenly between well-buttered popover pan or ten 6 oz. custard cups which have been placed on a baking sheet. Bake at 375° for 60 minutes. If a metal popover pan is used, reduce baking time to 40 minutes. Slit each popover open on one side to let the steam out. Return to oven and bake until well-browned, about 15 minutes more. Serve immediately. Wonderful, high altitude popovers. Makes 10 popovers.

Triathlon Popovers
Great as a bread dish or dessert.

1 ¼ cups flour
¼ tsp. salt
3 large eggs
1 ¼ cups milk (skim milk works)
1 Tbsp. unsalted butter, melted
2 Tbsp. unsalted butter, cut into 6 even pieces

Oil or spray popover pan. Set rack in middle of oven and preheat to 450°. Preheat popover pan in oven about 2 minutes. It will be smoking when removed. Blend flour, salt, eggs, milk, and melted butter until mixture is the consistency of heavy cream, about 1-2 minutes. Place 1 small piece of butter in each cup and place pan back in preheated oven until butter is bubbly, about 1 minute. Fill each cup half-full with batter and bake at 450° for 25 minutes. Reduce temperature to 325° and continue baking for 20 minutes. Do not peek until heat is reduced to 325°. Serve hot either plain, with jam, or honey. Makes 6 popovers. This batter can be made ahead of time and stored in the refrigerator, but it should be used at room temperature.

Cajun Cornbread
½ cup fried bacon, reserve fat
2 cups all purpose flour
1 Tbsp. baking powder
1 tsp. salt
¼ cup granulated sugar
2 cups stone ground cornmeal
5 eggs
½ cup salad oil
½ cup heavy cream
1 ½ cups milk
1 cup diced onion
3 jalapeño peppers, diced

Fry bacon and pour fat in preheated 9" x 13" baking pan. Return pan to 425° oven. Mix crumbled bacon and all dry ingredients in a large mixing bowl. Add wet ingredients and mix well. Pour into hot baking pan and bake approximately 40 minutes.

This recipe is adjusted for high altitude. For lower altitudes, use 4 eggs and 2 Tbsp. baking powder.

Garlic Cheese Bread

A quick bread for barbecues or company.

½ loaf French bread
¼ - ⅓ cup mayonnaise
¼ cup fresh Parmesan cheese, grated
½ tsp. dried parsley flakes
¼ - ½ tsp. garlic powder

Preheat broiler. Cut bread lengthwise in half. Broil bread 1-2 minutes until lightly browned. Combine remaining ingredients and spread over bread. Broil 2-3 minutes more until lightly browned. Slice bread. Best if mayonnaise mixture is made ahead of time to allow flavors to come through. Serves 4.

Carrot Zucchini Bread

Makes large loaves full of flavor.

2 ½ cups sugar
6 large eggs
2 ½ cups canola oil
1 ½ tsp. vanilla extract
4 cups all-purpose flour
4 tsp. baking powder
1 tsp. salt
3 tsp. allspice
2 cups grated carrots
2 cups grated zucchini
1 ½ cups chopped walnuts
1 tsp. orange zest

In a large bowl, beat sugar, eggs, oil, and vanilla until well-blended. Sift flour, baking powder, salt and allspice together. Add sugar and oil mixture to dry ingredients and mix until just well blended. Be careful not to overmix. Fold in carrots, zucchini, nuts, and orange zest. Pour into lightly greased 9" x 5" bread pans and bake at 350º for 50 minutes. Loaves are done when a toothpick inserted in the center comes out clean. Cool in the pans for 20 minutes. Turn out and cool completely before serving. Wrapped tightly, this bread will keep well for 4-5 days. Makes 2 loaves.

Super Wheat Germ Zucchini Bread

1 ½ cups wheat germ
3 cups flour
3 tsp. baking powder
1 tsp. salt
2 tsp. cinnamon
1 ½ cups chopped nuts
2 eggs
1 ¾ cups sugar
2 tsp. vanilla
⅔ cup oil
3 cups (about 3 medium size) zucchini, grated

Mix together wheat germ, flour, baking powder, salt, cinnamon and nuts. Beat eggs until light in color. Beat in sugar, vanilla and oil. Stir in zucchini. Gradually stir in wheat germ mixture. Turn into 2 greased and floured 8 ½" x 4 ½" loaf pans. Bake at 350º for 1 hour or until a toothpick inserted into center comes out clean. Cool for 10 minutes. Remove from pans and cool on rack. Makes 2 loaves.

Maple Zucchini Bread

Maple flavoring offers a new twist to an old favorite.

3 eggs, beaten
1 cup granulated sugar
1 cup brown sugar
1 cup cooking oil
3 tsp. maple flavoring
2 cups zucchini, coarsely grated, peeled and packed
2 tsp. baking soda
½ tsp. baking powder
2 tsp. salt
½ cup regular wheat germ
2 ½ cups flour, unsifted
1 cup chopped walnuts
⅓ cup sesame seeds

Beat together eggs, sugars, oil and maple flavor until foamy and thick. Stir in zucchini, soda, baking powder, salt, wheat germ and flour. Mix well. Stir in walnuts. Spoon batter into greased and floured 9" x 5" loaf pan. Sprinkle top with sesame seeds. Bake at 350º for 1 hour or until done. Cool for 10 minutes before removing from pan. Makes 2 loaves.

Grandma's Pumpkin Bread

1 ½ cups sugar
1 ⅔ cups flour, unsifted
¼ tsp. baking powder
1 tsp. baking soda
1 tsp. salt
1 ½ tsp. pumpkin pie spice
2 eggs
½ cup oil
⅓ cup water
1 ½ cups canned pumpkin
1 cup chopped walnuts

Mix sugar, flour, baking powder, soda, salt and spices together. Add eggs, oil, water and pumpkin and blend well. Add nuts. Pour into a 9" x 5" loaf pan and bake at 325° for 1 ½ hours. Test with toothpick for doneness. Let cool, then remove from pan. Serves 8-10.

Bashor Banana Bread

2 cups sugar
½ cup shortening
3 eggs
1 ½ cups white flour
1 cup wheat flour
½ cup bran
pinch of salt
1 ½ tsp. baking soda
1 cup buttermilk
3 extremely ripe bananas
½ cup chopped nuts
1 Tbsp. cinnamon
1 Tbsp. vanilla extract

Bashor Run on Mt. Werner was named after Carl Bashor, a colorful man who homesteaded 160 acres of land bisecting Giggle Gulch. He spent 60 years exploring Mt. Werner (formerly Storm Mountain) on skis and by horseback.

Cream sugar, shortening and eggs. Add remaining ingredients and mix well. Grease 2 loaf pans well. Bake at 375° for 40 minutes or until done. Freezes well. Makes 2 loaves.

Easy Banana Bread
Tastes just like fresh bananas.

½ cup butter, softened
½ cup sugar
1 egg
¾ tsp. baking soda
1 ½ cups flour
1 tsp. baking powder
½ tsp. salt
4 large, very ripe bananas, mashed

Preheat oven to 350°. Grease loaf pan. Mix butter and sugar; add egg and blend. Sift dry ingredients and add to butter and sugar mixture. Add bananas. Pour into pan and bake for 50-60 minutes. For variety, add nuts, seeds, yogurt, or chopped dried apricots to recipe.

Lemon Poppy Seed Bread
6 eggs
2 ½ cups granulated sugar
1 ½ cups milk
1 ¼ cups margarine
5 ¼ cups all purpose flour
1 ½ tsp. baking powder
6 ozs. poppy seeds
rind of 2 lemons, grated

Glaze:
juice of 2 lemons
1 cup granulated sugar

Cream eggs, sugar, milk and margarine until smooth. Combine remaining bread ingredients and add alternately with the egg mixture in 3 additions. Pour batter into greased and floured loaf pans. Bake at 350° for about 1 hour or until toothpick comes out clean. Remove breads from pans while still warm. Makes 2 loaves.

To prepare glaze, boil lemon juice and sugar together. Brush on bread loaves. (This recipe has been adjusted for high altitude. For low altitude cooking, use 5 cups flour and 1 Tbsp. baking powder.)

Crackle Poppy Seed Bread

Serve with orange-flavored whipped cream cheese.

1 ½ cups wheat flour
2 Tbsp. non-fat dry milk
½ cup sesame seeds
2 tsp. poppy seeds
1 ½ tsp. baking powder
½ tsp. salt
2 eggs, beaten lightly
½ cup honey
½ cup orange juice
2 Tbsp. melted, unsalted butter
2 Tbsp. vegetable oil

Combine first 6 ingredients. In separate bowl, combine remaining ingredients. Combine all and stir until just mixed. Spoon into 8½" x 4½" greased loaf pan and bake at 350° for 30-40 minutes. Cool 10 minutes; remove from pan to wire rack. Makes 1 loaf.

Encampment River and Meadows (Mt. Zirkel area) is so called because Indian tribes staked their summer tents on the broad meadow at the river ford where they lived off wild bounty.

Angler's Onion Dill Bread

3 cups flour
¼ cup instant dry milk
3 Tbsp. butter
2 Tbsp. sugar
1 tsp. salt
1 pkg. less 2 Tbsp. dry onion soup mix
2 tsp. dill weed
2 tsp. caraway seed
1 pkg. dry yeast
¾-1 cup lukewarm water

In food processor, mix first 8 ingredients about 10-15 seconds. Leave in bowl. Add yeast to ¼ cup lukewarm water and let sit until dissolved. With food processor running, add yeast mixture through food chute. In a slow steady stream, add just enough remaining water to form a loose ball. Remove dough and turn onto floured surface. Knead 8-10 times shaping into a ball. Place into greased bowl, cover with waxed paper and cloth. Let rise until doubled, about 1-2 hours. Turn onto floured surface. Punch down and knead until no longer sticky. Form into ball, cover with bowl and let rest 10 minutes. Shape into loaf and place in well-greased 9" x 5" loaf pan. Cover, let rise again 1-2 hours, until doubled. Bake at 375° for 40-45 minutes. Remove and cool on wire rack. Makes 1 loaf.

Hazie's Rolls

3 cups milk
½ cup sugar
1 tsp. salt
½ cup butter
2 pkgs. quick rise yeast
1 cup warm water
2 tsp. sugar
3 eggs
8 - 10 cups flour

In a medium saucepan, bring milk, sugar and salt to a boil. Remove from heat and add butter. While this cools, proof yeast with warm water and sugar. Beat eggs in a large bowl. Add cooled milk mixture and stir. Stir in yeast mixture. Add sifted flour, blending well with each cup added. Mix flour until dough is soft but not sticky. Place in an oiled bowl, cover and let rise until doubled. Punch down dough and let rise again. Roll out dough to ¾" thick and cut off pieces for rolls (size desired). Place on a greased baking sheet and let rise. Bake at 350° for 20 minutes or until rolls are lightly browned.

For cinnamon rolls: More sugar may be added to milk mixture if desired. After dough rises the second time, divide dough in 2 sections. Roll each section to ½" thick. Spread with ¼ cup softened butter. Sprinkle with a mixture of 1½ cup brown sugar and 2 heaping Tbsp. cinnamon. Roll dough up lengthwise into a long roll. Cut slices ½" to ¾" thick and place rolls on greased baking pan. Let rise until light and bake at 350° for 20-30 minutes until golden. Makes 45-75 rolls, depending on size.

Buddy Werner was America's first truly world class skier. Though Olympic medals eluded him in the games of '56, '60 and '64, he won nearly every other major championship. Buddy died in a Swiss avalanche in 1964, but his legendary style and sportsmanship continue to inspire all of Steamboat's youth.

Light Rolls

Regular Version:
1 pkg. yeast
¼ cup warm water
2 cups milk, warmed
2 tsp. salt
4 Tbsp. butter or margarine
4 Tbsp. sugar
3 eggs
5-6 cups flour

Low Cholesterol Version:
2 pkgs. yeast
⅓ cup warm water
2 cups water, warmed
2 tsp. salt
4 Tbsp. oil
4 Tbsp. sugar
1 egg
5-6 cups flour

Dissolve yeast in warm water. Combine with milk, salt, butter, sugar and eggs. Mix well. Stir in enough flour to make a soft, pliable dough. Knead until smooth and elastic. Let rise until doubled. Mold into round balls and place in a greased 13" x 9" pan. Let rise again. Bake at 400° for 12-15 minutes.

Light Crescent Rolls

These are incredibly light and airy rolls.

¾ cup milk
½ cup shortening
½ cup sugar
1 tsp. salt
2 pkgs. yeast
1 tsp. sugar
½ cup very warm water
4 ¼-4 ¾ cups flour
2 eggs
¼ cup butter, melted
2 Tbsp. sugar

Scald milk. Add shortening, sugar, and salt. Cool until lukewarm. Sprinkle yeast and sugar in warm water. Let proof. Add ½ cup flour to milk mixture and beat well. Beat in eggs and yeast mixture. Gradually add remaining flour. This is a soft dough that pulls away from the sides of the bowl. Knead 5-8 minutes. Place in a lightly greased bowl and turn dough once. Cover and let rise until double; about 1-1 ½ hours. Punch down dough. Turn on floured board and divide dough in half. Roll dough to about ⅓" thickness. Cut dough into 3" wide sections. Slice strips into pie shaped pieces about 3"x2½". Roll into crescents from wide end to point. Place on greased baking sheet and let rise 30-45 minutes. Bake at 375° for 12-15 minutes or until golden. Mix melted butter with sugar. Remove rolls from oven and brush rolls with butter mixture. Serve immediately. These are incredibly light, airy rolls. They can easily be made with quick rise yeast to reduce preparation time. Makes 2-3 dozen rolls.

60 Minute Rolls

2 pkgs. active dry yeast
⅓ cup warm water
1 ¼ cups milk
2 Tbsp. shortening
3 Tbsp. sugar
1 tsp. salt
1 egg
3 ½ cups flour

Dissolve yeast in warm water. Heat milk; add shortening, sugar, salt and egg; allow to cool. Add yeast. Add flour and beat well, dough will be sticky. Set dough in warm place and let rise 15 minutes. Punch dough down and knead lightly. Roll dough out to ¾" thickness and use round cookie cutter to make rolls. Place 1" apart on lightly greased cookie sheet; let rise 15 minutes and bake at 400° for 15 minutes. Yields 15 rolls.

Crescent Refrigerator Rolls
Wonderful to have on hand with a
houseful of company.

2 cups hot water
½ cup sugar
½ cup butter
1 tsp. salt
2 pkgs. dry yeast
2 eggs, beaten
6-6 ½ cups flour

Mix the first 4 ingredients in a large bowl. When cooled to lukewarm,
add yeast to the mixture. Add eggs, mix well and then gradually add
flour to make a very soft dough. Knead 5 minutes. Let rise until
doubled. Punch down. Put in refrigerator in a covered bowl
overnight. Divide dough into fourths. Roll each piece into pie rounds
and slice pie-shaped pieces. Roll from wide end to the point, tucking
point under. Place on lightly greased baking sheet. Bake at 400° for
15-20 minutes. Remove from oven and brush with melted butter.
This dough can be kept in the refrigerator for up to 1 week. If it rises
too much, just punch it down and return to the refrigerator. Makes
3 dozen rolls.

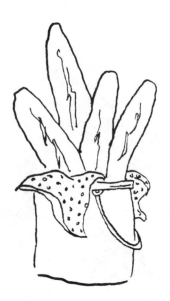

Easy French Bread
½ cup warm water
1 tsp. sugar
2 ½ tsp. yeast
3 cups flour
2 tsp. salt
1 tsp. sugar
1 scant cup warm water
cornmeal
1 egg white, mixed with water

Dissolve yeast and sugar in ½ cup warm water . Place flour, salt, and
sugar in a food processor with a steel blade. Turn on processor and mix
dry ingredients. With machine on, add yeast mixture and warm water,
a little at a time. Keep machine on. When a ball forms, about 2
minutes, count to 60 and turn it off. Place in an oiled bowl, cover, and
let rise. Punch down dough, cut in half, and form into long baguettes.
Place on greased cookie sheet, sprinkled with cornmeal. Let rise until
light. Bake at 400° for 30-45 minutes. Spray with a water bottle 3
times in the first 3 minutes. Halfway through baking, brush with egg
white mixture. Makes 2 loaves.

Quick French Bread

1 pkg. dry yeast
1 Tbsp. sugar
1 cup very warm water
1 Tbsp. vegetable oil
1 tsp. salt
2 ½ cups all-purpose flour

Combine the first 3 ingredients until yeast is dissolved. Stir in oil and salt. Stir in flour. Knead dough for 5 minutes. Place dough in a bowl and let rest for 20 minutes. Roll out dough into a rectangle, shaping into a long loaf. Place on a greased cookie sheet. Let rise for 30 minutes. Bake at 350° for 20-25 minutes. Makes 1 loaf.

Last Minute Pizza Dough

2 cups very warm water
2 pkgs. dry yeast
5 ¼ cups flour
1 tsp. salt
½ tsp. olive oil

Mix ingredients and knead for 5 minutes. Place in greased bowl, cover with towel. Place in oven that has been warmed to 200° degrees, then turned off. Let rise 20 minutes. Divide into 3 crusts. Top with pizza ingredients and bake at 450°. With leftover dough, roll into long skinny breadsticks, place on a cookie sheet, and bake with the pizza.

"Tillie and I stayed here all day by ourselves and were so busy we didn't get time to change our dresses or take down our frizzies. Tillie churned while I baked a cake, made light bread, etc."

From the diary of
Lulie Margie Crawford
Aug. 20, 1881

Italian Loaf

1 ¼ cups warm water
1 Tbsp. sugar
1 tsp. salt
1 pkg. dry yeast
1 Tbsp. vegetable oil
3 ½ cups flour
egg whites

Mix water, sugar, salt and yeast together. Let proof (yeast will bubble and rise for 5 minutes. Add 1 tablespoon vegetable oil and slowly mix in 3 ½ cups of flour. Knead well—dough will be slightly sticky. Place in an oiled bowl and let rise. Punch down, roll dough to fit in French loaf pan. Let rise. Slash 3 times and brush top with egg whites. Bake at 400° for 25 minutes. Makes 1 large loaf or two small loaves.

Olive Oil Bread

2 cups lukewarm milk
1 ½ Tbsp. dried yeast
1 ½ Tbsp. sugar
⅜ cup med. quality olive oil
2 tsp. salt
5-6 cups unbleached flour

Add yeast to warm milk, and sprinkle a pinch of sugar on top to help yeast dissolve. After mixture foams, about 10 minutes, add oil, sugar, salt and enough flour to make a thick batter. Continue to add flour gradually until you have a dough thick enough to be turned out onto a floured board. Knead, adding more flour as necessary to make an elastic, smooth dough, 5-10 minutes. Place dough in a greased bowl, turning the greased side upright, cover with plastic wrap, and place in warm place to rise. When dough has doubled in bulk, gently deflate, shape into loaves, place on greased baking sheets, and let rise again until almost doubled. If a shiny crust is desired, brush unbaked dough with egg wash made from an egg beaten with a little water. Bake at 350° for 25-40 minutes, depending on the shape and size of loaves. Makes 3 loaves.

To fill loaves for a main course, flatten pieces of dough into rectangles after first rising. Make an egg wash and brush on rectangle. Add filling lengthwise down the dough, and bring sides together, pinching them together securely as well as the ends, so filling is completely encased. Place seam side down, and let rise until almost doubled. Use a serrated knife to cut diagonally across the loaves, exposing the filling, and let dough rest 10 minutes before baking. Fillings can be anything from cheeses to mushrooms and green peppers, pesto, sliced salami, even peanut butter and jelly. Filling bread is a good way to use up leftover bits of ingredients.

Ranch House Bread

Six loaves and more for all your hungry help!

2 cups milk
¾ cup sugar
8 tsp. salt
¾ cup margarine
6 cups warm water
4 pkgs. dry yeast
24 cups unsifted flour (approx.)

Scald milk; stir in sugar, salt and margarine. Cool to lukewarm. Measure warm water into large warm bowl. Sprinkle in yeast; stir until dissolved. Add lukewarm milk mixture. Add 12 cups flour; beat until smooth. Add flour to make a stiff dough. Knead 10 minutes. Put in a greased bowl. Cover. Let rise 1 hour. Punch down. Cover. Let rest 15 minutes. Divide into pieces for loaves. Shape. Place in greased loaf pans. Let rise 1 hour. Bake at 400° for 30 minutes. Makes 6 loaves plus two round pans of rolls or one big pan of hamburger buns.

The Crawford family cabin, located at 12th and Lincoln, housed the first school as early as 1876. Most schools operated from September to May. A few operated only in the summer months because so many ranch children were isolated by the harsh winters.

Pearl Lake Oatmeal Bread
Wonderfully fragrant and hearty loaves.

4 cups boiling water
3 cups rolled oats
7 ½-8 cups all-purpose flour
5 tsp. dry yeast
1 Tbsp. salt
¼ cup salad oil
½ cup molasses

Lester Creek Reservoir is also called Pearl Lake for Pearl Hart who donated the land for the reservoir to the Colorado Division of Wildlife. The lake was filled in 1961 and is managed for quality fishing for native trout.

Pour boiling water over the oatmeal in a large bowl and allow to cool. Stir in 2 cups of the flour and the dry yeast. Place in a warm, draft-free spot. Allow this sponge to rise for 1-1 ½ hours. Stir down. Mix in salt, salad oil, molasses, and enough remaining flour to make a stiff dough. Knead at least 300 strokes. Divide dough into 3 equal portions. Form into loaves and place in 9" x 5" greased pans. Allow to rise again until doubled. Bake at 350° for 40-60 minutes or until it sounds hollow when tapped. This recipe also makes great rolls. Makes 3 loaves.

Whole Wheat Raisin Bread
This makes wonderful toast for breakfast.

3 cups water
3 cups raisins
2 Tbsp. honey
2 pkg. dry yeast
4 cups whole wheat flour
3-4 cups unbleached white flour
1 cup dry milk powder
2 tsp. salt
2 eggs
3 Tbsp. oil
1 ½ cups powdered sugar
¼ tsp. vanilla
4-6 tsp. water

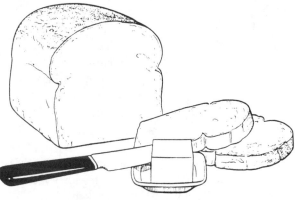

Bring water, raisins and honey to a boil. Drain off liquid and reserve. Set raisins aside. Cool liquid to 110°. Stir yeast into liquid until dissolved and bubbly. Combine whole wheat flour, 3 cups white flour, milk powder and salt in a large mixing bowl. Add eggs and oil to the yeast mixture. Add to the flour mixture. Stir in enough of the remaining white flour to make a soft dough. Turn out onto a floured surface and knead 8-10 minutes. Cover and let rise for about 1 ½ hours, or until doubled. Punch down dough. Divide into 2 equal pieces. Roll out each to ¾" thickness. Sprinkle half the raisins over each piece and roll up beginning with the long end. Place in greased 9" x 5" x 3" loaf pans. Cover; let rise until doubled, about 1 hour. Bake at 325° for 50 minutes. Remove from pans and allow to cool for 10 minutes. As loaves are cooling, combine powdered sugar, vanilla and water for a glaze. Drizzle over cooled loaves. Makes 2 large loaves.

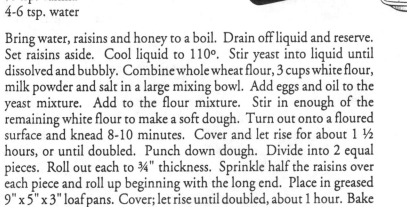

Whole Wheat Potato Bread

1 ½ cups water
1 ¼ cups milk
¼ cup margarine
¼ cup honey
3 ½ cups flour
1 ½ cups potato flakes
2 ½ tsp. salt
2 pkgs. dry yeast
2 eggs
2 ½-3 cups whole wheat flour

Heat first 4 ingredients in saucepan until warm and margarine has begun to melt. Combine in a large mixing bowl with 2 cups flour, potato flakes, salt, yeast and eggs. Beat 4 minutes at medium speed. Stir in remaining flour by hand. Knead until smooth and elastic. Let rise in a greased bowl, covered, until doubled. Punch down, divide and shape into 2 loaves. Place in two 9" x 5" loaf pans. Cover and let rise until doubled. Bake at 375° for 35-40 minutes. Remove from pans and let cool. Makes 2 loaves.

Pumpkin Seed Bread

1 cup pumpkin seeds
2 Tbsp. dry yeast
6 cups whole wheat flour
2 ½ cups milk
1 tsp. salt
2 Tbsp. oil
¼ cup honey

Chop pumpkin seeds in food processor; set aside. Using dough blade, mix together yeast and 2 cups of the flour. Mix together remaining ingredients and heat to lukewarm. Add to yeast mixture and run food processor to mix together. Add remaining flour and pumpkin seeds. Add a little more flour, if needed, to make the dough ball together in the food processor. Once it balls together, process about 1 more minute to knead the dough. Place the dough in an oiled bowl, turning dough to coat the top. Cover and let rise in a warm place until doubled, about 2 hours. Punch down and divide in half. Shape into 2 loaves. Place in oiled pans. Cover and let rise in a warm place until doubled, about 1 hour. Bake at 375° for 40-45 minutes. Cool loaves on a wire rack. Makes 2 loaves.

Wild West Wheat Bread

This moist bread is a good keeper.

12 oz. can evaporated milk
2 ⅔ cups water
1-1 ½ bananas, mashed
½ cup honey
8 oz. pkg. cream cheese
4 pkgs. dry yeast
1 cup warm water (80º-100º)
6 cups whole wheat flour
1 cup Quaker oats or 7-grain cereal
1 Tbsp. salt
5-6 cups white flour

Place milk, honey, cream cheese, and water in a medium saucepan. Heat slowly until barely warm. Stir together the yeast, 1 cup warm water, and a dab of honey in a 2-cup measuring cup; allow to stand until foamy. In a large electric mixing bowl, stir together the wheat flour, oats or 7-grain cereal, salt and about 1 cup white flour. Stirring very slowly, pour the warm honey mix, mashed banana, and then the yeast mixture into the flour. Beat for 3-5 minutes. Turn out onto a flour-covered surface and knead in remaining white flour. Place dough in a large, buttered bowl and brush the top with melted butter. Cover and allow to rise until double. Divide dough into 3 balls. Roll out each ball on a lightly floured surface, making a 9" x 16" rectangle. Beginning on the narrow side, roll up into a loaf. Place loaf, seam side down, into greased 9" x 5" bread pans. Brush top with melted butter, cover loosely with wax paper, and allow to rise. Bake in a preheated oven at 325º for 40-45 minutes, or until hollow sounding when gently tapped. Upon removing the loaves from the oven, brush with melted butter, then turn out onto a cooling rack. Cool slightly before eating. Makes 3 loaves.

Nick Cleaver began skiing in Australia at age 3. He moved with his family to Steamboat in 1982 and immediately joined the Winter Sports Club. Nick found his niche in freestyle and enjoyed much success in USSA competition. In 1991, at age 16, he returned to Australia to compete on their World Cup team. Several top 10 finishes earned him a spot on the 1992 Australian Olympic team which went to Albertville.

Whole Wheat Honey Bread

½ cup warm water
¼ tsp. ginger
1 tsp. honey
2 pkgs. dry yeast
2 cups whole wheat flour
½ cup dry milk
⅓ cup honey or molasses
1 cup warm water
1 tsp. salt
3 Tbsp. butter, melted
¾ cup water
4-5 cups all-purpose flour

Mix ½ cup water, ginger, honey, and yeast. Allow yeast to dissolve. Add whole wheat flour, dry milk, honey, and warm water. This will make a sponge. Cover and let rise 1 hour. Add salt, butter, water, and enough flour to make a firm dough. Knead 6-8 minutes. Cover and let rise until double. Shape into two loaves and place seam side down in greased 9" x 5" loaf pans. Bake at 375° for 45 minutes. Makes 2 loaves.

Sven Wiik has been called "the guru of American cross-country skiing." Born in Sweden in 1921, he came to Colorado in 1949 and skied cross-country for Western State College. Sven coached the U.S. Cross-Country Olympic team in 1960 and has been Steamboat's own guru since 1969.

Sven's Swedish Limpa

1 pkg. active dry yeast
¼ cup warm water
½ cup brown sugar, firmly packed
⅓ cup molasses
1 Tbsp. shortening
1 Tbsp. salt
2 tsp. caraway seeds
½ tsp. anise
1 ½ cups hot water
4 - 4 ½ cups flour, sifted
2 cups rye flour

Soften yeast in warm water and set aside. Mix next 6 ingredients in a large bowl. Add hot water and set aside until lukewarm. When lukewarm, blend in 1 cup flour until smooth. Stir softened yeast and add, mixing well. Add the rye flour and beat until very smooth. Beat in enough remaining flour to make a soft dough. Turn dough onto a very lightly floured surface. Allow to rest 5-10 minutes. Knead. Form dough into a large ball and put into a greased, deep bowl. Turn to bring greased surface to top. Cover with waxed paper and a towel and let stand in warm place until dough is doubled. Punch down dough; pull edges into center and turn completely over in bowl. Cover and let rise again until dough is nearly doubled. Punch down and turn out on a lightly floured surface. Divide dough into 2 portions and shape into balls. Cover and allow to rest 5-10 minutes. Remove to greased baking sheet. Cover and let rise until dough is doubled. Bake at 375° for 25-30 minutes, or until lightly browned. Cool completely on cooling racks. Makes 2 loaves.

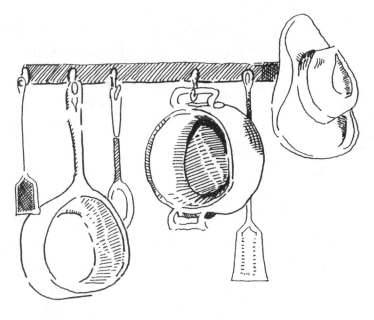

Soups

Soups

Cream of Cauliflower Soup

1 head cauliflower, chopped
1 medium onion, chopped
1 bay leaf
1 fresh sprig parsley
4 cups fresh chicken stock
2 Tbsp. butter
3 Tbsp. flour
1 cup light cream or evaporated milk
¼ tsp. white pepper
¼ tsp. salt
dash nutmeg
buttered croutons (garnish)

Combine cauliflower, onion, bay leaf and parsley with chicken stock in a medium saucepan. Cover and simmer 15 minutes or until vegetables are tender. Remove bay leaf and parsley. Melt butter in heavy skillet. Add flour and stir over low heat for 3 minutes. Do not brown. Add to soup and stir to blend. Purée soup in blender or food processor. Return to pan and add cream, pepper, salt and nutmeg. Heat, but do not boil. Garnish with buttered croutons. Serves 8.

Freestyle Creamed Soup

1 ½ cups chicken broth
½ cup chopped onion
desired vegetable and seasonings (see variations below)
2 Tbsp. butter or margarine
2 Tbsp. flour
½ tsp. salt
few dashes white pepper
1 cup milk

In a saucepan, combine chicken broth, onion and 1 of the vegetable-seasoning combinations. Bring to a boil. Reduce heat and simmer, covered, until vegetables are tender. Remove bay leaf if using broccoli. Blend mixture in a blender or food processor until smooth. In same saucepan, melt butter. Blend in flour, salt and pepper. Add milk and cook, stirring, until thickened and bubbly. Stir in vegetable purée. Heat through or chill for a cold soup (add 2 Tbsp. additional milk).

Kris Feddersen became hooked on freestyle at the Great Western Freestyle Center's summer training camp at age 12. En route to national aerial titles and World Cup success, he perfected triple-twisting triple-backflips and quadruple twisting triple-back-somersaults. He placed 4th in aerials at the Calgary Olympics in 1988, and he was 4th again in Albertville in 1992.

Variations:
• 2 cups chopped broccoli, ½ tsp. dried thyme, 1 small bay leaf, dash garlic powder
• 1 cup sliced carrots, 1 Tbsp. snipped parsley, ½ tsp. dried basil
• 1 ½ cups cut green beans, ½ tsp. dried savory
• 1 ½ cups shelled peas, ¼ cup shredded lettuce, 2 Tbsp. chopped ham, ½ tsp. dried sage
• 1 cup sliced potatoes, ½ tsp. dill weed

Wild Rice Soup

An elegant soup that goes well with game.

2 Tbsp. butter
1 Tbsp. onion, minced
¼ cup flour
4 cups chicken broth
2 cups cooked wild rice
½ tsp. salt
1 cup half and half
2 Tbsp. dry sherry
minced parsley or chives

Melt butter in 6 quart kettle and sauté onion until tender. Blend in flour, gradually add broth. Cook, stirring constantly until mixture thickens slightly. Stir in rice and salt. Simmer about 5 minutes. Blend in half and half and sherry. Heat to serving temperatures. Garnish with minced parsley or chives. Freezes well if you wish to prepare ahead. Serves 6-8.

Chilled Asparagus Soup

10 ½ oz. can condensed cream of asparagus soup
1 cup sour cream
dash of cayenne pepper
¼ tsp. onion salt
1 cup milk
2 Tbsp. chopped chives
pimentos (garnish)

Combine first 6 ingredients. Stir well and chill. Garnish with diced pimentos and serve. Serves 3-4.

Potage Creme D'or

2 Tbsp. butter
1 medium onion, chopped
1 lb. carrots, thinly sliced
5 cups chicken stock
1 cup fresh orange juice
1 cup cream
nutmeg, salt and pepper to taste
minced parsley or chives (garnish)

Melt butter in a stew pot. Add onions and carrots. Cover and stew slowly for 5-7 minutes. Pour in stock. Bring to a boil, and simmer until carrots are tender. Purée in food processor or blender. Return to clean pot and add orange juice, cream and seasonings. Heat, but do not boil. Serve with a sprinkle of chives or parsley. Serves 4-6.

Bear River Barley Soup

½ cup uncooked barley
hot water
8 oz. mushrooms, thinly sliced
6 carrots, thinly sliced
1 medium onion, chopped
1 Tbsp. oil
1 Tbsp. margarine
6 cups chicken broth
¼ tsp. coarsely ground black pepper
4 Tbsp. chopped fresh dill
2 Tbsp. fresh lemon juice

The Yampa River was once called the Bear River, leading people to believe that the Indian word for bear was yampa. However, yampa was a food that the Indians and pioneers used to survive on.

Soak barley in hot water for 20 minutes. Sauté mushrooms, carrots and onions in a combination of oil and margarine for 5 minutes, stirring occasionally. Drain barley. In a soup pot, combine chicken broth, barley, vegetables, pepper and 2 Tbsp. dill. Simmer 45 minutes. Add remaining dill and lemon juice. Simmer 10 minutes and serve. Serves 6.

Carrot Orange Soup

2 Tbsp. butter
2 Tbsp. safflower oil
2 cups yellow onions, finely chopped
12 large carrots (1 ½-2 lbs.), peeled and chopped
4 cups chicken stock, canned or homemade
1 cup freshly squeezed orange juice
salt and freshly ground black pepper to taste
grated fresh orange zest to taste
fresh minced dill, chives, or parsley; garnish

Melt butter in oil in a large pot. Add onions, cover, and cook over low heat until tender, about 20 minutes. Add carrots and chicken stock and bring to a boil. Reduce heat, cover, and simmer until carrots are tender, about 30 minutes. Pour soup through strainer and transfer solids to a food processor, fitted with a steel blade. Add 1 cup stock and process until smooth. Return puree to pot, add orange juice and additional stock (2-3 cups), until desired consistency. Season to taste. Garnish bowls with orange zest and chopped herbs. Serves 4.

Theodore Roosevelt hunted in the Flat Tops area in 1901.

Cheesy Chowder
A full meal with a salad and bread.

4 Tbsp. butter
½ cup onion, chopped
½ cup celery, chopped
½ cup green pepper, chopped
½ cup carrots, chopped
1 cup potatoes, chopped
1 cup corn
3 cups chicken stock
½ cup flour
2 cups milk
3 cups grated cheese

Sauté vegetables in butter in large kettle. Add chicken stock. Cook until vegetables are tender. Blend flour and milk and slowly stir into boiling soup to thicken. Stir in cheese. This recipe can be cooked in a crockpot all day. Add thickening and cheese right before serving. Serves 4.

French Onion Soup

2 Tbsp. butter
1 ½ to 2 lbs. (5 or 6) onions, thinly sliced
1 tsp. sugar
1 tsp. salt
¼ tsp. pepper
1 Tbsp. flour
5 cups beef stock
1 cup dry white wine
3 Tbsp. butter
12 thin slices stale French bread
1 cup Swiss cheese, grated

Melt butter in large, heavy bottomed saucepan. Add onions. Cook until translucent. Sprinkle with salt, pepper, sugar and raise heat to high. Cook, stirring occasionally until onions are golden. Sprinkle with flour and cook 3 minutes longer. Add beef stock and wine to onions. Bring to a boil, then simmer for 15 minutes. Butter bread on both sides. Preheat oven to 400°. Place bread on cookie sheet and put into oven for 5 minutes, turning over once. Pour soup into oven-proof tureen or bowls. Top with bread slices and cheese. Place under broiler until brown and bubbly. Serve at once. Serves 6.

German Cabbage Soup

2 large onions, diced
¼ cup butter
3-2 lb. cans stewed tomatoes
6 cups chicken stock
1 head green cabbage, chopped
½ cup lemon juice
½ cup brown sugar
1 Tbsp. caraway seed
salt and pepper to taste
1 lb. German sausage, sliced thinly

In a large pot, sauté onions in butter. Add remaining ingredients; bring to a boil. Reduce heat and simmer as long as you want, or until cabbage is tender. Adjust lemon juice and brown sugar to taste. Serves 8.

Miner's Potato Soup

2 chicken bouillon cubes
2 onions (white or yellow)
3 carrots
3 celery stalks
5 large red potatoes
¼ tsp. ground oregano
¼ tsp. pepper
¼ tsp. white pepper
16 ozs. medium Cheddar cheese, grated

Bring 3 qts. water to a boil. Add bouillon. Purée or mince vegetables and add to bouillon. Add spices. Simmer 30 minutes, covered, stirring frequently. Add cheese slowly while stirring. Simmer on low heat, covered, for 1 hour.

Coal was first mined to meet the needs of area residents who at one time were supplied by more than 70 "wagon mines." Oak Creek was the first to develop large mining operations because the railroad reached there in 1909.

Easy Tomato Soup

This soup freezes well and may be used later as the base for spaghetti sauce.
3 ozs. butter
1 large onion, minced
3 lbs. tomatoes (15-16 medium tomatoes)
2 tsp. basil, preferably fresh

Sauté onion in butter until transparent. Chop tomatoes and add to onions. Simmer until tomatoes turn a darker "tomato red," about 15 minutes. You may serve immediately. Or, you may cool and purée, then reheat. For a Cream of Tomato Soup, add ½ cup heavy cream right before serving.

Chili Grande

3-4 lbs. country style pork ribs
1 ½ lbs. ground round steak
3 medium onions, chopped
2-10 ½ oz. cans beef consomme'
1 can beer
1 cup red wine
2-10 ½ oz. cans whole tomatoes or 4 ½ cups chopped fresh
2 cans tomato paste
7 oz. can mild green chilies or 4-5 fresh, roasted and peeled
¼-⅓ cup chili powder
1 tsp. each cinnamon, cumin, and leaf oregano
2 cloves garlic
3 Tbsp. sugar
1 Tbsp. unsweetened cocoa
½ tsp. cayenne pepper
2-10 ½ oz. cans each red kidney beans and pinto beans

Brown ribs in a large kettle; remove and set aside. In same pot, brown ground steak and onions. Add ribs and consommé, beer, wine and broth. Mix well. Add remaining ingredients and simmer all afternoon. The longer it is allowed to cook, the better it is. At serving time, remove meat from ribs; discard bones. Serve with a dollop of sour cream and grated Cheddar cheese. Serves 15-20. Freezes well.

J. C. Trujillo's Green Chili Stew

2 - 4 lb. pork roasts
4 qts. water
3-4 cloves garlic, peeled and halved
1 Tbsp. chili pequin or chili rojo
2 tsp. salt
4 Tbsp. fat (bacon grease, vegetable oil or canola oil)
¾ cup flour
4 cups diced green chilies*
2 tsp. garlic salt
1 tsp. chicken bouillon granules
1 tsp. beef bouillon granules

Trim fat from roasts. Place roasts, water, garlic, chili and salt in a pressure cooker. Cook at medium heat for 2-2 ½ hours. If a pressure cooker is not available, simmer over low heat for 4-5 hours, until meat shreds from the bone. Remove meat, shred and debone. Strain the broth and skim off fat. Put fat in a clean stockpot, heat and whisk in flour. Begin adding broth to the roux 1 cup at a time, whisking constantly. When mixture thins out, add the remaining broth. Add meat to broth, add green chiles and seasonings. Simmer very gently for at least 2 hours. Serve with hot flour tortillas.

*Freshly-roasted green chilies make this dish extra-special.

Sopa de Lima (Mexican Lime Soup)

6 cups chicken stock
½ cup chicken, cooked and shredded
½ cup fresh tomato, diced
½ tsp. white pepper
½ cup fresh lime juice
1 ½ Tbsp. olive oil
¾ cup red onion, chopped
¾ cup diced green chilies
1 large fresh jalapeño pepper, minced
1 ½ tsp. minced garlic
1 lime slice per serving
6 corn tortillas
Picante sauce (optional)

Bring first five ingredients to a boil in a 4 quart pan. Simmer 20 minutes. Sauté next vegetables in olive oil in a large skillet until onions are tender. Add to broth. Simmer 30 minutes. Top each serving with a lime slice and ½ corn tortilla which has been cut in strips and lightly fried in oil. Pass picante sauce to season as desired. Serves 6-8.

Quick Draw Gazpacho

4 cups tomato juice
4 cups beef consommé
½ tsp. Tabasco sauce
3 Tbsp. olive oil
½ tsp. salt
½ cup fresh lemon juice
4 large cloves garlic
4 ice cubes
4 tomatoes, chopped
2 cucumbers, chopped
2 green peppers, seeded and chopped
10 green onions, chopped
½ cup minced parsley

Put first eight ingredients in blender or food processor, and blend for 1 minute. Or, mince garlic, omit ice cubes and add ½ cup water and mix ingredients by hand. Chill until serving time. Serve chopped vegetables in individual bowls for guests to add as they wish. Serves 8.

Soup and Salsa
In Mexico this soup is served with a wedge of lime.

4 chicken breasts
2 -10 ½ oz. cans chicken broth
1 cup water
¼ onion, sliced
1 cup rice
¼ cup butter
3 Tbsp. flour
1 cup milk
lime wedges
Salsa (recipe follows)

In large dutch oven parboil chicken breasts just covered in water.
Remove from water, debone and cut into small pieces. Return to
stock. Add chicken broth, water, onion and rice. In a small saucepan
melt butter. Add flour and stir until lightly browned. Add milk and
stir until thickened. Add to soup. Simmer soup until rice is done.
Serve with lime wedges and salsa.

Salsa:
2 tomatoes
¼ onion
fresh cilantro to taste
1 fresh jalapeño pepper, chopped
lime juice, a long squeeze
¼ tsp. garlic powder
¼ tsp. onion salt
¼ cup water

Chop and blend all ingredients. If using a blender, pulse to get a
chunkier salsa. Let stand, do not refrigerate. This salsa is best served
fresh at room temperature.

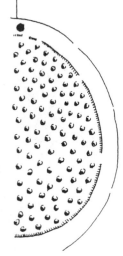

Wily Coyote Soup
2 lbs. ground beef (or turkey, venison, elk, etc.)
½ onion, chopped
2 ½ cups water
2-16 oz. cans whole peeled tomatoes
2-15 oz. cans dark red kidney beans, drained
16 oz. can tomato sauce
1 envelope taco seasoning
choice of toppings: avocado, grated cheese, tomatoes,
                              sour cream, corn chips, shredded lettuce

Brown beef with onion. Drain. Add remaining ingredients except
toppings. Simmer for 30 minutes. To serve, place soup in individual
bowls. Allow guests to add their own toppings. Serves 8.

Spanish Gazpacho

6 ripe tomatoes, peeled
2 green bell peppers, seeded
2 red bell peppers, seeded
4 cucumbers, peeled
1 clove garlic, minced
2 boiled eggs (yolks only)
1 tsp. olive oil
1 pinch dry mustard
1 pinch cumin
1 tsp. red wine vinegar
1 tsp. chopped chervil
1 tsp. chopped shallots
salt and pepper to taste
6 lemon slices (garnish)
1 cucumber, peeled, seeded and diced (garnish)

Cut peeled tomatoes in half and squeeze out seeds. Cut peppers in half and discard seeds. Cut peeled cucumbers in half lengthwise and scoop out seeds. Purée vegetables and garlic in blender until smooth. Mash egg yolks with olive oil to make paste. Add mustard and cumin. Add paste to the vegetable purée. Add vinegar, shallots, salt and pepper. Blend well. Keep chilled until served. Garnish with diced cucumber and a slice of lemon. You may add some hot peppers if you like it spicy.

"Oh, I haven't got but one comforter and I know most (likely) I'll freeze."

From the diary of
Lulie Margie Crawford
Jan. 10, 1881

Posole Stew

This is a traditional meal in New Mexico for feast days. Posole is said to bring good luck.

2 lbs. round steak, cubed
oil
1 ½ large onions, chopped
1 clove garlic, minced
5-10 oz. cans tomatoes with green chiles
2-10 oz. cans chopped green chiles
2 cups water
2 tsp. beef bouillon granules
2-16 oz. cans yellow hominy (posole), drained

Brown cubed steak slowly in a small amount of oil. Add onion, garlic, tomatoes and chiles. Simmer for 5 minutes. Add remaining ingredients. Simmer, covered, for 3 hours. Serves 4-6. Freezes well.

The deepest snowfall in Steamboat Springs was reported on March 2, 1929 when in a 24-hour period, 30" of snow fell on top of 27" already on the ground.

Winter Green Chile Stew

This is a great Sante Fe dish.

Its preparation is similar to French onion soup.

2 Tbsp. olive oil
1 lb. sirloin steak, cut into ½" cubes
2 yellow onions, diced
1 cup red wine
8 cups water
2 carrots, diced
2 potatoes, cut into ½" cubes
½ cup diced green chiles
1 cup beef stock
1 ½ tsp. cumin
1 ½ tsp. coriander
2 cups salsa, canned or your own
salt and pepper to taste
36 large garlic croutons (recipe follows)
3 ozs. grated Cheddar cheese
3 ozs. grated Monterey Jack cheese
sour cream
chili powder

In a large, heavy saucepan, heat oil. Sauté steak and onions for 2-3 minutes. Add wine and water. Bring to a boil, and simmer 15 minutes. Add carrots, potatoes, green chilies, beef stock, cumin, coriander and salsa. Simmer 1 hour. Season with salt and pepper. To serve, place stew in individual serving bowls. Top each with 6 croutons and a sprinkle of both cheeses. Broil until cheese melts. Top with sour cream and a sprinkle of red chili powder. Serves 6.

Garlic Croutons:

Melt ½ cup butter. Add a huge amount of minced garlic, a handful of parsley, a good dose of white pepper and salt. Pour this over some large French bread cubes and bake in the oven until they are brown and crunchy.

Egg Drop Soup

A great beginning to an oriental meal.

1 quart chicken broth
1 cup spinach, coarsely chopped
½ cup peas, frozen or freshly shelled
2 eggs, lightly beaten

Heat chicken broth. Add spinach and peas. Bring to a simmer. Slowly pour in eggs, stirring constantly. Serve immediately.

Hot and Sour Soup

½ lb. pork, cooked and shredded
6 ½ tsp. cornstarch
1 ½ tsp. salt
½ tsp. sherry
6 ozs. tofu
6 cups chicken broth
3 Tbsp. white vinegar
1 Tbsp. soy sauce
½ cup bamboo shoots, chopped
2 Tbsp. cold water
¼ tsp. pepper
2 eggs, slightly beaten
2 Tbsp. green onions, chopped
2 tsp. bottled red pepper sauce

Toss pork with ½ tsp. cornstarch, ½ tsp. salt and sherry. Cover and refrigerate 15 minutes. Cut tofu into ½" cubes. Heat broth, vinegar, soy sauce and remaining 1 tsp. salt to a boil. Stir in bamboo shoots, mushrooms, pork and tofu. Cover and reduce heat to simmer for 5 minutes. Mix remaining 6 tsp. (2 Tbsp.) cornstarch, water and pepper. Add to boiling soup, stirring continuously. Pour egg slowly into soup while stirring, until shreds form. Stir in onions and Tabasco, and serve. Serves 6-8.

Red and Yellow Pepper Soup

A nice first course soup.

¾ red bell pepper, chopped
¾ yellow bell pepper, chopped
2 Tbsp. chopped onion
½ clove garlic, minced
1 potato, cubed
2 Tbsp. butter
2 cups chicken broth
1 cup water
1 Tbsp. chicken bouillon granules
rosemary, thyme, cumin, pepper, salt, parsley to taste
plain yogurt or sour cream

Sauté peppers, onion, garlic and potato in butter. Add chicken broth, and simmer until vegetables are tender. Purée in blender or food processor. Return to pan and add water, bouillon and seasonings. Heat through. Serve with a dollop of yogurt or sour cream on top. Serves 4.

Tomato Cream Soup

Delicious on a snowy winter evening
with a salad and French bread.

¼ lb. bacon
2 - 28 oz. cans peeled tomatoes
1 onion, minced
2 celery stalks, thinly sliced
3 Tbsp. brown sugar
salt and pepper to taste
6 Tbsp. butter
3 Tbsp. flour
1 cup milk
1 cup half and half

Fry bacon. Drain and crumble and set aside. Blend tomatoes in food
processor or blender and put in 4 quart pan. Sauté onion and celery
until clear. Add to tomatoes along with brown sugar, salt and pepper.
Simmer 20 minutes. In saucepan melt butter. Add flour and brown
slightly on low heat. Slowly add milk and half and half. Cook until
bubbly. Add milk mixture and bacon to soup. Mix well and heat.
Serves 6.

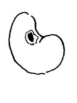

Anasazi Bean Soup

1 pkg. Anasazi beans
pot of water
1 Tbsp. beef bouillon granules
3 Tbsp. chicken bouillon granules
salt and pepper to taste
1 handful dried parsley
1 large onion, quartered
1 clove garlic, minced
1 carrot, grated
1 piece dried red chile
3-4 slices bacon, minced
3 ozs. tomato paste
4 oz. can diced green chilies
½ tsp. each, cumin, coriander, ground red chili powder
¼ cup cooking sherry
1 whole clove

Soak beans overnight in water. Drain. Fill pot with fresh water to
cover beans. Add next 10 ingredients. Boil for 3 hours. Add
remaining ingredients and boil another hour, making sure beans do
not get too soft. Serve with French bread sticks, green salad and beets.
Serves 6-8.

Frijoles Negros Soup

Even the kids will enjoy this prepare-ahead dish.

2 -15 oz. cans black beans
1 pt. beer
kernels from 2 ears fresh corn
1 pint cherry tomatoes
1 bunch cilantro, chopped
2-3 jalapeño peppers , minced
1 large white onion, chopped
sour cream (garnish, optional)
Cheddar cheese, grated (garnish, optional)

Put all fresh vegetables into a large, deep pan. Add jalapeños according to taste. Add beans and beer. Stir and simmer 4 hours. Serve with dab of sour cream on top of each bowl. Pass Cheddar cheese. Serves 4-5. Can be made ahead and frozen.

Bar 7 Bean Soup

A great hearty soup.
Pair it with sandwiches or hot French bread.

¼ cup each of 7 different type dried beans:
    pinto, navy, white, lima, split peas, black eyed peas,
    pearl barley, lentils, etc.
2 Tbsp. salt
2 qts. water
1 ham hock
1 large onion, chopped
juice of 1 lemon
1 tsp. chili powder
32 oz. can tomatoes
salt and pepper to taste

Wash beans thoroughly. Cover with water and salt; soak overnight. Drain beans. Add 2 qts. fresh water and ham hock. Bring to a boil. Reduce heat and simmer, covered, for 2 hours. Add remaining ingredients and simmer for 30 minutes. Remove ham hock and serve. Serves 6.

Speedy Spinach Soup

1 pkg. frozen spinach, chopped or leaf, thawed and squeezed
8 oz. pkg. cream cheese
14 oz. can chicken broth

Combine spinach and cheese in saucepan. Cook over low heat until cheese is melted. Add ½ of the broth. Purée in a blender and return to saucepan with remainder of broth. Heat and serve. Makes 3 cups.

A cowboy's life re-
volved around the
chuckwagon. The
term "chuck" being
synonymous with
food in cow coun-
try parlance, a
chuckwagon was
literally that: a
wagon in which
food and the para-
phernalia with
which to prepare
and serve it were
carried.

Red Park Lentil Soup

7 cups chicken stock
1 ½ cups red lentils (may substitute black lentils)
4 Tbsp. fresh cilantro
½ tsp. cumin
1 tsp. paprika
3 Tbsp. fresh oregano
⅛ tsp. cayenne pepper
1 ½ tsp. curry powder
6 cloves garlic, minced
1 carrot, diced
½ cup red pepper, diced
1 celery stalk with leaves, diced
½ yellow onion, diced
¼ red onion, diced
6 green tomatillos, chopped (may substitute 2 large red tomatoes)

Red Parks (Big and Little) take their names from the reddish-colored soil of the area, particularly along the banks of the creeks. Around the turn of the century the first confrontations between cattlemen and sheepmen took place in these parks.

Mix first eight ingredients in 4 quart pan. Cover and simmer 30 minutes. Add next five ingredients. Simmer 15 minutes. Add red onion and tomatillos. Simmer 5 minutes. Serve warm with French bread. Serves 4.

Senate Bean Soup

This is the traditional bean soup served in the Senate dining rooms in Washington, D. C.

1 lb. dry navy beans, rinsed
10 cups water
1 small ham hock
1 bay leaf
1 tsp. pepper
1 large onion, chopped
2 stalks celery, chopped
¼ cup parsley
2 cloves garlic, minced
1 tsp. each salt, oregano, basil
½ tsp. nutmeg

In a large pot, soak the beans overnight in 6 cups of water. Add remaining 4 cups water, ham hock, bay leaf and pepper. Bring to a boil. Reduce, cover and simmer 1 ¼ hours. Stir in remaining ingredients. Cover and cook 1 hour. Take out bay leaf. Cut meat from bone. Serves 4-6.

Silver Creek Steak Soup

1 lb. sirloin steak (may use elk steak), cut into 1" cubes
½ lb. lean ground beef (may use elk burger)
2 cloves garlic, minced
4 Tbsp. butter
6 Tbsp. flour
6 cups hot beef bouillon
½ tsp each: celery salt, garlic salt, seasoned salt, black pepper,
                red pepper (cayenne)
1 cup onion, chopped
1 cup celery, chopped
1 cup tomatoes, chopped (may use 8 oz. can peeled tomatoes)

Brown steak and burger in heavy skillet with garlic. Remove meat, but save drippings. Add butter to drippings. Mix in flour and stir to make a smooth roux. Add 3 cups bouillon and stir until smooth and fairly thick. Pour into soup pot or crockpot. Add spices, remaining bouillon, meat and vegetables. Simmer 1 ½ hours. This is equally good with beef or elk. Serve with fresh hot bread. Serves 4.

Poverty Flats, the village that became the town of Hahns Peak, was the campsite for miners conducting placer operations for the Hahns Peak Gold and Silver Mining Company at the Poverty Bar Placer Mine. A bar was a term used to describe an area of placer mining.

Mulligatawny Soup

⅓ cup diced small onions
2 medium stalks celery, diced small
4 Tbsp. butter or margarine
1 lb. spinach
2 small apples, peeled and diced small
2 Tbsp. flour
1 tsp. curry powder
salt and white pepper to taste
2 qts. hot chicken stock
½ medium green pepper, diced small
1 pint milk, hot
¼ cup light cream, hot
12 ozs. cooked medium noodles
1 cup diced chicken meat

Sauté onions and celery in butter in heavy soup pot until tender. Blanch spinach and apples separately in boiling salted water, about 5 minutes each; drain. Add flour, curry powder, salt and pepper to onions and celery; mix well. Cook over low heat 5-6 minutes. Do not brown. Add hot chicken stock gradually, stirring until thick and smooth. Return to boil and add green pepper and apples. Simmer until apples and green pepper are tender. Blend in scalded milk and cream. Add boiled noodles and diced chicken. Stir in spinach. Adjust seasoning and serve.

There were 35 children attending school in Steamboat Springs in 1888.

During the decades between the 1920s and the 1940s, 46 school districts operated more than 70 schools in Routt County.

Chicken a La Rhine Soup
A light soup with hearty flavor.

1 chicken breast
4 chicken bouillon cubes
1 quart water
3 Tbsp. butter
2 Tbsp. flour
1 Tbsp. onion, minced
1 Tbsp. green pepper, minced
1 Tbsp. pimento, minced
1 Tbsp. celery, minced
1 Tbsp. butter
½ cup cooked rice

Cook chicken breast in bouillon and water until tender. Remove chicken and dice. Melt 2 Tbsp. butter. Add flour and cook gently to make roux. Slowly stir into boiling chicken stock to thicken. Sauté vegetables in 1 Tbsp. butter until tender. Add vegetables, chicken and rice to stock. Simmer one hour. It freezes well. Makes 1 quart.

Chicken and Ham Gumbo
1 Tbsp. vegetable oil
1 large onion, chopped
1 clove garlic, minced
1 red cabbage, chopped
2 Tbsp. flour
1 ¾ cups chicken broth
1 cup water
¾ lb. boneless chicken breasts, skinned and cut into 1" pieces
½ cup diced ham
16 oz. can Italian stewed tomatoes
1 bay leaf
½ tsp. thyme
¼ tsp. black pepper
⅛ tsp. ground hot red pepper
½ cup rice, uncooked
5 ozs. okra, frozen or fresh, chopped (opt.)

Heat oil in a large saucepan, and sauté onion and garlic for 2 minutes. Add cabbage and sauté for 2 more minutes. Stir in flour until mixed. Add broth, water, chicken, ham, tomatoes, spices and rice. Bring to a boil. Then lower heat and simmer for 20 minutes. Add okra. Simmer 10 minutes and serve. Serves 4.

Chicken Enchilada Soup

4-6 chicken breasts
1 cup margarine
1 onion, diced
1 clove garlic, chopped
1 ½ cups flour
2 tsp. seasoned salt
2 tsp. paprika
2 pts. sour cream
¼ tsp. cumin
1 can green chilies

Cook chicken in 12-16 cups of water until done. Debone chicken and reserve broth. In a large sauté pan, combine margarine, onion and garlic. Gradually add flour, seasoned salt and paprika. This will make a white sauce. If too thick, add a little broth and stir. Add remaining broth and sour cream. Stir well. Add remaining ingredients and mix well. Cook until heated through and serve. Serve with tortilla chips, grated cheese, green onions and picante sauce.

Hawk Stew
Cooks while you play!

2 lbs. beef cubes
1 large onion, cubed
4 potatoes, cubed
5 carrots, cut into large cubes
4 celery stalks, cut into chunks
1 cup red wine
bay leaf
salt and pepper
thyme, basil and garlic to taste
8 oz. can tomato sauce
1 cup light sour cream

Combine all ingredients and pour into large baking dish. Bake at 325 for 5 hours. Add water or broth before serving, if needed to thin.

Pumpkin Oyster Soup

16 oz. can pumpkin
6 cups chicken stock
salt and freshly ground pepper to taste
⅜ cup dry sherry
½ lb. or ½ pint shelled oysters and their liquid
1 cup heavy cream

Place pumpkin in a large saucepan with stock; bring to a simmer. Season to taste with salt and pepper. Stir in sherry; add the oysters and cream, and cook just long enough for the edges of the oysters to curl and to heat the soup. Serves 4-6.

Key West Conch Chowder

Be sure to pass around the dry sherry for that extra special Key West flavor.

¼ lb. salt pork, diced
1 onion, chopped
1 large green pepper, chopped
4 cloves garlic, minced
16 oz. can tomatoes, or substitute fresh
6 oz. can tomato paste
2 qts. water
8 large conch
2 Tbsp. white vinegar
4 bay leaves
2 Tbsp. oregano
4 Tbsp. barbeque sauce
1 tsp. poultry seasoning
9 medium potatoes, diced
cayenne pepper (opt.)
dry sherry (opt.)

Sauté pork, onions, green peppers and garlic in a small amount of oil until transparent. Add tomatoes, tomato paste and water. Let boil while preparing conch. Tenderize conch by pounding, or chop into small pieces in a food processor. If pounding, chop conch into ½" pieces. Add conch, vinegar, bay leaves, oregano, barbeque sauce and poultry seasoning to pot. Season to taste with salt and pepper and simmer 2 hours. Add potatoes and cook until tender. Pass cayenne and sherry at the table. Serves 4-6.

Wren's Routt County Chowder

8 slices bacon, chopped
½ cup diced celery
1 cup thinly sliced green onions
4-6 ½ oz. cans chopped clams
8 oz. can tomato sauce
1 cup regular strength chicken broth
3 medium size potatoes (about 1 lb.), peeled and diced
2 cups half and half or light cream
salt and pepper to taste

Place bacon in a 5-6 quart pan and cook over medium heat until crisp, stirring occasionally. Discard all but 3 Tbsp. drippings, then add the celery and onions. Cook, stirring often until onions are limp. Stir in clams with their liquid, tomato sauce, broth and potatoes. Bring to a boil over high heat, cover. Reduce heat and simmer until potatoes are tender, about 10 minutes. Stir in half and half and season to taste. Heat until steaming. Serves 5-6.

Northwest Clam Chowder

4 slices bacon, diced
6 Tbsp. butter
1 medium onion, diced
3 stalks celery, diced
1 pinch each: minced fresh garlic, black pepper, cayenne pepper
1 tsp. marjoram
2 tsp. chopped fresh basil
1 tsp. Italian seasoning
½ tsp. thyme
2 bay leaves
⅓ cup flour
4 cups heavy cream
½ cup half and half
1 ½ cups clam juice or nectar
¼ lb. new potatoes
1 ½ cups clams, chopped, (fresh or frozen)
¼ tsp. dill
⅓ cup fresh parsley, chopped

Cook bacon until transparent. Add butter, onions, celery and all seasonings except dill and parsley. Cook until vegetables are tender. Add flour and cook 3-4 minutes, stirring continuously. Add cream, half and half, and clam nectar. Heat to just under the boiling point. Blanch new potatoes and cool. Cut potatoes into ½" cubes and add to soup with clams. Bring to a boil and slowly cook 2-3 minutes. Add dill and parsley, and serve. Serves 6-8.

When Colorado became a territory in 1861, the area of Routt and Moffat Counties lay in Summit County; later they were included in Grand County. Routt County was created by the first Colorado State Assembly less than a year after Colorado became a state. On January 29, 1877, Governor John L. Routt (1826-1907), the last territorial and first elected governor of Colorado, signed a bill establishing the county which bears his name. The Routt County created by this bill encompassed the entire area of today's Moffat and Routt Counties. Enormous distances and disputes over the location of a county seat prompted a division along existing county lines on February 27, 1911.

Bourbon Street Gumbo

In some areas of Southern Louisiana,
gumbo is eaten with potato salad instead of rice.

2 lbs. shrimp, peeled and deveined; save shells
8 cups water
1 ½ cups vegetable oil
1 ½ cups flour
1 large onion, diced
1 stalk celery, diced (optional)
1 small bell pepper, diced
3 cloves garlic, minced
4 Tbsp. salt
1 Tbsp. cayenne pepper
1 Tbsp. white pepper
½ cup chopped scallion tops
½ cup chopped parsley

In stock pot combine shells and water. Boil 1 hour. (If desired, this stock may be seasoned with an onion, 2 garlic cloves and a celery stalk). Strain stock and place back in pot. In 2 quart pan make roux with flour and oil by stirring together over medium heat. When roux is brown, add onions, celery and bell pepper and cook until "red like a copper penny." Add roux to stock one spoonful at a time until completely dissolved. Add garlic and seasonings. Simmer for 1 hour or more. (When simmered for longer periods, this dish will only improve in flavor. Add water when necessary.) Add shrimp and simmer 20 minutes. Adjust seasonings, add scallions and parsley and simmer 10 minutes. Serve with rice in your favorite bowls, with hot French bread and butter. Serves 8-10.

Variations:
1. Add 1 lb. crabmeat 10 minutes before serving.
2. Add 1 lb. crab claws 10 minutes before serving.
3. Add 1 lb. sliced smoked sausage after adding roux to stock.
4. Add 1 pint oysters with liqueur 5 minutes before serving.
5. Add 1 lb. can whole tomatoes and 4 cups sliced fresh okra after adding roux to stock. If using frozen okra, cover it with water and a little oil and soak until no longer slimy. Then add to gumbo.

Billy Kidd's Go-Fast Soup

1 pkg. miso soup
1 can fancy crabmeat
1 tomato, chopped
2 carrots, chopped
1 clove garlic, minced
1 yellow squash, chopped
1 zucchini, chopped

Combine all ingredients.   Cook on medium-high 5 minutes in saucepan.

Bisques from the 'Boat

Crab:
2 cups milk
1 Tbsp. flour
2 Tbsp. butter
1 tsp. salt
pinch pepper
⅔ cup cooked or canned crab meat
few sprays raw celery leaves

Fish:
2 cups milk
1 Tbsp. flour
2 Tbsp. butter
1 tsp. salt
pinch pepper
⅔ cup cooked or canned flaked fish
few sprays raw parsley

Billy Kidd, the first American male to win an alpine Olympic medal in skiing (a silver in Innsbruck in 1964), has called Steamboat his home since 1970. After a career of winning every major ski award, he continues to win the friendship and admiration of all those who meet him as he promotes the sport he loves.

Lobster:
2 cups milk
1 Tbsp. flour
2 Tbsp. butter
1 tsp. salt
pinch pepper
½ cup cooked or canned lobster meat
few sprays raw parsley

Place all ingredients for the variety of bisque desired in blender or food processor. Partially blend or process, approximately 15 seconds. Place purée into a pan and heat through. Each bisque yields 2 ½ cups.

More Bisques from the 'Boat

Oyster:
2 cups milk
1 Tbsp. flour
2 Tbsp. butter
1 tsp. salt
pinch pepper
3 raw oysters
few sprays raw celery leaves

The name Steamboat Springs was derived from the peculiar puffing sounds emitted by one of the springs, similar to the chugging sound of a Mississippi River steamboat.

Salmon:
2 cups milk
1 Tbsp. flour
2 Tbsp. butter
1 tsp. salt
pinch pepper
½ cup cooked or canned salmon
2 rings raw green pepper

Shrimp:
2 cups milk
1 Tbsp. flour
2 Tbsp. butter
1 tsp. salt
pinch pepper
⅔ cup cooked or canned shrimp
few sprays raw parsley

Thrifty Ann:
1 cup milk
1 cup broth
1 Tbsp. flour
2 Tbsp. butter
1 tsp. salt
pinch pepper
½ cup leftover beef, lamb, veal or ham, diced
few sprays raw celery leaves

Place all ingredients for the variety of bisque desired in blender or food processor. Partially blend or process, approximately 15 seconds. Place purée into a pan and heat through. Each bisque yields 2 ½ cups.

Salads

Salads

Rabbit Ears Salad

1 head Romaine lettuce, cut into 2" square chunks
½ head red leaf lettuce, cut into 2" square chunks
1 red bell pepper, seeded and cut into thin slivers
½ red onion, thinly sliced
½ cup pinon nuts, hulled and toasted
1 small raddichio

Combine all ingredients with Poppy Seed Dressing (recipe in this chapter) and toss well. Serves 6-8.

Whole Garden Salad

A refreshing salad for the whole family.

1 lb. variety of greens: Bibb, Romaine and/or spinach
11 oz. can mandarin oranges, drained
2 cups sliced seedless grapes or fresh plums
1 large tomato, sliced
2-3 scallions, sliced
¼ cup raisins
¼ cup walnut pieces
Poppy Seed Dressing

Rabbit Ears Pass was named by the Hayden Survey Expedition in 1873 for the formation of nearby Rabbit Ears Peak, resembling rabbit ears.

In a large salad bowl, mix greens of your choice. Toss with remaining ingredients except dressing. Chill covered. Serve with Poppy Seed Dressing (recipe in this chapter).

Salad with Montrachet and Walnuts

This is a very elegant salad.

salad greens: green leaf, red leaf and watercress
endive, trimmed
⅓ cup white wine vinegar
½ cup walnut oil
½ cup vegetable oil
1 Tbsp. finely chopped scallions
salt and pepper to taste
⅓ cup chopped walnuts, toasted
7 ozs. Montrachet, sliced into ½" rounds
seasoned breadcrumbs

Wash greens and divide among plates. Top with endive leaves. Whisk together vinegar, scallions, oils, salt and pepper. Cover and refrigerate until ready to use. Put Montrachet rounds into breadcrumbs and gently press each sides and edges. Place on greased cookie sheet and bake at 350° until soft to the touch. Toss the salad with walnut dressing; top with walnuts. Serve several warm Montrachet slices on the side. Serves 6.

Raspberry Spinach Salad

1 lb. spinach, washed and trimmed
⅓ cup salad oil
4 Tbsp. raspberry vinegar
¼ tsp. salt
⅛ tsp. pepper
½ pint raspberries, rinsed
3 kiwis, peeled and sliced

Place spinach in a large salad bowl. Combine oil, vinegar, salt and pepper. Pour half of dressing over spinach leaves and toss well. Divide among 4 salad plates. Arrange raspberries and kiwi slices over spinach leaves and top with remaining dressing. Serves 4-6.

Sioux Salad

Great for a potluck.

1 large bunch spinach
14 oz. can artichoke hearts, drained
6 oz. can pitted black olives, drained
½ lb. fresh mushrooms, sliced
2 firm tomatoes, cut into chunks
8 oz. bottle Italian dressing
freshly grated Parmesan cheese

Add any of the following: cauliflower bits; broccoli bits; sliced water chestnuts; small canned shrimp; anchovies; tuna; bacon; eggs.

Wash spinach and drain. Marinate artichoke hearts, olives, mushrooms, tomatoes, and your choice of optional ingredients in Italian dressing at least 12 hours. Toss marinated vegetables with salad greens when ready and serve. Pass freshly grated Parmesan cheese to sprinkle on top. Serves 6.

Carefree Spinach Salad

1 lb. fresh spinach, washed and trimmed
¼ cup sesame seeds
¼ cup sliced almonds
1 can mandarin oranges, drained
1 cup oil
⅓ cup red wine vinegar
2 Tbsp. soy sauce

Bake almonds at 350° for 10 minutes to toast. Mix spinach, sesame seeds, toasted almonds and oranges. Combine remaining ingredients, pour over salad and toss well.

The little settlement of Sidney (8 miles east of Steamboat Springs) was at one time a booming town. It boasted a school, a saloon, a church, blacksmith shop, creamery, boarding house, and a general store where dances were held on Saturday nights.

Sidney Spinach and Chutney Salad

1 lb. spinach, washed and trimmed
1 cup water chestnuts, sliced
2 small star fruit, sliced
½ cup Gruyère cheese, grated
1 small red onion, sliced
6 slices bacon, crumbled
¼ cup wine vinegar
1 clove garlic, minced
3 Tbsp. chutney
2 tsp. sugar
2 Tbsp. Dijon mustard
½ cup oil
salt and pepper to taste

Prepare spinach, water chestnuts, cheese, onion, and bacon. Blend vinegar, garlic, chutney, sugar, mustard, oil, and salt and pepper. Pour dressing over salad including star fruit slices; toss lightly. Serves 8-10.

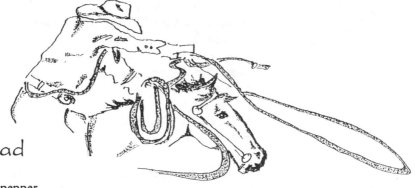

Caesar Salad

2 tsp. salt
1 tsp. freshly ground pepper
2 cloves garlic, crushed
1 tsp. anchovy paste
¼ tsp. dry mustard
½ tsp. Worcestershire sauce
1 Tbsp. freshly grated Parmesan
2 Tbsp. red wine vinegar
2 Tbsp. fresh lemon juice
½ cup olive oil
1 egg yolk
1 large head Romaine lettuce
homemade croutons
freshly grated Parmesan

Blend salt, pepper, and garlic together in a wooden salad bowl. Mash in anchovy paste. Add mustard, Worcestershire, and cheese. Mix well. Beat in vinegar, lemon juice, and oil. Add egg yolk and beat well. Add lettuce and toss. Sprinkle with croutons and Parmesan to taste. Serves 6-8.

Wither's Cole Slaw

¼-⅓ cup mayonnaise
2 Tbsp. vinegar
½ tsp. celery seed
⅓ cup sugar
½ cup sour cream or yogurt
4 cups chopped cabbage, (1 medium sized head)
½ green pepper, chopped
1 small onion, chopped fine

Blend first 5 ingredients and refrigerate overnight. Mix cabbage, green pepper and onion. Pour dressing over vegetables and serve. Serves 6.

"Mr. Reid thinks we will have trouble with the Utes in the spring. They say they are going to fight. Oh, I hope they won't."

From the diary of
Lulie Margie Crawford
April 8, 1882

Ramen Salad

A delicious salad to complement an oriental meal.

½ head cabbage, shredded
4 green onions, chopped
½ cup sliced almonds or sunflower seeds, toasted
2 Tbsp. sesame seeds, toasted
1 pkg. ramen noodles, uncooked, in small pieces
½ cup sunflower or canola oil
3 Tbsp. cider vinegar
2 Tbsp. sugar
1 pkg. chicken flavor ramen seasoning
dash Chinese sesame oil (opt.)

Mix cabbage, onions, almonds and sesame seeds in a salad bowl and refrigerate for 2-3 hours. Combine remaining ingredients except ramen noodles in a small mixing bowl and refrigerate for at least 1 hour before serving. Just before serving, combine salad, noodles and as much dressing as desired. A simple and delicious salad to complement an oriental style meal. Serves 4.

3 Bar A Salad

2 lbs. asparagus, cooked and chilled
2 medium avocados, peeled and cut into chunks
2 - 6 oz. jars marinated artichoke hearts, drained and reserved
1 head of Boston Bibb lettuce

Line a large platter with lettuce. Arrange asparagus, avocados, and artichokes on top of lettuce. Combine remaining artichoke marinade and either drizzle over salad or pass with salad at the table. Serves 8.

Raspberry Lemon Slaw

10 oz. pkg. fresh prepared cole slaw
1 large red delicious apple, chopped
8 oz. container lemon yogurt
3 Tbsp. lemon juice
3 Tbsp. raspberry jelly
⅛ cup chopped roasted almonds

Combine cole slaw and apple. Combine yogurt, lemon juice and jelly together. Add to slaw mixture. Top with almonds. Serves 4.

Pineapple Coleslaw Salad

A nice and fresh salad.

4 cups Napa Valley cabbage, shredded
1 cup fresh parsley, snipped
8 oz. can crushed pineapple, drained
8 oz. can sliced water chestnuts, drained
½ cup chopped green onions
½ cup Coleslaw Salad Dressing (recipe in this chapter)
1 tsp. grated fresh gingerroot or
1 ½ tsp. ground ginger

In large bowl, combine cabbage, parsley, pineapple, water chestnuts and onion. Cover and chill thoroughly. In a small bowl, combine coleslaw dressing and ginger. Cover and chill. Just before serving, pour dressing over the cabbage mixture and toss to coat. For added color, add 1 chopped red delicious apple to cabbage mixture. Serves 10-12.

Orchard Slaw

5 cups finely chopped cabbage
1 cup sliced celery
1 cup grated carrots
½ cup raisins
½ cup chopped pecans
2 Tbsp. lemon juice
½ tsp. salt
8 oz. orange, peach or pineapple yogurt
1 tart apple, chopped
1 tsp. poppy seeds

Mix cabbage, celery, carrots, raisins and nuts. In a separate bowl, mix lemon juice, salt and yogurt. Pour over cabbage mixture and mix well. Add apples and poppy seeds and toss gently. Chill for 2 hours before serving. Best if allowed to chill overnight.

Royal Hotel Fruit Salad
Great presentation—use the pineapple shell for a bowl.

1 lb. container low-fat cottage cheese
½ cup chopped pecans
1 Tbsp. chopped green onion
2 medium pineapples
1 pint strawberries, washed, hulled and halved
2 medium bananas, sliced
1 kiwi fruit, peeled and sliced
1 cup seedless green grapes, halved

Combine cottage cheese, pecans and green onions in a medium size bowl; cover; chill 30 minutes. Cut pineapples in half lengthwise including plume top. Cut pineapple away from rind out of each half with a sharp paring knife held at an angle. Cut each removed fruit section in half; slice off core; then cut pineapple crosswise in thin slices. Use half in the salad and reserve remainder for later use. Add strawberries, bananas, kiwi and grapes to pineapple chunks; toss gently. Divide fruit mixture evenly among the 4 pineapple half shells; top with scoops of cottage cheese mixture. Garnish with additional chopped pecans and green onions and sprigs of mint. Makes 4 generous servings.

Harvest Tomato Salad
6 ripe tomatoes, cut into wedges
1 small sweet red bell pepper, sliced or chunked
1 small sweet yellow bell pepper, sliced or chunked
1 small sweet green bell pepper, sliced or chunked
1 sweet Vidalia onion, sliced
1 cup sliced pitted black olives
1 cup sliced fresh mushrooms
⅔ cup oil
¼ cup vinegar
¼ cup fresh chopped parsley
¼ cup sliced green onions
¼ tsp. salt
¼ tsp. lemon pepper
1 tsp. sugar
1 tsp. dried basil

Prepare vegetables and combine in a salad bowl. Blend remaining ingredients and pour over vegetables. Cover and refrigerate for 3-4 hours. Serves 6.

Marinated Tomato/Cucumber Salad

This will remind you of a chunky gazpacho.

2 Tbsp. olive oil
2 Tbsp. red wine vinegar
½ tsp. minced garlic
¼ tsp. salt
2 medium cucumbers, quartered and chopped
2 medium tomatoes, cut into chunks
3 Tbsp. sliced green onions
1 cup halved cherry tomatoes
onion and garlic flavored croutons

Whisk oil, vinegar and garlic in a medium size bowl. Add remaining ingredients except croutons. Mix gently. Cover and refrigerate 2 hours or overnight. Sprinkle with croutons just before serving. Serves 4.

Toponas Tomato Salad

1 Tbsp. red wine vinegar
¼ cup olive oil
1 Tbsp. minced onion
1 Tbsp. minced fresh basil
¼ tsp. oregano
1 clove garlic, minced
6 tomatoes, sliced
 salt and pepper

Mix all ingredients and place in the refrigerator overnight. Serve chilled or at room temperature. Serves 4.

A sandstone rock, which from a distance resembles a lion lying with its head erect, prompted naming Toponas for the Indian word for "sleeping lion."

Broccoli and Sunflower Seed Salad

1 bunch broccoli, cut up
6 slices bacon, cooked and crumbled
½ cup raisins
1 cup sunflower seeds
1 small red onion, chopped

Dressing:
1 cup mayonnaise
2 tsp. vinegar
¼ cup sugar

Mix salad ingredients in 1 bowl. Mix dressing ingredients several hours before using; refrigerate dressing to blend. Toss dressing with salad at serving time.

Green Bean, Pecan, & Feta Salad

This is great served as a salad or a vegetable dish.

1 ½ lbs. fresh green beans
¾ cup olive oil
1 Tbsp. dill
¼ cup white wine vinegar
¼ tsp. salt
½ tsp. minced garlic
¼ tsp. pepper
1 cup chopped pecans, toasted
1 cup diced red onion
1 cup crumbled Feta cheese

Trim ends of the beans and cut in half crosswise. Bring 4 quarts of water to boil in a 6 qt. saucepan. Add beans and cook until crisp tender, about 4 minutes. Drain well; immediately plunge into cold water. Drain again and pat dry. Combine oil, dill, vinegar, salt, garlic, and pepper; blend. Arrange beans in a shallow glass serving bowl. Sprinkle with nuts, onion, and cheese. Just before serving, pour dressing over and toss thoroughly. This salad is just as delicious served leftover. Serves 4-6.

Southern Colorado Salad

3 cups broccoli flowerets
1 cup peeled and cubed jicama
1 cup Greek or Calamata olives
2 Tbsp. sliced green onion
⅓ cup Lime Mustard Vinaigrette (recipe follows)
3 large tomatoes, sliced
½ cup crumbled Feta cheese
2 Tbsp. minced cilantro or parsley
1 lime, sliced

Cook broccoli in small amount of boiling water for 5 minutes. Drain and chill. At serving time, combine jicama, broccoli, olives, onion and Lime Mustard Viniagrette and toss well. Spoon broccoli mixture on a serving platter. Arrange tomato slices around the edge. Sprinkle with cheese and cilantro. Garnish with lime slices. Serves 6-8.

Lime Mustard Vinaigrette:
⅓ cup olive oil or vegetable oil
3 Tbsp. lime juice
1 Tbsp. Dijon mustard
⅛ tsp. salt
dash pepper

In a cruet, combine all ingredients and shake well. Cover and chill until ready to serve.

Ute Orange Jicama Salad

4 Tbsp. white vinegar
4 Tbsp. oil
¼ tsp. paprika
¼ tsp. salt
¼ tsp. pepper
1 clove garlic, minced
2 tsp. sugar
4 seedless oranges, peeled and cut into small chunks
1 small jicama, peeled and sliced
lettuce leaves
parsley (garnish)

Prepare dressing by blending the first 7 ingredients. Place lettuce leaves on salad plates. Arrange oranges and jicama slices over lettuce leaves. Drizzle with dressing and garnish with parsley. Serves 4-6.

Pioneer routes into Routt County followed Ute Indian paths which trace game migration trails connecting warm lowlands with the wild mountain height.

Fresh Broccoli and Mandarin Salad

This pretty salad has many interesting textures.

4 cups broccoli flowerets
½ cups raisins
6 slices bacon, cooked and crumbled
2 cups sliced mushrooms
½ cup sliced almonds
1 cup mandarin oranges, drained
½ medium onion, sliced to ⅛"
Dressing:
1 ½ Tbsp. cornstarch
1 Tbsp. dry mustard
1 egg
1 egg yolk
½ cup sugar
¼ cup vinegar
½ cup water
2 Tbsp. butter or margarine

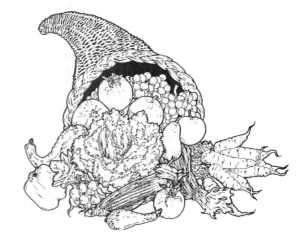

To prepare dressing, whisk together cornstarch, mustard, egg, egg yolk, and sugar in the top of a double boiler. Combine the vinegar and water; slowly whisk into egg mixture. Place over hot water and cook stirring constantly until mixture thickens. Remove from heat and stir in butter. Chill. Blanch broccoli and chill. When ready to serve, toss dressing and remaining ingredients in a serving bowl and serve. This is a very pretty salad with many interesting textures. Serves 10-12.

Wolcott Barley Salad

1 cup pearl barley
1 lb. green beans, trimmed and cut into 1" pieces
½ cup olive oil
⅓ cup red wine vinegar
1 Tbsp. minced fresh basil
1 tsp. salt
½ tsp. pepper
5 large ripe tomatoes, coarsely chopped
⅓ cup minced parsley
¼ cup sliced green onion

Place barley in boiling water and cook until tender, about 45 minutes. Drain well. While barley cooks, steam green beans until tender. Run under cold water and drain well. Cover and refrigerate until ready to serve. Combine oil, vinegar, basil, salt and pepper. Pour over barley and tomatoes and toss well. Cover and refrigerate 30 minutes. Just before serving, add green beans, parsley and green onions. Serves 8-10.

In 1888 the Whipple Stage was established from Wolcott with an overnight stop in McCoy and then on to Yampa and Steamboat Springs. This was a three-day trip. The stage was pulled by 4 to 6 horses and carried 14 passengers.

Spinach Rice Salad

A nice salad to accompany grilled fish or poultry.

1 cup rice, cooked
½ cup Italian dressing
1 Tbsp. soy sauce
½ tsp. sugar
2 cups fresh spinach, cut into thin strips
½ cup sliced celery
½ cup sliced green onions
⅓ cup bacon, cooked and crumbled

Place cooked rice in a salad bowl and cool slightly. Combine dressing, soy sauce and sugar. Stir into warm rice. Cover and chill. Fold in remaining ingredients just before serving. Serves 6-8.

Kashiwa Rising Sun Rice Salad

4 cups cooked brown rice (½ brown and ½ wild rice optional)
⅔ cup Kashiwa Shooting Star Sauce*
½ cup chopped red bell pepper
½ cup chopped green onions
1 small can water chestnuts, coarsely chopped
½ lb. cooked shrimp or scallops
cilantro for garnish

Cook rice and cool to room temperature. Combine rice with remaining ingredients, chill well before serving. Garnish with cilantro. Serves 6-8. *Hank Kashiwa's own! Available in specialty food stores.

Seafood Rice Salad
A great light meal.

½ lb. small shrimp, cooked
7 oz. can tuna, drained and flaked
3 cups cooked brown rice
½ cup finely chopped onion
½ cup finely chopped sweet pickles
1 ½ cups thinly sliced celery
¼ cup diced pimiento
1 Tbsp. lemon juice
1 cup mayonnaise
salad greens
3 eggs, hard cooked and chopped
tomato wedges

Thoroughly toss together first 7 ingredients. Stir lemon juice into
mayonnaise. Add to rice mixture, tossing thoroughly. Serve on salad
greens garnished with eggs and tomato wedges. Serves 6.

Appenzeller Salad
⅓-½ cup sour cream or plain yogurt
2 tsp. grated horseradish
1 tsp. dry mustard
1 tsp. cumin seed, coarsely ground
kosher salt or salt
dash pepper
3-4 cups greens for salad: Bibb, bok choy or Belgian endive
any 1 or more of the following:
thinly sliced cucumbers, slivered green peppers,
green onion tops or watercress
½ lb. Swiss Appenzeller cheese
4 hard boiled eggs, sliced

Combine ⅓ cup sour cream with horseradish, dry mustard, cumin
seed, salt and pepper. Set aside, covered. Toss greens and vegetables
in a large bowl. Sprinkle cheese and eggs on top. Adjust dressing to
taste adding more sour cream, if needed. Toss salad gently with
dressing and serve. Serves 4.

Battle Creek Black Bean Salad

Delicious, nutritious and easy. A nice potluck dish.

¼ cup salad oil
2 Tbsp. cider vinegar
1 tsp. prepared mustard
½ tsp. sugar
½ tsp. ground cumin
¼ tsp. Tabasco sauce
16 oz. can black beans, rinsed and drained
12 oz. can shoe peg canned corn, drained

Combine in large mixing bowl, first 6 ingredients. Add black beans and corn. Refrigerate until ready to serve. Serves 4.

Lentil, Bean, and Walnut Salad

A hearty, flavorful salad.

½ lb. Great Northern or Navy Beans, sorted and rinsed
1 clove garlic, peeled
2 bay leaves
1 Tbsp. dried basil
1 Tbsp. dried oregano
1 Tbsp. dried thyme
4 cups chicken stock
½ lb. lentils, sorted and rinsed
1 carrot, peeled and quartered
1 small onion, peeled
2 cups chicken stock
¾ cup thinly sliced scallions
½ cup finely chopped red bell pepper
1 cup walnut halves
Vinaigrette Dressing:
⅓ cup white wine vinegar
2 tsp. Dijon
2 cloves garlic, peeled
½ cup walnut oil

Bring beans, herbs, and chicken stock to a boil. Boil 5 minutes and cool. Return to heat and simmer 1 hour or until tender. Meanwhile, simmer lentils, carrot, and onion in 2 cups chicken stock for 20-25 minutes or until tender, but not mushy. Drain lentils and beans discarding onion, carrot, bay leaves, and garlic. Combine ingredients for the vinaigrette in a food processor or blender and whirl until smooth and creamy. Combine beans and lentils. Pour warm vinaigrette over warm beans and lentils. Season with salt and pepper. Cool to room temperature and then refrigerate for several hours or overnight. Add scallions, red pepper, and walnuts. Toss and serve. Makes about 3 quarts.

Bean Sprout /Water Chestnut Salad

1 lb. bag fresh bean sprouts
½ cup sliced water chestnuts
1 cup pineapple chunks
½ cup thinly sliced green pepper
2 cups mayonnaise or part plain yogurt
2 tsp. soy sauce
2 tsp. curry powder
toasted almonds

Rinse bean sprouts and drain well. Toss with water chestnuts, pineapple chunks and green pepper. Combine mayonnaise, soy sauce and curry powder. Pour dressing over the sprout mixture and toss well. Arrange in a lettuce lined bowl or divide among salad plates. Sprinkle with toasted almonds. Serves 6-8.

Garden Pasta Salad

Makes a colorful salad for a large group.

1 lb. spaghetti, cooked
1 bunch broccoli, cut into flowerets
3 tomatoes, chopped
4 cucumbers, sliced
1 large onion, chopped
2 green peppers, cut in thin strips
2.5 oz. bottle McCormicks Salad Supreme, or to taste
8 oz. bottle Viva Italian Dressing

Mix spaghetti and vegetables together. Add Salad Supreme and Italian Dressing. Mix well. Marinate in refrigerator overnight. Serves 8-10.

Skroodle Salad

½ cup white vinegar
¼ tsp. salt
½ tsp. Accent (optional)
¼ cup sugar
½ tsp. pepper
½ tsp. garlic salt
8 oz. package curly noodles
1 tsp. mustard
¼ onion, chopped
½ green pepper, chopped
½ jar pimientos
8 oz. package crab or imitation crab

Heat together first 6 ingredients while boiling curly noodles in salted water. To vinegar mixture add mustard, onion, green pepper, pimientos, and crab. Combine with cooked and drained noodles. Marinate refrigerated overnight. Serves 6-8.

Battle Creek and Battle Mountain were first homesteaded in 1883. The residents constructed a church and school which are now listed on the Colorado Inventory of Historic Sites. Battle Creek was named for the mountain which is in Carbon County, Wyoming. The area was the site of a skirmish between trappers and hostile Indians on August 21, 1841 when Jim Baker and Henry Farbe, with 23 trappers and a band of Shoshones withstood 40 charges by 500 Cheyenne, Arapahoe and Sioux. Casualties included ten trappers and an estimated 100 Indians. Fearing another attack, the trappers left the area.

Round Up Pasta Salad

Serve as main dish with hard rolls.

⅓ cup canola or olive oil
2 Tbsp. water
5 Tbsp. red wine vinegar
½ tsp. salt
¾ tsp. dried basil
¼ tsp. oregano
5-8 drops Tabasco or to taste
1 clove garlic, minced
6 oz. linguini, broken into thirds, cooked, drained, and cooled
½ cup sliced celery
1 firm tomato or 10 cherry tomatoes, peeled, seeded, and chopped
½ cucumber, cut in half lengthwise, thinly sliced
10 black olives, sliced
1 ½ cups roast beef or left over steak, sliced thinly and cut into strips
2.5 oz. jar of whole canned mushrooms, drained and cut in half
¼ cup grated carrot

Combine oil, water, vinegar, salt, spices, and Tabasco in a jar with a tight fitting lid. Shake well and set aside. Prepare remaining ingredients and combine in a large bowl with cooled linguini. Toss with dressing. Refrigerate for several hours or overnight. Makes 10 one cup servings.

South of the Border Pasta Salad

An unusual, colorful twist to macaroni salad.

12 ozs. elbow macaroni
1 3.8 oz. can sliced black olives
½ Bermuda onion, chopped
½ red bell pepper, chopped
½ yellow bell pepper, chopped
2 stalks celery, chopped
¼ to ⅓ cup minced cilantro

Dressing:
¼ tsp. cayenne pepper
½ cup mayonnaise
3 Tbsp. red wine vinegar
1 Tbsp. sugar (optional)
½ tsp. garlic salt
1 tsp. pepper

Some of the famous bucking horses (broncs) at the turn of the century were "Carrie Nation," "General Pershing," and the famous "Pin Ears."

Boil macaroni according to package directions until al dente. Drain and cool. In a small bowl, mix dressing ingredients together until well blended. In a large bowl, toss macaroni with black olives, onion, red and yellow peppers, and celery. Add dressing and toss, add cilantro and toss lightly. Serve garnished with some cilantro, black olives or slices of bell pepper. Serves 6-8.

Orange Shrimp Salad

4 oranges, peeled and sectioned
2 cups cubed avocado (1 ½ medium size)
1 lb. shrimp, cooked and peeled
2 bunches watercress, cleaned and stemmed*
Orange Avocado Dressing (recipe follows)

Combine all ingredients except dressing and set aside.

Orange Avocado Dressing:
5 Tbsp. orange juice
½ medium avocado, mashed
¼ cup mayonnaise or yogurt
2 tsp. white vinegar
¼ tsp. salt
¼ tsp pepper

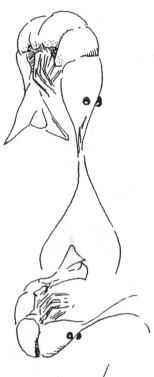

Combine all ingredients in a blender and whirl. Pour over salad, toss and serve. Serves 4-6. *A combination of salad greens may be used in place of watercress.

Baja Shrimp Salad

3 cups shrimp, shelled and deveined
½ lime
½ red onion, finely chopped
2 stalks of celery, finely minced
¼ tsp. cayenne
½ cup mayonnaise
½-1 tsp. jalapeño pepper, minced
salt and pepper to taste

Drop shrimp in 2 quarts of boiling water. Boil until orange in color, about 5 minutes. Do not overcook. Immediately drain and rinse shrimp in ice cold water until well chilled. Place in a medium sized bowl. Squeeze juice of lime over the shrimp. Add remaining ingredients and toss well. Season to taste. Chill thoroughly before serving. Can be garnished with lime wheels and a sprinkle of minced cilantro.

Chicken n' Cabbage Salad

2 whole chicken breasts, cooked
1 head cabbage, chopped
1 cup slivered almonds
6-8 Tbsp. sunflower seeds
1 ½ bunches green onion, chopped
8 oz. bottle Italian dressing

Remove chicken from bones and chop. Add next 4 ingredients. Pour Italian dressing over all and toss. Serves 4-6.

Chinese Chicken Salad

1 chicken breast, cooked and shredded
1 small head lettuce or bok choy, shredded
½ cup chopped green onion
½ cup sunflower seeds
¼ cup cashews
2 Tbsp. sugar
½ tsp. salt
¼ tsp. pepper
¼ cup salad oil
1 tsp. soy sauce
3 Tbsp. cider vinegar
¼ tsp. ginger

Toss first 5 ingredients together in a salad bowl and set aside. Combine the remaining ingredients and allow to sit for 30 minutes to enhance flavor. Just before serving, pour over salad and toss. Serves 4.

Luau Chicken Salad

2 cups diced chicken
1 apple, peeled and diced
1 cup chopped celery
1 cup halved green grapes
1 banana, sliced
1 cup fresh pineapple pieces
1 cup mayonnaise or ½ cup lowfat plain yogurt and ½ cup mayonnaise
3 Tbsp. pineapple juice
1 Tbsp. curry powder

Combine first 6 ingredients together. Stir in remaining ingredients. Decorate with grapes and parsley.

Chicken Salad in Pita Pockets

1 ¾ lb. chicken, cooked and cut into pieces
2 stalks celery, diced
½ - 1 jar chutney, to taste
1 cup mayonnaise
¼ - ½ cup lemon juice
2 - 3 tsp. curry powder, to taste
salt and pepper to taste
½ tsp. celery salt
1 apple, chopped
1 cup green grapes, halved
¼ cup sliced almonds
½ cup sliced water chestnuts
1 package pita bread pockets

Combine chutney, mayonnaise, lemon juice, curry powder, salt, pepper and celery salt. Toss remaining ingredients and serve in pita bread pockets. Serves 6.

Head lettuce was Routt County's first proven cash crop. Unlike grain which was traded among local ranchers or exchanged for goods and services elsewhere, lettuce sold for cash on eastern slope markets.

Sauce Vinaigrette

1 Tbsp. wine vinegar
3 Tbsp. oil
pinch black pepper
¼ tsp. salt

Beat all thoroughly with a fork. Add 1 or more of the following ingredients, if desired: 1 tsp. tarragon; 1 tsp. chopped shallots; 1 tsp. Dijon mustard; 1 tsp. chopped chives; garlic, pressed or chopped.

Garlic Dijon Vinaigrette

1 cup safflower oil (or canola oil)
½ cup water
½ cup white vinegar
2 Tbsp. Dijon mustard
8 cloves garlic, minced
dash cayenne

Blend together all ingredients in blender or food processor. Store in refrigerator. Makes 2 cups. For Mexican flavor, add fresh cilantro, salsa, cumin, and chili powder. For Italian flavor, add chopped fresh oregano, chives, and parsley.

Lemon Buttermilk Dressing

1 cup salad oil
½ cup freshly squeezed lemon juice
½ cup cultured buttermilk
2 large cloves garlic, pressed
2 tsp. dried dill weed
1 tsp. each salt, pepper, and sugar

Put all ingredients in a jar with a tight fitting lid; shake well. Always shake well before using and keep refrigerated. This will keep 1-2 weeks. Makes about 2 cups.

Poppy Seed Dressing

⅓ cup sugar
2 tsp. dry mustard
2 tsp. salt
⅔ cup vinegar
2 cups salad oil
1 tsp. poppy seeds
½ medium onion, finely chopped

Mix first 4 ingredients. Add oil slowly. Stir in seeds and onion. Makes about 3 cups.

Green Goddess Salad Dressing

1 avocado, chopped
1 cup mayonnaise
½ cup sour cream
½ cup tarragon vinegar
¼ cup wine
1 can anchovies, drained and chopped
2 Tbsp. sliced green onions
1 Tbsp. lemon juice
1 clove garlic, minced
salt and pepper to taste

Combine all ingredients in a blender. Chill until ready to use. Makes about 3 cups.

Dressing for Coleslaw

This was Gramma Werner's recipe.

1 pt. whipping cream
1 Tbsp. sugar
salt and pepper
1 Tbsp. vinegar

In a medium bowl, mix cream, sugar, salt and pepper. Stir well. Add vinegar just before adding one head of finely shredded cabbage.

Swiss Dressing

⅓ cup sunflower oil
1 Tbsp. white wine vinegar
2 tsp. Maggi Seasonings
1 tsp. mustard
2 Tbsp. sour cream
Salt and pepper

Blend all ingredients with a wire whisk until light and well mixed. Toss with a salad of mixed greens. Makes about ⅔ cup.

Kashiwa Sesame Sword Dressing

½ cup Teriyaki
½ cup rice vinegar
1 Tbsp. fresh lemon juice
2 tsp. sesame seeds
½ tsp. brown sugar
2 Tbsp. sesame oil
hot chili oil to taste (optional)

Combine ingredients in a small jar and shake well. Toss with your favorite salad. Keeps in refrigerator indefinitely. Makes approximately 1 cup.

Roast Tenderloin of Beef with Horseradish

4 lb. beef tenderloin
1 ½ cups beer
½ cup oil
2 cloves garlic, minced
salt and pepper to taste
horseradish sauce (recipe follows)

Combine all ingredients except tenderloin. Place tenderloin in pan, cover with marinade and refrigerate about 4 hours. Grill over hot coals for 12 minutes on each side. Serve with horseradish sauce. Serves 6-8.

Horseradish sauce:
1 cup sour cream
1 Tbsp. onion, grated
1 ½ Tbsp. Dijon mustard
3 tsp. prepared horseradish

Combine all ingredients and chill until ready to serve.

Filet Mignon with Danish Herb and Bleu Cheese Sauce

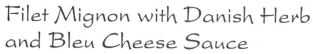

2 Tbsp. Danish cream cheese with herbs and spices
1 Tbsp. plus additional Danish Bleu cheese, crumbled
2 Tbsp. butter
2 small filet mignon steaks, cut 1 ¼" thick and trimmed
2 Tbsp. dry white wine
2 Tbsp. water
freshly ground pepper to taste
2 slices bacon, crisply cooked and drained

On a small plate mash herbed and spiced cheese with 1 Tbsp. Bleu cheese and set aside. Warm serving plates in a slow oven. In small skillet over moderate heat, melt butter. Add steaks. Brown on both sides then cook to desired doneness. Transfer to heated plates and keep warm. Add wine to drippings in skillet. Increase heat until mixture boils. Boil for 1 minute and reduce heat to low. Stir in cheeses, mixing well with a fork. Blend in water and pepper. Simmer gently one minute, stirring several times. Thin to desired consistency with additional water if necessary. Pour sauce over steaks and top each with bacon strip. Serve with additional Bleu cheese. Serves 2.

"Dave brought all the herd of horses up, and Pa and Elmer caught Kit, Bess, and Frank, and hauled some poles with the team. Logan rode Kit first, and then I rode her and went almost up to Spring Creek and back here and up Soda Creek a ways."

(It had been five months since the children had had a horse to ride!)
From the diary of
Lulie Margie Crawford
May 14, 1881

Chilled Fillet of Beef
with Sour Cream Dressing

Salt/pepper
3 lbs. beef tenderloin
4 Tbsp. butter
1 carrot, finely chopped
1 leek, white part only, finely chopped
1 stalk celery, finely chopped

Salt and pepper the beef and dot with 2 Tbsp. butter. In a small roasting pan melt the remaining butter and sauté carrots, leek, and celery over low heat for 8 minutes. Add the beef and place the pan in a preheated 500° oven for 25 minutes. Remove the beef from the oven and cool for 1 hour in the pan juices.

Sour Cream Dressing:
1 Tbsp. oil
1 clove garlic, crushed
¾ lbs. bacon, cut in 1" pieces
¼ lbs. fresh mushrooms, sliced
1 ½ cups sour cream
2 Tbsp. grated onion
1 Tbsp. fresh parsley, finely chopped
1 tsp. dried thyme
1 tsp. dried basil

In a heavy medium-sized skillet, heat the oil and garlic over moderate heat for 1 minute, then add the bacon. Sauté the bacon until barely crisp. Remove the bacon and drain on paper towel. Pour off all but 3 Tbsp. of the fat and sauté mushrooms in the remaining fat over moderate heat for 3 - 5 minutes. Drain the mushrooms and set aside.

After the meat has cooled, remove it to a cutting board. Pour the pan juices into a medium-sized mixing bowl and add sour cream, horseradish, onion, parsley, thyme, and basil, blending well. Add the bacon bits and mushrooms. Salt and pepper to taste.

To stuff, slice a 1" wide, 1" deep wedge along the top length of the fillet and remove the wedge. Fill the cavity with 3 Tbsp. of the dressing. Replace the wedge in the fillet. To serve, cut through the fillet in complete ¾" slices and serve accompanied by the additional dressing.

Pepper Steak

4 sirloin steaks (8 oz. each)
1 tsp. salt
2 Tbsp. black peppercorns
2 Tbsp. white peppercorns
4 Tbsp. plus 1 tsp. butter
1 Tbsp. oil
1 tsp. flour
¼ cup beef broth
2 Tbsp. heavy cream
1 tsp. Dijon mustard
½ cup brandy
Watercress sprigs

Sprinkle steaks with salt on both sides. Place peppercorns in a small plastic bag and pound with a hammer or rolling pin. Spread crushed peppercorns on a cutting board and press one side of each steak in them. Melt 4 Tbsp. butter and brush the other side of each steak. Chill the steaks slightly to set the butter. When ready to serve, sauté steaks in the oil in a large skillet, butter side down, for 5 minutes over moderate heat. Turn the steak and sauté 5 minutes on the other side. Remove steaks to a serving platter and keep warm. Add 1 tsp. butter, the flour, beef broth, cream, mustard, and brandy to the pan. Simmer, stirring for 3 - 5 minutes. Serve the sauce over the steaks. Garnish with watercress. Serves 4.

Cattle were the mainstay of the county's economy between 1880 and 1920 when seasons were marked by the "shove up" to summer ranges and the "shove down" to the mesas. Despite high profits during World War I, cattle prices fell sharply during the 1920s and smaller ranches replaced the few vast holdings, but the cattle industry today remains an integral part of the county's economy.

New York Pepper Steak

Pepper Blend:
3 parts coarse black pepper
1 part granulated garlic
1 part paprika
1 part salt

steaks, cut about 1" thick
2-3 Tbsp. butter
1 oz. brandy for each steak
sliced mushrooms

Combine ingredients for pepper blend and press into both sides of steak. Heat butter in skillet until melted. Cook steak on first side hot and avoid burning butter. Turn steak and cook until just about done. Add brandy, mushrooms, cover, and reduce heat. Let simmer until desired doneness and mushrooms are done. Serve steak with mushrooms over top and pour remaining sauce on steak and enjoy.

Steak Ore House

6-9 oz. filet mignon
smoked bacon
2-3 ozs. crab meat (not imitation)
3-4 ozs. sautéed mushrooms
1 - 1 ½ ozs. Béarnaise sauce

Trim all excess fat from steak. Wrap slice of bacon around perimeter of steak and secure with a large wooden pick. Grill fillets over hot mesquite coals until desired doneness. Meat is best if cooked hot and fast.

While fillets are cooking, heat crab meat. To serve, top steaks with crab meat, surround with sautéed mushrooms and apply a good scoop of Béarnaise sauce over the works. Serve with steamed broccoli or another green vegetable and a fresh baked russet potato.

Crockpot Steak Diane

1 ½ lbs. beef tenderloin, fat trimmed
2 cups thinly sliced fresh mushrooms
1 small white onion, sliced
3 cloves garlic, crushed
1 tsp. lemon juice
3 Tbsp. Worcestershire sauce
¼ cup soy sauce
¼ cup butter, melted
2 Tbsp. fresh snipped parsley
oregano
½-¾ cup red wine or cooking sherry

Place meat in the bottom of a crockpot. Place the remaining ingredients on top and stir. Turn crockpot on low or simmer and cook for 5 hours. Remove meat and slice into 8 thin slices. Place meat on a serving platter and pour juices from crockpot over and serve. Great served over rice or noodles. Serves 4-6.

Braciole Meat Roll

2 thin sliced round steaks (2 lbs.)
1 cup Parmesan cheese
3 cloves garlic, minced
3 Tbsp. parsley
1 ½ cups breadcrumbs
1 Tbsp. basil
salt and pepper
1 Tbsp. dried onion
oil
1 qt. spaghetti sauce or beef bouillon

Pound steaks with meat hammer. Mix next 7 ingredients, moisten with a little water. Spread over steaks leaving edges dry. Roll meat as a jelly roll. Tie with string. Brown in oil. Top with 2 cups spaghetti sauce or 2 cups beef bouillon and bake at 325º, covered, for 1 hour. Slice and serve with pasta or rice and additional sauce.

Barbecued Beef Slices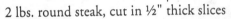

2 lbs. round steak, cut in ½" thick slices
3 Tbsp. oil
2 medium onions, grated
2 Tbsp. Worcestershire sauce
1 tsp. salt (optional)
¼ tsp. hot sauce (optional)
¾ cup ketchup
1 tsp. chili powder
¾ cup water

Generously cover steaks in flour and brown in oil. Combine remaining ingredients and mix well. Pour over browned meat, cover and simmer. Do not let boil. Can be transferred to a crockpot at this point, cooked on low for 6-8 hours. Good served over rice. Serves 4-6.

B-B-Q Beef

Place on timed bake and dinner cooks while you ski.

3 lbs. beef chuck roast
1 large onion, diced
½ cup red wine vinegar
2 Tbsp. sugar
1 tsp. salt
½ cup diced celery
2 tsp. prepared horseradish
14 oz. bottle barbecue sauce

Trim meat and cut into 3" pieces. In oven-proof casserole, combine meat along with remaining ingredients and mix well. Cover and bake at 300º for 4-5 hours. Mash with potato masher to shred meat. Serve on buns. Serves 8.

Matt Grosjean began skiing with the Steamboat Springs Winter Sports Club as a preschooler in the mid '70s. His standout technical ability propelled him quickly and successfully along the path from junior racer to U.S. Ski Team member. In 1992, Matt had several top 10 finishes in World Cup competition and placed 10th in slalom at the Albertville Olympics.

Barbecued Beef Brisket

8-10 lb. beef brisket, trimmed
½ cup ketchup
½ cup Worcestershire sauce
½ cup barbeque sauce
½ cup water
½ cup brown sugar
½ tsp. salt
¼ tsp. pepper

Preheat over to 475º. Place brisket in 13" x 9" pan and bake for 30 minutes uncovered. Meanwhile, combine remaining ingredients in saucepan and mix well. Bring to a boil for 1 minute. Remove brisket and pour sauce over meat and cover with foil. Reduce heat to 250º and bake for 6-7 hours. Slice thin, preferably with electric knife. Serves 10-12.

Phippsburg and Yampa were railheads for the great cattle herds being driven from the White River Valley.

By 1913, more cattle were shipped from Steamboat Springs than from any other single point in the United States.

Sauerbraten

Serve with potato pancakes & sweet and sour cabbage.

4 lbs. top round roast, beef, elk or deer

Marinade:
2 cups cider vinegar
2 cups Port wine
1 large onion, sliced
1 green pepper, sliced
2 medium carrots, thinly sliced
8 sprigs parsley, chopped
1 bunch celery, leaves only
1 tsp. whole black pepper
2-4 bay leaves, crumbled
1 tsp. salt
2 tsp. marjoram, leaf
4 cloves garlic, minced and mashed
2 tsp. rosemary, leaf
2 tsp. sweet basil, leaf
3 Tbsp. butter
5 gingersnaps, crushed
½ pt. sour cream

Combine marinade ingredients and mix well. Place meat in marinade. Marinate meat refrigerated for 4-5 days, turning twice daily. Remove meat, drain, and brown in butter, add marinade and simmer 3-4 hours. Strain marinade from meat and discard or use as extra sauce. Add gingersnaps and sour cream to pot. Stir until thick and smooth, do not boil, serve while hot or cold.   Serves 8.

Belgian Goulash

½ cup sifted flour
2 ½ tsp. salt
½ tsp. pepper
2 lbs. beef chuck or arm roast, cut into bite size pieces
½ cup salad oil
2 lbs. yellow onions, halved and sliced
1 clove garlic, minced
1 can beer
1 Tbsp. soy sauce
1 Tbsp. Worcestershire sauce
1 Tbsp. steak sauce
2 bay leaves
½ tsp. dry thyme
fresh parsley (garnish)

Combine salt, pepper and flour and mix well. Roll meat in flour, coat well and brown in oil. Add remaining ingredients except parsley to pan. Stir well to mix, cover and simmer slowly until tender, stirring occasionally. Serve over flat, buttered noodles or rice with fresh grated Parmesan. Garnish with fresh parsley. Serves 4-6.

Burgess Creek Beef Fondue

2 lbs. beef tenderloin
3 quarts beef broth
1 cup dry white wine
2 cloves garlic, minced
2 Tbsp. fresh ginger, minced
½ pound snow peas
cocktail onions
1 cup thinly sliced green onions

Make sauces (below) to accompany fondue. Cut beef into ¾ inch cubes and chill. Snap ends off of snow peas and remove strings. Combine broth, ginger, garlic and wine in an attractive pot. Heat to boiling. Put sauces in separate serving bowls. Serve snow peas and onions in separate serving bowls. Put pot of broth on a tabletop burner on the dinner table. Adjust the heat to keep the broth simmering. To cook, each guest spears beef on long fondue fork and immerses it in simmering broth until cooked to desired temperature. Dip meat in sauces and eat. When broth has been reduced and appetites are fairly filled, add snow peas and cocktail onions to individual soup bowls and ladle broth into bowls. Season with sauces and enjoy. Fondue is great with a crusty French bread. If a tabletop burner is not available, use a conventional fondue pot but the chef must periodically pre-cook meat chunks for 1-2 minutes in a pot on the stovetop. Guests may then heat or cook the meat to desired temperature in the broth in the fondue pot. Serves 6-8.

Sundried Tomato Sauce
½ cup sundried tomatoes in oil
¾ cup red wine vinegar
2 Tbsp. minced fresh basil
Drain tomatoes and reserve 2 Tbsp. of tomato oil. Blend tomatoes, oil, and vinegar in a food processor. Stir in basil and refrigerate until used.

Vegetable Herbed Cheese Sauce
½ lb. carrots, peeled and chopped
1 small onion, peeled and chopped
2 Tbsp. olive oil
4 ozs. soft herb flavored cheese
¼ cup plain yogurt
Mix carrots and onions with oil and spread level in an 8" x 10" pan. Roast vegetables uncovered in a 350° oven for 45 minutes or until softened. Let cool. In a food processor purée vegetables with cheese and yogurt. Serve chilled or warm.

Herbed Lime Dip
½ cup minced cilantro
¾ cup lime juice
salt and pepper
Mix lime juice and cilantro together, season to taste. Serve immediately or cover tightly and chill until used. This is also great used as a marinade for grilled chicken or beef, just add ½ cup oil and 1 or 2 cloves garlic.

Burgess Creek was named for Perry A. Burgess of Bates County, Missouri. He was one of the founders of the original Steamboat Springs Townsite in 1875.

Beef Stew with Dill and Artichokes

4 - 6 Tbsp. vegetable oil
2 cloves garlic, split
2 large onions, sliced
2 ½ lbs. stewing beef, cut in 1 ½" cubes
⅓ cup flour
½ tsp. salt
½ tsp. pepper
½ tsp. dried dill
1 cup burgundy
1 ¼ cups beef stock
18 fresh mushrooms, quartered
4 Tbsp. butter
8 fresh artichoke hearts, halved, or a 9 oz. pkg. frozen artichoke hearts, thawed
2 ½ cups biscuit dough or enough to make approximately 16 biscuits
¼ cup butter, melted
¼ cup freshly grated Parmesan cheese

Heat 4 Tbsp. of the oil in a heavy 3 qt. pot over medium heat. Sauté the garlic and onion 6 - 8 minutes or until soft. Remove onion and garlic with a slotted spoon and set aside. Dredge the meat in the flour, salt, and pepper. Brown meat, ⅓ at a time, over moderate-high heat, using the cooking oil from the onion and adding 1 - 2 Tbsp. more oil as needed. Remove the meat and set aside as you brown. When all the meat is browned, return it to the pan along with the onion and garlic. Add dill, wine, and stock. Cover the pot and simmer 2 hours or until the meat is tender.

Sauté the mushrooms in the butter over moderate-low heat 2 - 3 minutes. Add mushrooms and artichoke hearts to the meat. Remove the garlic halves and place the stew in a 2 ½ qt. casserole. Cut the biscuit dough into rounds and place on top of the stew. Bake in a preheated 400° oven 20 minutes. Remove the casserole from the oven and brush the top with the melted butter and sprinkle with cheese. Return to the oven for 5 minutes. Serve with additional biscuits and tossed green salad. Serves 6.

South American Beef Stew
This stew is served in a pumpkin.

2 lbs stewing beef, cut in 1 ½" cubes
½ cup olive oil
3 - 4 cloves garlic, chopped
2 onions, chopped
2 green or red peppers, chopped
3 carrots, grated or chopped
2 sweet potatoes, mashed
½ cup raisins
½ - 1 cup apricots, chopped
2 cans whole tomatoes
2 bouillon cubes
1 cup red wine (optional)
bay leaf
salt/pepper to taste
1 tsp. allspice
fresh parsley, chopped
sweet basil

Sauté beef with chopped garlic in olive oil. Add remaining ingredients. Cook on low heat 2 hours or more. Serve in a cleaned-out pumpkin shell. Serves 6-8.

It was illegal for cowboys to hold bucking contests and horse races on Main Street Sunday mornings because it frightened the ladies on their way to and from church.

Vermicelli with Sweet-Hot Beef
7 ozs. vermicelli, uncooked
1 lb. lean ground chuck
¼ cup raisins
1 ¼ tsp. black pepper
1 ¼ tsp. ground cumin
½ tsp. salt
¼ tsp. ground cinnamon
⅛ tsp. ground red pepper
½ cup water
8 oz. can unsalted tomato sauce
2 tsp. lemon juice
fresh parsley, chopped (opt.)

Cook vermicelli according to directions, omitting salt and fat. Drain and set aside. Cook ground chuck in a large skillet over medium high heat until browned, stirring to crumble. Drain well. Return meat to a clean skillet; add raisins and next 7 ingredients, stirring well. Cook over low heat for 15 minutes, stirring occasionally. Stir in lemon juice. Serve over vermicelli. Sprinkle with chopped parsley, if desired. Serves 5.

Sweet and Sour Beef and Vegetables

2 lbs. round or chuck steak, cut into 1" cubes
2 Tbsp. vegetable oil
2 - 8 oz. cans tomato sauce
¼ cup soy sauce
⅛ cup sugar
½ tsp. salt
¼ cup vinegar
½ cup light molasses
2 cups sliced carrots
2 cups small white onions, peeled
1 green pepper, cut into 1" squares

Brown meat in hot oil in a skillet and transfer to a crockpot. Add remaining ingredients and mix well. Cook 6-7 hours on low setting (4 hours on high). Serve with macaroni or noodles. Serves 6.

Hot and Spicy Orange Beef

¼ cup orange juice
1 Tbsp. hoisin sauce
1 Tbsp. dry sherry
1 Tbsp. soy sauce
½ tsp. grated orange peel
½-¾ tsp. red pepper flakes
1 Tbsp. cornstarch
¾ lb. flank steak, sliced thin
3 Tbsp. salad oil
2 tsp. minced fresh ginger
3 cups shredded bok choy
½ cup grated carrots
4 green onions, sliced thin
4 ozs. firm tofu, cut into strips
hot cooked rice

In a small bowl, combine first 6 ingredients and 1 tsp. of cornstarch. Toss beef with remaining 2 tsp. cornstarch; set all aside. In wok or skillet, heat 2 Tbsp. oil. Add ginger and cook over medium high heat for 1 minute. Add bok choy, carrots and green onions. Stir fry 2-3 minutes, until tender crisp. Remove from wok. Add remaining 1 Tbsp. oil to wok. Add meat and stir fry until lightly browned, about 2 minutes. Gently stir in tofu. Stir orange juice mixture; add to wok and continue cooking 1 minute or until thickened. Return vegetables to wok; heat through. Serve over rice. Serves 4.

Hank Kashiwa won the World Professional Championships in 1975. He was a member of the U.S. Ski Team from 1967-1972 and competed in the 1972 Olympics. He also competed on the professional circuit for nine years.

Hank is as well-known in the kitchen as he is on the slopes with his cooking products line.

Kashiwa's Teriyaki Fajitas

2 whole boneless, skinless chicken breasts, cut into ½" strips
or 1 lb. favorite cut of beef in ½" strips
¼ cup Teriyaki sauce
1 bell pepper, sliced into ¼" strips
1 small onion, sliced into ¼" strips
2 Tbsp. sesame oil or vegetable oil
8 flour tortillas, warmed

Marinate meat in sauce for at least 30 minutes. Sauté meat in sauce and a few drops of oil over medium heat for 5 minutes, until tender. Keep warm. Sauté vegetables in Teriyaki sauce and a few drops of oil until tender-crisp. Combine meat, vegetables, and accompaniments (guacamole, chopped lettuce, chopped tomatoes, refried beans, sour cream, grated cheese, salsa, chopped black olives) in warm tortilla. Roll and serve. Serves 6.

Caballeros Casserole

Great for potlucks.

1 ½ lbs. lean ground beef
1 small onion, chopped
1 clove garlic, minced
1 ½ cups picante sauce
10 oz. pkg. frozen spinach, thawed and squeezed dry
8 oz. can tomato sauce
2 medium tomatoes, chopped
1 large red bell pepper, diced
4 oz. can diced green chilies
1 Tbsp. lime juice
½ tsp. garlic salt
dash cumin
½ teaspoon cayenne pepper
¼ cup Jalapeño pepper, diced
12 corn tortillas
1 cup sour cream
¾ cup Monterey Jack cheese, grated
¾ cup Cheddar cheese, grated
shredded lettuce
½ cup ripe black olives, sliced

Brown meat with onion and garlic and drain. Add next 11 ingredients and simmer, uncovered for 15 minutes, stirring occasionally. Arrange 6 tortillas on bottom of greased 13" x 9" baking dish, overlapping as necessary. Top with half meat mixture. Spread sour cream over meat. Top with remaining tortillas and meat. At this point, it may be refrigerated up to 6 hours. Allow to stand at room temperature 30 minutes before baking. Bake at 350° for 30 minutes, or until hot and bubbly. Remove from oven and sprinkle cheeses on top. Let stand 10 minutes. Serve with lettuce and olives and extra picante sauce, if desired. Serves 8-10.

Fajitas

2 lbs. round or skirt steak
4 Tbsp. oil
4 Tbsp. lemon juice
4 tsp. Worcestershire sauce
4 cloves garlic, minced
salt to taste
2 Tbsp. chili powder
4 tsp. cumin
3 onions, sliced
2 green peppers, sliced

Grill meat quickly on both sides, then slice thinly. Combine next 7 ingredients and mix well. Pour over meat and toss until well coated. Marinate, covered, in the refrigerator 3-4 hours. When ready to serve, sauté onions and peppers in a small amount of oil until slightly limp; set aside. Quickly reheat meat over high heat. Serve with onions, peppers, tortillas, sour cream, guacamole and any other favorite condiments. Serves 6.

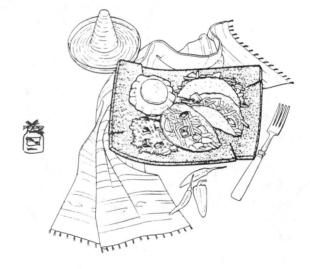

Mexican Meat Mix

6 lbs. chuck or pork roast
1 pkg. dry onion soup mix
2 cups water
3 onions, chopped
4 oz. can diced green chilies
16 oz. green chile salsa
1 tsp. garlic salt
4 Tbsp. flour
salt to taste
1 tsp. cumin
29 oz. can tomatoes, slightly puréed
juices from the roasts

Brown meat in a pressure cooker. Add water and top with onion soup mix. Cook at 15 lbs. pressure for 1 hour and 45 minutes. Cool and shred. Sauté onions and chilies; add salsa, flour and spices. Stir until blended. Add meat, puréed tomatoes, and meat juices. Simmer, covered, for 30 minutes. Allow to cool. Divide into 3 portions and freeze in quart containers. This mix is good in making burritos served with cheese, lettuce, sour cream and salsa. Makes 3 quarts.

Marvin Crawford, an outstanding competitor in downhill, slalom, jumping and cross-country, was never defeated in four-way competition. He capped a brilliant collegiate career by placing 23rd in nordic combined in the 1956 Cortina Olympics.

Marv's sons, Rod, Greg, and Gary have followed their father to skiing acclaim. Gary Crawford, a nordic combined star, skied in both the Lake Placid Olympics of 1980 and in the 1988 Olympics in Calgary.

German Burgers

2 pkgs. 12 count frozen white dinner rolls
1 lb. premium ground beef
1 small head cabbage, finely chopped
1 medium onion, finely chopped
½ lb. mushrooms, sliced
3-4 Tbsp. soy sauce
salt and pepper to taste
mayonnaise
Dijon mustard

Thaw dinner rolls on 2 greased cookie sheets until doubled in size. In a 5 qt. saucepan, brown the ground beef. Add the cabbage, onion, mushrooms, soy sauce, salt and pepper and cook, covered, over medium-low heat until cabbage is well cooked. Mixture should be moist but not too liquid. Cook uncovered until excess liquid is gone. On a floured surface, knead 2 rolls together and roll out with a rolling pin to the size of a large thick tortilla, approximately 8". Repeat until you have 12 circles. Spoon about ⅓ cup of the meat mixture into the center of each circle. Pick up edges and enclose the mixture by pinching all edges together. Place pinched side down on a greased baking sheet, 6 burgers per sheet. Bake at 350° (375° for altitudes over 6000') for 20 minutes or until golden brown. Mix equal parts of mayonnaise and Dijon mustard and serve as a dip for the burgers. For vegetarian burgers, cook cabbage mixture in a little oil, substitute ground beef with ½ cup sunflower seeds. These should be added after the cabbage mixture is well cooked. Makes 12.

Sven Wiik's Favorite Burgers
Amazingly tasty, even kid approved!

1 lb. lean ground beef
1 egg
½ - ⅔ cup consommé
1 ½ tsp. salt
¼ tsp. white pepper
2 Tbsp. onion, chopped
⅔ cup mashed potatoes
½ cup diced pickled red beets
3 Tbsp. juice from beets

Sauté the onions. In a mixing bowl, combine ground beef, egg, mashed potatoes, consommé, a little at a time. Add beets, beet juice, white pepper and sautéed onions and mix well. Form mixture like thick hamburgers and grill or fry in a frying pan. This dish is traditionally served with sliced, fried or finely cut potatoes. Serves 6.

Kashiwa's Marinated Hamburgers

1 lb. lean ground beef
⅓ cup Teriyaki sauce

In mixing bowl, thoroughly combine ingredients. Lightly shape into patties and grill on barbeque or under broiler. Place on toasted bun. As a garnish, sauté bell peppers, onions, mushrooms, celery in Teriyaki sauce and add to burgers. Makes 3 - 4 burgers

Crawford Boys' Sloppy Joes

2 lbs. ground round or better
1 small bottle ketchup
1 small bottle yellow mustard
5 oz. bottle Worcestershire sauce
½ cup margarine
1 cup sugar

Brown meat. Add remaining ingredients and simmer for 30 minutes. Toast buns and serve. Serves 6-8.

Soupçon Meatloaf

2 lbs. lean ground beef
1 lb. ground pork or ground veal or combination
1 cup bread crumbs (seasoned) or crushed croutons
2 eggs
1 large onion, chopped
½ cup ketchup
¼ - ½ cup horseradish
¼ cup Worcestershire or soy sauce
¼ cup Dijon mustard
salt/pepper
basil

Mix all ingredients and put in loaf pan. Bake in 350° oven for 1 hour. After 30 minutes, cover meatloaf with sauce and bake for remaining 30 minutes. Serves 8-10.

Sauce:
½ cup ketchup
2 Tbsp. brown sugar
1 Tbsp. Worcestershire or soy sauce

Brandied Barbequed Pork Tenderloin

2 pork tenderloins, or pork loin
⅔-¾ bottle teriyaki baste and glaze
¼-⅓ cup apricot brandy or peach brandy
¼-⅓ cup white wine, not too dry
4 ozs. apricot or apricot/pineapple preserves
2-3 sticks cinnamon, broken into large pieces
6-8 cloves
2 cloves garlic, sliced in half
3-4 bay leaves

Combine all ingredients except pork. Add pork and marinate in refrigerator for at least 1 hour; overnight is better. Grill 10-12 minutes on each side, depending on thickness. Reserve marinade to baste during grilling. Cook any remaining marinade over low heat while grilling. Drizzle over cut meat and serve extra on the side. Serves 6-8.

Grilled Oriental Pork

½ cup soy sauce
¼ cup sake or dry sherry
¼ cup salad oil
2 cloves garlic, crushed
1 tsp. powdered ginger
2 pork tenderloins (about ¾ lb. each)
1 cup converted rice
1 Tbsp. butter
1 tsp. salt
2 ¼ cups water
¼ cup sliced green onion tops
5 oz. can water chestnuts, diced

"It snowed last night about 2 inches. Oh, I hope my shoes and dress (ordered from Montgomery Ward) will come soon for I need them awfully."

From the diary of
Lulie Margie Crawford
May 18, 1881

Prepare marinade for pork by combining first 5 ingredients; mix well. Cut pork crosswise into ½" slices. Pour marinade over pork in shallow dish or bowl. Cover and refrigerate 4 hours, turning meat occasionally. Drain off and reserve marinade. Half an hour before serving, prepare rice by placing rice, butter, salt, water and ¼ cup reserved marinade in a saucepan; bring to a boil. Cover, and cook over low heat until rice is tender and all liquid has been absorbed, about 25 minutes. Just before serving, add green onions and water chestnuts; toss gently to mix well. Arrange pork slices flat side up and thread horizonally on skewers; use 2 parallel skewers through slices to make turning easy. To cook, broil 5" from heat source, turning 3 times and brushing lightly each time with remaining reserved marinade, about 15 minutes or until done. Serve with rice. Serves 4-6.

Herbed Garlic Pork Loin

3-5 lb. pork loin roast or thick chops
orange juice
Old Bay Seasoning
basil
Italian herbs
fresh ground black pepper
¼ cup prepared crushed garlic
¼ cup cooking sherry
¼ cup olive oil

Pour orange juice over meat. Sprinkle with generous amount of Old Bay Seasoning, basil, Italian herbs and pepper. Spread on garlic and sprinkle with cooking sherry and olive oil. Marinate several hours if desired. Bake at 325° for about 1 ¼ - 1 ½ hours. For thick chops, bake at 350° for 35-45 minutes. Can be prepared on the grill if preferred. Serves 6.

Ryan Heckman, "The Speck from Winter Park," began training with the Winter Sports Club in 1990. His diminutive size (hence the nickname) belies a gigantic ski-jumping ability. Ryan, at 17, was named to both the Nordic Combined team and Special Jumping team for the Albertville Olympics of 1992.

Santa Fe Ribs

1 cup orange juice
1 cup grapefruit juice
1 cup lime juice
½ tsp. cayenne pepper
½ tsp. basil
1 tsp. oregano
3 ozs. chipotle pepper
3 tsp. minced garlic
½ cup vegetable oil
baby back pork ribs

Blend all ingredients except ribs. Pour over ribs. Refrigerate and marinate for at least 4 hours or overnight. Grill over medium coals until done.

Quick Pork Chops a L'Orange

5 pork chops
1 ⅓ cups uncooked rice
1 cup orange juice
1 ½ cups chicken stock

Brown pork chops on both sides. Put uncooked rice in a casserole dish, pour in orange juice and place chops on top. Pour chicken stock over the chops and cover. Bake at 350° for 45 minutes. Uncover and bake for 10 minutes more. Serves 3-4.

Brandied Apple Pork Chops
Very quick, easy and elegant.

6 center cut pork chops, 1-1 ½" thick
fresh thyme
⅓ cup olive oil
2 apples, cored and sliced
1 onion, sliced
1 Tbsp. flour
½ cup apple juice
½ cup cream
2-3 Tbsp. brandy
salt and pepper to taste

Heat ½ the oil in a large sauté pan. Sauté onions and apples until soft. Remove from pan and keep warm. Add remaining oil and heat; place chops on top of thyme in the sauté pan. Brown the chops until done, about 8-10 minutes per side. Remove from pan and keep warm. Add flour to remaining juices in pan, stir over medium heat, slowly add apple juice, stirring constantly. Add remaining ingredients and season to taste. Remove thyme from chops. To serve, top each pork chop with apples, onions and pour sauce over. Serves 6.

Pinnacle Peak Pork Chops

6 thick cut pork chops
6 large onions, sliced
⅓ cup brown sugar
¼ tsp. salt
½ tsp. garlic salt
⅛ tsp. pepper
1 ½ Tbsp. lemon juice
⅓ cup chili sauce

Pinnacle Peak is a 12,200 foot peak believed to have been named by Scotchman George Morrison for the high grade of coal mined in the area.

Arrange pork chops in a large casserole dish. Top each chop with one onion slice. Combine remaining ingredients and pour over chops. Bake at 350° for 1 ½ hours. Serves 6.

Bavarian Pork Chops

4 pork chops, trimmed of fat
4 potatoes, peeled and quartered
1 large can sauerkraut
1 tsp. caraway seeds
salt and pepper to taste
½ cup water

In a large skillet, brown pork chops in salted pan. Add potatoes, sauerkraut, caraway seeds, pepper and water and simmer, covered, for 45 minutes or until potatoes are tender. Serves 4.

Sweet and Sour Pork Kabobs

½ cup apricot preserves
½ cup tomato sauce
¼ cup brown sugar
½ cup dry red wine
2 Tbsp. lemon juice
2 Tbsp. vegetable oil
2 tsp. grated onion
2 lbs. lean, boneless pork, cut into 1 ½" cubes
4 large carrots, cooked, cut into 1" pieces
1 green pepper, cut into 1 ½" pieces
1 red pepper, cut into 1 ½" pieces
1 pt. cherry tomatoes
15 ¼ oz. can pineapple chunks
salt and pepper to taste

Combine first seven ingredients in saucepan. Boil uncovered for 10-15 minutes. Thread pieces of pork onto four skewers. Season with salt and pepper. Thread pieces of carrots, peppers, pineapple and tomatoes, alternating on 4 additional skewers. Season with salt and pepper, set aside. Grill and turn meat only once over medium coals for 10 minutes. Add vegetable skewers to grill. Brush meat and vegetables with sauce and grill 15 minutes more. Remove from skewers and put on serving platter. For variation, add quartered, precooked new potatoes. Serves 4-6.

Grilled Pork with Cranberry Sauce

¾ cup minced onion
1 Tbsp. olive oil
3 Tbsp. cranberry juice
1 tsp. crumbled leaf oregano
1 tsp. crumbled leaf thyme
¼ tsp. salt
⅛ tsp. pepper
2 lbs. boneless pork, trimmed of fat and cut into 1 ½" cubes
3 green onions, minced (garnish)
hot cooked rice
cranberry sauce (see recipe below)

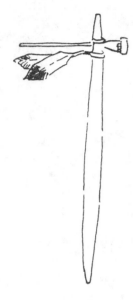

Combine first 7 ingredients in a plastic bag. Add pork cubes; close bag with wire. Marinate in refrigerator for at least 5 hours. Remove meat from marinade. Thread onto skewers. Broil for about 30 minutes, or until pork is thoroughly cooked, rotating skewers several times. Remove from skewers, garnish with chopped green onion. Serve over rice with cranberry sauce on the side. Serves 6-8.

Cranberry Sauce:
12 oz. can frozen cranberry juice cocktail concentrate
⅓ cup sugar

Combine concentrate and sugar in a small saucepan. Boil gently until mixture is reduced by ⅓; cool. Sauce will thicken as it cools.

Gourmet Chile Verde

1 ½ lbs. boneless beef chuck & 1 ½ lbs. pork shoulder cut into 1" cubes
    OR 3 lbs. pork or beef roast
2 cloves garlic, minced
2 large (28 oz.) cans tomatoes
4 oz. can chopped green chilies
⅓ cup chopped parsley
1 ½ - 2 tsp. ground cumin
1 cup dry red wine
salt to taste

Brown approximately ¼ of the meat at a time on all sides. Remove with a slotted spoon and reserve. In pan drippings, sauté garlic until soft. In a large pot combine tomatoes and their liquid, green chilies, parsley, seasonings and wine. Bring tomato mixture to a boil, then reduce heat to a simmer. Add browned meats and their juices plus the garlic. Cover and simmer for 2 hours, stirring occasionally. Remove cover, simmer 45 minutes more or until sauce is reduced to desired consistency. Taste and adjust seasonings as needed. Serving suggestions: serve in bowls with flour tortillas or serve over rice or reduce until very thick and use as a filling for flour tortillas as burritos. Leftover meat from roasts can be used, simply shred. Cooking the meat in a pressure cooker or a crock pot first makes it tender. Once it's cooled, just shred and add to the tomato mixture. Makes 4 qts.

Indonesian Pork with Peanut Sauce

¼ cup walnuts
1 Tbsp. coriander
3 cloves garlic
1 onion, coarsely chopped
½ tsp. red pepper flakes
1 cup orange juice
2 Tbsp. brown sugar
2 Tbsp. soy sauce
2-3 lb. pork tenderloin
hot peanut sauce (recipe follows)

Put first 8 ingredients in a blender and blend well to make marinade.
Pour over pork tenderloin and marinate several hours or overnight.
Grill over medium coals about 25 to 30 minutes or until desired
temperature. Slice and serve with hot peanut sauce. Garnish with
fresh parsley or cilantro. Serves 4-6.

Hot Peanut Sauce:
2 Tbsp. butter
1 small onion, chopped
6 Tbsp. chunky peanut butter
2 Tbsp. soy sauce
½ tsp. red pepper flakes
1 cup milk
Place all ingredients in blender and purée thoroughly. Transfer to
saucepan and heat. Serve hot.

*It was the Crawford
home that served as a
fort for Hayden and
Yampa River settlers
during Indian scares
in September and
October of 1879 fol-
lowing the Meeker
Massacre.*

Ranch House Ham and Beans

4-5 lb. boneless ham
2 large onions, sliced
4 large celery stalks
4 carrots
6 whole cloves
1 large pkg. dried great northern white beans
water

Place all ingredients in a large pot with just enough water to cover.
Bring to a boil. Turn off heat, cover, and let sit overnight refrigerated.
Next day, bring to a boil and cover. Reduce heat to low and cook,
slowly, all day, until beans are right texture. Turn heat off and allow
to sit until ready to serve. Break ham up with a fork; serve. Serves 8.

For American style pork and beans: make the above recipe, put half of
the beans into a separate pot. Add 1 cup ketchup, 2 Tbsp. mustard,
½ cup molasses, 1 canned pineapple, 2 Tbsp. Worcestershire sauce,
and brown sugar to desired sweetness.

Baked Ham

14 lb. bone-in sugar cured ham
whole cloves
1 cup brown sugar
½ cup sherry
½ cup Dijon mustard
½ cup apricot jelly

Bake ham at 325° for 2 hours with fatty side up. Meanwhile, combine remaining ingredients as glaze. Remove ham from oven and score top in a diamond pattern. Insert cloves in center of diamonds. Brush glaze over ham and return to oven. Continue baking for 1 ½ - 2 hours. Glaze occasionally while baking. Slice thinly and serve with a wine raisin sauce (recipe follows).

Wine Raisin Sauce:
2 cups dry white wine
½ cup water
1 cup sugar
4 Tbsp. Dijon mustard
½ tsp. salt
1 cup raisins
3 Tbsp. arrowroot, dissolved in ¼ cup water

In a 2 qt. saucepan, mix the wine, water, sugar, mustard and salt with a wire whisk until well mixed. Add raisins and simmer over low heat for 30 minutes. Add dissolved arrowroot and bring sauce to a slow boil and simmer until slightly thick. Serve with pork or ham.

Hoe-Down Sauerkraut & Sausages

A hearty, simple meal—especially on winter nights.

4 lbs. fresh sauerkraut, cold water rinsed
2-3 cloves garlic, minced
chicken or beef broth
freshly ground black pepper
selection of poached sausages: knockwurst, frankfurters, Italian cotechino, Polish kielbasa

Place sauerkraut in a large pot. Add garlic and enough broth to cover. Bring to a boil; reduce heat to low. Simmer 2-3 hours, adding more broth as needed. Add pepper to taste. Serve on a large platter with a selection of sausages. Serve with Dijon mustard, Dusseldorf, rye bread, beer or Alsatian white wine.

Skis were first used in Routt County to carry mail in the early 1880s.

Early skiers used a single pole as a brace, a rudder, or to drag between the legs to slow speed.

In the 1920s, some hearty souls would ski to Denver when they were without train service. The trip was a two-week journey.

Grilled Butterflied Leg of Lamb

5-7 lb. leg of lamb, deboned and butterflied.
Your choice of marinade as follows:

Herb Marinade:
1 cup dry red wine
¾ cup beef stock
3 Tbsp. orange marmalade
2 Tbsp. red wine vinegar
1 Tbsp. minced dried onion
1 Tbsp. dried marjoram
1 Tbsp. dried rosemary
1 large bay leaf, crumbled
1 tsp. seasoned salt
¼ tsp. ginger
1 clove garlic, crushed

Combine all ingredients except the lamb in a 2 qt. saucepan and simmer, uncovered, for 20 minutes. Place the lamb in a medium-sized 13"x 9" roasting pan or a broiler pan. Pour the hot marinade over and marinate at room temperature for 6-8 hours, turning frequently.

Soy Honeyed Marinade:
¾ cup hot water
⅓ cup soy sauce
¼ cup honey
2 Tbsp. oil
2 Tbsp. lemon juice
3 cloves garlic, crushed
rosemary (optional)
black pepper (optional)

Make sure all fat is trimmed from lamb. Place lamb in a pan just large enough to hold it. Combine remaining ingredients and pour over meat. Refrigerate about 8 hours, turning lamb occasionally .

Minted Marinade:
1 cup Zinfandel or dry red wine
¾ cup soy sauce
6 cloves garlic, sliced
½ cup chopped fresh mint leaves
1 ½ Tbsp. fresh rosemary or 2 tsp. dried, chopped
1 Tbsp. freshly ground black pepper

Combine all ingredients except lamb. Trim fat from lamb. Place lamb in pan with marinade, cover and refrigerate about 8 hours, turning lamb occasionally.

Grilling Directions:
Grill over hot coals for about 20 minutes on each side, basting with marinade. Lamb should be rosy pink in the middle. Serve immediately in thin slices. Serves 10-12.

Grilled Marinated Lamb Chops

8 double rib lamb chops, well-trimmed

Marinade:
2 cups peanut or corn oil
¼ cup honey
¼ cup tamari or soy sauce
1 medium onion, thinly sliced
1 cup fresh basil, minced
1 Tbsp. sesame oil
1 Tbsp. rice wine vinegar

Sesame Butter:
½ cup unsalted butter, softened at room temperature
1 ½ Tbsp. sesame seeds, toasted
2 drops Asian sesame oil
2 drops chile oil
1 Tbsp. fresh cilantro, minced
salt and freshly ground pepper to taste
2 Tbsp. black sesame seeds

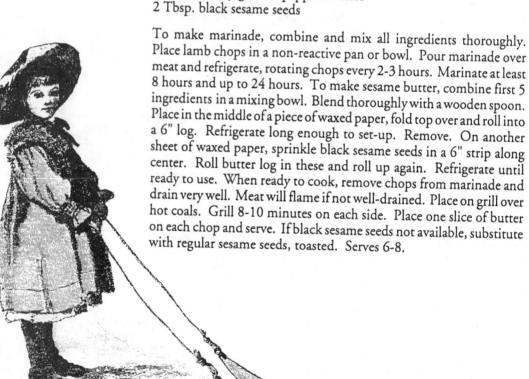

To make marinade, combine and mix all ingredients thoroughly. Place lamb chops in a non-reactive pan or bowl. Pour marinade over meat and refrigerate, rotating chops every 2-3 hours. Marinate at least 8 hours and up to 24 hours. To make sesame butter, combine first 5 ingredients in a mixing bowl. Blend thoroughly with a wooden spoon. Place in the middle of a piece of waxed paper, fold top over and roll into a 6" log. Refrigerate long enough to set-up. Remove. On another sheet of waxed paper, sprinkle black sesame seeds in a 6" strip along center. Roll butter log in these and roll up again. Refrigerate until ready to use. When ready to cook, remove chops from marinade and drain very well. Meat will flame if not well-drained. Place on grill over hot coals. Grill 8-10 minutes on each side. Place one slice of butter on each chop and serve. If black sesame seeds not available, substitute with regular sesame seeds, toasted. Serves 6-8.

Rack of Lamb Persillee

This makes a juicy, tender rack of lamb.

1 six-rib rack of lamb
1 cup fresh breadcrumbs
½ cup finely chopped parsley
salt and pepper to taste
1 cup chicken or beef broth

Rub the rack with salt and pepper. Place in a roasting pan, meaty side down. Add broth, and roast at 450° for 25 minutes. Meanwhile, combine the breadcrumbs and parsley and place on a piece of foil. Remove pan from oven. Holding the rack by the ribs, press the meaty side firmly into crumbs and parsley until thoroughly coated. Baste with a spoonful or 2 of the pan juices. If not fat enough, place a dot of butter or 2 on the crumbs. Bake 5-6 minutes more until crumbs are nicely browned. Serves 2.

Babotie

This recipe is commonly served in Africa.

2 lbs. lean ground lamb or beef
2 onions, finely sliced
2 Tbsp. butter
2 Tbsp. curry
2 Tbsp. sugar
2 Tbsp. vinegar
2 slices white bread, soaked in milk, squeezed dry
2 eggs
2 tsp. salt
¼ tsp. cloves
¼ tsp. nutmeg
¼ tsp. ginger
¼ tsp. pepper
½ cup raisins
6 bay leaves
1 cup milk

Heidi Bowes grew up skiing on a 360-foot slope in the backyard of her cozy Strawberry Park home. She was named to the U.S. Ski Team in 1979 and enjoyed national and international success before retiring in 1990.

Brown onion and meat in butter. Add curry, sugar, vinegar, bread, 1 beaten egg, salt, cloves, nutmeg, ginger, pepper and raisins. Stir well. Pour into well-buttered baking dish. Bake at 350° for 20 minutes. Beat remaining egg and 1 cup milk. Pour over meat mixture. Insert bay leaves in an upright position. Bake 15 minutes more or until top is set. Remove bay leaves before serving. Good served over rice. Serves 8.

Greek Meatballs

Excellent served with hot mustard sauce.

½ lb. ground beef
½ lb. lean ground lamb
1 large onion, chopped fine
2 eggs
1 slice bread, soaked in water
1 medium potato, grated
1 Tbsp. Greek oregano
1 Tbsp. thyme

Combine all ingredients in a large mixing bowl. Shape into little footballs. Fry 5-10 minutes in hot oil and serve with French fries or rice. Serves 4.

Saltimbocca

4 veal chops, Frenched and butterflied
4 slices prosciutto
4 slices Fontina
1 tsp. fresh sage, chopped
6 oz. fresh mushrooms, sliced
1 tsp. shallots, minced
1 tsp. garlic, minced
salt and pepper to taste
6 oz. demi glace sauce mix
¼ cup heavy cream
⅓ cup Marsala
4 Tbsp. fresh sage

Rub inside of each chop with ¼ tsp. fresh, chopped sage. Roll prosciutto and Fontina and stuff chops. Brown in olive oil, remove and bake at 350° for 45 minutes. Meanwhile, sauté mushrooms, shallots, garlic, herbs, salt and pepper. Deglaze with Marsala. Add demi and heavy cream and garnish with sage leaf. Serves 4.

Escalopes de Veau Henriette

4 veal scallops, about 4" square and thinly sliced
salt and freshly ground pepper to taste
1 egg, lightly beaten
bread crumbs
3 Tbsp. butter
1 Tbsp. oil
½ lb. mushrooms, thinly sliced
¼ cup beef broth or 2 Tbsp. each broth and red or white wine
¼ cup grated imported Parmesan cheese

Pound veal as thin as possible. Season with salt and pepper. Dip each piece in beaten egg until lightly coated on both sides, letting any excess egg drip off. Then coat lightly on both sides in bread crumbs. Heat butter and oil in a large heavy skillet and fry veal over medium heat until browned on both sides (about 2 minutes on each side). As each piece is browned, place in an oven proof casserole. Fry the mushrooms in the same skillet for 1-2 minutes adding more butter if necessary . Add mushrooms to casserole, pour in the broth and sprinkle with cheese. Bake at 375°, covered, for 5-7 minutes. Serves 2.

When the Crawfords arrived at Steamboat Springs, fewer than 200 members of the Yampa and Uintah bands of Utes were camped along the Yampa River in the area of the present city park.

Veal Piccata

2 lbs. veal scallops, pounded to ⅛" thick
½ tsp. salt
¼ tsp. freshly ground black pepper
½ cup all-purpose flour
2 Tbsp. unsalted butter
2 Tbsp. olive oil
½ cup dry white wine
½ cup chicken broth
2 Tbsp. lemon juice
1 lemon, thinly sliced (garnish)

Season veal with salt and pepper, and dredge in flour, shaking off excess. In a large skillet over moderately high heat, melt butter with the oil. Cook meat a few pieces at a time until lightly browned on both sides, about 5 minutes. Remove to a serving platter, and keep warm. Pour out remaining fat. Over high heat, add wine and broth to the skillet. Bring to a boil, and cook for about 2 minutes. Stir in lemon juice. Pour sauce over veal. Garnish with lemon slices and serve. Serves 4.

Viennese Goulash

1 onion, chopped
2 Tbsp. butter or olive oil
½ lb. veal
½ lb. pork
¾ lb. sauerkraut
1 Tbsp. caraway seeds
½ cup white wine
½ pt. sour cream

Trim meat and cut into 1" cubes. Sear with onions. Add sauerkraut, caraway seeds and white wine. On low heat, cook for 45 minutes, covered. This can also be baked at 325° degrees. Add sour cream and heat through. Serves 4.

" 'Snow, the beautiful white snow' still continues to fall. Most of the hay for the cow is gone. Mail has not got in from either direction. We have taken turns reading. All the family have retired but me and I still have to fix Dave's supper in case he comes in late."

From the diary of
Lulie Margie Crawford
March 11, 1881

Mom's English Mustard Sauce

½ cup sugar
½ cup flour
½ tsp. salt
½ cup dry mustard
½ tsp. turmeric
boiling water
vinegar

Mix sugar, flour, salt, mustard and turmeric in a saucepan. Add enough boiling water to make a thick paste. Cook on very low temperature for 30 seconds. Thin with vinegar. This is a hotsy-totsy sauce! Great on meat sandwiches.

Hot Mustard Sauce

Serve with sandwiches or as a vegetable dip.

1 can consommé
1 cup dry mustard
1 - 2 lb. bag brown sugar
2 Tbsp. flour
1 cup vinegar
3 beaten eggs

Mix ingredients together in a saucepan. Cook over medium heat until thick, stirring constantly. Store covered in refrigerator for two to three months. Makes 6 cups.

Mustard Aioli

1 large head garlic
⅓ cup coarsely ground mustard
¼ cup mayonnaise
¼ cup sour cream

Cut 1 large head of garlic in half crosswise. Lay cut side down in an oiled 8 inch pan. Roast in a 350° oven for 50 minutes. Squeeze garlic from skin and put in a food processor or blender. Add remaining ingredients and pulse until just chopped and blended. Serve chilled or warm. Makes about 1 cup.

Chicken or Steak Fajita Marinade

12 oz. apricot nectar
10 oz. soy sauce
16 oz. Italian dressing

Mix all ingredients and use as marinade for chicken or steak fajitas. Makes about 4 cups.

Fresh Horseradish Sauce

1 horseradish root (about 1 lb.)
1 cup white vinegar
1 tsp. salt
½ tsp. sugar
1 small turnip, peeled and cubed

Scrub and peel horseradish. Cut into cubes. In blender, combine vinegar, salt and sugar. Add ⅓ each horseradish and turnip and blend well, continuing to add ⅓ of each at a time. Cover tightly and refrigerate for up to 3 months. Makes 3 cups.

Sundried Tomato Sauce

6 shallots
6 garlic cloves
1 ½ cup sundried tomatoes (softened in red wine or oil)
whole colored peppercorns
2 ½ - 3 cups dry white wine
4 Tbsp. butter
½ Tbsp. flour (optional)

Cut shallots, garlic and 1 cup tomatoes in small pieces and just cover with about ½ cup white wine. Let sit at room temperature overnight. In a medium saucepan, heat all ingredients. Add ½ cup dried tomatoes (chopped) to give sauce more chunkiness. Add 1 cup white wine and let reduce. Add a dash of salt and another cup of white wine and allow this to cook. Add 4 Tbsp. butter. Add 1 - 2 Tbsp. flour to make sauce thicker. Bring to a boil, mixing thoroughly. To make sauce richer, add sautéed, sliced mushrooms. Serve over beef tenderloin, salmon, or chicken breasts.

Poultry

Poultry

Brittany Style Roast Chicken

Excellent served with roasted potatoes.

2 ½ lb. whole chicken
½ bottle Muscadet
⅓ cup Madeira
1 carrot, sliced
1 Tbsp. unsalted butter
½ Tbsp. flour
3 shallots, chopped
1 clove garlic, chopped
salt and pepper
oil

Prepare a marinade with the Muscadet, Madeira, carrot, salt and pepper. Place the chicken in the marinade. Remove after 2 hours. Drain and pat dry. Strain the marinade and set aside. Place the chicken in a heavy skillet. Brush with oil and sprinkle with a little salt and pepper. Roast at 375° for 40 minutes. Remove the chicken and cut into 4 pieces. Keep warm and set aside. Add butter to the skillet. When melted, blend in flour. Mix with a wire whisk and cook for 2 minutes. Pour in the strained marinade, stirring constantly. Add the shallots and garlic. Cook slowly for 10 minutes. Put the chicken back in the sauce and heat through. Serves 4.

Sunday's Roast Chicken

1 roasting hen
½ lemon, sliced
2 Tbsp. minced garlic
1 small yellow onion, sliced
6 sprigs fresh rosemary
salt and lemon pepper
2 cups dry white wine
2 cups chicken broth
1 ½ Tbsp. cornstarch

Trim excess fat around belly and neck area of hen. Rub garlic over hen, inside and out. Put remaining garlic in the bottom of a roasting pan. Salt and pepper the bird inside and out. Place in pan. Place 2 sprigs rosemary, 2 slices onion, and 1 lemon slice inside the bird. Place remaining lemon and onion in the roasting pan. Strip needles from remaining rosemary and sprinkle over and around bird. Pour liquids in the pan. Bake for 1 ½ hours at 375°, until hen is tender and falls from the bone. Pour juices, rosemary and onion into saucepan. Simmer for 5 minutes. Mix ¼ cup of juice with cornstarch and return to saucepan, blending well. Cook until slightly thickened. Adjust thickness by adding wine and water. Remove meat from bones. Serve with rice or pasta. Serves 6.

"I went up in the cherry bushes and read a story. I got a gooseberry limb and tied some white flowers and violets to it and made a wreath for my head. Ma and the boys and I went to hunt Snip (a cow) but didn't find her."

From the diary of
Lulie Margie Crawford
Sunday, May 29, 1881

Teriyaki Cornish Game Hens

4 Cornish game hens
1 Tbsp. oil
3 Tbsp. soy sauce
3 Tbsp. teriyaki sauce
2 Tbsp. honey
1 Tbsp. lemon juice
2 cloves garlic, chopped.

Remove liver and neck from hens and discard. Wash hens and pat dry. Combine remaining ingredients to make marinade. Place hens in 2 plastic bags and add marinade. Marinate overnight, turning bags occasionally. Remove from marinade and place in roasting pan. Bake at 400° for 1 hour, turning once. Baste with marinade occasionally. To check for temperature, pierce with a fork. When juices run clear, birds are done. Serves 4.

The Chief Theatre was established in the late 1920s by Mr. Harry Gordon.

Spicy Southern Fried Chicken

3 eggs, lightly beaten
½ cup + 2 Tbsp. buttermilk
¾ tsp. hot pepper sauce or to taste
1 ⅞ cup flour
1 heaping Tbsp. salt
1 heaping tsp. pepper
¾ tsp. Hungarian hot paprika or to taste
10 chicken parts, skin on, soaked in warm salt water and rinsed or 1 frying chicken
oil
gravy (recipe follows)

In bowl, mix eggs, buttermilk and hot sauce; set aside. Pour flour, salt, pepper and paprika in large paper bag. Hold top and shake to combine. One at a time, dip chicken into egg mixture, allowing excess to drip off. Put into bag and shake; remove to tray. Heat oil in cast iron skillet (1 ½" deep) over medium high heat. Cook chicken 10 minutes per side. Drain on paper towels. Serve with gravy.

Gravy for Chicken:
2 Tbsp. cooked fat
½ cup flour
¼ cup milk
¼ cup cream
salt and white pepper

Make roux with fat and flour. Lower heat where chicken cooked and slowly add milk and cream, whisking constantly until smooth. Add salt and pepper to taste.

Honey Curried Chicken

¼ cup butter
½ cup honey
1 tsp. prepared mustard
1 tsp. salt
1 tsp. curry powder
3 lbs. chicken, cut into pieces

Melt butter. Add honey, mustard, salt and curry powder; mix well.
Coat chicken with honey mixture. Place in baking pan, skin side
down. Skinless chicken may be used as well. Bake at 375° for 30
minutes. Turn chicken over and bake 30 minutes more. Good served
with rice. Serves 4.

Vermont Maple Chicken

A nice meal you can make ahead.

3 ½ lbs. chicken, cut up
1 cup maple syrup
1 Tbsp. oil
4 Tbsp. white wine vinegar
14 ozs. tomato purée
½ cup dry sherry
2 tsp. hot curry powder
1 tsp. marjoram
1 Tbsp. soy sauce
4 whole cloves
salt and pepper
1 medium onion, chopped
⅓ cup mushrooms, cut in half
2 tsp. raisins
⅔ cup almonds
1 green pepper, chopped
2 celery stalks, diced

Place chicken pieces in large cooking pot. Cover with next 9
ingredients. Add a pinch of salt and pepper. Mix well and marinate
at room temperature for 4 hours. Simmer over low heat 30 minutes.
Add remaining ingredients and cook another 30 minutes. Serve over
noodles or rice. Serves 6-8.

Back Country Marinated Chicken
Excellent on the grill or for camping trips.

3 lbs. chicken, skinned
⅓ cup soy sauce
2 Tbsp. lemon juice
¼ tsp. onion powder
¼ tsp. garlic powder
¼ tsp. poultry seasoning
2 Tbsp. minced parsley

Place chicken in a dish . Combine remaining ingredients and pour over chicken. Let marinate 8-24 hours, turning every few hours. Place chicken in a greased baking pan and sprinkle with paprika. Cover with foil and bake at 375° for 1 hour. Can be made ahead and frozen in marinade. Serves 6.

For camping, microwave chicken for 15 minutes, skin chicken, then pour marinade and chicken into sealable plastic bags. Shake well and freeze until ready to go camping.

Dakota Ridge Chicken with Herbs

5 whole boneless chicken breasts, skinned
½ cup butter
1 tsp. dried oregano
1 tsp. fine herbs
1 tsp. dried marjoram
½ tsp. salt
1 Tbsp. fresh parsley, minced
¼ lb. cheese (Jack, Gruyère, Camembert), cut into sticks
½ cup flour
2 eggs
2 Tbsp. water
1 ½ tsp. oil
1 cup bread crumbs
1 cup freshly grated Parmesan cheese
1 cup chablis wine

Place breasts between waxed paper and flatten until about ¼" thick. Melt butter with herbs and brush some on the inside of each breast, reserving the rest. Combine eggs, water and oil and set aside. Mix bread crumbs and Parmesan and set aside. Place a stick of cheese on each breast, roll and secure with toothpicks. Coat each roll with flour, then the egg mixture, then the bread crumbs and Parmesan. Place in a baking pan, making sure rolls do not touch. Bake, uncovered, at 350° for 20 minutes. Combine reserved butter with herbs and wine. Pour over chicken and continue baking for 15 minutes. Place under broiler for a few minutes to brown. Serve with sauce over a bed of fettuccine noodles. Serves 6-8.

Cajun Chicken Stew

1 fresh hen, approximately 5 lbs.
2 Tbsp. salt
1 Tbsp. red pepper
2 tsp. black pepper
2 tsp. white pepper
3 large onions, finely chopped
2 large bell peppers, finely chopped
2 ribs celery, finely chopped
2 qts. chicken stock
2 cups mushrooms (opt.)
1 cup chopped parsley

Roux:
5 cups flour
3 ½ cups oil

Wash hen and cut into pieces. Reserve neck and back pieces for chicken stock. Mix seasonings together in a bowl and use approximately ⅓ to season to chicken. Brown chicken in skillet using as little oil as necessary. Remove chicken pieces and set aside. Add 3 ½ cups of oil and 5 cups of flour to skillet and brown over low heat until "red like a copper penny." Add all vegetables and remove from heat, stirring often. This will sauté vegetables and cook the roux. In a 6-8 qt. stock pot, bring stock to a boil and add roux, 1 cup at a time, until well mixed and dissolved. After roux is dissolved, reduce heat to medium and simmer for 30-45 minutes. Add chicken and cook for 1 hour or until tender, skimming surface often to remove oil. Add mushrooms and parsley and cook for 10 minutes prior to serving. Serve with rice. Serves 6-8.

Note: The gravy in this recipe will be slightly thicker than gumbo stock. Thickness can be adjusted by increasing or decreasing roux, or adjusting amounts of stock. A lighter color gravy can be achieved by cooking roux to a lighter color. For best flavor, don't rush this dish.

Chicken Cassis

Double or triple this recipe for a large party.

4 chicken breasts
4 Tbsp. Creme de Cassis
½ cup orange juice
1 tsp. basil
1 tsp. paprika
salt and pepper

Skin chicken breasts if desired and place in an 8" baking dish. Salt and pepper to taste. Mix Creme de Cassis and orange juice and pour over chicken. Add salt and pepper. Crush herbs and sprinkle over chicken. Cover and bake at 350° for 40-45 minutes. Serve on a large platter over a bed of rice and garnish with parsley and orange rounds. Serves 3- 4.

Rabbit Ears Pass was built in 1913 and was used for summer travel only. It is named for the rock formation to the north of the pass summit which resembles a rabbit's ears. Meadows Campground, near the west summit, was an early Indian campsite.

Chicken Cacciatore

Serve chicken pieces with sauce over
cooked whole wheat spaghetti.
2 onions, thinly sliced
3 lb. broiler fryer chicken, skinned and cut up
2 cloves garlic, minced
1 lb. can tomato sauce
1 tsp. salt
¼ tsp. pepper
3 tsp. crushed oregano leaves
½ tsp. crushed basil
½ tsp. celery seed (opt.)
1 bay leaf
¼ cup dry white wine

Place onions in bottom of slow cooker. Add remaining ingredients.
Cover and cook on low for 8 hours. Serves 4.

Chicken and Sundried Tomatoes

4 boneless chicken breast halves
1 ½ Tbsp. butter
1 large shallot, minced or 2 Tbsp. minced onion
1 Tbsp. + 1 tsp. Dijon mustard
1 cup heavy cream
3 Tbsp. dry vermouth or white wine
1-2 tsp. dried tarragon (opt.)
3 ozs. dried tomato halves, soaked in boiling water for 2 minutes

Skin chicken breasts and cut each breast into 6 pieces. Melt butter in
skillet and sauté chicken for 4-5 minutes. Remove chicken with
slotted spoon to a platter. Add shallots, sauté 1 minute, then add
remaining ingredients. Simmer and stir until sauce thickens slightly.
Return chicken to skillet, simmer until heated. Serve with rice or pasta
(great with brown rice) and asparagus or green beans. Serves 4.

Chicken Teriyaki
¼ cup firmly packed light brown sugar
¼ cup soy sauce
3 Tbsp. lemon or lime juice
3 Tbsp. water
¼ tsp. garlic powder
dash ground ginger
2 ½ - 3 ½ lb. chicken, cut into pieces
¼ cup flour (opt.)
¼ cup water (opt.)

Mix first 6 ingredients until smooth. Pour over chicken, cover, and marinate in refrigerator several hours or overnight. Place chicken and marinade in crockpot and cook on low for 6-8 hours. If a thicker gravy is desired, make a paste of flour and water. Stir into crockpot, cover, and cook on high for additional 15 min. or until thickened. Serves 4.

Pollo San Marino
4 boneless chicken breasts, skinless
8 slices paper thin prosciutto ham
8 slices Fontina cheese
½ cup flour
2 eggs, beaten with ¼ cup milk
½ cup Italian seasoned breadcrumbs
⅛ cup olive oil
Cynari Sauce (recipe follows)

Pound chicken with mallet until ¼" thick. Place 2 slices prosciutto and 2 slices Fontina on each breast. Fold chicken in half. Dip chicken in flour until coated. Dip chicken in egg and milk mixture, then seasoned breadcrumbs. Pan fry in olive oil until brown. Remove chicken and place in baking pan and bake at 400° for 15 minutes. Remove from oven and place on warm plates. Spoon Cynari Sauce over chicken breasts and serve. Serves 4.

Cynari Sauce:
¼ lb. mushrooms, sliced
2 large cloves garlic, pressed
4 Tbsp. unsalted butter
2 Tbsp. flour
14 oz. can artichoke hearts and its liquid, chopped
2 pints heavy cream
salt and freshly ground white pepper
¼ tsp. whole rosemary

Sauté mushrooms and garlic in 2 Tbsp. butter; set aside. Melt remaining butter and add flour, stirring constantly to make roux. Add liquid from artichokes to roux and let thicken. Add cream and artichoke hearts. Stir in rosemary, salt and pepper to taste. Add sautéed mushrooms and garlic; heat through. Serves 4.

For a short time Oak Creek was called Belltown for store owners Sam and Ed Bell, but the thick scrub oak on the banks of the creek running through town prompted the official name.

New Orleans Chicken

8-5 oz. chicken breasts, skinned
2 fresh crawfish tails
1 lb. lump crab meat, chopped and cleaned
1 cup butter
2 bunches green onions, chopped
1 small white onion, chopped
2 Tbsp. garlic, chopped
1 cup pecan pieces
1 cup chopped watercress
2 Tbsp. black pepper
½ tsp. salt
1 cup white wine
1 cup chicken broth
20 ozs. Italian breadcrumbs
8 slices mozzarella cheese
2 egg whites plus 2 Tbsp. water
waxed paper
New Orleans Chicken Sauce (recipe follows)

Place waxed paper over each chicken breast. Pound chicken with mallet to flatten, do not smash. Place a slice of cheese over each breast. Set aside. Purée crawfish tails, pulsing in a food processor. Blend in crab meat. Melt butter and lightly sauté green onions and onions for 5 minutes. Combine puréed crawfish tails and crab meat, sautéed onions, garlic, pecans, watercress, pepper, salt, white wine and chicken broth for stuffing. With stuffing make a ball about 2 ozs. in weight and place on top of cheese on chicken and roll chicken to make a ball. Secure with a toothpick. Beat egg whites with water. Roll chicken ball in flour, drop in egg wash and roll in breadcrumbs. Fry chicken in 1" hot oil until light golden brown. Remove and finish cooking in a microwave oven for 6 minutes, or regular oven at 350° for 15 minutes. Serve on a bed of rice with sauce.

New Orleans Chicken Sauce:
1 cup chicken broth
½ cup white wine
1 cup whipping cream
½ cup chopped parsley
½ tsp. chopped garlic
1 tsp. black pepper
⅓ cup olive oil
½ tsp. salt

In olive oil, sauté parsley and garlic for 2 minutes. Add all ingredients and cook for 15 minutes over medium heat. Thicken sauce with a mixture of 3 Tbsp. melted butter to 3 Tbsp. flour. Add mixture slowly until desired thickness.

Lingonberry Chicken
A great, easy meal for company.

4 whole chicken breasts, skinned
4 Tbsp. unsalted butter
½ cup minced onion
½ tomato, minced
8 Tbsp. red wine or raspberry vinegar
½ cup chicken broth
½ cup heavy cream
½ cup lingonberry sauce

Cut breasts into halves removing any extra fat. Flatten and pound each piece. Melt the butter in a large skillet. Raise heat and cook breast about 5 minutes on each side. Remove from skillet. Add minced onion and cook until glossy. Add vinegar to pan and heat uncovered until vinegar begins to reduce, 5-7 minutes. Whisk in chicken broth, heavy cream and tomatoes. Slowly stir in lingonberry sauce, simmer 10-15 minutes. Return breasts to pan and simmer in the sauce 5 minutes more, do not over cook. Arrange chicken breast on a platter and top with sauce. Serve immediately. Serves 4-6

Rick Mewborn began jumping at Howelsen Hill when he was 13. Since then, he has been the U.S. National Champion, the Canadian National Champion, and he competed in the Calgary Olympics in 1988. After ski jumping the world over, he has returned to Howelsen Hill to coach young jumpers.

Roma Chicken
Great with pasta ...

4 chicken breasts, skinned
1 Tbsp. oil
1 qt. stewed tomatoes or tomato sauce
2 Tbsp. packed brown sugar
1 Tbsp. red wine vinegar
salt and pepper to taste
1 clove garlic, finely chopped
½ tsp. basil
½ tsp. oregano
2 carrots, cut into ¼" slices
1 onion, sliced
½ cup lightly packed celery leaves
4 oz. mozzarella cheese, cut into thin strips

Brown chicken in skillet in 1 Tbsp. oil. Combine next 7 ingredients, mix well and pour over chicken. Place carrot slices, onion slices and celery leaves around chicken in skillet, cover and simmer for 20 minutes, stirring occasionally. Place mozzarella strips on each piece of chicken, cover and heat 2-3 minutes until cheese melts. Serve chicken with sauce and vegetables. Serves 4.

Bow Tie Chicken

¼ cup butter
4 cups sliced mushrooms
2 tsp. pepper
2 tsp. Mrs. Dash seasoning
1 pt. heavy cream
1 cup skim milk
½ cup parsley, chopped
2 cloves garlic, finely chopped (or 2 tsp. prepared crushed garlic)
4 ozs. prosciutto ham
2 lbs. boneless chicken breasts
1 lb. bow tie noodles

Cut chicken breasts into bite-sized chunks and cook 8 minutes over low heat in 2 Tbsp. butter. Remove from pan. Add remaining 2 Tbsp. butter and sauté mushrooms over medium heat. Add pepper, Mrs. Dash seasoning, heavy cream and skim milk, simmering slowly. Slice prosciutto ham very thin and cut into strips. Add chicken and ham to the mushroom and cream mixture and simmer slowly until thick. If not thick enough, you may need to add a little cornstarch. Blend together parsley and garlic and add to chicken. Serve immediately over freshly cooked bow tie noodles, or any desired pasta. Top with freshly grated Parmesan cheese. Serves 4-6.

A restored saloon and general store in Columbine (Hahns Peak area) are reminders of this bustling camp that served as a major way-stop for travelers.

Lemon Herb Chicken

4 whole chicken breasts, skinned
garlic powder
onion powder
basil and oregano (if dried, crumble to release flavor)
black pepper
salt (optional)
fresh lemon juice (enough for 1 Tbsp. juice per breast)

Sprinkle chicken with all seasonings, to taste, except lemon. Microwave the seasoned chicken in a covered microwave dish on high for approximately 8 minutes. Remove chicken and place in pan for broiling, reserving juices for later. Place under broiler for 5 to 7 minutes, until lightly browned. Remove and immediately squeeze juice from fresh lemon over chicken. Combine reserved juices with lemon juice in broiler pan and pour over chicken. This recipe can also be cooked in a conventional oven, baking in an open baking pan at 350° for 45 minutes, and finishing with fresh lemon juice. Serve with rice. Serves 6-8.

Columbine Chicken

8 boneless chicken breast halves
⅓ cup butter
½ lb. mushrooms, sliced
⅓ cup flour
¼ tsp. salt
13 ¾ oz. can chicken broth
2 Tbsp. half and half

Fry chicken in butter, remove and set aside. Sauté mushrooms in the pan, remove and set aside. Blend flour and salt in pan drippings and mix until blended. Gradually add broth and half and half. Stir over medium heat until thickened, stirring constantly. Add chicken and mushrooms. Reduce heat to low, cover and simmer 20 minutes. Excellent served over rice. Serves 6-8.

Arriba Enchiladas

These enchiladas can easily be frozen.

3 cups chicken broth
⅓ cup flour
12 oz. jar salsa
4 oz. can diced green chilies
1 cup chopped onion
1 garlic clove, chopped
1 tsp. sugar
1 tsp. ground cumin
½ tsp. basil
½ tsp. oregano
salt and pepper to taste
12 corn tortillas
3 lb. whole chicken, cooked, deboned and cut into small pieces
Monterey Jack cheese, cut into strips
¾ cup sour cream
1-1 ½ cups grated Monterey Jack cheese

In a saucepan, blend chicken broth and flour. Cook, stirring, until broth begins to thicken. Add salsa, chilies, onion, garlic, sugar and seasonings, mix well. Soften the tortillas by dipping them into the hot mixture. Place a spoonful of chicken and a slice of cheese in each tortilla. Roll and place enchiladas in a greased 13" x 9" baking dish. Add the sour cream to the hot mixture, mix thoroughly and pour over enchiladas. Top with grated cheese. Bake at 400° for 15 minutes. Enchiladas can be easily frozen. Serves 6.

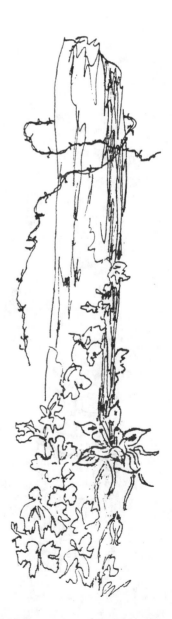

Monterey Chicken

8 boneless chicken breast halves, skinned
7 ozs. chopped green chilies
½ pound Monterey Jack Pepper Cheese
½ cup bread crumbs
⅓ cup freshly grated Parmesan cheese
1 to 3 tsp. chili powder
½ tsp. salt
¼ tsp. cumin
¼ tsp. pepper
3 Tbsp. butter or margarine, melted
3 Tbsp. extra virgin olive oil
Mexicali Sauce (recipe follows)

Pound chicken breasts until thin. Cut cheese into 2 inch strips.
Combine breadcrumbs, Parmesan cheese, chili powder, salt, cumin
and pepper in a shallow dish Blend oil and butter in a separate bowl.
Spread each breast with 1 Tbsp. green chilies. Place one cheese slice
on chilies. Roll up each breast and secure with toothpick. Dip each
breast in the oil butter mixture then dip in breadcrumb mixture,
coating well. Bake at 400° for 30 minutes. Serve with Mexicali sauce
and garnish with limes slices and sour cream. Serves 6-8.

Mexicali Sauce:
15 ozs. plain tomato sauce
½ tsp ground cumin
⅓ cup sliced green onions
juice of one lime
1 clove garlic, minced

Mix all ingredients in a small sauce pan. Simmer about 10 minutes to
blend flavors. Serve hot with the chicken.

Cortina Chicken

4 boneless chicken breasts, skinned
1 bottle Italian dressing
1 ¾ cups buttery crackers, crumbled
1 cup grated Parmesan cheese
½ cup unsalted butter
2 Tbsp. lemon juice

Pound chicken breasts and place in container to marinate. Pour Italian
dressing over chicken, making sure all sides are coated well. Marinate
for 3-4 hours, stirring once each hour. Combine cracker crumbs and
Parmesan cheese. Coat each chicken breast with crumb mixture. Place
in baking dish. Bake at 350° for approximately 20 minutes. Do not
overcook. If desired, broil for a few minutes to brown. While baking,
combine butter and lemon juice in saucepan and simmer gently.
Season to taste. Drizzle lemon butter over chicken; serve. Serves 4.

Chicken Bundles

Dough:
2 cups warm water
½ cup sugar
2 pkgs. dry yeast
2 tsp. salt
3 cups whole wheat flour
1 egg
¼ cup oil
3 ½ cups unbleached white flour
Chicken Filling (recipe follows) or
Mock Hollandaise Sauce (recipe follows)

Dissolve yeast in warm water. Add sugar and stir to dissolve. Add salt and whole wheat flour and beat for two minutes. Add egg, oil and flour, mix well and turn onto a floured surface. Knead for about 5 minutes. Place in a greased bowl, cover and let rise in the refrigerator for 2 hours or overnight. Divide dough into 4 equal parts. Roll out each part into a thin rectangle. Divide the rectangle into 8 equal squares. Fill each square with 2 Tbsp. of filling, draw up corners and pinch closed. Place on a greased cookie sheet and let rise 20 minutes. Bake at 350° for 15-20 minutes. Makes 32.

Chicken Filling:
1 3 lb. chicken
2 cups grated Swiss cheese
2 egg yolks
¼ cup sour cream
2 tsp. lemon juice
1 bunch broccoli, cooked until tender, drained and chopped
salt and pepper to taste
Cook and debone chicken, dice and mix with remaining ingredients.

Mock Hollandaise Sauce:
1 cup sour cream
2 egg yolks
2 Tbsp. lemon juice
1 tsp. Dijon mustard
½ tsp. salt

Combine all ingredients in top of double boiler over medium heat. Stir until thick and hot. Serve with chicken bundles. Makes 1 ½ cups.

"The boys drove the chickens up the creek and some of them flew across and old Lamey got in and I guess drowned. Ma gave the boys a good whipping. We have just been weighing the butter. There is 38 pounds. Ma, Dave, and the boys found Snip with a calf in Soda Park. Snip's calf has glass eyes. Dave made some milk stools."

From the diary of
Lulie Margie Crawford
May 30, 1881

Tender Breaded Chicken Breasts

4 boneless chicken breast halves
juice of 1 lemon
seasoning salt
basil or marjoram
Italian breadcrumbs
2 eggs, beaten
olive oil

Thoroughly pound each chicken breast on both sides. Squeeze lemon juice over chicken. Combine seasoning salt, basil and breadcrumbs. Dip each breast first in beaten egg, then in breadcrumb mixture. Fry in lightly oiled frying pan, browning on both sides. Serves 4.

Mediterranean Tart

One of Soupçons most popular specials.

3 Tbsp. butter
1 cup chopped onion
2 tsp. flour
1 cup chicken stock
2 medium tomatoes, diced
3 ½ cups chicken pieces, cooked
1 cup black olives, pitted
1 Tbsp. anchovy paste
salt and pepper to taste
¾ cup butter, melted
16 sheets phyllo
½ cup freshly grated Parmesan cheese
sauce (recipe follows)

Sauté onion in butter. Stir in flour and cook for about 2 minutes. Stir in chicken stock, tomatoes, chicken, olives and anchovy paste. Season with salt and pepper. Preheat oven to 350°. Brush bottom and sides of a 12"x 7"x 2" pan with melted butter and line with one phyllo sheet. Brush phyllo with melted butter and sprinkle with Parmesan cheese. Repeat with 8 sheets of phyllo, spoon chicken filling in and repeat phyllo process with 8 more sheets. Brush top with butter and bake for 50 minutes. Serve with sauce. Serves 6-8.

Sauce:
1 lb. mushrooms, sliced
2 cups chicken stock
½ cup diced onions
1 tsp. flour
1 tsp. sherry

Sauté onions in butter. Stir in flour and cook over low heat for 2 minutes. Add mushrooms, chicken stock and sherry and simmer until slightly thickened.

Jon and Jere Elliott were both talented four-way skiers. After making the U.S. Ski Team in 1959, Jon focused on jumping and was an alternate to the Squaw Valley Olympics of 1960. His brother, a Ski Team member from 1965-69, specialized in giant slalom and downhill and competed in Grenoble in the '68 Olympics.

Montezuma Pie

½ cup oil
18 corn tortillas
2 cup shredded cooked chicken
Green Chile Sauce (recipe follows)
1 cup sour cream
Tomatillo Sauce (recipe follows)
2 cups grated Cheddar cheese

Heat oil in an 8" skillet over moderate heat. Fry 1 tortilla at a time for 15 - 20 seconds on each side until limp but not crisp. Drain tortillas between paper towels.

Spread 6 tortillas on the bottom of a greased 3½" - 4" deep and 10" in diameter casserole dish. Spread ⅓ of chicken, ⅓ of Green Chile Sauce, ⅓ of sour cream, ⅓ of Tomatillo Sauce, and ⅓ of the cheese. Repeat the layers 2 more times. Bake uncovered in a preheated 350° oven for 25 minutes. Serve casserole with rice.

Green Chile Sauce:
8 oz. whole green chilies
3 Tbsp. oil
½ onion, thinly sliced
½ tsp. salt

Wash chilies, remove seeds, and dry chilies thoroughly. Heat oil over medium heat in a skillet. Slice the chilies into thin strips and cook them in the oil along with onion slices and salt until the onions are limp (about 6 - 8 minutes).

Tomatillo Sauce:
2 cups fresh tomatillos or 3 - 12 oz. cans tomatillos, drained
2 cloves garlic, minced
¼ tsp. sugar
½ tsp. salt
½ cup water
2 Tbsp. cilantro, chopped
½ cup chopped onion
2 Tbsp. oil

Blend tomatillos, garlic, sugar, salt, water, cilantro, and onion in a blender at medium speed until smooth, about 30 seconds. Heat oil over moderate heat in skillet and add the tomatillo mixture. Cook the mixture for 10 minutes, stirring occasionally. Serves 6.

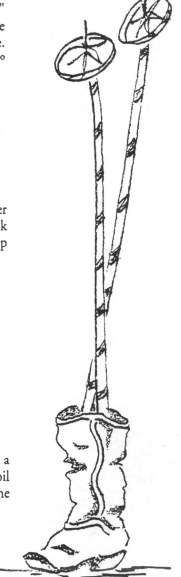

Popover Chicken with Mushrooms

6 boneless chicken breasts, skinned
4 Tbsp. olive oil
1 ½ cups milk
1 ½ cups flour
¾ tsp. tarragon
½ tsp. salt
3 eggs, beaten
Mushroom Sauce (recipe follows)
parsley for garnish

Brown chicken in 3 Tbsp. oil. Season with salt and pepper and place in a greased 13" x 9" baking pan. Combine milk, remaining 1 Tbsp. oil, flour, tarragon and salt. Add eggs and mix until smooth. Pour over chicken and bake at 350° for 1-1 ¼ hours. Spoon mushroom sauce over chicken when serving. Garnish with parsley. Serves 6.

Mushroom Sauce:
4 Tbsp. butter
1 cup sliced mushrooms
2 Tbsp. flour
½ tsp. salt
dash pepper
1 cup milk

Melt 2 Tbsp. butter in heavy saucepan. Sauté mushrooms 2-3 minutes. Remove mushrooms with slotted spoon and set aside. Melt remaining 2 Tbsp. butter in same saucepan and stir in flour, salt and pepper. Gradually add milk. Cook over medium heat, stirring constantly, until thickened. Add mushrooms and heat through.

Fiesta Chicken

4 boneless chicken breasts, skinned and cut in half
1 cup salsa
2 pkgs. fast cooking long grain wild rice (makes 4-6 cups)
1 medium onion, sliced and quartered
1-2 medium tomatoes, sliced and quartered
1 medium green or red bell pepper, chopped
1 cup grated Cheddar or mozzarella cheese
sour cream

Place chicken on foil and cover with ¼ cup of picante sauce, wrap in foil and bake at 350° for 30 minutes. Meanwhile, boil water for rice, adding ½ onion, ½ tomatoes and bell pepper at the same time as rice. When rice is cooked, pour into an 8" square baking dish. Place chicken over a bed of rice. (Chicken should be ¾ cooked). Top with remaining onion, tomatoes and picante sauce. Sprinkle with cheese and bake approximately 30 minutes. Serve with sour cream. Serves 6.

Spicy Gazebo Springs Chicken

1 lb. boneless chicken breasts, skinned
2 Tbsp. corn oil
¼ cup slivered orange peel
1 clove garlic, minced
¾ tsp. ground ginger
2 Tbsp. cornstarch
¼ cup dry sherry
1 cup chicken broth
⅓ cup soy sauce
⅓ cup orange marmalade
¾ tsp. dried crushed red pepper

Thinly slice chicken. In a wok or large skillet, heat corn oil over medium high heat. Add chicken, a few slices at a time. Stir fry 3 minutes or until browned. Return all chicken to wok. Add orange peel, garlic and ginger. Stir fry 1 minute. Stir together remaining ingredients in a small bowl. Stir into chicken. Stirring constantly, bring to a boil over medium heat and boil several minutes. Serve over rice or pasta. Serves 4.

Across from the Bud Werner Memorial Library, Soda Spring bubbles with highly effervescent carbonic gases which provided a favorite drinking water sometimes added to soft drink mixes by local youngsters. The spring has subsided in both volume and carbonation in recent years. In 1906, after a pavillion was erected over the spring, a group of Steamboat Springs youngsters—spearheaded by Bob Swinehart—put a haywagon on top of it as a Halloween prank.

Chicken Breasts in Wine Sauce

6 boneless chicken breasts
1 ½ Tbsp. lemon juice
4 Tbsp. butter
¼ cup chicken stock
¼ cup dry white wine
1 cup heavy cream
black olives, sliced (garnish)
chopped parsley (garnish)

Sprinkle chicken breasts with lemon juice. Melt butter in heavy skillet, making sure not to brown. Roll chicken in butter, coating all sides. Cover and place skillet in 375° oven for 7-8 minutes, until cooked. Transfer chicken to a platter and keep warm. Place skillet over high heat, pour in broth and wine and cook until liquid is syrupy. Whisk in cream and reduce, stirring constantly, until the cream begins to thicken. Pour sauce over chicken. Garnish with sliced black olives and/or chopped parsley. Serves 6.

Curried Apple Chicken

1 ½ lbs. fresh mushrooms, sliced
¾ cup butter
⅔ cup minced onion
2 cups peeled and diced Jonathan or Granny Smith apples
6 Tbsp. flour
2 tsp. salt
dash pepper
3 Tbsp. curry powder
1 ½ cups half and half
1 ½ cups chicken stock
6 cups cooked and diced chicken

Sauté mushrooms in half of the butter until tender. Remove and set aside. Add remaining butter, apples and onions. Sauté until soft and put in top of double boiler. Put pan over boiling water and add flour, salt, pepper, curry powder and blend. Add half and half and chicken stock, slowly, stirring constantly until thickened. Lower heat and cook 10 minutes. Add mushrooms and chicken and blend. Pour into a casserole dish and heat. Can be made ahead of time and reheated. Serve over rice with condiments such as: chopped green onions, chutney or peanuts.

Almost all chuckwagon cooks were short tempered and not without cause. Their day began around 3:30 a.m. which is in itself sufficient enough to sour a man's disposition.

Chutney Chicken

An elegant, quick dinner.

2 large chicken breasts, halved lengthwise
¾ cup orzo
2 Tbsp. snipped parsley
1 Tbsp. olive oil
⅓ cup chutney
1 Tbsp. white wine or water
12 ozs. snow peas, cooked until tender crisp

Place chicken, skin side down, on rack of broiler pan. Broil 5-6" from heat for 10 minutes. Turn, broil 10 minutes more. Cook orzo according to package directions. Drain; toss with parsley and oil. Keep warm. Combine chutney and wine in a saucepan; heat through. Brush chicken with chutney mixture; broil 5 minutes. Serve chicken over orzo which has been arranged on top of a bed of snow peas. Spoon remaining chutney over chicken. Serves 4.

Chuckwagon Cheddar Chicken

8 boneless chicken breasts
½ cup butter
4 cloves garlic, minced
¾ cup Italian seasoned breadcrumbs
¼ cup grated Parmesan cheese
⅛ tsp. pepper
1 ½ cups grated Cheddar cheese

Melt butter, add garlic. Mix breadcrumbs, Parmesan, pepper and Cheddar cheese in a bowl. Dip chicken in garlic butter, then dip in breadcrumb mixture, coating well. Put into a baking dish. Pour any extra butter or breadcrumb mixture over chicken. Bake, uncovered in a 9" x 13" baking dish, at 350° for 45 minutes. Serves 4-6.

Chicken Piccata

Great served with pasta or rice.

4 whole skinless chicken breasts, deboned
salt and pepper
½-1 cup flour
6 Tbsp. butter
2 Tbsp. olive oil
3 garlic cloves, minced
1-1 ½ lbs. mushrooms, thinly sliced
4 tsp. lemon juice
¾ cup dry white wine
1 Tbsp. capers
lemon wedges (garnish)

Pound chicken breasts until ¼" inch in thickness or less. Dredge in flour mixed with salt and pepper. Shake off excess. Melt butter in olive oil over medium heat. Sauté garlic. Add chicken and sauté until browned. Remove chicken and keep warm. Sauté mushrooms; return chicken to pan. Add lemon juice and wine and stir. Cover and simmer until cooked, approximately 15 minutes. Add capers and cook 2-3 minutes more. Place chicken on a platter and pour mushroom sauce over and serve. Serves 6-8.

Kayaker's Chicken Pasta

1 lb. rotini
¼ cup olive oil
2 cloves garlic, minced
1 ½ lbs. boneless chicken breasts, cut into bite size chunks
½ red bell pepper, sliced
½ yellow bell pepper, sliced
2 cups snow peas, cleaned and trimmed
¾ cup grated Parmesan cheese
½ cup toasted almonds

Cook pasta according to directions; drain. Heat ½ the olive oil in a large sauté pan. Add garlic and sauté 3 minutes. Add chicken pieces and sauté 8-10 minutes, turning occasionally. Remove chicken and keep warm. Add remaining olive oil, red and yellow peppers and sauté over medium heat for 5 minutes. Add snow peas, sauté 3-5 minutes. Add chicken and heat quickly. Stir in Parmesan cheese and almonds. Toss pasta with chicken mixture; serve immediately. Serves 4-6.

Chicken and Sausage Jambalaya

2 chicken breasts, diced
seasoned salt mixture
pepper to taste
vegetable oil spray
½ large onion, coarsely chopped
1-2 cups coarsely chopped celery
6 - 8 mushrooms, coarsely chopped
½ - 1 red bell pepper, coarsely chopped
½ tsp. basil
½ tsp. parsley
½ tsp. Italian herbs
½ garlic clove, minced
4 smoked beef weiners or sausage, cut up
1 can consommé soup
1 can zesty tomato soup
2 - 15 oz. cans Italian or Mexican tomatoes, cut up
dash of Worcestershire sauce and Tabasco sauce
2 bay leaves

Season the chicken breasts with seasoned salt mixture and pepper. Spray a small amount of cooking oil spray in a large frying pan and brown the chicken breasts. Add onion, celery, mushrooms, red pepper, basil, parsley, Italian herbs and garlic. Simmer 10 min. Add weiners and simmer 15 min. Add remaining ingredients and simmer until heated through. Serves 6.

Turkey Tostados

3 - 8 oz. cans tomato sauce with cheese
1-1 ½ tsp. chili powder
½ tsp. oregano
3 cups cooked and cubed turkey
12 tortillas
cooking oil
2 large avocados, peeled and sliced
garlic salt
6 Tbsp. minced onion (opt.)
shredded lettuce
1 cup grated Cheddar cheese
sour cream (opt.)

Combine tomato sauce, chili powder, oregano and turkey. Simmer, covered. Fry tortillas in about ¼" hot cooking oil until crisp; drain on paper towels. For each serving, top a tortilla with avocado slices, garlic salt and onion. Top with a little turkey mixture. Top with another tortilla, turkey mixture, then lettuce and cheese. Serve with a side of sour cream, if desired. Serves 6.

Parmesan Turkey

1 lb. turkey breast
¼ cup butter, melted
2 Tbsp. grated Parmesan cheese
½ tsp. dry mustard
⅛ tsp. garlic powder

Cut turkey into ½" slices. Combine remaining ingredients together. Brush turkey slices with mixture. Broil for 5 minutes. Turn and repeat. Serves 4.

Turkey with Tomato Basil Sauce

1 lb. turkey breast
½ cup mayonnaise
½ cup milk
¼ tsp. dried basil leaves
1 small tomato, chopped
1 green onion, chopped

Cut turkey into ¼" slices. Place slices in covered skillet with small amount of melted butter and cook on medium heat for 10 minutes. Combine mayonnaise, milk and basil in a saucepan. Cook on medium heat until thickened. Stir in half of tomato and onion, and heat through. Pour sauce over turkey. Garnish with remaining tomato and onion and serve. Serves 4.

The first sign of growth came in the summer of 1883 when H. Suttle brought a sawmill to Steamboat Springs. With the capacity to produce logs for homes and stores, develop-ment was assured.

Tomahawk Roast Turkey

A great recipe for a moist turkey.

10 lb. turkey
giblets, neck and tail
½ tsp. sage
1 tsp. thyme
1 tsp. basil
1 tsp. marjoram
1 large onion, stuck with 3 whole cloves
1 bay leaf
pepper to taste, preferably fresh ground
apples, sectioned

Gravy:
flour
2 dashes Worcestershire sauce
2 dashes soy sauce
chicken bouillon granules to taste

Cover giblets, neck and tail with water in a large soup kettle. Add sage, thyme, basil, marjoram, onion and bay leaf. Add pepper to taste. Simmer 2 - 4 hours. Place turkey in a roasting pan. Stuff with apples and dot turkey with butter. Make a tent with aluminum foil and tuck tightly around the pan. Try not to let the foil touch turkey. Bake at 350° for 2 ½ hours. Remove foil, increase heat to 450° and brown about 20 minutes. Remove from oven and let set for 15 minutes before carving.

Separate fat from the turkey juices. Return juice to roasting pan. Strain and add giblet water. Boil and whisk while slowly adding flour to thicken. Add 2 dashes Worcestershire, 2 dashes soy sauce and chicken bouillon granules to taste.

Wild Rice Stuffing

⅔ cups wild rice
3 cups water
4 tsp. instant beef bouillon granules
4 slices bacon
1 medium onion, chopped
½ lb. mushrooms, sliced
1 tsp. crushed leaf oregano
3 ribs celery, chopped
2 cups bread crumbs
salt and pepper to taste

Run cold water through wild rice in a colander until water runs clear. Stir the rice into the water in a 3 qt. heavy saucepan and stir in the bouillon granules. Bring to a boil, stirring to dissolve bouillon. Reduce heat, cover, and simmer until rice is tender, about 40 minutes. Meanwhile, cut the bacon into 1" pieces and fry, adding the onion and mushrooms to sauté with the bacon. Cook until the bacon pieces are crisp and the onions and mushrooms, soften slightly. Add to cooked rice, along with oregano, celery and bread crumbs. Adjust seasonings with salt and pepper. Also great in cornish game hens. Substitute ½ lb. cooked, crumbled and drained sausage for the bread crumbs. This heartier stuffing goes well with ducks and geese. Makes enough stuffing for a 10 lb. turkey.

"Great goodness alive! Mr. Moon skipped the country. Mr. Goodson came with the mail. Our two pair of shoes came and Pa's overalls and John's too. The men branded the cattle. Ma and I helped them. Had a terrible time. Uncle Henry was knocked down and kicked under the chin and got a tooth broken."
(Note: Uncle Henry's fiddle and a horse had also disappeared with Mr. Moon.)

From the diary of
Lulie Margie Crawford
May 19, 1881

Classic Turkey Gravy

turkey neck and giblets
3 cups chicken broth
1 large onion, sliced
½ cup carrot, peeled and sliced
½ cup dry white wine
⅓ cup celery and leaves
3 Tbsp. all purpose flour
salt and pepper

Put turkey neck and giblets in a medium saucepan. Add next 5 ingredients. Bring to a boil and reduce heat, simmer uncovered for 1½ hours. Strain broth. Add enough water to make 4 cups broth. Chop giblets and set aside. Discard vegetables. Pour off all but 3 Tbsp. fat drippings from roasting pan. Blend flour with the fat and whisk for 3-5 minutes. Slowly blend in broth, whisking constantly. Stir in chopped giblets, if desired. Season with salt and pepper. Serve hot over turkey and dressing.

Grilled Turkey Breast

½ turkey breast
lime juice
Italian herbs
cheese and garlic Italian dressing
hot and spicy barbeque sauce

Cover turkey breast with lime juice. Shake on Italian herbs, cover with dressing and brush on barbeque sauce. Let marinate 2-3 hours. Grill over medium coals for 30 minutes. Brush on additional barbeque sauce each time turned. Serves 4.

Rodeo Marinade for Chicken

1 cup picante sauce
3 Tbsp. brown sugar
4 tsp. Dijon mustard

Combine all ingredients and mix well. Use half to marinate chicken and other half as sauce for serving. Excellent marinade for grilling.

Barbeque Marinade

½ cup honey
½ cup soy sauce
2 lemons
3 cloves garlic, chopped
2 tsp. dry mustard

In a saucepan, combine all ingredients and heat through. Great marinade for chicken or beef on grill.

Red's Barbeque Sauce

½ cup butter or margarine
1 cup red wine vinegar
1 cup water
2 Tbsp. Worcestershire sauce
2 Tbsp. fresh lemon juice
1 Tbsp. dry mustard
2 Tbsp. chili powder
1 Tbsp. black pepper
1 Tbsp. salt (optional or use ½)
2 bay leaves, crushed
4 cloves garlic, sliced

Melt the butter in a saucepan. Add liquid ingredients. Mix well and add dry ingredients. Simmer uncovered for 10 minutes. Do not let boil. Excellent sauce for barbecued chicken. Makes 2 cups.

Game

Game

A Few Helpful Game Hints

Elk and Deer:
Must be gutted and skinned immediately to allow to cool. The meat should hang for at least a week at 36° to 40°, longer for older animals.

When butchering the meat, all fat must be removed, even the slightest trace because game fat is what causes the "gamey" taste. If a locker processes the meat for you, it is very easy to remove all fat after the package of meat has been thawed.

Ducks and Geese:
Many hunters like to hang their ducks for about three days in a cool place. Plucked—but not gutted—ducks and geese come out cleaner if they are dipped in a bucket of hot wax, then dunked in a bucket of ice water. The hardened wax is then peeled and returned to the hot bucket. The birds are now ready to gut, using a spoon and making sure all entrails are removed. Before freezing the birds, they should be sealed very well in an airtight cellophane wrap, and wrapped again with freezer paper, as birds get "freezer burn" very easily.

To remove the "liver" taste in dark-meated birds, soak the thawing birds three times, ten minutes each, in 3 cups of water and ½ tsp. soda.

Grouse, Pheasant and Quail:
To remove any gamey taste in pheasant, doves, quail and chukars, soak the semi-frozen birds in half and half until thoroughly thawed.

Fish:
Because gills start to deteriorate as soon as the fish die, they need to be cleaned and put on ice as soon as possible. It is important not to overcook fish. As soon as the meat loses its translucent color, it's done!

Hospitality in the early years was as freely accepted as it was offered. Occasionally someone would bring a deer, grouse, or chopped a little wood in exchange for a room. On the frontier, offer of payment would have been considered a discourtesy.

Game Marinade

⅓ cup soy sauce
2 cloves garlic, minced
⅓ cup olive oil
2 Tbsp. lemon juice
1 Tbsp. Worcestershire sauce
1 tsp. black pepper (fresh ground is best)
salt (optional)
1 tsp. chili pepper
1 Tbsp. barbeque sauce
fresh ginger root or fresh herbs (optional)

Combine all ingredients and mix well. Excellent as marinade for venison or elk. Also good with chicken. Grill meat to desired temperature. Makes enough for 2 lbs. meat.

Game with Wild Mushrooms

This recipe can also be prepared with beef steaks.

10-15 peppercorns
3 Tbsp. white wine tarragon vinegar
1 ½ ozs. dried cepes or boletus; porcinis give best flavor
3 cups water
¼ cup onion, chopped
2 Tbsp. clarified butter
1 tsp. sugar
1 tsp. salt
1 Tbsp. soy sauce
1 oz. sherry or madeira
1 ½ Tbsp. arrowroot, mixed in ¼ cup water
4 steaks, trimmed well
pepper
2 cloves garlic, thinly sliced

"Ma rode Coaly and Pa rode Bess and went hunting. They brought in a deer. Haven't seen or heard of that wretch Moon. Warm this eve."

From the diary of
Lulie Margie Crawford
May 20, 1881

Soak peppercorns in vinegar overnight. Grind peppercorns and vinegar in a blender until liquefied and set aside. Reconstitute dried mushrooms in water by bringing to a boil and then simmer for 10-15 minutes. Cool caps, then slice, reserving liquid in which they were boiled. Sauté onions in butter until transparent. Add mushrooms, mushroom liquid, sugar, salt and soy sauce. Simmer until volume of liquid reduces to 2 cups, being careful not to reduce too far. Add sherry and 2-3 tsp. of the peppercorn mixture and simmer 1 minute. Strain through a fine sieve. Heat the liquid and thicken with arrowroot mixture. Return mushrooms to liquid and keep warm. Sprinkle steaks with pepper. Add slivers of garlic clove into holes cut in the meat. Broil meat and serve with sauce. Serves 4.

Foiled Game Roast

Juices make an excellent gravy for rice or potatoes.

6 lb. roast, venison or elk
10 oz. can cream of mushroom soup
1 pkg. dry onion soup mix
1 tsp. marjoram

Lay roast on a large piece of aluminum foil. Pour the soups over the meat and sprinkle with marjoram. Seal the foil and place in a roasting pan. Bake at 350 for approximately 2 ½ hours. Serves 6-8.

Venison or Elk Steaks Supreme

1 cup cracker crumbs
1 cup flour
½ tsp. salt
½ tsp. pepper
1-1 ½ lbs. elk or venison steaks
1 egg, beaten
¼ cup oil
1 Tbsp. butter
½ cup chopped onion
½ cup chopped carrots
2 cans golden mushroom soup
½ cup milk
½ cup water

Combine cracker crumbs, flour, salt and pepper. Dip meat in beaten egg, then coat with cracker crumb mixture. Fry in oil until browned. Remove and pat dry. In a large pan sauté onions and carrots in butter. Add soup, milk and water. Heat to a boil. Add meat and simmer, covered, for 45 min. to 1 hour, or until meat is very tender. Serves 6.

Elk Stroganoff

2 lbs. elk steak, cubed
vegetable cooking spray
¼ cup water
1 large yellow onion, chopped
3-4 cloves garlic, pressed
1 lb. fresh mushrooms, cleaned and stemmed
2 - 10 oz. cans cream of mushroom soup (or white sauce)
3 Tbsp. Worcestershire sauce
salt and pepper to taste
2 cups sour cream or part plain yogurt
1 lb. prepared pasta (preferably fresh) or rice

Liberally spray a large skillet with vegetable spray. Add ¼ cup water. Over medium heat sauté onion until translucent. Add meat and garlic. Cook until meat is browned, about 5 minutes. Add mushroom caps, cream of mushroom soup and Worcestershire sauce. Add salt and pepper to taste. Cover, reduce heat to medium low and simmer for 15 minutes. Meanwhile, prepare pasta and drain. Just before serving, add sour cream to stroganoff mixture. Stir thoroughly and bring to a boil. Serve immediately by spooning over pasta or rice. Serves 8.

Antelope a la Pizzaiola

6 slices antelope or elk, venison or beef, cut ¼" thick
olive oil
2 cloves garlic, diced
1 stalk celery, sliced
1 onion, sliced thin
4 cloves shallots, minced
16 oz. can stewed tomatoes, coarsely chopped with their juice
12 black Greek olives, pitted and halved
½ lb. fresh mushrooms, sliced
1 cup white wine
½ tsp. oregano
salt and pepper to taste
3 Tbsp. chopped parsley

In a large skillet, brown meat quickly on both sides in oil. Remove and keep warm. In same oil, sauté onion, garlic, celery and shallots until soft. Add tomatoes and cook 15 minutes. Add olives, mushrooms, wine, oregano, salt and pepper and cook 15 minutes more. When ready to serve, add meat to skillet and heat through. Place on a warm platter; garnish with parsley. Serve with rice or egg noodles. Serves 6.

Pot au Wild Feu

Excellent—cooks while you enjoy the great outdoors!

1 lb. sliced elk or venison steaks
1 pheasant, cut up
½ lb. Kielbasa sausage, cut into 1" pieces
3 carrots, cut into 3" pieces
2 onions, peeled, halved and stuck with a whole clove each
2 stalks celery, cut into 2" pieces
10 oz. can beef bouillon
1 bay leaf
6 peppercorns
½ tsp. thyme
4 cloves garlic, minced

In a crock pot, alternate layers of meats with sausage on top. Add vegetables on the side to fill. Add bay leaf, peppercorns, thyme and garlic. Pour bouillon over the top. Cover and cook on low for 12-18 hours. Can easily be doubled. Serves 6.

Teriyaki Roast

2 lb. elk or venison roast
1 cup teriyaki sauce
¼ cup lemon juice
1 tsp. chopped garlic

Marinate roast in teriyaki sauce in refrigerator for 24-48 hours. Place in roasting pan and bake at 400° for 20 minutes. Reduce heat to 350° and bake additional 45 minutes for medium rare meat. Serves 4.

Eagle Ridge Rollettes

2 lbs. elk round steak, ½" thick
¼ cup mustard
salt and pepper
6 slices bacon or Canadian bacon
6 pickle slices
flour
¼ cup butter
10 oz. can beef broth
1 cup sour cream

Cut steak into 6 equal pieces and pound each to ¼" thickness. Sprinkle each with salt and pepper, and spread mustard on top side. Lay a strip of bacon and 1 pickle slice on each piece and roll up securing the roll with a toothpick. Flour the meat and sauté in butter. Stir in broth, reduce heat, cover and simmer 1-1 ½ hours. Stir in sour cream until well blended. Serve over rice, noodles or mashed potatoes. Serves 6.

Elk River was named for the many elk that roam the area. It was in the Elk River Valley ranchers discovered that grain and hay crops such as alfalfa and red clover would grow despite the high altitude and short growing season.

Elk River Chili

2 Tbsp. oil
2 green peppers sliced in large rings
3 onions sliced in large rings
2 cloves garlic diced
2 lbs. elk meat (either ground or sliced in small strips)
3 12 oz. cans tomato sauce
2 12 oz. cans water
3 Tbsp. chili powder
salt and pepper to taste
1 can beer
2 15 oz. cans dark red kidney beans

In large skillet put oil, green peppers, onions and garlic. Cook until soft. Add meat, brown, and leave in big chunks. Add tomato sauce and water, salt and pepper and chili powder. Cover and simmer for 20 minutes. Add beer and beans (undrained). Simmer uncovered for 20 minutes. Serves 8.

Wild Game Chili
Beef can be substituted for the venison or elk

1 lb. ground meat (venison or elk)
1 lb. sausage
1 large onion
2 28 oz. cans stewed tomatoes
¼ cup chopped green pepper
3 cloves garlic, minced
4 oz. can chopped green chilies
15 oz. can kidney beans
2 Tbsp. cumin
½ tsp. seasoning salt
2 Tbsp. chili powder
1 Tbsp. coriander, ground
1 cup ketchup

Sauté onion, green pepper and garlic until tender. Brown meats and drain. Place all ingredients in a large pot and bring to a boil. Reduce heat to a slow boil and cook for 30 minutes. Serves 6.

Green Chili and Tortillas
Butter and oil
1 ½ to 2 lbs. elk meat, diced
flour
7 oz. can green chilies
½ of 4 oz. can chopped jalapeños
1 tsp. each of salt and pepper
1 tsp. garlic, chopped
1 medium onion, diced
water to cover meat
package of flour tortillas

Brown meat in a little butter and oil, sprinkle with flour and brown again.   Add rest of ingredients, cover meat with water and simmer slowly for 2 to 2 ½ hours in covered pan, until meat shreds easily. Serve with flour tortillas. Serves 4.

Mad Creek Meatballs

1 to 1 ½ lbs. elk burger
½ cup rolled corn chips
½ onion, minced
3 tsp. cumin
1 tsp. garlic salt
4 Tbsp. chopped fresh cilantro
pepper to taste
2 Tbsp. butter
1 can Cheddar cheese soup
1 cup mild picante sauce

Combine meat, rolled chips, onion, cumin, garlic salt, fresh cilantro, and pepper. Roll into tight balls. Brown meatballs in hot butter in hot skillet. Add soup and salsa, stirring gently to mix. Let simmer covered for 20 min. Serve over rice or roll meatballs in flour tortillas. Serves 4.

Brown's Park Jerky

2 lbs. lean meat cut in ⅓" strips.
½ tsp. garlic powder
1 ½ tsp. onion powder
1 ½ tsp. season salt
1 ½ tsp. liquid smoke
1 tsp. vinegar
¼ cup soy sauce
½ cup Worcestershire sauce
1 tsp. fresh ground black pepper
1 ½ tsp. crushed red pepper
6 Tbsp. molasses (optional—for sweetness)

"We saw 6 deer across Bear River. Pa set out cabbages and fixed the gate to the corral and made posts for the yard. No news from Moon."

From the diary of
Lulie Margie Crawford
May 21, 1881

Marinate above ingredients for 2 days in refrigerator. Arrange meat on rack in the oven in single layers. It will drip, so put aluminum foil on rack directly below the meat. Bake on warm (150º) for about 12 hours or until chewy. Store in refrigerator in an airtight container.

Pheasant Piccata

1 whole pheasant, deboned
2 Tbsp. butter
2 shallots, chopped
2 cloves garlic, minced
2 Tbsp. soy sauce
½ lemon
¼ cup white wine
2 Tbsp. capers

Slice pheasant breasts into 6 steaks. Discard legs. Hammer meat to flatten pieces to ¼" thick. Sauté shallots and garlic in butter. Leave in hot pan and add dark pieces of meat first, then white. Cook dark meat 3 minutes, white 2 minutes on first side. Turn and sprinkle with wine, soy sauce, lemon and capers. Cook another 2 minutes. Serve immediately. Serve with wild rice and fresh vegetables. Serves 2.

Although predominantly a Ute Indian hunting ground, Routt County was also visited by the Arapahoe, Gros Ventre, Sioux, Shoshone and Cheyenne. Control of the area was hotly contested—the "mountain men" (beaver trappers) allied themselves with local Indians, but in so doing became the enemies of rival tribes. Battle Creek, near Slater, was the scene of an 1842 skirmish which killed 27 trappers and an estimated 100 Indians.

Stuffed Grouse or Pheasant

4 grouse or pheasant
6 whole club crackers, crumbled
¼ small loaf of French bread, chopped
3 small apples, chopped and peeled
handful of golden raisins
pepper
¾ tsp. garlic salt
1 ½ Tbsp. poultry seasoning
chicken broth for right moisture or melted butter

Sauté and add to stuffing:
4 chopped green onions
1 Tbsp. chopped parsley
¾ cup chopped celery
¾ cups sliced mushrooms
½ cup chopped zucchini

Gravy:
1 can chicken stock
1 Tbsp. flour
water
half and half to taste

Brown grouse at 400° for 10 minutes in large baking pan. Remove and stuff birds with stuffing. Cover with foil and cook 350° for about 2 hours. Make gravy by removing birds from pan and using drippings, adding chicken stock, flour and half and half. Serves 8-10.

Out of This World Pheasant

2 cans cream of mushroom soup
1 cup sour cream
1 cup milk
1 bay leaf, broken up
8 large pheasant breasts, deboned and skinned
8 slices bacon
2 ½ oz. jar chipped beef (optional)

Combine first 4 ingredients to make a sauce. Roll breasts up and wrap each in a slice of bacon. Shred chipped beef and place in bottom of greased 13" x 9" baking dish. Place breasts over beef and cover with sauce. Bake, uncovered, at 350° for 2 ½ hours. Baste 3-4 times during baking with sauce. Great with wild rice casserole. Serves 8.

Roasted Pheasant
Succulent and tender ...

1 pheasant, whole or 2 quail
2 Tbsp. butter
2 Tbsp. minced shallots
1 Tbsp. minced garlic
¾ cup small white pearl onions, peeled
¾ cup small mushrooms
½ cup dry white wine
¼ cup chicken stock
½ tsp. dried thyme
1 Tbsp. minced parsley
¼ cup half and half

Brown pheasant in 1 Tbsp. butter, in hot roasting pan. While browning, sauté shallots, garlic, onions and mushrooms in 1 Tbsp. butter. Pour vegetables over pheasant. Add wine, chicken stock and thyme. Cover and bake at 400° for 55 minutes for pheasant or 20 minutes for quail. Add half and half to juice to make sauce. Garnish with parsley. Serve with wild rice and seasoned vegetables. Serves 2.

Jack's Duck Lunch ⏱
So simple, but so good!

2 duck breasts
olive oil
1 tsp. butter
½ tsp. salt
½ tsp. pepper
½ cup flour

Combine flour, salt and pepper. Dip duck breasts in the flour mixture and coat well. Heat oil in skillet until hot. Add ½ tsp. butter under each duck. Cook 3 minutes on each side for medium rare. Should be cooked hot and quick. Remove from heat and let cool. To serve as an appetizer, fan the breasts out into fingers shaped like a hand and serve with horseradish. Serves 2 - 4.

Duck with Orange Sauce
3 ducks, whole
1 orange, sliced

Sauce heated in pan:
½ cup red wine
3 Tbsp. honey
2 Tbsp. vinegar
½ can concentrated orange juice
1 Tbsp. Worcestershire sauce

Push orange slices up under duck skin, especially over breast. Brush duck with sauce and brown ducks in baking pan 20 minutes at 400°. Drain grease from pan and brush ducks again with sauce and return to oven 350° for 1 hour. Reduce temperature to 300°, brush ducks again and bake 20 minutes more. Serve ducks with remainder of heated sauce. Do not use drippings from pan, as they are too greasy. Serves 3.

The Best Wild Duck You Ever Ate

One large Northern Mallard (ones with very orange feet)
50/50 mixture of Tamari Soy Sauce and olive oil
(use about ¼ to ½ cup for 2 birds)
any old apples and oranges
sweet hot mustard
"Fines Herbs" (Spice Island or similar)

Have frozen ducks thaw slowly, as this will tenderize the bird. Rub inside and out with olive oil/soy mixture, be liberal (make a mess). Stuff cavity full of apple and orange slices. Arrange breast up on cooking sheet and spread all visible duck parts with sweet-hot mustard (use plenty). Sprinkle ducks liberally with Fines Herbs. Cooking: The secret is "fast and furious" (very hot). Preheat oven all the way to 550°+, hopefully top and bottom elements will remain on. Place ducks on lower rack and turn on the kitchen fan! Depending on how hot your oven can get, cooking time is about 14 minutes for two ducks and 16 to 18 for four (they will be rare, the best way). If you prefer medium, try 20 to 22 minutes. When the mustard is brown and crackling, they're done!   1 mallard serves 2 people.

Loris Werner, like many of Steamboat's greatest, was an accomplished four-way skier, beginning as a jumper and later focusing on downhill. In his nine years on the U.S. Ski Team, he was a jumping alternate for the Innsbruck Olympics in 1964, and he competed in the '68 Grenoble Olympics on the alpine squad.

How to "Cook your Goose"

by Loris "Bugs" Werner

7 to 9 lb. skinned goose
1 large can concentrated orange juice
⅛ cup teriyaki sauce
⅛ cup Worcestershire sauce
1 tsp. garlic powder
1 tsp. Greek seasoning
½ tsp. creole seasoning

Marinate above ingredients for 12 hours, breast side down.

Stuff bird with:
1 apple thinly sliced
1 orange, thinly sliced
1 white onion, thinly sliced
4 celery stalks, cut 3-4 inches long
3-4 pineapple slices
4-5 bacon strips (to place over breast)

Place in large cooking bag (using direction on package). Pre-heat oven to 300°. Cook 2 ½ to 3 hours or until meat reaches 180°. Serves 4-6.

Good Ol' Fried Fish

fresh fish fillets
2 eggs beaten
2 Tbsp. milk
½ tsp. salt
½ tsp. pepper
¾ cup flour
¼ cup butter
lemon wedges
fresh parsley

Fish Creek was named by the James Crawford family for the many fish they caught in the creek.

Beat eggs and milk in flat dish, add all dry ingredients in another flat dish. Dip fillets in egg mixture, then roll in dry mixture. Cook in hot butter at medium heat about 3 minutes each side. Serve with lemon wedges and fresh parsley. Serves 4.

Pan Fried Trout with Walnuts

3 Tbsp. walnut oil
6 fresh brook trout
½ cup walnuts
1 Tbsp. fennel seeds
salt and pepper to taste
juice of lemon

Put the oil in a large skillet and heat until hot. Reduce heat to medium; add the trout and cook until golden brown, about 3 to 4 min. on each side. Remove and keep warm. Return the pan to heat and add walnuts, fennel, salt and pepper, cook until the walnuts are slightly browned. Top the trout with the walnuts, fennel seeds, and a squeeze of lemon. Serves 6.

"Mama went fishing this morning but didn't get a bite. I commenced to sew a cardboard motto, 'Home Sweet Home.' We had supper of graham mush and milk."

From the diary of
Lulie Margie Crawford
March 29, 1881

Teriyaki Trout

whole trout
tin foil
squeeze of lemon
green peppers diced
slivered almonds
diced green onions
teriyaki sauce (Trader Vic's is best)
garlic diced fine, or garlic powder

Lay trout on tin foil. Sprinkle inside of trout with squeeze of lemon, green peppers, slivered almonds, green onions, teriyaki sauce, and garlic. Wrap and bake 12 minutes at 400°. Or place on grill 6 minutes each side (more or less depending on size of fish). Serves 1.

Delicious Stream-Side Trout

one native trout per person (about 12-14 inches)
orange meated variety is best
foil sheets (heavy duty, about 3 to 4 inches longer than the fish)
two bacon slices per fish
two yellow onion slices per fish, cut in half
three or four red potato slices per fish
1 tsp. Fines Herbs (Spice Islands or similar)
1 tsp. lemon herb seasoning (or fresh lemon if convenient)
Lawry's seasoned salt

Do all this ahead of time before you go fishing: Roll your bacon up in the individual foil sheets, slice and bag the onions and potatoes, mix the dry spices together and put in a small bag or bottle. Catch fish and clean (don't throw guts in lake!). Open up foil with bacon and stack as follows: bacon slice, halved onion slices, potato slices, fish (in the middle, well-seasoned inside with dry mixture) more potato slices, halved onion slices, and the other bacon slice. Sprinkle seasoning mix during process and add lemon juice. Seal foil well, trout can be kept in "tubes" overnight for breakfast or cooked immediately. Where small campfires are permitted, bury the foil tubes in coals, about 10 minutes side one, 10 minutes side two, and 3 minutes original side up, i.e. turn twice in hot fire. Eat it all with your fingers! If baking at home, cook in very hot oven (450° to 500°) for 15 to 20 minutes, or until bacon is cooked. Serve on a plate—be more civilized—use forks and knifes, add Chardonnay, wild asparagus, eh!

Danish Cheesy Trout

6 medium size fresh trout, cleaned
2 Tbsp. butter
dill weed
1 egg, beaten
¼ cup milk
¾ cup fine bread or club cracker crumbs
⅓ cup grated Havarti or Swiss Cheese
¼ tsp. salt
dash cayenne
2 Tbsp. melted butter

Put teaspoon butter and a dash of dill weed inside each fish. Blend together egg and milk in a shallow dish. Combine bread crumbs, half of the cheese, salt, and cayenne in another dish. Dip fish in each dish coating well. Lay fish in greased pan. Cook at 500° for approximately 15 min. Sprinkle with remaining cheese for last 5 minutes. Serves 6.

Shrimp and Crab Stuffed Trout

2 Tbsp. butter
1 clove garlic, crushed
1 small onion, chopped
½ medium green pepper, minced
¼ lb. cooked crab, flaked
¼ lb. tiny shrimp
¼ - ½ cup fine bread crumbs
1 Tbsp. minced parsley
1 Tbsp. minced chives
¼ tsp. salt
⅛ tsp. pepper
4 - 10" trout

Melt butter in large fry pan. Add garlic and onions and sauté. Add green peppers, crab, shrimp, bread crumbs, parsley, chives, salt and pepper. Mix well adding more crumbs if necessary to hold mix together loosely. Brush trout with additional melted butter and then pile stuffing in cavities. Place fish on greased pan with tight-fitting lid. Bake covered 350° about 15 min. Uncover and bake until trout flakes easily (about another ½ hour). Can also be baked in a clay pot as follows: covered at 375° for 30 min. Any extra stuffing can be baked in pan with fish. Double the amount of shrimp may be substituted for crab. Serves 4.

The wild meadows around the Crawford cabin contributed dock, yampas, wild onions, strawberries, chokeberry and sarvice berries to the Crawford's dinner table.

Ceviche Trucha (Trout Ceviche)

2 - 3 orange-meated trout
lime juice, enough to cover trout, fresh is best, about ½ cup
salt, enough to neutralize the lime juice, 2 to 3 teaspoons
dill to taste, about tsp.
diced onions, wild if available in Spring, or small white onion
½ tsp. black pepper, or thin sliced fresh chili (deseeded)

Fillet meat off both sides of trout (bones are not part of ceviche). Skin the fillets, holding knife flat just between skin and meat at the tail, then pull skin out from under meat. Dice trout meat into ½" pieces or smaller. Marinate for 30 minutes with all other ingredients. Stir the mix occasionally. Don't use a metal bowl—plastic or glass is best. Lay a plate over the fish to keep it down in the lime mixture. Serve cool with brown bread or corn chips. Serves 4.

Pasta

Pasta

Twentymile Pasta

⅓ cup olive oil
4 cloves garlic
crushed red pepper to taste
15 oz. can artichoke hearts
½ cup sun dried tomatoes in oil, drained
½ - 1 cup black olives
1 lemon
2 Tbsp. chopped parsley
¾ - 1 lb. pasta
freshly grated Parmesan cheese
pine nuts, toasted (opt.)

Crush garlic, sauté in olive oil over low heat. Add red pepper to taste. Drain and chop artichokes, sun dried tomatoes and olives. Add to garlic. Squeeze lemon into pan and add chopped parsley. Stir gently. Serve over warm pasta and sprinkle with Parmesan cheese and pine nuts. Serves 4.

Variations: Add drained tuna; boneless chicken breasts, chopped and sautéed in oil and herbs.

Twentymile Park, lying between Yampa, Hayden, and Steamboat Springs, was probably named by early cowboys who rounded up their herds and branded in a large white adobe flat located approximately 20 miles from each town.

End-of-Summer Pasta

Use any vegetables of the season in this dish.

½ cup olive oil
8 garlic cloves
2 lbs. ripe plum tomatoes, seeded and chopped OR
    2 - 15 oz. cans no salt tomatoes, drained and chopped
2 medium zucchini, cut into thin matchsticks
¼ lb. mushrooms, sliced
¼ lb. snow peas
1 pound fusilli or rotelle
8 large scallions, white and 2" of green, thinly sliced
1 ½ cups coarsely chopped fresh basil
1 tsp. each salt and pepper
2 cups freshly grated Parmesan cheese

Preheat oven to 375°. In a large casserole or baking dish, combine the garlic cloves and olive oil. Bake 10 to 15 minutes, until garlic is golden. Remove from oven and, using a slotted spoon, remove and discard garlic cloves. Add tomatoes, zucchini, mushrooms, snow peas and toss well. Return to the oven and bake for 10 minutes longer or until vegetables are slightly softened. Cook pasta according to package directions until al dente. Drain and add to vegetables in the casserole. Add scallions, basil, salt and pepper, and 1 cup of Parmesan and toss well. Serve warm or at room temperature. Pass remaining Parmesan at the table. Serves 4-6.

Vegetable Pasta

1 lb. spiral pasta
½ lb. sliced bacon
½ cup walnuts
½ eggplant, peeled and sliced
2 red or yellow bell peppers, seeded and cut into strips
2 small zucchini
½ cup pinon nuts
½ cup grated Parmesan cheese
½ cup grated Romano cheese
olive oil

Cook bacon in frying pan until brown and crisp. Remove and drain. Break into 1" pieces. In the same pan, sauté the walnuts over high heat until fairly dark brown. Remove and drain. Pour off bacon grease and season pan with olive oil. Heat the oil and sauté eggplant and peppers for 8 minutes. Add zucchini. Sauté for 5 minutes more or until browned and tender. Prepare pasta al dente; drain. Return to warm pot. Stir in vegetables, walnuts, pinon nuts and cheeses. Toss well. Toss in bacon. Serve. Serves 4 - 6.

The Antlers Hotel in Yampa was the largest hotel in Routt County until the Cabin Hotel was built in Steamboat Springs. It served as the main overnight stage stop between Steamboat Springs and Wolcott.

Ceci Bean Macaroni

1 lb. small pasta shells
15 oz. can ceci beans (garbanzo beans)
⅓ cup olive oil
5 cloves garlic, crushed
½ onion, finely chopped
3 fresh tomatoes, chopped
½ tsp. salt
½ tsp. pepper
2-5 dry serranno peppers, crushed
1 tsp. oregano
1 tsp. basil
½ tsp. thyme
1 Tbsp. anchovy paste
Parmesan cheese (garnish)

Cook pasta shells in a 5 quart pot in boiling salted water until al dente. At the same time, add ceci beans to the boiling water to heat along with the cooking pasta. Sauté garlic and onions in olive oil in a large pan, until the onions are translucent. Add tomatoes and seasonings. Add serranno peppers to taste. They are quite hot. 1-2 peppers will be mild, 3 will be medium, 4-5 will be hot. Cook until tomatoes are soft. Add the anchovy paste, stirring in well, and cook for 1 more minute. Drain the pasta and beans and toss with the sauté mixture. Garnish with Parmesan cheese and serve immediately. For variations, add steamed broccoli or spinach with the tomatoes. Serves 3-4.

Pasta Primavera

½ cup butter
⅛ cup olive oil
1 bunch green onions, minced
3 cloves garlic, minced
2-3 zucchini, cut in quarter rounds
½ lb. mushrooms, thinly sliced
½ lb. small shrimp, peeled and deveined
6 oz. bottle clam juice
2 cups heavy cream
4-5 tomatoes, cut in sixths
3-4 Tbsp. basil leaves, chopped
salt and fresh pepper
1 ½ lbs. fettuccine noodles
1 cup freshly grated Parmesan cheese

In large skillet, sauté onion and garlic in butter and oil until onion is translucent. Add zucchini and mushrooms and sauté until zucchini is tender (about 2-3 minutes). With a slotted spoon remove vegetables and set aside. Add shrimp and sauté 2-3 minutes, being careful not to overcook. Remove and set aside. Add clam juice and cream to skillet and allow to reduce by about half simmering on low heat. At this point, have water boiling for pasta and cook as directed. Drain and set aside. Add vegetables, shrimp and tomatoes with cream and clam juice. Add pasta and season with basil, salt, pepper and Parmesan cheese. Toss vigorously. Serves 4-6.

Pasta Fresca

Add grilled, sliced steak or chicken for a main dish.

2 lbs. tomatoes or plum tomatoes, chopped
½-¾ cup chopped fresh basil
3 Tbsp. raspberry vinegar or red wine vinegar
2 garlic cloves, minced
¾-1 cup extra virgin olive oil
salt
freshly ground pepper
1 lb. fettuccine or linguine

Combine tomatoes, basil and garlic. Marinate at room temperature 2 - 3 hours or overnight in refrigerator. Blend vinegar, salt and pepper into tomato mixture and heat through. Boil pasta according to directions and drain. Transfer to a large bowl. Add ¼ cup olive oil and toss pasta. Add tomato mixture, remaining olive oil, toss and serve. For variation, try adding roasted red and yellow peppers to the tomatoes and marinate or add stir-fried snow peas to the sauce and heat through. Serves 6-8.

Priest Creek Primavera

1 cup zucchini, chopped
1 ½ cups chopped broccoli
1 ½ cups snow peas
1 cup baby peas
6 stalks asparagus, cut into 1" pieces
10 large mushrooms, sliced
1 lb. spaghetti
12 cherry tomatoes
3 Tbsp. olive oil
2 tsp. chopped garlic
¼ cup chopped fresh parsley
salt and pepper to taste
⅓ cup butter
¼ cup grated Parmesan cheese
1 cup sour cream
1 Tbsp. dry basil

Steam the first 6 vegetables until tender crisp and drain. While spaghetti is cooking, sauté the tomatoes in the olive oil with the garlic and parsley. Season with salt and pepper. Melt butter and add Parmesan cheese, sour cream, and basil. Keep warm. Drain spaghetti and toss all ingredients together. Serves 4-6.

Priest Creek was named after the first settler on the creek, Chester F. Priest.

Pasta with Herb Sauce

1 ½ cups heavy cream or half evaporated skim milk and half cream
4 Tbsp. unsalted butter
½ tsp. salt
⅛ tsp. nutmeg
pinch cayenne pepper
¼ cup freshly grated imported Parmesan cheese
1 cup finely chopped mixed herbs (mint, cilantro, basil or parsley with chives or green onion tops)

Combine cream, butter, salt, nutmeg and cayenne in a heavy saucepan and cook for 15 minutes or until sauce is slightly reduced and thickened. Whisk in Parmesan and fresh herbs and simmer 5 minutes more. Taste and correct seasonings, if necessary. Serve immediately over linguine or other fine pasta. Makes 2 cups sauce.

Anchovy Garlic Sauce with Pasta

1 cup olive oil
1 cup hot water
8 cloves garlic, minced
2 - 2 oz. cans anchovies, in oil
½ bunch fresh parsley, chopped
1 lb. pasta, spaghetti or linguine, cooked

Heat the oil in a large skillet. Add garlic and anchovies, with their oil, and sauté 2-3 minutes, mashing the anchovies. Add parsley and hot water and cook over medium heat for about 10 minutes. Serve over cooked pasta. Serves 4-6.

Simply Delicious Pasta

2 lbs. Italian sausage
1 large onion, chopped
1 red bell pepper, chopped
½ -1 cup mushrooms, sliced
½ cup olive oil
2-3 Tbsp. finely chopped garlic
1 Tbsp. basil
Parmesan cheese

Heat oil and garlic. Add sliced sausage and cook 10 minutes. Add onions, red pepper, basil and mushrooms and sauté until lightly cooked but crisp tender. Toss with cooked pasta of your choice. Top with fresh Parmesan cheese. Serves 4-6.

Chicken Pesto Pasta

1 lb. boneless chicken breasts, skinned and cut into chunks
olive oil
4 ozs. pesto
1 lb. fettuccine or spaghetti
Parmesan cheese (garnish)
pine nuts (garnish, optional)

Prepare pasta according to pasta directions. Sauté chicken in olive oil in large frying pan for about 8 minutes, until just cooked. Add pesto and cooked and drained pasta. Toss thoroughly, heating through. Garnish with Parmesan and pine nuts. Serves 4.

Variations: Add mushrooms sautéed with chicken; black olives; fresh tomato chunks add with pesto; or all of these.

Pasta Pesto

8 ozs. fresh basil leaves
8 ozs. pine nuts
3 cloves garlic, chopped
4 ozs. grated Romano cheese
2 cups olive oil

In a food processor, grind basil leaves with ½ cup olive oil until basil just turns to a paste. Scrape into a mixing bowl. Repeat with pine nuts and ½ cup oil. Scrape into same bowl. Combine ground basil and nuts with grated cheese and gradually add remaining olive oil until mixture is a thin paste. Add garlic, a little at a time, tasting as you add. Refrigerate until ready to serve. To serve, boil pasta of your choice until al dente. Add cold pesto to hot pasta, 2 Tbsp. pesto per serving, and mix well.

Van Card, born in Steamboat in 1939, was a formidable competitor in both alpine and jumping events. He won the Junior Nationals slalom championship in 1957 and was named an alternate to the U.S. jumping team for the 1964 Olympics in Innsbruck.

Spinach Pesto

2 cups fresh spinach leaves, firmly packed
¼-½ cup parsley
3 Tbsp. toasted pine nuts
3 cloves garlic, minced
3 Tbsp. fresh basil
¾ tsp. salt
¾ cup olive oil
¾ cup Parmesan cheese

In a food processor, process first 5 ingredients in small batches until finely minced, pulsing. Add remaining ingredients and pulse until just blended. Do not over process or pesto will lose its lovely green color. Makes 3 cups pesto. Serves 1¾ - 2 lbs. pasta.

Basil Spinach Pesto

1 cup fresh basil
¼ cup fresh spinach
¼ cup pine nuts
¼ cup olive oil
10 cloves garlic

Purée all ingredients in a blender. Thin with warm water. Keeps for weeks in a jar. Use in sauces, salad dressings and soups. Makes 4 cups.

Tomato Basil Sauce

20 plum tomatoes, blanched, peeled and seeded
½ cup carrot juice
¼ cup olive oil
½ cup fresh basil
10 cloves garlic
4 shallots, minced
¼ cup fresh oregano
cayenne to taste

Purée all ingredients in a blender. Transfer to a saucepan and cook slowly for 45 minutes. Can be thickened with a little unsalted tomato paste. Makes 4 cups.

Putanesca Sauce

This sauce is best when served over Penne Rigate macaroni noodles.

2 - 6 oz. cans chopped black olives
10 oz. green olives, chopped
24 oz. can whole tomatoes
1 can anchovies in oil
½ of a 3 oz. jar capers
2 Tbsp. chopped garlic, or to taste

In a large pot, smash the tomatoes and add all the other ingredients. Cook over medium heat for 15 to 20 minutes, stirring occasionally. This will cover 1 lb. of pasta. Serves 4.

Steamboat Springs has been the site of nine American distance ski jumping records on the 90-meter hill.

No Cook Spaghetti Sauce

2 large tomatoes, cut into chunks
2 Tbsp. garlic
10 large leaves basil, chopped or ½ Tbsp. dried basil
6 oz. can chopped black olives
½ cup olive oil

Combine all ingredients in a large bowl and let sit for about 2 hours. When ready to serve, heat through and serve over noodles or spaghetti. Serves 2.

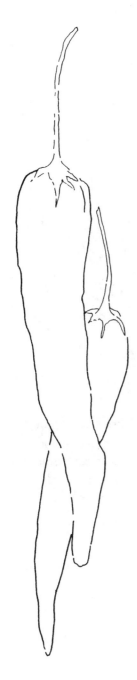

Ziti Salad with Basil Vinaigrette
A great summer meal.

1 ½ cups olive oil
⅓ cup red wine vinegar
¼ cup lemon juice
¼ cup chopped fresh basil
1 ½ tsp. salt
1 tsp. pepper
1 tsp. garlic salt
1 ½ lbs. zucchini, cut into 1 ½" x ¼" sticks
1 lb. carrots, peeled and cut same as zucchini
1 lb. ziti macaroni noodles

Combine olive oil, vinegar, lemon juice, basil, salt and pepper in a blender or food processor. Whirl on low speed until smooth, stopping 2-3 times to scrape down sides with rubber spatula. Cook ziti according to directions. Drain, but do not rinse. Transfer to bowl. Sprinkle ziti with garlic salt. Pour basil vinaigrette over hot pasta; toss gently to coat. Cool to room temperature. Cover; refrigerate overnight. Blanch zucchini and carrots in boiling salted water until vegetables brighten in color and are crisp tender (about 2 minutes). Drain, and rinse under cold water to cool. To serve; remove pasta from refrigerator; let stand 15 minutes. Add zucchini and carrots; toss gently to mix. To make a 1 course meal, add ¾ lb. cooked ham, roast beef or chicken, cut into ½" cubes and serve with bread. Serves 6.

Tortellini with Chili Tomato Sauce

2 qts. water
1 Tbsp. oil
1 ½ pkgs. dry tortellini
2 Tbsp. pine nuts
1 Tbsp. olive oil
½ cup chopped onions
1-2 Tbsp. chilies or jalapeño peppers (optional)
1 tsp. garlic powder
16 oz. can tomatoes, undrained
½ cup sliced black olives
1 ½ cups grated mozzarella cheese

Add tortellini to boiling water and oil. Cook until al dente. Brown pine nuts in oil in medium saucepan , set aside. Drain tortellini, rinse with warm water and place in serving dish and keep warm. Sauté onions, chilies and garlic in olive oil until onion is soft. Add tomatoes, breaking up while stirring. Simmer gently for 5 minutes. To serve, top tortellini with ¾ cup of cheese, tomato sauce, pine nuts and olives. Sprinkle remaining cheese over the top. Serves 6.

Angel Hair Pasta With Shrimp

2 Tbsp. butter or margarine
2 Tbsp. vegetable oil
12 ozs. medium size shrimp, peeled and deveined
2 large cloves garlic, crushed
8 oz. package angel hair pasta
¾ cup heavy cream
½ cup dry white wine
1 cup frozen peas, thawed
¼ cup chopped fresh parsley
½ cup grated Parmesan cheese
½ tsp. dried basil
¼ tsp. crushed red pepper (opt.)

Prepare pasta, according to package directions. Melt butter and oil in 12" skillet over medium heat. Add shrimp and garlic and cook 6 minutes, stirring frequently, until shrimp are pink. Using slotted spoon, remove shrimp and keep warm. Add cream, wine, peas, parsley, ¼ cup of the Parmesan, basil and red pepper to the skillet. Blend well and bring to a boil over medium high heat. Reduce heat and simmer for 5 minutes, stirring occasionally. Add pasta and shrimp. Toss until well mixed. Serve immediately with remaining Parmesan. Serves 6.

Maggie Crawford had become an enthusiastic convert to her husband James's dreams of a wonderful town to be called Steamboat Springs. In helping to fulfill that dream, she gave to this raw new land what was most needed—her skill as a cook, and her talents as a homemaker.

Steamboat Alfredo

Try this Alfredo—Steamboat Style!

10 ozs. medium size shrimp, peeled and deveined
10 ozs. sea scallops
¼ cup butter
2 Tbsp. cream sherry
½ cup heavy cream
1 lb. fettuccine, cooked
¾ cup grated Romano and Parmesan cheese
1 egg beaten well
2 cloves garlic, minced
salt, pepper to taste
parsley

Sauté seafood in butter 3 - 6 minutes until scallops turn white. Add sherry and simmer for about 1 minute. Add cream and bring to a slow boil, stirring constantly. Add egg, garlic, salt, pepper and a bit of fresh parsley. Stir in cheese until smooth. Add cooked fettuccine and toss well. Garnish with lemon wedges and fresh parsley. Serves 4.

Soda Creek Lasagne

6 lasagne noodles
2 egg whites, slightly beaten
1 ½ cups lowfat ricotta cheese
dash pepper
5 green onions, sliced
3 Tbsp. water
1 cup skim milk
4 tsp. cornstarch
⅛ tsp. nutmeg or to taste
1 ½ cups grated part skim mozzarella cheese
10 oz. package frozen chopped spinach, thawed and drained
½ cup freshly grated Parmesan cheese

Cook lasagne noodles, drain, rinse with cold water and drain again. Stir together egg whites, ricotta cheese and pepper. Set aside. Steam onions in ½ cup water, covered, about 3-4 minutes or until tender. Blend milk, cornstarch and nutmeg. Add to onions. Cook over medium heat until bubbly. Gradually add 1 cup mozzarella cheese and stir until melted. Add thoroughly drained spinach and mix well. Spray 10"x6" baking dish with non-stick spray. Place two lasagne noodles in dish. Spread ⅓ of ricotta cheese mixture over noodles. Top with ⅓ of spinach sauce. Repeat 2 more times. Top with Parmesan cheese and remaining mozzarella cheese. Cover with foil and bake at 350° for 30 minutes. Remove foil and bake 5-10 minutes more until cheeses are melted and bubbly. Let stand 10 minutes before serving. Serves 5-6.

Soda Creek was named as such because it ran near Soda Springs. Just above its banks, the Crawfords built their first cabin along with the community's first sawmill, and a one-room schoolhouse.

Lighted Man Lasagne

1 lb. ground turkey
½ lb. ground turkey sausage (Italian)
½ tsp. salt
1 clove garlic, minced
1 Tbsp. basil
12 oz. can tomato sauce
16 oz. can tomatoes, cut up
8 wide lasagna noodles
3 ⅓ cups lowfat cottage cheese
2 eggs, beaten
½ tsp. pepper
2 Tbsp. dried parsley flakes
½ cup grated Parmesan cheese
1 lb. mozzarella cheese, grated

Brown ground turkey and turkey sausage in a heavy skillet. Drain. Add salt, garlic, basil, tomato sauce and tomatoes. Simmer, uncovered, until sauce is thick. While sauce is thickening, cook noodles. In a separate bowl, combine cottage cheese, eggs and seasonings. Add Parmesan cheese. Place 4 noodles in a 13" x 9" baking dish, sprayed with vegetable oil. Spread ½ of the cheese mixture over the noodles. Spread ½ of meat sauce over cheese. Spread ½ of mozzarella cheese over meat. Repeat, ending with cheese. Bake at 350° for 40 minutes, or until set. Let stand 10 minutes before serving. Serves 6-8.

Lasagne with Pesto Sauce

1 lb. ricotta cheese
1 ½ cups grated Parmesan cheese
1 cup minced mozzarella cheese
½ cup fresh minced parsley
½ cup minced green onion
1 egg yolk
½ tsp. marjoram
½ tsp. minced garlic
½ tsp. dried basil
¼ tsp. oregano
salt and freshly ground black pepper
¾ lb. lasagne noodles, cooked
1 recipe Pesto Sauce (recipe follows)

Preheat oven to 350°. Grease a shallow 2½ quart baking dish. Combine first ten ingredients in a large bowl. Salt and pepper to taste and blend well. Spread filling on noodles and roll up jelly roll fashion. Stand up in baking dish and pour the pesto sauce over all. Bake until bubbly, about 30 minutes. Serves 4-6.

Pesto Sauce:
2 cups basil leaves
2 cloves garlic
1 tsp. salt
3 oz. pine nuts
1 Tbsp. Parmesan cheese
1 Tbsp. Romano cheese
¾ to 1 cup olive oil

Place the basil, nuts and garlic in a food processor and turn to mush. Add the cheeses. Dribble in the oil. Mixture should be fairly thick when done. This will cover 2-3 lbs. of noodles and can be frozen.

After World War II, a night show featuring skiers carrying flares and fireworks and jumping through flaming hoops became part of the Winter Carnival; and during the 1940s the "Lighted Man" — Claudius Banks descending the hill with 100 pounds of battery-powered flashing lights and Roman candles — was added to the tradition.

Lulie's Lasagne

2 Tbsp. olive or salad oil
1 lb. ground beef or Italian sausage
1 onion, chopped
2 - 3 garlic cloves, minced
6 oz. can tomatoes
2 - 6 oz. cans tomato paste
2 tsp. oregano
1 ¾ tsp. salt
⅛ tsp. cayenne pepper
1 bay leaf
2 tsp. sugar
1 cup white wine
16 ozs. lasagna noodles
2 eggs, beaten
3 cups ricotta or cream style cottage cheese
½ cup grated Parmesan or Romano cheese
2 Tbsp. parsley flakes
1 tsp. salt
½ tsp. pepper
1 lb. mozzarella cheese, thinly sliced

In a large saucepan cook meat, onion, garlic and oil over medium heat until meat is well browned. Drain excess fat. Stir in chopped tomatoes with liquid, tomato paste, oregano, salt, pepper and bay leaf. Add sugar and enough white wine to reduce thickness. Reduce heat to low. Cover and simmer 35 minutes, stirring occasionally. Meanwhile, cook noodles as directed; drain. Combine eggs and remaining ingredients except mozzarella cheese. Layer 4 noodles in a greased 13" x 9" casserole dish. Spoon meat sauce over noodles. Place approximately 9 mounds of egg and cheese mixture over noodles, placing a slice of mozzarella over each mound. Repeat until casserole is full, about 4 layers. Bake, covered, at 375° about 30 minutes. Let stand 10 minutes before serving. Serves 8-10.

"I went up on Lookout Mountain (Woodchuck Hill near the present Colorado Mountain College) and read The Cricket on the Hearth.*"*

From the diary of
Lulie Margie Crawford
April 20, 1881

Savory Cannelloni

A great meal—serve with garlic bread,
salad and a nice dry white wine.

Sauce:
¼ cup butter
1 clove garlic, crushed
¼ cup flour
1 ½ tsp. instant chicken bouillon
⅛ tsp. white pepper
2 cups light cream or half and half
½ cup combined grated Parmesan and Romano cheese

Filling:
6 cannelloni shells
2 Tbsp. butter
3 Tbsp. sliced green onion
10 oz. package frozen spinach, thawed and well drained
1 cup cooked and finely chopped chicken
1 cup cooked and finely chopped ham
½ cup combined grated Parmesan and Romano cheese
2 eggs, beaten
¾ tsp. Italian seasoning
¼ tsp. pepper

To prepare sauce, sauté garlic in butter for 3 minutes. Stir in flour, chicken bouillon and pepper. Remove from heat. Gradually stir in cream. Bring to a boil over medium heat. Boil and stir for 1 minute. Reduce heat to low, stir in cheeses until melted. Set aside.

To prepare filling, parboil shells according to directions, rinse and drain. Sauté onions in butter until tender, about 3 minutes. Remove from heat; stir in remaining ingredients. Preheat oven to 350°. Fill shells. Place in a greased 2 quart rectangular baking dish. Spoon sauce over filled cannelloni. Bake for 20 minutes. Then broil several inches from source of heat for 5 minutes, or until sauce becomes golden and bubbles. Serve immediately. Serves 4.

Perry-Mansfield Manicotti

For vegetarian manicotti, substitute
mushrooms for the meat in this recipe.

1 lb. lean ground beef or turkey
½ cup chopped onion
2 - 3 cloves garlic, minced
4 cups canned tomato juice
6 oz. can tomato paste
1 tsp. oregano
1 tsp. sugar
1 tsp. salt or to taste
¼ tsp. pepper
1 tsp. basil or fennel seed
8 ozs. manicotti shells
3 cups grated mozzarella cheese
15 ozs. ricotta or cottage cheese
10 oz. package frozen chopped spinach, thawed and drained
2 eggs, beaten
½ cup grated Parmesan cheese

To prepare meat sauce, sauté together ground beef, onions and garlic.
Pour off fat. Add 2 cups tomato juice, tomato paste, spices and sugar.
Simmer while preparing filling. In a large bowl, combine 2 cups
mozzarella, ricotta, spinach, eggs, and Parmesan cheese. Mix well and
stuff into uncooked manicotti shells. Arrange in a greased 13"x 9"
baking dish. Spoon meat sauce over shells and pour over remaining
2 cups tomato juice. Cover with foil and bake at 350° for 1 hour. Top
with remaining mozzarella cheese and let stand 15 minutes before
serving. Serves 6-8.

*Perry-Mansfield
Camp in Strawberry
Park was founded by
Charlotte Perry and
Portia Mansfield
who pioneered pro-
fessional instruction
in dance theater and
horsemanship.*

Seafood

Seafood

Spicy Clams and Sausage

2 Tbsp. minced garlic
2 cups chopped onion
2 cups chopped sweet red pepper
½ lb. hot Italian sausage, crumbled
⅓ cup olive oil
1 ½ cups dry white wine
6 cups chicken or fish stock
2 cups fresh plum tomatoes, seeded and chopped
dried red pepper flakes to taste
5-6 dozen small to medium clams, cleaned and scrubbed
chopped parsley

In a large skillet, sauté garlic, onions, red pepper and sausage in oil until sausage is cooked. Add wine. Stir and scrape bottom of pan. Add stock and simmer until somewhat reduced, about 20-30 minutes. Add chopped tomatoes and pepper flakes. Can be prepared ahead of time to this point. Fifteen minutes before serving, add clams to boiling broth. Cover and cook 6-10 minutes, until clams have opened. Ladle clams and broth into bowls and sprinkle with parsley. Serves 4-6.

Littleneck clams work well in this recipe.

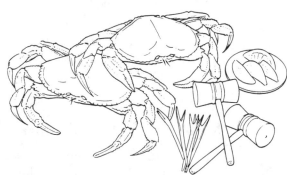

Crab Pilaf

6 slices bacon
2 medium onions, chopped
1 clove garlic, minced
½ lb. smoked ham, julienned
1 ripe tomato, peeled, seeded and chopped
3 Tbsp. tomato purée
1 lb. crabmeat
⅓ cup rum or cognac, warmed
1 cup dry white wine
2 Tbsp. chopped parsley
⅛ tsp. sugar
⅓ cup heavy cream

In a large skillet sauté bacon until crisp. Remove and crumble; set aside. Add onion and garlic to skillet. Cook over low heat until barely golden. Add ham and heat. Add tomato and cook down for about 5 minutes. Add tomato purée and crabmeat. Pour warmed liquor over and ignite. Shake to extinguish flame. Add wine, parsley and sugar. Simmer for 15 minutes. Add bacon and cream. Blend and heat through. Serve with rice. Serves 4-5.

Jalapeño Crab Cakes
Incredible crab cakes with a Mexican twist.

3 Tbsp. butter
3 shallots, finely chopped
2-3 jalapeño peppers, seeded and minced
⅔ cup finely chopped celery
2 large eggs, beaten
¾ cup heavy cream
1 cup fresh breadcrumbs
3 cups fresh crabmeat
1 Tbsp. Dijon mustard
2 Tbsp. fresh lemon juice
2 Tbsp. chopped cilantro
1 Tbsp. chopped parsley
salt and pepper to taste
flour
butter

Melt butter in small skillet. Sauté shallots until softened. Add jalapeños and cook for 2 minutes. Add celery and cook for 2 more minutes. Remove from heat and cool slightly. Stir vegetables into beaten eggs. Blend in next 8 ingredients. Chill for 2-4 hours. Form into 8 three inch cakes. If too dry, add a bit more cream. If too moist, add more breadcrumbs. Dust with flour and fry in melted butter 4 minutes on each side. Serve with lime and lemon wedges. Serves 4.

Soft Shelled Crabs
Soft shelled crabs are a real treat.
Be sure to try them during their short season.

12 fresh soft shelled crabs, cleaned
½ cup butter
flour
salt and pepper
juice of 1 lemon
½ cup dry white wine

Melt 2 Tbsp. butter in a large skillet. It may be necessary to use 2 skillets, as the crabs must be cooked in a single layer. Lightly dredge crabs in flour. When the butter is hot and foamy, add the crabs. Cover and cook for 1 minute. Sprinkle with salt and pepper and cook, covered, for 2 more minutes. Turn crabs. Add more butter, if necessary. Sprinkle with salt, pepper and lemon juice. Cover and cook 1 minute. Pour in wine and cook, uncovered for about 2 more minutes, basting frequently. Serve with lemon wedges. Serves 4-6.

Magnificent Mussels

A quick and succulent way to prepare mussels.

4 Tbsp. butter
½ cup minced onions
2 medium cloves garlic, minced
⅛ tsp. thyme
1 Tbsp. minced parsley
1 cup dry white wine
3 lbs. mussels, cleaned

Melt butter and cook onions, garlic, thyme and parsley until onions and garlic are soft. Add wine. Boil until liquid is reduced by ⅓. Add mussels, cover pot, and steam until shells are open, 5-7 minutes. Serve mussels and broth in bowls with French bread for dunking. Serves 4.

Coquilles St. Jacques Parisienne

1 cup dry white wine
1 bay leaf
4 shallots, finely chopped
2 lbs. bay scallops, or sea scallops, halved
1 lb. mushrooms, sliced
6 Tbsp. butter
6 Tbsp. flour
1 cup milk, boiling
4 egg yolks
1 cup creme fraiche or heavy cream
½ cup grated Gruyère
2 Tbsp. butter

Simmer first 3 ingredients in medium saucepan for about 5 minutes. Add scallops and mushrooms with enough water to cover all ingredients. Cover and simmer for 5 minutes. Remove scallops and mushrooms with a slotted spoon; set aside. Reduce cooking broth to about ¾ cup. Reserve. Melt butter in heavy saucepan. As soon as it begins to bubble, add flour and cook over low heat for 1 or 2 minutes, stirring constantly. Add milk and reserved broth to flour mixture. Bring to a boil and boil slowly, stirring constantly, for 2-3 minutes or until thickened. Mix yolks and cream and gradually add to sauce. Stir in mushrooms and scallops and spoon into buttered baking shells or a baking dish. Sprinkle with cheese and dot with butter. Broil until bubbly and cheese begins to brown. Serves 6.

Slalom Scallops

2 Tbsp. butter
2 cups chopped mushrooms
1 clove garlic, minced
4 green onions, chopped
1 lb. scallops
½ cup dry white wine
juice of ½ lemon
½ tsp. DaVinci Italian Seasoning
⅓ cup whipping cream

Sauté vegetables in butter. Add scallops. Stir and cook for 1 minute. Stir in wine, lemon juice and seasoning. Add cream and stir. Cook until scallops are done and sauce is thoroughly heated. Adjust seasonings before serving. Serves 4.

Chris McNeil moved to Steamboat when he was 6 months old and immediately learned to walk and ski. Jumping came next at age 6. A member of the U.S. jumping team from 1972-80, he placed 23rd in 70-meter jumping in the Lake Placid Olympics of 1980.

Scallop Creole

2 cups minced onions
1 cup minced celery
2 Tbsp. butter
1 ½ cups chopped green pepper
3 cloves garlic, minced
1 tsp. dried thyme
1 tsp. dried basil
½ tsp. cayenne pepper
½ tsp. black pepper
1 bay leaf
2 cups peeled, seeded, and chopped tomatoes
1 cup tomato sauce
½ cup dry white wine
½ tsp. sugar
Tabasco
salt
1 ¼ lbs. sea scallops, halved

Sauté onion and celery in butter over medium heat until onion is golden. Add green pepper and cook, stirring until softened. Add seasonings and bay leaf and cook, stirring for 1 minute. Add tomatoes, tomato sauce, wine, sugar. Add salt and Tabasco to taste. Simmer, stirring occasionally for 20 minutes. Add scallops and cook about 5 minutes until scallops are opaque and just firm. Serve over rice. Serves 4.

BBQ Shrimp

5 lbs. shrimp
1 ½ cups melted butter
Louisiana Tabasco Sauce to taste
½ tsp. black pepper
1 Tbsp. salt
1 tsp. paprika
1 tsp. onion salt
4 Tbsp. powdered BBQ spice
⅛ tsp. cayenne pepper
⅛ tsp. oregano
1 clove garlic, minced
1 onion, cut in half and thinly sliced
juice of 2 lemons

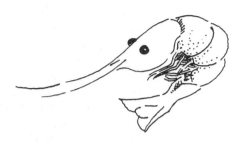

Lay shrimp flat in large baking pans. Combine remaining ingredients
and pour over shrimp. Bake at 350° for approximately 45 minutes.
Serve with French bread. Serves 8-10.

Hot Chinese Shrimp Stir Fry

6 Tbsp. oil
1 ½" piece ginger, peeled and chopped
6 cloves garlic, smashed and chopped
7 hot dried chili peppers or 1 tsp. red pepper flakes
1 ½ - 2 lbs. medium to large shrimp, peeled and deveined
¼ tsp. salt
2 Tbsp. rice wine or dry sherry
2 green onions, chopped
¼ cup water
1 tsp. sugar
4 ribs celery, sliced in ¼" pieces
1 sweet red pepper, julienned
1 bunch broccoli, flowerets only
2 Tbsp. cornstarch, dissolved in 2 Tbsp. water

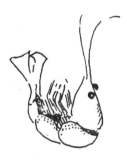

Heat oil in wok or skillet until very hot. Stir fry garlic and ginger for
30 seconds. Add peppers and stir fry for 30 seconds. Add shrimp and
salt. Stir fry for about 1 ½ minutes. Add wine and stir fry 30 seconds.
Add green onions and water. Stir occasionally for 2 minutes. Cover
and cook for 2 minutes. Uncover, add sugar and stir fry 45 seconds.
Add cornstarch, celery, pepper, and broccoli. Stir fry about 2 minutes
more until sauce thickens. Serve over rice.

Have all ingredients ready in small bowls before beginning. This
recipe also works well with cubed chicken breasts.

Shrimp Donatello a la Gallery

The Gallery was one of Steamboat's first great gourmet restaurants. This shrimp dish was their most requested recipe.

3 cups rice, cooked
2 ½ lbs. jumbo shrimp, peeled and deveined
5 qts. boiling salted water
8 oz. pkg. cream cheese, softened
5 ozs. Roquefort or Bleu cheese, crumbled
½ cup light cream
½ cup Madeira wine
1 Tbsp. chopped pimientos
1 tsp. anchovy paste
salt, pepper, Worcestershire sauce to taste
3 Tbsp. chopped clams
3 Tbsp. grated Parmesan cheese
Sherry wine

Place rice in bottom of casserole dish. Cook shrimp in water until just tender; place over cooked rice. Combine next 7 ingredients in mixing bowl; spread over top of shrimp. Bake at 375° until sauce bubbles. Sprinkle clams and Parmesan cheese over dish; brown under broiler. Sprinkle sherry over all. Serve immediately. Serves 4-6.

Grilled Shrimp

These are tasty served with salsa or a conventional cocktail sauce.

jumbo shrimp or tiger prawns, deveined and butterflied
fresh lemon juice
Old Bay Seasoning
dill seed
minced garlic

Cover shrimp with lemon juice. Sprinkle lightly with Old Bay and dill seed. Top with plenty of fresh minced garlic. Marinate for at least 4 hours. Grill on slow fire for approximately 10 minutes.

Baked Stuffed Shrimp

2 lbs. jumbo shrimp
5 Tbsp. butter
2 Tbsp. shallots, minced
¼ cup scallions, minced
1 green or red pepper, minced
1 cup bread crumbs
1 egg, beaten
½ to 1 tsp. cayenne pepper
pepper
salt

Shell, devein, and split shrimp open lengthwise, leaving tail intact.
Cook 6 shrimp in 3 Tbsp. butter until just pink. Finely chop cooked
shrimp. Add scallions, pepper and shallots to pan. Cook until almost
soft. Add remaining butter, melt. Remove pan from heat. Stir in
bread crumbs, chopped shrimp, remaining butter, egg and seasonings.
Stuff remaining shrimp with a heaping portion of stuffing. Bake in
a 400° oven for 8-12 minutes, until stuffing is lightly browned. Serve
hot, garnished with lemon wheels and parsley. Serves 4.

Shrimp Cakes with Chipotle Sauce

1 lb. raw, peeled and deveined shrimp
1 Tbsp. sugar
1 Tbsp. lemon juice
1 tsp. Worcestershire
1 Tbsp. mayonnaise
1 Tbsp. chopped parsley
1 Tbsp. baking powder
1 egg
2 slices white bread with crusts removed, finely chopped
½ medium red onion, finely diced
1 tsp. Dijon
½ tsp. black pepper

*Phippsburg, once named
Wilson, was renamed in
honor of Senator
Lawrence Phipps who
was instrumental in
bringing the railroad into
Northwest Colorado.*

In food processor, coarsely chop the raw shrimp. Turn into a mixing
bowl and add remaining ingredients. Mix thoroughly. Shape into
small patties and put in an oiled, hot sauté pan. Brown on both sides.
Serve with chipotle sauce.

Chipotle Sauce:
4 oz. sour cream
a few chipotles*, finely chopped
splash lemon juice

Blend all ingredients together. *Chipotles are very hot. Vary the
quantity according to personal taste.

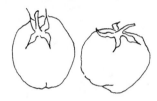

Calamari with Seafood Stuffing in Tomato Sauce

This recipe has been passed down through generations of an Italian family we know, and it is served as part of their traditional Christmas Eve feast.

Tomato Sauce:
#10 can whole tomatoes
2 Tbsp. basil
2 Tbsp. oregano
3 bay leaves
2 Tbsp. chopped garlic
salt and pepper
1 can anchovies (opt.)

Stuffing:
1 cup breadcrumbs
2 eggs
½ bunch fresh parsley, chopped
2 Tbsp. chopped garlic
1 lb. salad shrimp, crabmeat, or combination

24 whole squid, cleaned and prepared as pockets
(Ask your fish vendor to do this)

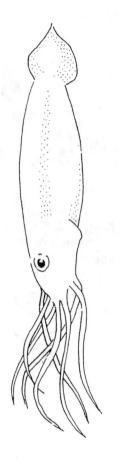

To prepare tomato sauce, drain tomatoes and purée in a food processor. Put tomatoes and remaining ingredients in a large pot and cook down over low heat.

To prepare stuffing, thoroughly combine all ingredients.

Stuff the squid pockets with the stuffing and secure the tops with toothpicks. Put the squid into the prepared tomato sauce and cook over low heat for 1 hour. Some of the squid may split open, but it will only enhance the sauce. Serves 8-12.

Zesty Broiled Fish

A fast and delicious dish for olive lovers.

12 Kalamata olives, chopped
6 Tbsp. chopped sun-dried tomatoes
2 Tbsp. sliced scallions
2 Tbsp. olive oil
juice of 1 lemon
6 fresh fish steaks or thick fillets (tuna, swordfish, etc.)

Combine first 5 ingredients and set aside. Broil fish about 5 minutes per side. During the last 2 minutes, top with olive mixture.

Lightning Fish

As quick and easy as the name implies.

Fish fillets (halibut, sole, cod, scrod)
dry white wine
mayonnaise
Parmesan cheese, grated
salt and pepper
paprika
garlic salt

Place fillets on a baking pan covered with foil. Sprinkle with wine. Spread with mayonnaise. Sprinkle liberally with Parmesan and spices to taste. Bake at 350° for 20 minutes. Broil until browned, about 3-5 minutes.

Anno's Famous Fish

fresh fish (yellow fin tuna or mahi mahi)
fresh lemon juice
1 tsp. soy sauce per serving
lemon pepper
Old Bay Seasoning
Italian herbs
dried basil
mayonnaise

Sprinkle fish liberally with lemon juice and soy sauce. Lightly cover each side of steak or fillet with the dry spices. Cover each side with mayonnaise. Grill over moderately hot coals, 3-4 minutes on each side. Fish may also be broiled.

Glazed Salmon

4 salmon steaks or fillets
¼ cup butter
¼ cup brown sugar, firmly packed
2 Tbsp. lemon juice
salt and pepper to taste
crushed red pepper flakes (optional)

In small saucepan, combine all ingredients except salmon and melt. Marinate salmon in glaze for 1 hour. Arrange salmon on lightly greased broiler pan. Brush with glaze. Broil 5" - 6" from heat, 8-10 minutes on each side or until fish flakes easily, brushing occasionally with remaining glaze. Place salmon on serving platter and spoon over any leftover glaze. Serve with lemon wedges. This dish is also great when cooked on a grill. Serves 4.

"Have just come in from covering up the plants on top of the house, and Ma from covering up the old fort. We all went fishing this morning and took our dinner (had eggs) and gathered wild onions and ate under a large tree. Ma fished some at the bluff but without any luck. Fine day."

From the diary of
Lulie Margie Crawford
April 26, 1881

Grilled Sesame Salmon

4 salmon steaks
juice of 1 lemon
¼ cup soy sauce
¼ cup sesame oil
1 Tbsp. freshly grated ginger
pepper

Place salmon in baking dish. Sprinkle with lemon juice, soy sauce, sesame oil, pepper and ginger. Cover and refrigerate overnight or at least 2 hours. Grill over hickory chips that have been soaked in water. Grill, covered, for 8 minutes per side. Garnish with lemon wedges. Serves 4.

Salmon Spuds

A great lunch or light dinner using leftover salmon.

1 lb. smoked salmon or leftover cooked salmon
4 baking potatoes (about 2 ½ lbs.)
½ cup milk
¼ cup butter
½ cup freshly grated Parmesan cheese
¼ cup minced green onion
1 tsp. thyme, crumbled
½ tsp. salt
dash black pepper
½ cup frozen peas, thawed

Wash, oil and prick skin of potatoes. Bake in 400° oven 1 hour or until soft. Cool enough to handle. Cut the tops off the potatoes lengthwise. Scoop out pulp being careful not to break potato skin. Mash potatoes. Heat milk and butter; beat into potatoes. Beat in cheese, onion, thyme, salt and pepper. Stir in salmon and peas. Spoon mixture into potato skins, mounding tops. Bake at 350° for 20 minutes. Serves 4.

Salmon Moose

30-50 lbs. salmon (must catch yourself)
2 heads garlic, outer skin peeled
4 cups Colorado butter
fistful of salt
2 cups low cholesterol cooking oil
1 cup Kashiwa teriyaki sauce

Butterfly salmon and remove bones and save. Mix remaining ingredients in blender or food processor. In a well ventilated area, place salt water soaked alder chips (from Washington) in an airtight smoker on hot charcoals so they will smoke a lot. Place salmon 24" above the heat, skin side down and smothered with sauce. Include the bones. After 1 hour, remove bones for hors d'oeuvres and add any remaining sauce. Cook should remain at smoker at all times. Cold beer helps!

Moose Barrows has been living and skiing in Steamboat since he was seven. One of the U.S. Ski Team's greatest downhillers, his "thrill of victory and agony of defeat" run in the Grenoble Olympics of '68 will never be forgotten. He displays the same wild abandon in preparing his famous smoked salmon.

Red Snapper in Parchment
These luscious packages are sure to be a hit!

parchment paper
3 Tbsp. butter
4 red snapper fillets or halibut, sole, cod, etc.
8 very small new red potatoes, halved (quartered if not too small)
2 medium carrots, cut in large julienne strips
½ cup chopped red onion
fresh thyme
fresh dill
salt and pepper
lemon juice
white wine

Cut 4 - 16" circles from parchment paper. Butter one side. Place a fish fillet on ½ of the buttered side of each circle. Divide vegetables evenly over fish. Sprinkle liberally with fresh herbs, salt and pepper to taste. Dot with remaining butter. Sprinkle with lemon juice and a bit of white wine. Fold over parchment and crimp edges to seal. Place packages on baking sheet and bake at 350° for 12 to 15 minutes or until parchment is puffed. Place packages on individual dinner plates and serve immediately. Serves 4.

Snapper Baked in Chili Cream

6 fresh green chilies or canned green chilies
3 Tbsp. unsalted butter, softened
3 Tbsp. flour
1 cup half and half
2 cups sour cream
2 cloves garlic, minced
salt and white pepper
3 lbs. red snapper fillets
all purpose flour for dredging)
3 Tbsp. butter
3 Tbsp. olive oil
1 cup grated Monterey Jack cheese
1 cup grated Cheddar cheese

Roast green chilies, if fresh, in a 450° oven until slightly blackened and blistered. Transfer to a paper bag. Tightly close bag and let sit for 15 minutes. Peel and seed chilies and cut into strips. Melt 3 Tbsp. butter in a large saucepan. Whisk in 3 Tbsp. flour and slowly add half and half; whisk in sour cream. Add salt, pepper and garlic. Simmer for 15 minutes, stirring occasionally. Dredge fish fillets in flour. Heat butter and oil in skillet. Add fillets and sauté about 4 minutes on each side. Remove fish from pan. Add chilies and heat thoroughly. Place fillets in a 13"x9" baking pan, add chilies on top, cover with sour cream mixture and top with cheeses. Bake until cheese is melted, about 10 minutes. Place under broiler if more browning is needed. Serve immediately. Serves 5 - 6.

Snapper Diablo

1 tsp. Old Bay Seasoning
1 tsp. cayenne pepper
1 tsp. white pepper
1 tsp. black pepper
1 tsp. garlic powder
1 tsp. Worcestershire sauce
1 tsp. A1 Steak Sauce
juice of 1 lemon
olive oil
4 fresh red snapper fillets, skinned and deboned
white wine
1 cup heavy cream

Combine first 9 ingredients in a shallow bowl, adding enough olive oil to make a liquid consistency. Heat a large sauté pan until very hot. Dip each fillet into bowl and coat fish on both sides. Sauté fish in pan until done, turning once. Remove fish to 4 individual serving plates. Deglaze sauté pan with white wine and add 1 cup heavy cream. Reduce until thick. Pour sauce over fish and serve with rice and steamed vegetables. Serves 4.

Sole Elegante
An elegant dinner that can be made in minutes.

4 sole fillets
1 cup cream
½ cup sherry
salt and pepper to taste
1 cup shrimp or lobster, cubed
1 cup green grapes

Poach fillets in cream and sherry for 6 minutes. Add salt and pepper
to taste. Remove to bake-proof flat dish. Arrange shrimp or lobster
with grapes on top. Cook sherry and cream down until thick. Cover
the fish and grapes with the sauce. Place the fish under the broiler for
several minutes, until sauce bubbles. Serve immediately, garnished
with parsley and fresh grapes. Serves 4.

Swordfish Oriental

4 cloves garlic, minced
1 Tbsp. fresh ginger, minced
1 tsp. dry mustard
¼ cup Chinese hot oil
¾ cup salad oil
juice of 1 lemon
2 Tbsp. rice wine vinegar
2 Tbsp. brown sugar
1 ½ lbs. fresh swordfish, mahi mahi, tuna, marlin or any steak-like fish

For the marinade, combine all ingredients except fish. Marinate fish
in ginger-soy mixture for 1-2 hours, refrigerated. Grill on hot grill for
4-5 minutes per side. Serve with vegetable brochettes which have been
marinated in the same ginger-soy marinade. Serves 2-4.

Marinade can be frozen and reused once or twice depending on the
freshness of the fish.

Snappy Swordfish Steaks
Marinade:
1 pkg. dry Italian Dressing Mix
3 cups olive oil

4-8 oz. swordfish steaks, ½" thick
4 slices Monterey Jack cheese
seasoned fine breadcrumbs (opt.)

Combine marinade ingredients and marinate fish, covered, refrigerated for 4 hours or more. Broil fish 10-12 minutes, turning once
during cooking. Place a slice of cheese on each steak and melt. If
desired, sprinkle breadcrumbs over cheese once melted and serve.
Serves 4.

Tropical Tuna with Coconut Sauce

4 tuna steaks
14 ozs. unsweetened coconut milk
1 Tbsp. vegetable oil
1 Tbsp. lemon grass
1 tsp. shallots, minced
1 tsp. shrimp sauce
2 tsp. fresh lime juice
1 tsp. minced fresh ginger
¼ tsp. chili oil or chili paste
salt and pepper to taste

Simmer coconut milk in heavy saucepan until reduced to about 1 cup, reserve. Heat oil in large skillet. Add shallots and lemon grass, sauté 1 minute. Add coconut milk, shrimp sauce, lime juice, ginger and chili oil. Bring to a boil. Season to taste. Prepare grill and grill tuna about 5 minutes per side. Transfer tuna to plates or serving platter and top with sauce. Serves 4.

Tuna Piquanté

2 Tbsp. olive oil
2 cups finely chopped tomatoes (or canned tomatoes in chunks)
5-8 cloves garlic, peeled
dried red pepper flakes, to taste
salt and pepper
coriander, cilantro or parsley
Hungarian paprika
4 fish steaks (tuna, sword, mahi mahi, tile, shark, etc.)

In an ovenproof baking dish, combine 1 Tbsp. olive oil, 1 cup tomatoes, hot pepper flakes and garlic cloves. Lay the fish on top. Sprinkle with salt and pepper. Put the remaining tomatoes on top of the fish along with chopped coriander. Make a mixture of 1 Tbsp. olive oil and a pinch or 2 of Hungarian paprika and smooth over the top with the back of a spoon. Cover with foil and cook for 5 minutes on top of stove to get everything hot. Uncover and bake at 400° for 15 minutes. Serves 4.

Vegetarian

Vegetarian Entrées

Broccoli Cheese Stromboli

6 dried mushrooms
1 medium onion, chopped
14 ½ oz. can Italian style or plain stewed tomatoes
½ cup chopped broccoli
½ tsp. Italian seasonings
¼ tsp. pepper
¼ cup chopped red or green sweet pepper
¼ cup sliced pitted black olives
10 oz. pkg. refrigerated pizza dough
1 cup grated low-fat mozzarella cheese
milk
sesame or poppy seeds

Soak dried mushrooms in enough warm water to cover for about 30 minutes or until rehydrated. Squeeze to drain thoroughly. Thinly slice mushrooms, discarding stems. For filling, in a medium skillet cook onion until tender. Stir in undrained tomatoes, broccoli, Italian seasonings, and pepper. Bring to a boil; reduce heat. Simmer, uncovered, about 15 minutes or until most of liquid has evaporated, stirring occasionally. Stir in sweet pepper, olives and mushrooms. Cool slightly. Spray a 15" x 10" x 1" baking pan with non-stick spray; set aside. On a lightly floured surface, roll pizza dough into a 14" x 12" rectangle. Cut dough into four 7" x 6" rectangles. Down the center of each triangle, spoon ¼ of filling. Sprinkle with cheese. Moisten the edges with milk. Bring the long edges together over filling; stretch and pinch to seal. Fold up ends and over seam; seal. Arrange rolls, seam side down, on the prepared baking pan. If desired, use hors d'oeuvre cutters to make 2-3 cutouts in tops or prick with a fork. Brush tops with milk; sprinkle with sesame or poppy seeds. Bake, uncovered, at 375° for 25-30 minutes, or until brown. Serves 4.

Rudy's Cheese Ravioli with Tomato Spinach Sauce

½ cup chopped walnuts
1 clove garlic, minced
3 Tbsp. oil
15 oz. can tomato sauce
10 oz. pkg. frozen chopped spinach, cooked and well drained
15 oz. pkg. frozen cheese ravioli, cooked and drained
2 Tbsp. grated Parmesan cheese

In a medium saucepan, sauté walnuts and garlic in oil until walnuts are lightly toasted. Stir in tomato sauce and spinach until well mixed; cook until heated through. Arrange hot ravioli in greased 11" x 7" baking dish. Pour sauce over ravioli; sprinkle with Parmesan. Broil 3 minutes or until cheese is lightly browned. Serves 4.

Snowshoes or skis were usually made of hickory, white pine, or spruce boards measuring 3-4 inches wide and eight to twelve inches long and secured by a toe and sometimes a heel strap.

Shiitake and Cheese Cannelloni

2 ozs. dried shiitake mushrooms (about 2 ½-3 cups)
1 ½ lbs. regular mushrooms, rinsed and ends trimmed
7 Tbsp. butter or margarine
1 clove garlic, minced or mashed
3 Tbsp. white wine vinegar
1 ½ Tbsp. soy sauce
⅔ cup dry sherry
4 ½ tsp. minced fresh ginger
1 ¼ tsp. dry mustard
1 ¾ tsp. ground coriander
¼ cup all purpose flour
1 ½ cups regular strength vegetable broth
¾ cup milk
¾ lb. muenster cheese, grated
8 egg roll wrappers, each about 6" square

Put shiitake mushrooms in warm water to cover; let stand for 20 minutes. Gently work softened shiitake mushrooms with your hands to release any grit, then lift them from water; discard water. Cut off and discard stems. Set aside 8 small shiitake caps. Thinly slice remaining shiitake and regular mushrooms. Melt 4 Tbsp. butter in a 5-6 qt. pan over medium high heat. Add sliced mushrooms and garlic; cook, stirring often, until liquid has evaporated and mushrooms are browned, about 25 minutes. Add vinegar, soy sauce, ⅓ cup sherry, 3 tsp. ginger, ¾ tsp. mustard, and 1 tsp. coriander. Cook, stirring, until liquid evaporates, about 5 minutes; set aside. In a 3-4 qt. pan over medium high heat, melt remaining 3 Tbsp. butter. Blend in flour, remaining ginger, mustard, and coriander; cook, stirring, until bubbly. Remove from heat and smoothly whisk in broth and milk. Return to heat and cook, stirring, until mixture reaches a rapid boil, about 3 minutes. Remove from heat and add 1 cup cheese and remaining sherry; stir until cheese melts. Stir 1 cup sauce into mushrooms.

Lay wrappers out flat. Along 1 end of each, spoon ⅛ of the mushroom mixture. To shape cannelloni, roll each wrapper to enclose filling. Spread ½ cup sauce in a 9" x 13" baking dish; add cannelloni, seams down, side by side. Spoon remaining sauce evenly over cannelloni to cover, then sprinkle with remaining cheese. Garnish with reserved shiitake caps. If made ahead, cool, cover, and chill as long as overnight. Bake, uncovered, at 425° for 10-12 minutes, or until sauce is bubbly. Serves 4.

Escarole and Cannellini with Pasta

1 bunch (about 1 ½ lbs.) escarole, cored and washed
2 cloves garlic, minced
2 Tbsp. oil, preferably olive
1 tsp. salt
16 oz. can tomatoes, cut up, undrained
20 oz. can cannellini (white kidney beans), undrained
2 cups cooked elbow macaroni
crushed red pepper
grated Parmesan cheese

Separate leaves on escarole, discarding tough outer ones. In a large kettle or large heavy pot, sauté garlic in oil until lightly browned. Add ½" water, salt and escarole. Bring to a boil; cover tight; reduce heat and simmer 15 minutes. Add tomatoes and cannellini. Simmer, uncovered, 5-10 minutes, or until escarole is tender. Stir in macaroni; simmer just until macaroni is heated. Serve with red pepper and Parmesan. Serves 4.

"Mr. Snook brought the mail down. Aunt Nannie and I went up to the bath house on snowshoes. Had about 50 falls off in the snow more or less. Had a good time though"

From the diary of
Lulie Margie Crawford
Jan. 17, 1881

Southwestern Beans and Rice

½ red bell pepper, cut into chunks
½ green bell pepper, cut into chunks
¼ yellow onion, cut into chunks
10 plum tomatoes, peeled and minced
8 Tbsp. cilantro, chopped
8 Tbsp. fresh oregano
1 Tbsp. cumin
2 Tbsp. chili powder
dash cayenne
8 cloves garlic, chopped
½ cup water
2 Tbsp. unsalted tomato paste
2 Tbsp. lemon juice
2 cups canned beans (kidney, chili, pinto, black)
10 green tomatillos, chopped
¾ cup red onion, chopped
3 cups cooked brown rice
¾ cup grated Cheddar cheese
4 Tbsp. chopped green onion

Sauté peppers and yellow onion. Add next 10 ingredients and mix well. Stir in beans and simmer 20 minutes on low heat. Add tomatillos and red onion. Pour over rice which has been placed in a casserole dish. Best if refrigerated at this point for 24 hours. Remove and top with cheese and green onion. Reheat in microwave or oven until heated through. Serves 4 as a main course, 6-8 as a side dish.

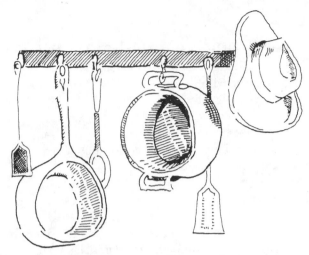

Black Bean Vegetable Chili

1 medium-sized eggplant, cut into ½" cubes
1 Tbsp. coarse (kosher) salt
½ cup olive oil
2 medium-sized yellow onions, peeled and cut into ¼" chunks
2 zucchini, cut into ¼" chunks
1 red bell pepper, seeded, cored and cut into ¼" chunks
4 large cloves garlic, peeled and coarsely chopped
8 ripe plum tomatoes, cut into 1" cubes
1 cup vegetable broth (use a vegetable bouillon cube)
1 cup chopped Italian parsley
½ cup slivered fresh basil leaves
3 Tbsp. chili powder
1 ½ Tbsp. ground cumin
1 Tbsp. dried oregano
1 tsp. freshly ground black pepper
½ tsp. crushed red pepper
salt to taste (opt.)
2 cups cooked black beans
1 ½ cups fresh corn kernels (removed from 2 cobs)
½ cup chopped fresh dill
¼ cup lemon juice
sour cream (garnish)
grated Monterey Jack cheese (garnish)
3 scallions, thinly sliced (garnish)

Place eggplant in colander; toss with salt and let sit for 1 hour to remove moisture. Pat dry. Heat ¼ cup olive oil in a large casserole. Sauté onions, zucchini, peppers and garlic for 10 minutes. Place remaining ¼ cup oil in a skillet. Over medium high heat, cook eggplant until just tender, about 10 minutes. Remove with slotted spoon to casserole. Add tomatoes, broth, ½ cup parsley, basil and spices. Cook over low heat for 30 minutes, stirring occasionally. Add black beans, corn, dill and lemon juice. Cook additional 15 minutes. Adjust seasonings and stir in remaining ½ cup parsley. Serve hot, garnished with a generous dollop of sour cream and/or Monterey Jack cheese and sliced scallions. Serves 8.

Italian Artichoke Pie

eggs, beaten
oz. pkg. cream cheese with chives, softened
/4 tsp. garlic powder
½ cups grated mozzarella cheese
cup ricotta cheese
½ cup mayonnaise or salad dressing
3 ¾ oz. can artichoke hearts
cup cooked garbanzo beans
½ cup pitted black olives
oz. jar diced pimientos, drained
Tbsp. snipped parsley
unbaked 9" pastry shell
⅓ cup grated Parmesan cheese
tomato slices, halved

Combine first 3 ingredients and ¼ tsp. pepper. Stir in 1 cup mozzarella and next 2 ingredients. Drain artichokes; quarter 2 hearts; reserve. Chop remaining hearts; fold into cheese mixture along with next 4 ingredients. Turn into pastry shell. Bake at 350° for 30 minutes. Top with remaining cheeses. Bake 15 minutes more until set. Let stand 10 minutes. Top with quartered artichokes and tomato. Serves 8.

In Brown's Park, Fort Davy Crockett served the fur trade from 1837-1841. Jim Baker, Kit Carson and Joe Meed "over-wintered" there. Located on The Outlaw Trail between Hole in the Wall (Wyoming) and Robber's Roost (Utah), this park became a haven for "bad-men" and free range cattle operations and outlaws flourished.

Spinach and Orzo Pie

2 eggs, beaten
3 cups cooked orzo (1 ½ cups uncooked)
15 ½ oz. jar chunky spaghetti sauce
⅓ cup grated Parmesan cheese
10 oz. pkg. frozen chopped spinach, cooked and drained
½ cup ricotta cheese
¼ tsp. ground nutmeg
½ cup grated Fontina or mozzarella cheese

In a medium bowl, combine eggs, cooked orzo, ½ cup spaghetti sauce and Parmesan cheese. Spread mixture over bottom and up sides of a greased 9" pie plate to form a shell. Stir together spinach, ricotta cheese and nutmeg. Spoon into bottom of pasta-lined plate. Spread remaining spaghetti sauce over filling. Cover edge of pie with foil. Bake at 350° for 30 minutes. Remove from oven and top with grated cheese. Return to oven and bake for 3-5 minutes more or until cheese is melted. Transfer to a wire rack; let stand for 5 minutes before serving. Serves 6.

Vegetable and Cheese Phyllo Pie

½ cup chopped onion
2 cloves garlic, minced
1 tsp. vegetable oil
10 oz. pkg. cauliflower, chopped, thawed and drained
10 oz. pkg. frozen spinach, chopped, thawed and drained
8 oz. carton part skim ricotta cheese
4 ozs. Cheddar cheese, grated
¼ cup Italian breadcrumbs
3 eggs
2 tsp. Italian seasoning
1 tsp. black pepper
¾ tsp. cayenne pepper or to taste
butter flavored vegetable cooking spray
12 sheets frozen phyllo pastry, thawed

Sauté onion and garlic in oil; transfer to large bowl. Add next 9 ingredients and mix well; set aside. Coat a round cake pan with cooking spray. Place 1 phyllo sheet in pan (keep remaining phyllo covered). Coat phyllo with cooking spray. Layer 7 more sheets on first sheet, coating each layer with cooking spray, and fanning each slightly to the right. Gently press into pan forming a large shell; fill with vegetable cheese mixture. Top with 5 more sheets, coating each with spray and fanning slightly to the right. Tuck top sheets down around filling. Fold edges over top to enclose filling. Spray top with cooking spray. Bake, uncovered, at 400° for 25 minutes. Cover and bake an additional 35 minutes. Let stand 15 minutes. Remove from pan. Serve warm. Serves 8.

Summer Vegetable Bake

1 lb. small zucchini, thinly sliced
4-5 medium ears corn, corn removed from cob (2 ½-3 cups)
¾ cup chopped green peppers
3 medium tomatoes, peeled and coarsely chopped
2 Tbsp. vegetable oil
1 tsp. salt (opt.)
¼ tsp. pepper
1 onion, chopped
1 clove garlic, chopped or ½ tsp. garlic powder
1 tsp. Italian seasoning
1 ½ cups cubed bread
½ cup grated part skim mozzarella cheese

In flameproof casserole, cook first 10 ingredients over medium heat for 10-12 minute, or until zucchini and corn are just cooked. Sprinkle vegetables with bread and cheese and bake at 350° until cheese melts and bread is crisp, 20-30 minutes. Serve hot. Serves 6.

Dill Gulch Zucchini Pie

7 ½ cups grated unpeeled zucchini
1 medium onion, chopped
2 Tbsp. butter
1 lb. Feta cheese, rinsed, drained and crumbled
½ cup chopped fresh dill or 3 Tbsp. chopped fresh parsley
   and 2-3 Tbsp. dried dill
3 eggs, beaten
½ tsp. nutmeg
pinch pepper
½ cup fine breadcrumbs
14 phyllo leaves
½ cup melted butter or margarine

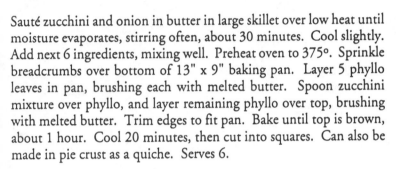

Sauté zucchini and onion in butter in large skillet over low heat until moisture evaporates, stirring often, about 30 minutes. Cool slightly. Add next 6 ingredients, mixing well. Preheat oven to 375º. Sprinkle breadcrumbs over bottom of 13" x 9" baking pan. Layer 5 phyllo leaves in pan, brushing each with melted butter. Spoon zucchini mixture over phyllo, and layer remaining phyllo over top, brushing with melted butter. Trim edges to fit pan. Bake until top is brown, about 1 hour. Cool 20 minutes, then cut into squares. Can also be made in pie crust as a quiche. Serves 6.

Green and Gold Casserole

2 pkgs. (16) refrigerated crescent rolls
½ cup grated Parmesan cheese
1 ¼ lbs. zucchini (3-4 medium), halved lengthwise and sliced ¼" thick
3 cups sliced fresh mushrooms
1 large onion, halved lengthwise and sliced
16 oz. carton dairy sour cream
¼ cup all purpose flour
¼ tsp. salt
⅛ tsp. pepper
6 oz. jar marinated artichoke hearts, drained and chopped
1 cup grated Monterey Jack cheese

International Camp, the first gold camp in Routt County (near the present town of Hahns Peak) was established to house miners who called it "Bug Town" because of the big bugs.

Lightly grease a 13" x 9" x 2" baking pan. Unroll 1 package crescent rolls; press evenly in pan to cover bottom, sealing perforations. Sprinkle with ¼ cup Parmesan cheese. Bake at 350º for 10-15 minutes, or until golden. Meanwhile, place zucchini, mushrooms and onion in a large steamer basket over boiling water. Cover; steam 8-10 minutes or until crisp-tender. Remove; set aside. In a large bowl, stir together sour cream, flour, salt and pepper. Stir in zucchini mixture and artichokes. Turn into pan; spread evenly over crust. Top with Monterey Jack cheese. Unroll remaining crescent rolls; separate into triangles. Arrange on top of cheese. Sprinkle with remaining Parmesan. Bake at 350º for 30-40 minutes, or until top is golden and filling is heated through. Serves 10-12 as side dish.

Hearty Spinach and Tofu Risotto

8 ozs. tofu, drained
1 medium onion, chopped (½ cup)
1 clove garlic, minced
2 Tbsp. cooking oil
14 ½ oz. can Italian tomatoes, cut up
1 tsp. dried oregano, crushed
2 cups cooked brown rice
10 oz. pkg. frozen chopped spinach, thawed and drained
½ cup grated Swiss cheese
1 Tbsp. toasted sesame seeds

Place tofu in blender, cover, blend until smooth. In a large saucepan, cook onion and garlic in hot oil until onion is tender. Add undrained tomatoes and oregano. Bring to boiling; reduce heat. Simmer, uncovered, about 3 minutes. Stir in tofu, rice, spinach, ¼ cup cheese, ½ tsp. salt, and ¼ tsp. pepper. Divide mixture into 4 individual greased casseroles or place all the mixture in a greased 1 ½ qt. casserole. Bake, uncovered, at 350° for 30 minutes or heated through. Top with remaining cheese and sesame seeds. Serves 4.

David Moffat built the famous Moffat Tunnel which connected Denver to Salt Lake City. This project required many people with varied skills to complete the massive project to forge the Continental Divide.

Vegetable Tabbouleh

1 cup bulgar
1 cup cold water
1 cup canned water chestnuts, drained and chopped
    OR 1 cup peeled chopped jicama
½ cup minced green onion
½ cup chopped carrot
⅓ cup minced fresh mint
¼ cup each olive oil and lemon juice
salt
small Romaine leaves, washed and crisped (garnish)
mint sprigs (garnish)

In a strainer, rinse bulgar well; drain. In a bowl, combine bulgar with cold water and let stand until grain is soft to bite, about 1 hour. Drain off any remaining liquid. Mix bulgar with water chestnuts, green onion, carrot, mint, oil and lemon juice. Add salt to taste. Spoon into a wide, shallow bowl and garnish with Romaine and mint sprigs. Serves 6-8.

Eggplant Parmesan

1 large eggplant
2 eggs
½ cup seasoned flour (flour plus ½ tsp. black pepper)
vegetable oil to cover bottom of automatic frying pan
1 large clove garlic, thinly sliced
¾ lb. Mozzarella, thinly sliced
½ cup grated Parmesan cheese

Tomato Sauce:
1 - 1 lb. can (2 cups) tomatoes
2 - 6 oz. cans (1 ⅓ cups) tomato paste
1 clove garlic, minced
1 Tbsp. chopped parsley
1 Tbsp. basil
1 tsp. salt (optional)

Beat the eggs slightly. Mix the flour well with the black pepper. Peel and slice the eggplant in ¼" to ⅜" slices. Sauté the thinly sliced garlic in the oil on low temperature; the garlic should become transparent but should not brown. Remove garlic and set aside. Dredge the eggplant in the beaten egg and then in the flour. Sauté the dredged eggplant in the pan, turning it once so that it is golden brown on both sides. Remove each layer as it is cooked, and blot well with paper towels and set aside. If you need to add oil (you probably will), place the sautéed garlic back in the pan to flavor the new oil. (Do not substitute garlic salt.)

Very lightly oil a 9" x 12" x 2" baking pan. Layer the eggplant, the mozzarella cheese, the tomato sauce, and the grated Parmesan, mixing the last layer of tomato sauce and Parmesan together. You should get about three layers. Bake for about 45 minutes in a 350° oven, or until it bubbles. Let it stand for about 10 minutes after cooking. Serve with tossed salad and hard rolls.

Spaghetti Squash Lasagne

1 medium spaghetti squash
1 lb. ricotta cheese
½ lb. grated mozzarella cheese
1 6-oz. can black olives, sliced
¼ lb. mushrooms, sliced and sauteed
16 oz. can whole tomatoes, drained
Parmesan cheese
basil, oregano, garlic, salt, pepper to taste or
dill, garlic, salt, pepper to taste

Cook and remove insides of squash. Put in a large bowl and combine with remaining ingredients. Mix well. Put into a large greased baking dish. Sprinkle top with Parmesan cheese. Bake at 350 for 45 minutes, until bubbly. Serves 6.

Cream Cheese and Mushroom Enchiladas

½ cup onion, chopped
1 clove garlic, minced
1 Tbsp. cooking oil
28 oz. can tomatoes, cut up
1 Tbsp. honey
1 Tbsp. chili powder
½ tsp. ground cumin
½ tsp. ground coriander
dash ground red pepper
12 ozs. fresh mushrooms, sliced
2 ¼ oz. can black olives, sliced
2 Tbsp. butter or margarine
8 oz. pkg. cream cheese, cut up
1 cup sour cream
¾ cup green onions, thinly sliced
8 - 7" flour tortillas
1 large can black olives, sliced
¾ cup Monterey Jack cheese or Monterey Jack with jalapeño peppers, grated

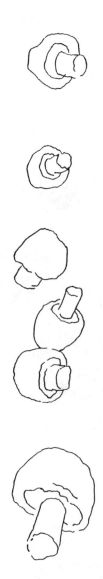

Cook onion and garlic in hot oil until tender. Stir in undrained tomatoes, honey, 1 tsp. of the chili powder, cumin, coriander and pepper. Bring to a boil, reduce heat, simmer, uncovered, about 30 minutes, stirring occasionally. Set aside. In a small saucepan, cook mushrooms and the remaining chili powder in butter on medium heat about 10 minutes until mushrooms are tender. Reduce heat. Stir in cream cheese until melted, mix in sour cream and green onions. Dip 1 side of each tortilla in the juice of the tomato mixture. Spoon ⅓ cup of the cheese mixture onto center of the dry side of each tortilla. Sprinkle black olives, dividing equally, over cheese mixture on each tortilla. Roll up; place seam side down, in a greased 12" x 7 ½" baking dish. Spoon tomato mixture over tortillas. Cover and bake at 350° about 30 minutes or until heated through on the top shelf of your oven. Top with cheese. Bake, uncovered, 4-5 minutes or until cheese melts. Serves 5.

Wheat and Lentil Pilaf

6 oz. wheat pilaf mix
19 oz. can lentil soup
1 ⅔ cups water

Combine all ingredients in a baking dish. Bake at 375° for 1 hour. Serves 4-6 as a side dish.

Vegetables & Side Dishes

Vegetables & Side Dishes

Tomato Halves with Bleu Cheese

Great with baked chicken or grilled chops.

6 medium tomatoes (about 2 lbs.)
¼ cup butter
6 ozs. Bleu cheese, crumbled
¼ cup half and half
2 Tbsp. finely chopped parsley
½ tsp. salt
¼ tsp. pepper

Preheat oven to 250°. Halve tomatoes crosswise. Melt butter in 10" skillet over medium-high heat. Add tomatoes, cut side down; cook 3 minutes. Turn tomatoes over; cook 2-3 minutes. Remove to serving platter; keep warm in oven. Stir cheese, half and half, parsley, salt and pepper into skillet. Cook over medium heat, whisking constantly until smooth and bubbling slightly. Pour over tomatoes and serve hot. Serves 6.

Brooklyn Broiled Tomatoes

¼ cup mayonnaise
¼ cup freshly grated Parmesan cheese
¼ cup minced shallots or green onions
2 Tbsp. minced parsley
2-3 large ripe tomatoes, sliced into thirds or halved

Preheat broiler. Combine all ingredients except tomatoes and blend well. Gently spread mixture about ¼" thick on tomatoes. Broil 4 inches from heat for 2-3 minutes, or until lightly browned. Watch carefully. Serve immediately. Serves 6.

By the 1900s, a number of saloons and "fancy houses" had sprung up on the unincorporated south side of the river across from the town of Steamboat Springs. Residents dubbed this "red light district" Brooklyn. It consisted of one unnamed street lined with saloons and Hazel McGuire's popular parlor. Changes in the state liquor laws closed all of the saloons by 1914.

Spinach Souffle

8 oz. pkg. cream cheese
1 pt. sour cream
3-4 eggs
1 pkg. dry onion soup mix
2 pkgs. frozen spinach, thawed, drained and chopped
1 cup grated Sharp Cheddar cheese

Mix cream cheese, sour cream and eggs in a food processor or mixer. Transfer to a mixing bowl. Blend in soup and spinach and mix well. Pour mixture into a greased 1 quart casserole. Sprinkle cheese on top. Bake at 350° for 1 hour. Serves 4-6.

Oriental Celery Sauté

Great with an oriental entrée.

¼ cup butter
2 cups sliced celery, (slice diagonally)
½ cup sliced green onions
1 cup sliced mushrooms
8 oz. can sliced water chestnuts
¼ cup sliced almonds
salt and pepper

Melt butter in a large skillet. Add remaining ingredients. Sauté about 5 minutes or until crisp and tender. Serves 4.

Cross Country Carrots

Kids love these and it's an easy dish for guests.

"We had cucumber for dinner—first one for Steamboat Springs."

From the diary of
Lulie Margie Crawford
Aug. 17, 1881

1 lb. carrots, peeled
1 cup water
1 ½ tsp. salt
1 ½ Tbsp. honey
½ tsp. nutmeg
1 Tbsp. butter, softened
salt and pepper to taste

Cut carrots on the diagonal in ½" thick slices. Place in a saucepan with water and salt. Bring to a boil. Cover and simmer about 15 minutes, or until just tender. Drain. Return carrots to pot, add remaining ingredients, and heat through. You may add 1 Tbsp. freshly grated ginger and 2 Tbsp. lime juice for an interesting variation. Serves 4-6.

Carrots Madeira

1 ½ lbs. carrots, sliced diagonally
1 Tbsp. butter
½ cup chicken stock
2 egg yolks
⅓ cup Madeira wine
2 Tbsp. chopped parsley
1-2 tsp. honey

Sauté carrots in butter 10 minutes or until crisp-tender. Add chicken stock, cover, and simmer 5-7 minutes. Beat egg yolks and Madeira. Slowly stir into carrots, and cook on low heat for a few minutes. Do not boil. Transfer to serving dish and garnish with parsley. Serves 6.

Sweet-Sour Cucumbers

2 cucumbers, peeled
¼ cup sugar
½ cup vinegar
½ tsp. salt
¼ tsp. black pepper
¼ tsp. dried tarragon, crushed
¼ tsp. dried parsley

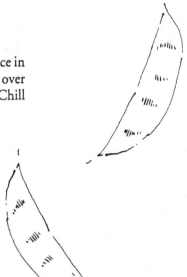

Score cucumbers lengthwise with a fork and slice paper thin. Place in a plastic storage container and pour remaining ingredients over cucumbers. Cover with a tight fitting lid and shake to mix. Chill several hours. Makes 6 servings.

Snow Pea Sauté

1 lb. snow peas
1 clove garlic, minced
2 Tbsp. olive oil
1 red bell pepper, thinly sliced lengthwise
1 tsp. basil
freshly ground salt and pepper

Break off stems of snow peas and remove strings. Sauté garlic 2 minutes in hot oil. Add red pepper and sauté 5 minutes. Add snow peas, sauté about 4-5 minutes. Snow peas should retain their bright color and still have crunch. Add basil and freshly ground salt and pepper and stir. Serve immediately.

Lemon Green Beans with Almonds

2 lbs. fresh green beans
4 quarts boiling water
1 ½ tsp. salt
juice of 1 lemon
1 cup toasted almonds
2-3 Tbsp. butter
salt and pepper

Clean and trim beans. Drop beans into boiling salted water. Cook beans for 15 minutes or until tender crisp. Drain beans. Toss beans with butter and lemon juice over very low heat until butter is melted. Toss in toasted almonds. Season to taste with salt and pepper. Serves 8.

Sesame Green Beans

1 lb. fresh green beans
1 Tbsp. vegetable oil
pinch of nutmeg
4 large mushrooms, sliced or ¼ cup almonds, sliced
1 Tbsp. sesame seeds

Steam the green beans until tender crips. Combine the oil and nutmeg in a large skillet over medium heat. Add mushrooms and sauté until tender. Add green beans and mix lightly. Add sesame seeds and toss. Serves 4-6.

Marinated Green Beans

1 lb. green beans, steamed until tender crisp
2 cups sliced mushrooms
1 cup chopped red cabbage
½ cup chopped onion
2 tsp. minced garlic
½ cup Italian dressing

Combine all ingredients. Refrigerate 2-3 hours or until chilled throughout. Serves 6.

Green Beans with Artichoke

1 lb. green beans
2 small jars marinated artichoke hearts

Clark began as a stage stop in the early 1800s. The Clark community consisted of various sawmills, a blacksmith shop, and a community hall built by Woodsman of the Year in 1912.

Break beans into ½"-¾" pieces. Cook in boiling water until crisp tender. Drain and return to pan. Toss with artichoke hearts with their oil. Heat through and serve. Serves 4.

Clark Corn Souffle

½ cup flour
1 ½ tsp. baking powder
2 cups milk
3 large eggs, beaten until frothy
15 oz. can creamed corn
salt
2 Tbsp. sugar

Mix flour, baking powder and milk with a wire whisk. Add beaten eggs; stir in corn, salt and sugar. Pour into buttered casserole or souffle dish. Bake at 375° for 1 ½ hours. Serves 6-8.

Macque Choux

A Cajun corn dish of Indian and Spanish influence.

24 ears fresh corn or 8 cups frozen
1 cup butter
2 medium onions, diced
2 large bell peppers, diced
6 large ripe tomatoes or 1 lb. can whole tomatoes, diced
2 tsp. salt
2 tsp. black pepper
1 tsp. cayenne pepper
1 tsp. white pepper
1 cup water or chicken stock

Shuck corn and cut off cob, reserving as much corn milk as possible. (The best way to do this is to remove the kernels in two cuts and run knife along cob to force out juices.) Melt butter in large skillet or saucepan. Add onions and bell peppers and sauté until transparent over medium heat. Add corn and stock and bring to a boil. Add tomatoes and seasonings and reduce heat. Cover and simmer for 45 minutes or until tender. Serve with rice. Serves 6-8. This dish can also be served as a main dish by adding chicken or shrimp. If using chicken, brown chicken and then sauté vegetables. Add back in before stewing. If using shrimp, add peeled shrimp while stewing.

Jalapeño Corn Casserole

Great to serve with a Mexican entrée.

2 - 16 oz. cans white or yellow corn, drained
8 oz. container cream cheese with chives and onions
3-4 fresh jalapeño peppers, seeded and chopped or 4 oz. can chopped

Preheat oven to 350°. Combine all ingredients in a greased 1 ½ quart casserole. Bake, covered, for about 30 minutes or until heated through. Serves 6-8.

Werner's Holiday Sauerkraut

A Steamboat tradition.

2 - 1 qt. jars sauerkraut, drained
3 small potatoes, peeled and diced
4 smoked pork chops, cubed
1 Tbsp. caraway seeds
1 apple, peeled and diced
2 - 10 oz. cans chicken broth
1 Tbsp. brown sugar

Combine all ingredients except brown sugar in slow cooker or crock pot. Simmer on low heat all day. Add sugar to taste before serving. Serves 10-12.

"Skeeter" Werner, first-born of the three Werner Olympians, began skiing when she was one and was the "Queen of the Junior Nationals Circuit" by the time she was in high school. "Skeeter," placing 10th, had the highest American finish in the Cortina downhill in the '56 Olympics.

Chilled Yogurt Asparagus

1 ½ lbs. fresh asparagus
Dressing:
1 cup plain non-fat yogurt
2 tsp. minced fresh parsley
1 tsp. Dijon mustard
2 tsp. snipped fresh chives
½ tsp. dried crumbled tarragon leaves
½ tsp. sugar
¼ tsp. paprika
cayenne pepper to taste
dash of salt (opt.)

Steam asparagus to tender crisp. Cut into 2" pieces and chill
Combine dressing ingredients, mix and refrigerate for 1 ½ hours o⟩
longer. When ready to serve, toss asparagus with yogurt dressing, serve
on bed of lettuce and garnish with parsley.

"Another New Year and this time we are at Steamboat Springs— home. It has been snowing all day, but now the stars are shining. Dave came in with the mail. He brought bad news. One of the mail carriers is lost and hasn't been seen or heard of since last Tuesday. Was lost in that dreadful hard storm. Poor fellow! Pa received a letter from Elmer saying the cattle and horses are doing well."

From the diary of
Lulie Margie Crawford
Jan. 1, 1881

Asparagus Oriental

1 ½ lbs. fresh asparagus, tender part only*
salt and pepper
3 Tbsp. butter
1 Tbsp. soy sauce
2 tsp. lemon juice

Rinse asparagus under cold water. Cut stalks into thin diagonal slices.
Place in a skillet in a single layer. Sprinkle with salt and pepper. Add
water to the skillet to a depth of ¼". Cover and cook on high heat.
After the water boils, cook 2 minutes or until asparagus is tender crisp.
Combine remaining ingredients in a small saucepan and bring to a
boil. Remove from heat. Drain asparagus and put in serving dish.
Pour sauce over asparagus and toss well. Serve immediately. Serves 6.
*Grasp asparagus spears lightly at both ends and gently bend. The
spear will snap, separating the tender from the tough.

Pepper Sautéed Broccoli

2 lbs. broccoli, cut into spears
2 Tbsp. olive oil
1 small red bell pepper, minced
salt and pepper to taste

Steam broccoli until tender-crisp. Heat oil in a large skillet, quickly
sauté red pepper for a few moments. Add broccoli, salt and pepper and
heat through. Serves 6-8. Broccoli may be steamed and refrigerated
one day ahead.

Broccoli with Almonds in Cream

3 cups chopped broccoli, cooked and drained
3 Tbsp. chopped onions, cooked with broccoli
¼ cup butter
¼ cup flour
1 cup light cream (half and half)
¾ cup hot water
1 beef bouillon cube
2 Tbsp. cooking sherry
2 Tbsp. fresh lemon juice
pepper to taste
1 cup grated Sharp Cheddar cheese
¼ cup blanched almonds

Arrange cooked broccoli and onions in a 9" shallow quiche pan. In a small saucepan, melt butter and blend in flour. When mixture is smooth, add cream and hot water in which bouillon cube has been dissolved. Stir constantly until mixture is smooth and thickened. Add sherry, lemon juice and pepper. Add half the cheese. When all is blended, pour sauce over broccoli and sprinkle with remaining cheese and almonds. Bake at 350° for 20 minutes. Serves 6. Parmesan cheese may be used instead of Sharp Cheddar. Use only ¼ cup and only sprinkle on top.

Broccoli Helene with Lime Sauce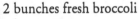

2 bunches fresh broccoli
salt
2 cups mayonnaise
2 cups sour cream or plain yogurt
⅓ cup lime juice
1 Tbsp. lime zest
2 tsp. horseradish
2 tsp. Dijon mustard
½ tsp. salt

Cut broccoli into spears and cook in boiling salted water 12-15 minutes or until tender-crisp. Immediately plunge into ice water; drain and refrigerate. To prepare lime sauce, combine remaining ingredients. Serve broccoli with a dollop of sauce and a sprinkling of lime zest. Serves 6-8.

Cauliflower Gratineé

1 head cauliflower
1 ½ cups warm beer and 1 chicken bouillon cube
OR 6 ozs. beer and 6 ozs. chicken stock
½ cup seasoned breadcrumbs
¼ cup grated Parmesan cheese
⅛ tsp. salt
⅛ tsp. pepper
½ cup Monterey Jack cheese

Place whole cauliflower, beer and bouillon in covered pot and steam for 15-20 minutes, until tender. Remove from pot and put in baking dish. Pour in liquid from steaming. Sprinkle cauliflower with remaining ingredients. Place under broiler for 2-3 minutes, until cheese melts. To serve, slice cauliflower like a cake. Serves 6.

Tangy Mustard Cauliflower

1 medium cauliflower
¼ cup water
½ cup light mayonnaise
1 tsp. finely chopped onion or dried minced onion
1 tsp. mustard, dried or prepared
½ cup grated part-skim mozzarella cheese
¼ tsp. salt (opt.)

Place whole cauliflower and water in a 1 ½ quart casserole. Microwave, covered, 9 minutes on high. Combine remaining ingredients in small bowl. Spoon onto cauliflower and microwave 1 ½ - 2 minutes to heat topping and melt cheese. Let stand 2 minutes. Serves 6.

Brussels Sprouts & Red Grapes

A succulent twist to a traditional
Thanksgiving vegetable.

2 pints Brussels sprouts, trimmed and halved lengthwise
2 cups seedless red grapes
2 ½ Tbsp. unsalted butter
1 Tbsp. fresh lemon juice
½ tsp. salt
¼ tsp. freshly ground black pepper

In a steamer basket, steam the Brussels sprouts, covered, until tender (approximately 15 minutes). Add the grapes and steam 1 minute longer. Drain well. Put the Brussels sprouts and grapes in a serving bowl. Add the butter, lemon juice, salt and pepper. Toss well. Serves 6-8.

Eggplant au Gratin

1 medium eggplant
1 large onion, chopped
¼ cup butter
½ lb. Sharp Cheddar cheese, grated
2 eggs
cracker crumbs
butter
salt and pepper to taste
paprika or fresh parsley (garnish)

Peel, chop and boil eggplant in slightly salted water until soft. Drain water, making sure to squeeze all excess water out. Mash eggplant. Sauté onions in 2 Tbsp. butter. Beat eggs and grated cheese together. Combine eggplant, onion, eggs and cheese. Place in a greased casserole dish. Cover with crumbs. Salt and pepper and dot with remaining butter. Bake at 350° for 45 minutes. Garnish with paprika and/or fresh parsley. Serves 4-6.

Cyclone Eggplant

A good vegetable dish to accompany Chinese food.

8 oz. sweet Italian sausage
2 tsp. soy sauce
¼ tsp. ground ginger
¼ tsp. black pepper
1 Tbsp. cornstarch
1 Tbsp. finely chopped scallions
1 tsp. curry powder
1 tsp. dry sherry or Vermouth (opt.)
½ tsp. sugar (opt.)
4-5 small, narrow Japanese eggplants or 1 lb. regular eggplant
2 eggs, well beaten
1 cup lightly seasoned breadcrumbs

Chop sausage a few times to loosen. Place in a bowl, add the seasonings and the cornstarch in the order listed, stir until well-mixed. The consistency will be on the dry side. Cut off the stems and peel the eggplants. Cut crosswise into ¼" thick slices. Spread meat mixture between two slices of eggplant to make a sandwich. Roll in the egg and then in the breadcrumbs, coating well. Place singularly on a plate until ready to deep fry. The above can be done several hours in advance; cover and refrigerate. They can also be prepared and frozen to use at a later date. When ready to cook, heat 4 cups oil in wok or heavy pot to 375°. Lower eggplant piece by piece and deep fry for about 4 minutes, until they are golden brown and crisp, turning gently all the while. Drain on paper towels. Serve as a hot appetizer, a main dish or a side dish. Zucchini may be substituted for eggplant (but do not freeze). A hot sweet and sour sauce may accompany this dish.

Cyclone Park was named for the sound of the wind in the pines. In the early 1900s a wealthy Chicago clothier named Zwick built an elaborate home here. Knowing nothing about cattle, he went broke.

Zirkel Zucchini

2 small zucchini, sliced lengthwise
salt
coarse black pepper
garlic salt
oregano
2 tomatoes, sliced
1 medium onion, sliced
6-8 slices Sharp Cheddar cheese
4-6 bacon strips, partially cooked

Mount Zirkel and the wilderness area was named after an old explorer who settled at the foot of the 12,200 foot peak.

Put zucchini in a shallow baking dish and season with salt, pepper, garlic salt and oregano. Place sliced tomato over zucchini and season as above. Layer sliced onion over tomatoes and season again. Layer cheese over onions. Top with sliced bacon. Bake, uncovered, at 350° for 30-45 minutes, until zucchini is fork tender and bacon is cooked. Serves 2-4.

Zucchini Pesto

Great with grilled meats, roasted chicken or ragout.

¼ cup freshly grated Parmesan cheese
¼ cup olive oil
3 Tbsp. minced fresh basil or 1 Tbsp. dried, crumbled
1 clove garlic, minced
2 Tbsp. olive oil
3 medium zucchini, cubed
1 onion, minced
3 medium tomatoes, cubed
1 tsp. salt
fresh parsley (garnish)

Combine first 4 ingredients in food processor or blender and mix well; set aside. Pour oil into a large skillet and heat until very hot, about 30 seconds. Add zucchini and stir fry 3 minutes. Add onion and continue stirring 3 minutes. Add tomatoes and salt; stir fry an additional 3 minutes. Remove from heat and blend in pesto sauce, stirring briskly until thoroughly mixed. Turn onto heated platter, garnish with parsley. Serve immediately. Serves 4-6.

Scalloped Summer Squash

3 Tbsp. butter
1 onion, minced
1 clove garlic, minced
1 green pepper, chopped
4 medium tomatoes, peeled and chopped
½ tsp. salt
pepper to taste
1 ½ lbs. summer squash
1 cup grated Parmesan cheese

Heat butter. Add onion, garlic and green pepper and sauté until tender and lightly browned. Add tomatoes, salt and pepper and cook, stirring occasionally. Slice or cube squash. In a medium saucepan, add ½ cup boiling water and squash, and cook until tender. Drain well. Preheat oven to 350°. Turn half the squash into a casserole dish. Cover with ½ of the tomato mixture and cheese and repeat. Bake until cheese is bubbly. Serves 6.

The Zirkel Wilderness area includes 27,500 acres straddling the Continental Divide. It consists of 14 peaks and more than 65 lakes.

Southwestern Squash

2 cloves garlic, minced
1 Tbsp. melted butter or margarine
3 medium yellow squash, sliced
6 green onions with tops, very finely minced
⅓ cup whipping cream
¼ tsp. salt
¼ tsp. white pepper
12 oz. can whole kernel white corn, drained
4 oz. can diced green chilies
½ cup grated Monterey Jack cheese

Sauté garlic in butter 1 minute in a large, heavy skillet. Add squash and green onion; sauté 5 minutes. Stir in cream, salt and white pepper. Cook 5 minutes over low heat, stirring occasionally. Stir in corn and green chilies; cook 1 minute. Remove from heat and stir in cheese until melted. Serve immediately. Serves 6.

Seedhouse Summer Squash

1 ½ lbs. yellow squash
2 cloves garlic, minced
½ tsp. dried rosemary leaves
1 Tbsp. olive oil
1 Tbsp. butter
2 Tbsp. chopped parsley
1 Tbsp. lemon juice
¾ tsp. salt
¼ tsp. pepper

Cut squash lengthwise into ¼" slices. Cut crosswise into ¼" strips. Sauté garlic and rosemary in oil and butter in a large skillet. Add squash; cook, stirring constantly, until crisp tender, about 4 minutes. Add parsley, lemon juice, salt and pepper. Toss. Transfer to plate and serve. Serves 4.

Seedhouse was built in 1912 by the Forest Service to collect and dry seeds from spruce and pine cones, but the operation proved too costly and was abandoned. After 1913 the building was used as a temporary ranger station, and a co-educational summer camp operated nearby between the early 1930s and 1945 when it was sold.

Timberline Tempura Vegetables

Tempura Batter:
1 cup flour
1 tsp. baking powder
¼ tsp. salt
1 cup beer
1 egg

Mix flour, baking powder and salt; add beer and mix well. Add egg and mix well. Let stand for 30 minutes before using. Dip each vegetable in batter and fry in oil at 375° until golden, approximately 5-7 minutes.

Suggested Vegetables for Tempura:
*   cauliflower or broccoli - cut into small flowerets
*   carrots - sticks or slices
*   mushrooms - whole, halved or quartered
*   zucchini - sticks or slices
*   okra - whole

Suggested Dips for Tempura Vegetables:
*   dash of Oyster Sauce
*   dash of Honey Mustard Dip: combine ¼ cup Dijon mustard, 2 Tbsp. mayonnaise and 2 Tbsp. honey.
*   dash of Sweet and Sour Chili Dip: combine 1 cup water, ⅓ cup red wine vinegar, ¼ cup honey, 1 small jalapeño, de-stemmed and cut into ½" pieces. Bring to boil and simmer 10 minutes. Purée in blender, strain, return to pot and add 4 tsp. arrowroot which has been dissolved in ¼ cup water, stirring constantly. Remove from heat when thickened.

Mom's Chinese Vegetables

¼ cup chopped green onion
2 Tbsp. butter
1 tsp. garlic salt
½ lb. snow peas
1 cup sliced mushrooms
8 oz. can water chestnuts
2 tsp. cornstarch
⅔ cup cold water
1 tsp. instant chicken bouillon
2 tsp. soy sauce
2 Tbsp. almonds, toasted

Cook onion in butter and garlic salt in sauté pan or wok until tender. Add snow peas and mushrooms. Cook for 1 minute. Toss in water chestnuts and stir. Remove from pan. Mix together cornstarch, water, chicken granules and soy sauce in a small saucepan. Heat, stirring until thick. Add sauce to vegetables, stir to coat. Top with toasted almonds. Serve with rice. Serves 5.

Indian Vegetable Biryani

2 Tbsp. margarine
1 cup chopped onions
2 cloves garlic, crushed
3 tsp. curry powder
¾ tsp. cinnamon
⅛ tsp. ground cloves
2 cups water
1 tomato, peeled, seeded and chopped
1 cup diced carrots
1 ½ tsp. salt
1 cup long grain rice
2 ½ cups cauliflower, broken into small flowerets
½ cup seedless raisins

Heat margarine in a 3 quart saucepan. Add onions and garlic and sauté until translucent, about 5 minutes. Add curry, cinnamon and cloves. Cook for 2 minutes. Add water, tomato, carrots and salt. Bring to a boil. Add rice, cauliflower and raisins. Cover, reduce heat and simmer 30 minutes. Slice bananas and shredded coconut may be served with this dish. Serves 10-12.

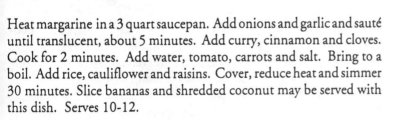

Stuffed Artichoke

2 artichokes, tips cut
1 cup cooked brown rice
2 Tbsp. diced carrot
4 Tbsp. diced celery
2 Tbsp. diced red onion
4 Tbsp. diced broccoli
4 Tbsp. diced cauliflower
¼ cup grated soy mozzarella
2 Tbsp. Basil Pesto (see recipe in Pasta chapter)
4 Tbsp. Tomato Basil (see recipe in Pasta chapter)

Boil artichokes 45 minutes or until done. Cool and remove very center leaves only. Very carefully scrape hair from heart with a spoon. Fill with rice, vegetables, cheese, Basil Pesto and ¼ cup of the Tomato Basil Sauce. Put in a baking pan with a little water on bottom and reheat in the oven. Spoon ½ cup Tomato Basil Sauce on each plate and set artichoke on top. Serves 2.

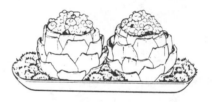

Mediterranean Roasted Vegetables

2 ½ Tbsp. pure olive oil
2 medium red onions, thinly sliced
1 Tbsp. chopped fresh thyme or 1 tsp. dried
½ lb. small yellow squash, thinly sliced
½ lb. small zucchini, thinly sliced
3 medium tomatoes (about ¾ lb.), thinly sliced
½ tsp. freshly ground pepper
2 tsp. extra virgin olive oil
1 Tbsp. chopped fresh basil
1 Tbsp. chopped fresh mint

In a large skillet, warm the olive oil. Add onions and thyme and cook over low heat, stirring occasionally, until the onions are soft, about 10 minutes. Spread the onion mixture in an even layer over the bottom of a large shallow baking dish. Preheat oven to 450°. Beginning with squash, arrange the squash, zucchini and tomato slices in slightly overlapping rows across the dish. Keep them neat and tight by pushing the rows close together as you go. Bake the vegetables on the upper rack of oven until tender and golden brown, about 25 minutes. To serve, season with pepper and drizzle olive oil on top. Sprinkle with basil and mint. Serve hot or at room temperature. Serves 4.

Stuffed Vegetable Casserole

4 medium zucchini, sliced ¼" thick
¾ cup grated carrots
¾ cup chopped onion
3 Tbsp. + 1 tsp. butter
2 ½ cups herbed stuffing
¼ cup sour cream or plain yogurt
¼ cup milk

Cook zucchini until tender by boiling or steaming. In a saucepan, cook carrots and onions in 4 tsp. butter until soft. Remove from heat and stir in 1 ½ cups of the stuffing. Combine milk and sour cream and add to stuffing mixture. Gently fold in zucchini and turn into a 1 ½ quart casserole. Melt remaining butter and mix with remaining stuffing and sprinkle on top. Bake at 350° for 35-40 minutes. Can be prepared ahead, refrigerated, and baked later in the day.

Potatoes Gratin Dauphinois

4 cups thinly sliced potatoes
1 tsp. salt
½ tsp. freshly ground pepper
⅛ tsp. freshly grated nutmeg
2 cloves garlic, minced
1 ¼ cups grated Gruyère cheese
4 Tbsp. butter
2 eggs, lightly beaten
1 cup heavy cream
2 Tbsp. freshly grated Parmesan cheese

Preheat oven to 375°. In a large bowl, toss potatoes to coat with ½ the salt and pepper, and all the nutmeg and garlic. Place ⅓ of the potatoes in the bottom of a well buttered baking dish. Sprinkle with ⅓ Gruyère cheese; dot with ⅓ butter. Repeat 2 more times. In a small bowl, beat eggs, cream and remaining salt and pepper. Pour evenly over potatoes and sprinkle with Parmesan cheese. Bake, covered, for 35 minutes. Remove cover and bake another 10 minutes or until potatoes are soft and top is golden. Serves 6-8.

Lowfat Potato Strips

3 baking potatoes
vegetable cooking spray
Parmesan cheese or salt

Rinse and stab potatoes. Cook in microwave for 10 minutes on high heat. Rinse to cool. Cut into fries. Place onto a cookie sheet which has been sprayed with vegetable spray. Sprinkle Parmesan or salt on fries. Bake at 400° for 10 minutes. Serves 4.

Chorizo Potatoes

Can be served as vegetable dish or main dish.

4 medium potatoes, peeled and sliced ¼" thick
1 lb. chorizo, sliced
salt and pepper to taste
6 Tbsp. flour
butter
2 cups heavy cream
2 cups grated Swiss cheese

Place a layer of potato slices in a buttered 2 quart casserole. Add a layer of sausage, then sprinkle with salt, pepper and flour. Dot with butter. Repeat layers, ending with top layer of potatoes. Add cream and sprinkle top with 1 ½ cups of cheese. Bake, covered, at 375° for 35 minutes or until potatoes are tender. Uncover, add remaining cheese, and place back in oven for 10 minutes, so cheese becomes crusty. Serves 4-6.

Herbed Home Fries

Boil potatoes ahead of time—makes serving a snap.

4 lbs. new potatoes
3 cups finely chopped onion
½ cup olive oil
1 tsp. dried rosemary or thyme
¼ cup minced fresh parsley
salt and pepper

Completely cover potatoes with water in a large pot. Simmer for 20 minutes until they are just tender. Drain potatoes and cool. Cut potatoes into 1 inch chunks. Heat oil in a large skillet until very hot. Add potatoes, onion, rosemary and salt and pepper to taste. Cook potatoes for 15 minutes, or until potatoes are golden, stirring frequently. Toss the potatoes with parsley and serve. Serves 8.

Saddle Up Sweet Potatoes
A great holiday treat.

3 cups mashed sweet potatoes (approximately 4 large)
2 eggs, beaten
⅓ cup milk
⅓ cup butter
1 tsp. vanilla

Topping:
⅓ cup butter, melted
1 cup light brown sugar
½ cup flour
1 cup chopped pecans

Peel, boil and mash potatoes. Beat in eggs, milk, butter and vanilla. Beat until mixture is quite light on medium speed. Spread in 13" x 9" ungreased baking pan. Mix topping ingredients and crumble on top of potato mixture. Bake at 350º for 25 minutes. Serves 10-12.

Bulgar Pilaf
Use as a main dish or with chicken or lamb.

1 tsp. olive oil
1 small finely chopped onion
1 cup medium or coarse bulgar
2 cups hot defatted chicken stock
¼ cup currants
2 Tbsp. pine nuts

Preheat oven to 350º. In a heavy 2 ½ -3 quart saucepan, heat oil over moderate heat. Add onion and sauté, stirring, until soft but not brown, about 2-4 minutes. Add bulgar and sauté 1 minute, stirring constantly, until the grains are coated with oil.

Add stock and currants and bring to a boil, stirring. Cover and bake for 40 - 45 minutes, or until all the liquid has been absorbed and the bulgar is tender. Do not stir at this time. Fluff the pilaf by tossing it briefly with a fork. In a large, dry skillet, toast the pine nuts over medium heat for about 3 - 5 minutes, stirring several times. Stir into pilaf. Taste and adjust seasonings, adding salt if necessary. Serves 4.

Whether he planned to be absent 6 hours or 16, a cowboy rarely thought of lugging a lunch with him. His attention was centered on his work and he was reconciled to going without food and water all day if need be.

Soubise

A great onion casserole!

½ cup long grain rice
6 Tbsp. butter
6 cups thinly sliced onions
2 cloves garlic, chopped
salt and pepper to taste
¼ cup grated Swiss cheese
1 Tbsp. chopped parsley

Precook rice in 1 ½ cups boiling water for 5 minutes. Drain well. Melt butter in ovenproof pan over medium heat. Stir in onions and garlic. Add rice, salt and pepper. Stir to coat well. Cover and bake at 300° for 1 hour. Stir in cheese and parsley and serve. Serves 6.

Lemon Dill Rice

An elegant, healthy rice dish.

2 cups chicken broth
½ tsp. salt
1 clove garlic, minced
1 cup long grain brown rice
1 Tbsp. finely grated lemon zest
2 Tbsp. chopped fresh dill
2 Tbsp. unsalted butter
freshly ground pepper to taste
grated Parmesan cheese

Heat broth, salt and garlic in a heavy saucepan. Bring to a boil. Stir in rice, cover, and simmer about 50 minutes, until liquid is absorbed. Remove from heat. Stir in lemon zest and let stand, covered, for 5 minutes. Stir in dill, butter and Parmesan cheese. Season with pepper. Serve immediately. This can easily be made ahead and microwaved before serving. It also freezes well. Serves 4-6.

Wild Rice Casserole

1 cup wild rice
1 cup grated Sharp Cheddar cheese
1 cup chopped onions
1 cup chopped tomatoes
½ lb. mushrooms, chopped
½ cup butter, melted
1 can black olives, chopped
1 tsp. salt

Prepare wild rice and drain. Add remaining ingredients and mix well. Pour mixture into a 13" x 9" baking dish or casserole. Bake, covered, at 350° for 1 hour. Serves 8-10.

Wild Bunch Wild Rice

1 lb. link sausages
1 lb. fresh mushrooms, sliced
1 cup chopped onion
2 cups wild rice
¼ cup flour
½ cup heavy cream
2 ½ cups chicken broth
½ tsp. oregano
½ tsp. marjoram
½ tsp. thyme
¼ tsp. pepper
½ cup slivered almonds

Sauté sausage, drain on paper towels and break into small pieces. Sauté mushrooms and onions in skillet with sausage drippings. Return sausage to skillet. Rinse rice thoroughly and cook 15 minutes in boiling water. Drain well. Add rice to sausage mixture. This can be done up to a day ahead. Blend flour and cream in heavy saucepan over low heat until smooth. Add chicken broth and cook slowly until thickened. Add seasonings. Pour into sausage and rice mixture and mix well. Place in a 2 ½ to 3 quart casserole dish. Bake at 350° for 45 minutes. Sprinkle almonds on top. Wild rice should have a slight crunch to it. Serves 10-12.

Notorious outlaws David Lant and Harry Tracy (who was a member of Butch Cassidy's Wild Bunch) broke out of the Hahns Peak jail in 1898 only to be recaptured boarding a stage outside Steamboat. The pair was transferred to the Aspen jail to await trial, but two weeks later they escaped again.

Sherried Wild Rice

1 cup wild rice
½ cup butter
½ cup slivered almonds
2 Tbsp. minced onion
¼ lb. fresh mushrooms, sliced
2 Tbsp. sherry
3 cups chicken or beef broth

Pour boiling water over rice and let stand for 30 minutes. Drain. Repeat; when cooled, drain well. In heavy frying pan, melt butter. Stir in rice, almonds, onion and mushrooms. Sauté about 5 minutes, without browning the onion and almonds. Stir in sherry. Turn into a lightly greased 2 ½ quart casserole dish and pour broth over. At this point, casserole can be covered and refrigerated or frozen. When ready to serve, bring casserole to room temperature. Bake, covered, at 350° for 1 hour. Uncover and bake 15 minutes longer or until rice is tender and liquid is absorbed. Serves 6-8.

Barley Pine Nut Casserole

A nice change from rice ...

1 cup pearl barley
2 Tbsp. pine nuts
2 tsp. butter
1 medium onion, chopped
3 cups hot, defatted chicken stock
¼ cup finely chopped scallions
⅓ cup finely chopped parsley
salt and freshly ground black pepper to taste

Preheat oven to 350°. Rinse barley, drain, and set aside. In a small, dry skillet, toast pine nuts, stirring over medium heat for 3 - 5 minutes, or until lightly browned. Set aside. Melt butter in a 1 ½ quart flameproof casserole dish over medium heat. Add onions and cook until softened, about 2 minutes. Add barley and continue cooking, stirring constantly, until the barley is coated with butter, about 1 minute. Stir in stock and scallions. Mix well, bring to a boil, cover and bake for one hour, or until barley is tender and liquid is absorbed. Add parsley and pine nuts. Fluff with a fork and turn out into a warm serving dish. Serves 6.

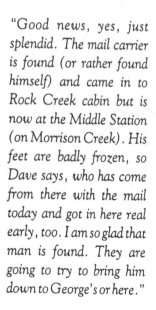

Saas-Fee Spaetzle

Add ham and Parmesan cheese to make a main dish that kids love.

1 ¾ cup flour
4 eggs
¾ tsp. salt
¼ cup water
nutmeg, grated
unsalted butter
8 quarts boiling water

Beat eggs, stir in flour and salt, then gradually add water until well mixed. To grate into boiling water, use a spaetzle grater or place colander over pot of boiling water. Put dough in colander, with a rubber spatula press dough through holes dropping pieces into water. Stir to separate. Boil for 5 to 7 minutes. Drain, toss with butter, nutmeg, salt and pepper and serve; or rinse with cold water, drain well and refrigerate until ready to serve. Before serving, sauté lightly in butter. Serves 4.

"Good news, yes, just splendid. The mail carrier is found (or rather found himself) and came in to Rock Creek cabin but is now at the Middle Station (on Morrison Creek). His feet are badly frozen, so Dave says, who has come from there with the mail today and got in here real early, too. I am so glad that man is found. They are going to try to bring him down to George's or here."

From the diary of
Lulie Margie Crawford
Jan. 4, 1881

Gourmet Sheepherder Beans
Great for a barbeque or Mexican dinner.

1 lb. pinto beans
1 pkg. dry onion soup mix
7 ozs. salsa
1 ham hock
1 tsp. pepper
1 Tbsp. soy sauce
2 Tbsp. Worcestershire
2 Tbsp. A-1 Steak Sauce
2 Tbsp. garlic powder
1 Tbsp. oil
3 cups water
1 tsp. vinegar

Combine all ingredients in a pressure cooker and cook for 1 hour 15 minutes at 15 lbs. of pressure. Serves 6-8.

Calico Beans
An excellent dish to take along for a barbeque.

1 lb. bacon
2 lbs. lean ground beef
1 ½ cups chopped onion
1 ½ cups chopped celery
2 large cans baked beans
15 oz. can kidney beans
15 oz. can black eyed peas
15 oz. can pinto beans
1 ½ cups ketchup
2 tsp. dry mustard
1 ½ cups brown sugar
6 Tbsp. vinegar

Brown bacon, crumble and set aside. Brown together ground beef, onion, and celery; drain and put in bottom of crock pot. On top of ground beef mixture, pour all beans and peas, undrained. Combine ketchup, mustard, brown sugar and vinegar and pour over beans. Place the bacon on top and cook 6-10 hours on low. Serves 12.

Black Beans and Rice

1 lb. black beans
5 oz. yellow rice, flavored with saffron
1 large onion, chopped
2 green, red or yellow peppers, chopped
12-16 ozs. pepperoni, chopped
olive oil
red wine vinegar

Rinse and sort beans; soak overnight in water that covers beans by several inches. Do not drain. Add enough water to allow the beans to boil. Cover and simmer 3-4 hours, until tender, stirring occasionally and adding more water when necessary. Prepare rice according to directions. Set up "buffet style" to serve. Guests start with a bowl of beans topped with rice. Garnish with onions, green peppers, and pepperoni. Add a splash of oil and vinegar. If yellow rice is not available, substitute with brown rice. Serves 6-8.

County Fair Baked Beans

Makes enough to feed a big crowd!

6 lbs. beans, cooked
32 ozs. ketchup
24 ozs. molasses
1 ½ lbs. bacon
2 lbs. brown sugar
2 lbs. onions, chopped
24 ozs. mustard
8 ozs. garlic salt or to taste
32 ozs. vinegar
onion salt to taste
10 ozs. soy sauce

Combine all ingredients in a large Dutch oven and cook at 325° for several hours, preferably all day.

Cheese Sauce

⅓ cup butter
⅓ cup flour
1 quart milk, scalded
½ lb. Sharp Cheddar cheese, grated
⅓ cup white wine
½ tsp. dry mustard
dash Tabasco
dash white pepper

Melt butter in saucepan and add flour, and mix well. Turn heat off. Add scalded milk, a little at a time, stirring constantly with wire whisk and scraping sides continually. Return to heat, stirring constantly until thickened (about 15 minutes). Add seasonings and cheese. Can be prepared 2 hours ahead of serving time; cover with plastic wrap and refrigerate. To serve, reheat slowly while whisking constantly.

Desserts

Desserts

Basic Pie Crust

2 ½ cups flour
1 tsp. salt
2 tsp. sugar
½ cup unsalted butter, chilled and cut into bits
5 Tbsp. vegetable shortening, chilled
6-8 Tbsp. ice water

Combine dry ingredients in bowl. Work in butter and shortening until crumbly. Sprinkle with 1-2 Tbsp. ice water and toss. Continue adding water until the dough can be gathered into a ball. Place dough on lightly floured surface and knead briefly to blend. Divide in half and flatten each piece and wrap in plastic. Refrigerate for 30-60 minutes. Roll each piece out on floured surface and fit into 9" pie pans. Prick bottom. Line with foil and fill with pie weights or dried beans. Bake at 375° for 8 minutes. Remove weights and foil and continue baking for 10-13 minutes for baked pie shell, or 2 minutes for partially baked shell. Makes 2 single crusts or 1 double crust.

Pâte Brisée (Short Pastry)

1 ½ cups sifted flour
1 Tbsp. sugar
8 Tbsp. butter or margarine
5 Tbsp. iced water

Place the flour and sugar in a large bowl. Sliver the butter over flour mixture and work lightly with fingertips until mixture looks like cornmeal. Add water and work quickly into a ball. Turn the dough onto a floured surface, and quickly knead with the heel of palm until dough is smooth (9-10 times). Wrap in waxed paper, flatten, and place in refrigerator for one hour before use. Roll out on floured surface. Makes one 8" crust.

Old Fashioned Apple Pie

9 inch unbaked pie crust
6 large tart apples, peeled, cored and thinly sliced
½ cup sugar
1 tsp. cinnamon
½ cup sugar
¾ cup flour
⅓ cup cold butter

Combine apples with ½ cup sugar and cinnamon. Place in pie shell. Combine ½ cup sugar and flour. Cut in butter until sandy in texture. Sprinkle over apples. Bake at 450° for 10 minutes. Reduce heat to 350° and continue baking for 40 minutes. Serve with vanilla or cinnamon ice cream.

Refreshing No-Sugar Peach Pie

5-6 firm ripe peaches, peeled, quartered or smaller pieces
⅔ of a 6 oz. can unsweetened frozen apple juice concentrate (thawed)
2-3 Tbsp. cornstarch (use more for a firmer pie, less for a juicy pie)
9" double crust uncooked pie shell

Arrange peaches in bottom shell. Combine juice and cornstarch in a small saucepan and stir until starch is completely dissolved. Heat to a boil. Boil 2-3 minutes stirring constantly. Pour over peaches. Cover with top crust, wrapping the upper edge under the edge of the lower crust and flute. Cut 4 tear-shaped slits in the top crust. Place pie pan on cookie sheet or large piece of foil to avoid a big cleaning job later, bake at 400° for 45-60 minutes until crust is golden brown and flaky. Cool completely before cutting. (Bottom crust will cook better in a glass pie pan.) For a delicious no-sugar cherry pie, substitute 3 cups of pitted cherries for the peaches.

Aunt Barbara's Famous Peach Grace Pie

This beautiful pie earned high praise from our testers.

Crust:
1 cup flour
1 ½ tsp. sugar
½ tsp. salt
½ cup vegetable oil
2 Tbsp. milk

Filling:
1 cup water
1 cup sugar
2 Tbsp. cornstarch
3 Tbsp. peach gelatin (½ pkg.)
3-4 drops red food coloring
6-8 fresh peaches, sliced
whipping cream

To prepare crust: Combine flour, sugar and salt. Whisk together oil and milk and blend into flour mixture. Press into a 9" pie plate and bake at 425° until golden brown, about 10-15 minutes. Cool.

To prepare filling: Bring water, sugar and cornstarch to a boil; cook until clear. Add gelatin and food coloring. Fill cooled crust with peaches. Pour gelatin mixture over peaches. Chill for at least 4 hours. Top with whipping cream and serve. Fresh strawberries and strawberry gelatin may be substituted for the peaches.

Fresh Kiwi Pie

Gorgeous, green and great!

12 medium kiwis, peeled
1 cup water
3 Tbsp. cornstarch
1 cup sugar
pinch of salt
1 Tbsp. lemon juice
1 tsp. butter
1 - 2 drops green food coloring
9" baked pie shell

Cut 9 kiwis in half and blot with paper towel. Blend the remaining 3 kiwis with water in blender or processor. In a saucepan, combine blended kiwi mixture with cornstarch, sugar and salt. Cook until thickened. Remove from heat and add butter and food coloring. Arrange halved kiwis in pie shell. Pour glaze over kiwis, coating them well. Chill for several hours. Serve with whipped cream, if desired.

Pleasant Valley Plum Kuchen

Kuchen Pie Shell:
1 ½ cups sifted flour
¼ tsp. baking powder
dash of salt
½ cup margarine, softened
1 egg
⅓ cup sugar

Filling:
1 ½ lbs. ripe Italian plums, washed, halved and pitted
½ cup granulated sugar
1 ½ tsp. grated orange peel
½ tsp. cinnamon
confectioners sugar

Pleasant Valley was named in September 1886 by Mrs. Henry C. Monson when she first saw the valley from the summit of Yellowjacket Pass and was reminded of Pleasant Valley, California. The Monson family was one of the first to settle in the valley, and their daughter, Laura, was the first teacher in the original Pleasant Valley School.

To prepare pie shell, sift flour, baking powder and salt. With electric mixer, blend in margarine until smooth. Beat egg until frothy. Add sugar and beat until lemon colored. Add to flour mixture, and blend until smooth. Turn dough into center of a greased 9" pie pan. Pat dough evenly over bottom and sides of pan but not on the rim. Refrigerate until ready to fill.

To prepare filling, make a ½" slit on pointed end of each plum. Arrange plums, in shell, in tight circular rows. Sprinkle with sugar, cinnamon, and orange peel. Bake at 400° for 15 minutes. Reduce heat to 350° and continue baking for 45 minutes. Cool partially and sprinkle with confectioners sugar.

Italian plums are available towards the end of summer, the riper, the sweeter. Great with vanilla ice cream.

Sour Cream Pear Pie

Nut Crust:
1 cup flour
¼ cup powdered sugar
¼ cup finely chopped filberts or walnuts
½ cup butter or margarine, chilled

Pear Filling:
½ cup sugar
2 Tbsp. flour
¼ tsp. salt (opt.)
1 egg
½ tsp. vanilla
1 cup sour cream
4 cups peeled, cored and sliced ripe pears (4-5 large)

Crumble Topping:
¼ cup butter or margarine, chilled
¼ cup flour
2 Tbsp. sugar
½ tsp. cinnamon

To prepare crust, combine flour, sugar and nuts in a bowl or processor. Add butter and blend until dough holds together. Press into bottom and sides of a 9" pie pan. Cover and chill until ready to use. This can be made 1 day ahead.

To prepare filling, combine sugar, flour and salt. Add egg, vanilla and sour cream and stir briskly to blend. Gently stir in the pear slices. Pour mixture into prepared shell. Bake at 400° for 30 minutes. As the pie bakes, prepare the topping. In a bowl or food processor, combine topping ingredients until evenly blended. Remove pie from oven and scatter topping over pear custard. Return to oven and bake for 25-30 minutes or more, until topping is golden brown. If the crust gets too brown around the edges, cover with strips of foil. Cool pie for 20 minutes on a rack to serve warm, or cool completely and serve at room temperature.

Japanese Fruit Pie

½ cup butter, melted
½ cup sugar
2 eggs
½ cup nuts, walnuts or pecans
½ cup coconut
½ cup raisins
½ tsp. vinegar
1 pie crust, unbaked

Blend butter, sugar and eggs. Add remaining ingredients and mix.
Pour into pie crust and bake at 325° for 1 hour or until golden brown
on top.

Lemon Stack Pie

9" pie shell and 2-6" rounds of crust, baked
2 tsp. unflavored gelatin
⅓ cup fresh lemon juice
3 eggs, beaten
1 ½ cups sugar
1 ½ Tbsp. butter
1 lemon rind, grated
1 cup whipping cream, whipped
grated lemon rind (garnish)

Soften gelatin in lemon juice and combine with next 4 ingredients in
a saucepan. Cook over low heat, stirring constantly until thickened.
Remove from heat.   Cool until mixture mounds slightly when
dropped from spoon. Fold half of the whipped cream into the cooled
lemon mixture. Spread ⅓ of lemon filling in pie shell. Top with 1
round of crust. Spread with ⅓ more filling, and top with second round
of crust. Spread with remaining filling; top with remaining whipped
cream and garnish with grated lemon rind. Serve well-chilled.

*Crosby Perry-Smith be-
gan skiing in 1929 in his
hometown of Lake
Placid. After serving in
the Army's 10th Moun-
tain Division in World
War II, he came to
Steamboat to train for
the National Jumping
Championships in 1946
and decided to stay. He
was an alternate to the
Oslo Olympics of 1952.*

Macadamia Nut Pie

A testing committee favorite!

¾ cup sugar
⅔ cup melted butter
7 eggs
2 tsp. vanilla
1⅓ cup light corn syrup
1⅓ cup dark corn syrup
½ lb. chopped macadamia nuts
2 - 8" unbaked pie crusts

Whip sugar, butter, eggs and vanilla together until light. Blend in light
and dark corn syrups. Sprinkle nuts evenly in both pie crusts. Pour
filling over nuts, dividing evenly between both crusts. Bake at 350° for
45 minutes. Makes 2 - 8" pies. Serves 16.

Chocolate Pecan Pie

So easy and so-o-o delicious.

1 ½ cups coarsely chopped pecans
6 oz. pkg. semi-sweet chocolate chips
8" pie shell, partially baked
½ cup light corn syrup
½ cup sugar
2 large eggs
¼ cup butter or margarine, melted and cooled
½ cup kahlua

Sprinkle pecans and chocolate chips evenly in pie shell. Blend corn syrup, sugar, and eggs. Mix in kahlua and melted butter. Pour mixture evenly into pie shell. Bake at 325° until firm, about one hour. Serve at room temperature. Top with whipped cream or ice cream, if desired. Recipe serves 8.

Pumpkin Pecan Pie

A great blend of two holiday favorites.

3 eggs, beaten
1 cup plain canned pumpkin
⅓ cup sugar
1 tsp. pumpkin pie spice
⅔ cup corn syrup
½ cup sugar
3 Tbsp. butter, melted
½ tsp. vanilla extract
1 cup pecan halves
1 9" pie shell, unbaked

Stir together 1 slightly beaten egg, pumpkin, ⅓ cup sugar and pie spice. Spread over bottom of pie shell. Combine 2 beaten eggs, corn syrup, ½ cup sugar, butter and vanilla. Stir in nuts. Spoon over pumpkin mixture in pie shell. Bake at 350° for 50 minutes or until filling is set and pie crust is golden.

Blueberry Clafouti

Tart Shell:
¾ cup cold unsalted butter, cut into bits
1 Tbsp. sugar
pinch salt
1 ½ cups flour
1 large egg
1 Tbsp. milk

Filling:
3 large eggs
½ cup sugar
½ cup finely ground blanched almonds
1 tsp. vanilla
6 Tbsp. unsalted butter, melted and cooled
½ cup plus 2 Tbsp. heavy cream
¼ cup fresh orange juice
2 cups fresh blueberries

To prepare crust: In a food processor, process butter, sugar and salt. Add flour and pulse a few times. Beat egg with milk. With processor running, pour egg mixture through feed tube. Process only until mixture forms small granules. Form into flattened ball. Wrap and refrigerate 2 hours. Roll dough ⅛" thick. Place in lightly buttered 11" tart pan. Chill ½ hour. Prick with fork, line with foil, and fill with dried beans or pie weights. Bake at 325° for 20 minutes. Remove foil and weights. Cool.

To prepare filling: Beat eggs, sugar and almonds. Stir in vanilla, butter, cream and juice. Place blueberries in crust and pour batter over. Bake at 350° for 40-45 minutes. Cool until set. Serves 8-10.

Anne Batelle, a Vermont native, came to Steamboat to train with the Winter Sports Club freestyle team in 1989. Anne's unique abilities led to World Cup success after only one year of major mogul competition. She was named to the U.S. Olympic team in 1992 and competed in Albertville.

Raspberry Creek Fruit Tart

1-12" x 12" sheet frozen puff pastry
1 egg yolk
1 egg
⅓ cup sugar
1 Tbsp. flour
2 Tbsp. unsalted butter, melted
¼ cup heavy cream
½ cup ground almonds
2-3 cups assorted fruits (strawberries, raspberries, blueberries)
seedless grapes, star fruit, sliced plums, etc.
apricot preserves (or your choice), melted and strained

Cut a 12" circle from puff pastry and place on cookie sheet. Cut remaining pastry in ¼" strips. Brush edge of pastry circle with egg yolk and put strips on top around edge to make a rim. Prick bottom with fork and refrigerate 1 hour. Mix egg, sugar, flour, butter, cream and almonds. Set aside. Bake tart at 400° for 10 minutes until it rises and becomes slightly golden. Add filling and bake 10 minutes more until filling is set. Arrange fruits decoratively on top, and brush with preserves.

Strawberry Raspberry Crunch

Topping:
6 Tbsp. margarine
6 Tbsp. unsweetened apple juice concentrate
½ tsp. vanilla extract
¼ tsp. almond extract
1 ¾ cups unsweetened muesli or granola
3 cups fresh hulled strawberries
2 cups fresh raspberries
3 Tbsp. unsweetened apple juice concentrate
1 Tbsp. unsweetened muesli or granola

In a 2½ quart microwave safe casserole, cook margarine and apple juice concentrate on high for 2 minutes uncovered. Stir in extracts and cereal. Cook uncovered on high for 5 minutes, stirring and breaking up mixture after 3 minutes. Transfer to bowl and set aside. In casserole dish, toss fruit with remaining ingredients. Cook uncovered on high for 6 minutes. Stir. Sprinkle evenly with granola mixture. Cook on high for 3 minutes longer. Cool slightly. Serve with ice cream. Serves 8-12.

L. R. Remington grew strawberry plants a foot tall and berries "too big to fit into water glasses." The berry was later given his name.

The Routt County Strawberry Company was formed in 1910 and the first 528 crates were loaded on a train leaving Steamboat Springs in 1911. Strawberry farms prospered in Strawberry Park until 1916, when early frosts ruined the crops.

Ski Camp Fruit Crisp

This crisp earned all-star approval from young skiers.

4 ½ cups (about 2 lbs.) pears, peaches, or apples: peeled, cored, thinly sliced
1 tsp. grated lemon rind
1 Tbsp. lemon juice
2 Tbsp. sugar
¼ tsp. ground cinnamon

Topping:
½ cup rolled oats
¼ cup whole wheat flour
¼ cup brown sugar
½ tsp. ground cinnamon
3 Tbsp. butter or margarine

Combine first 5 ingredients. Toss gently. Spoon into greased 8" square pan.

To prepare topping, combine first 4 ingredients. Cut in butter until mixture is crumbly. Sprinkle over fruit. Bake at 350° for 45 minutes. Serve warm with ice cream. Serves 6.

Strawberry Rhubarb Almond Crisp

A great combination with an added attraction.

4 cups diced rhubarb
4 cups sliced strawberries
¼ cup Grand Marnier
½ cup sugar
3 Tbsp. cornstarch
zest of 1 orange
2 cups Amaretti cookies, coarsely broken
1 cup rolled oats
¼ cup brown sugar
2 tsp. cinnamon
½ cup coarsely chopped almonds
¾ cup cold unsalted butter, cut into bits
1 egg, beaten

Combine first 6 ingredients. Place in well buttered 13"x9" baking dish; set aside. In a bowl, mix cookies, oats, sugar, cinnamon and almonds. Work in butter until crumbly. Lightly stir in egg. Sprinkle over fruit mixture. Bake at 350° for 45-50 minutes until bubbly.

Juicy Fruit Cobbler

½ cup butter
¾ cup flour
2 tsp. baking powder
¼ tsp. salt
½ cup sugar
1 cup milk
4 cups fresh fruit alone or in combination (peaches, strawberries, blueberries,
    raspberries, plums, or rhubarb)
½ - ¾ cup sugar
juice and grated zest of 1 lemon
cinnamon to taste

Melt butter in 13"x9" pan in 350° degree oven. Remove from oven. Sift together dry ingredients. Add milk and stir until just mixed. Pour mixture into melted butter. DO NOT STIR. Toss fruit with remaining ingredients. Place on top of milk mixture. DO NOT STIR. Bake at 350° for 40 minutes until top is golden. Serves 8.

Cranberry Walnut Tart
A delightfully different holiday dessert.

Tart Shell:
1 ⅓ cups flour
2 Tbsp. sugar
¼ tsp. salt
½ tsp. cinnamon
½ cup cold unsalted butter, cut into small pieces
1 large egg yolk
1 ½ Tbsp. ice water

Filling:
3 large eggs
⅔ cup brown sugar, packed
⅔ cup light corn syrup
¼ cup unsalted butter, melted and cooled
½ tsp. salt
1 tsp. vanilla
1 ¼ cups coarsely chopped cranberries
1 cup coarsely chopped walnuts

To prepare tart shell: Stir together first 4 ingredients. Blend in butter until mixture resembles coarse meal. Mix yolk and water and toss with flour mixture until incorporated. Form dough into ball, dust with flour, wrap in plastic wrap and chill for 1 hour. Roll out ⅛" thick on a floured surface and fit into 11" tart pan with removable bottom. Chill 30 minutes. Line with foil and fill with dried beans or pie weights. Bake at 425° for 15 minutes. Remove foil and weights and bake 5-10 minutes more until pale gold. Cool.

To prepare filling: Whisk together first 6 ingredients. Stir in cranberries and walnuts. Pour into shell. Bake at 350° for 40-45 minutes. If edges of pastry become too brown, cover with strips of aluminum foil. Cool completely.

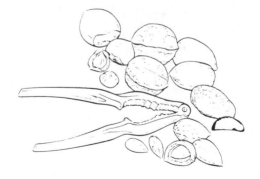

Poppy Seed Torte

A local favorite from the late, great Soupçon

⅓ cup poppy seeds
¾ cup milk
¾ cup butter, softened
1 ½ cups sugar
1 ½ tsp. vanilla
2 cups flour
2 ½ tsp. baking powder
¼ tsp. salt
4 egg whites, reserve yolks
¼ cup confectioners sugar

Filling:
½ cup sugar
1 Tbsp. cornstarch
1 ½ cups milk
4 egg yolks
1 tsp. vanilla
¼ cup chopped walnuts

In a small bowl, soak poppy seeds in milk for 1 hour. Cream butter until light. Add sugar, vanilla and poppy seed mixture. Add dry ingredients. Beat egg whites until stiff. Fold carefully into batter. Pour into 2 greased and floured 8" cake pans. Bake at 375° for 20-25 minutes. Cool cakes in pans, remove, and cut each in half horizontally to make 4 layers.

To prepare filling: mix sugar, cornstarch, milk and yolks in a saucepan. Cook, stirring constantly over medium-low heat until mixture thickens and boils. Remove from heat and stir in vanilla and walnuts. Cool. Spread filling between each layer of torte and sift confectioners sugar over the top.

Chocolate Gateau

Serve small pieces of this extremely rich cake—
you will savor every bite!

⅔ cup semi-sweet chocolate chips
¼ cup unsalted butter
⅔ cup sugar
rind of 1 orange, grated
1 Tbsp. orange liqueur
3 eggs, lightly beaten
1 ½ cups very finely chopped pecans (chop in processor)
pecans (garnish)

Chocolate Glaze:
1 cup semi-sweet chocolate chips
3 Tbsp. unsalted butter
1 Tbsp. light corn syrup

Early settlers found the Indians peaceful, friendly, and frequent beggars for sugar, biscuits, and medical attention in return for meat, moccasins, bows and arrows.

Butter an 8" springform pan. Line with waxed paper; then butter and flour the paper. Set aside. Melt chocolate and butter in a double boiler over hot, not boiling water, stirring until smooth. Remove from heat. Mix in sugar and rind. Add liqueur and eggs and mix well. Stir in chopped pecans. Pour batter into prepared pan. Bake at 375° for 25-30 minutes. Cool 15 minutes in the pan on a rack. Cake will settle as it cools. Remove from pan and cool completely on rack.

To prepare glaze, melt chocolate and butter in double boiler over hot water. Stir until smooth, then stir in corn syrup. Pour over cooled cake. Garnish with pecans, if desired. Serves 10-12.

Cold Oven Pound Cake

Wonderful with fresh fruit. Makes a great shortcake.

1 ¾ cup butter
3 cups sugar
2 Tbsp. almond extract
7 eggs
4 ¼ cups flour
1 tsp. baking powder
1 tsp. salt
1 cup evaporated milk

Cream butter and sugar. Add almond extract. Add eggs, one at a time, beating one minute after each addition. Sift dry ingredients together. Add alternating with milk. Mix well. Pour into greased and floured 9 inch tube pan. Place in cold oven and set to 325°. Bake for 1 hour, reduce heat to 300° and bake until done, about 30-40 minutes more. Let stand in pan 20 minutes before removing.

Variations: Add 1 cup mini chocolate chips. Dredge with flour so they don't sink to the bottom. Substitute 2 Tbsp. lemon extract for the almond.

Vanilla Crumb Cake

1 ½ cups sugar
1 cup butter
6 eggs
12 oz. box vanilla wafers, crushed
½ cup milk
7 oz. bag Angel Flake coconut
1 cup chopped black walnuts

Blend sugar and butter. Add eggs, 1 at a time, blending after each addition. Add wafers and milk alternately, blend. Add coconut and nuts, stirring well. Bake in greased and floured tube or springform pan at 325° for 1 ½ hours. Cool slightly, then turn out of pan.

Granny's Chocolate Sheet Cake

A four generation winner!

2 cups sugar
2 cups plus 2 Tbsp. flour
1 cup margarine
4 Tbsp. cocoa
1 cup water
½ cup buttermilk or ½ cup milk and 1 tsp. lemon juice
2 eggs, beaten
1 tsp. baking soda
½ tsp. cinnamon
1 tsp. vanilla extract

Icing:
½ cup margarine
4 Tbsp. cocoa
⅓ cup milk
1 lb. powdered sugar
1 tsp. vanilla extract
nuts (opt.)

Melt margarine with water and cocoa; bring to a boil. Pour over flour and sugar; blend well. Add remaining ingredients and mix well. Pour into greased and lightly floured 13"x9" baking pan. Bake at 400° for 25 minutes.

To prepare icing, melt margarine with cocoa. Add remaining ingredients. This makes more than needed for one cake, so save ⅓ for ice cream topping.

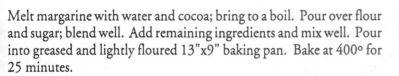

Hummingbird Cake

3 cups flour
2 cups sugar
1 tsp. salt
1 tsp. baking soda
1 tsp. cinnamon
3 eggs
1 ½ tsp. vanilla
1 ½ tsp. salad oil
18 ozs. crushed pineapple
1 cup chopped pecans,
2 cups crushed bananas
½ cup coconut flakes

Icing:
2 - 8 oz. pkgs. cream cheese, softened
1 cup butter
1 tsp. vanilla
1 cup chopped pecans
2 - 16 oz. boxes powdered sugar

Glen Eden was homesteaded before 1901 and named by George Franz because the beauty of the area reminded him of the Garden of Eden.

Combine all cake ingredients and mix thoroughly. Pour into 3 greased and floured cake pans or 1 Bundt pan. Bake at 350° for 30 minutes for cake pans; 1 hour for Bundt pan. Remove and cool completely. Combine all icing ingredients. Blend well and frost cooled cake.

Apple Cake with Sherry Cream

½ cup vegetable oil
2 cups sugar
2 eggs
2 tsp. vanilla
2 cups flour
2 tsp. baking soda
½ tsp. salt
2 tsp. cinnamon
4 cups grated tart apples (4-6 apples)
1 ½ cups chopped walnuts
½ cup raisins
confectioners sugar

Sherry Cream Sauce:
3 egg yolks
6 Tbsp. confectioners sugar
5 Tbsp. sherry
1 cup whipping cream

Cream together oil and sugar. Mix in eggs and vanilla. Add dry ingredients. Fold in apples, raisins and nuts. Spoon batter into greased and floured Bundt pan. Bake at 350° for 1 hour. Cool in pan for 10 minutes. Turn out onto plate, dust with confectioners sugar. Sauce: whisk yolks until light, whisk in sugar and sherry. Whip cream until stiff. Fold in yolk mixture. Chill well. Serve cake and pass the sauce!

No Cholesterol Apple Cake

¼ cup sugar
¼ cup brown sugar
¼ cup vegetable oil
3 egg whites
⅔ cup white flour
⅔ cup whole wheat flour
½ cup oat bran cereal, uncooked
1 ½ tsp. baking soda
1 tsp. cinnamon
¼ tsp. allspice
3 cups grated unpeeled apples

Mix first 4 ingredients. Combine dry ingredients and blend into sugar mixture. Stir in apples. Spread batter in greased 13 x 9" pan. Bake for 25- 30 minutes at 350º. Top with warm unsweetened applesauce if desired. Serves 12.

Carrot Coconut Cake

Even non-coconut lovers rave about this cake.

2 cups flour
2 tsp. baking soda
2 tsp. cinnamon
½ tsp. salt
3 eggs
¾ cup oil
¾ cup buttermilk
2 cups sugar
2 tsp. vanilla
8 ½ oz. can crushed pineapple, drained; reserve juice
3 cups grated carrots
1 cup grated coconut
1 cup chopped nuts

Frosting:
8 ozs. cream cheese, softened
½ cup butter, softened
1 lb. box confectioner sugar
3-6 Tbsp. pineapple juice

Sift dry ingredients together. Set aside. Beat eggs. Mix in oil, buttermilk, sugar and vanilla. Add to dry ingredients, blending well. Mix in drained pineapple, carrots, coconut and nuts. Pour batter into 2 well-greased 9" cake pans. Bake at 350º for 35-40 minutes. Cool and frost.

To prepare frosting, cream butter and cream cheese together. Add sugar slowly. Add as much juice as necessary to make a spreadable frosting.

Silver City Creek was named by early prospectors who after establishing silver claims, built several cabins in the 1870s which were burned by the Indians. A succession of rapids and water tumbling from high falls give the creek a silver appearance.

Silver City Squash Cake

3 cups finely ground squash (zucchini, yellow, or combination)
3 cups sugar
1 ½ cups oil
4 eggs
3 cups flour
1 tsp. soda
1 tsp. salt
1 ½ tsp. cinnamon
3 tsp. baking powder
1 cup coarsely chopped pecans
1 cup raisins

Frosting:
3 oz. cream cheese
1 tsp. vanilla extract
2 cups powdered sugar
½ cup butter, softened

Combine first 4 ingredients. In a separate bowl, combine dry ingredients. Add to squash mixture. Stir in nuts and raisins. Pour into greased and floured bundt pan. Bake at 300° for about 1 ½ hours. Cool before frosting.

To prepare frosting, beat all ingredients with electric mixer until smooth and fluffy.

Pineapple Cheesecake

Enjoy this cheesecake without guilt!

1 cup graham cracker crumbs
2 Tbsp. margarine
1 Tbsp. oil
1 pkg. unflavored gelatin
1 cup boiling water
1 lb. low fat cottage cheese, drained
⅓ cup sugar
2 tsp. grated lemon rind
1 Tbsp. lemon juice
1 tsp. vanilla
8 oz. can pineapple, crushed, in its own juice
3 tsp. cornstarch dissolved in 1 Tbsp. water

To prepare crust, mix graham cracker crumbs, margarine and oil. Press into the bottom of an 8" spring form or pie pan. Chill. Dissolve gelatin in boiling water; cool. Combine the next 5 ingredients in a blender or food processor and process until smooth. Slowly add gelatin while blending. Pour cheese mixture into crust; chill until firm. Combine pineapple and cornstarch in a small saucepan. Bring to a boil, stirring constantly; cool. Spread over cheesecake and chill at least 1 hour.

Nancy's Cheesecake

Nancy Kramer, former owner of the In Season, has
mailed this cheesecake to connoisseurs nationwide.

Crust:
1 cup graham cracker crumbs
1 Tbsp. powdered sugar
1 Tbsp. butter or margarine, melted

Filling:
1 ½ lbs. cream cheese
1 cup sugar
1 Tbsp. vanilla extract
3 eggs

Topping:
32 ozs. sour cream
2 Tbsp. sugar
1 tsp. vanilla extract

Crust: Blend all ingredients and pat into bottom of a 9" springform
pan. Bake at 325° until firm.

Filling: With mixer, blend cream cheese, sugar and vanilla. Add eggs,
1 at a time and mix thoroughly after each addition. Pour mixture into
pan and bake at 325° approximately 45 minutes or until center is firm.
Turn off oven and open door. Let cake sit for 15 minutes in oven.
Remove from oven and turn oven to 375°.

Topping: Mix all ingredients and spread evenly on top of filling. Place
in oven for 5-6 minutes, just until top is set. Remove from oven and
chill thoroughly before removing from pan.

If desired, drizzle raspberry sauce over cake before serving.

Raspberry Sauce:
10 oz. can frozen raspberries, thawed
5 oz. water
1 heaping Tbsp. cornstarch
2 Tbsp. sugar
⅛ tsp. almond extract

Combine raspberries and water in saucepan. Combine cornstarch and
sugar and add to saucepan. Bring to boil over medium heat, whisking
frequently. When sauce has thickened, remove from heat and add
almond extract.

Butterscotch Cheesecake

Crust:
1 ½ cups vanilla wafer crumbs, crushed very fine
½ cup powdered sugar
4 Tbsp. melted butter or margarine

Filling:
12 oz. pkg. butterscotch chips
3 - 8 oz. pkgs. cream cheese, softened
14 oz. can Eagle Brand sweetened condensed milk
4 eggs
3 tsp. vanilla

whipping cream (garnish)
chocolate curls (garnish)

It was a standing joke that the first thing the Crawfords always invited any guest to do was to take a bath. This invitation was readily accepted since to soak in a big, bubbling spring of comfortable hot mineral water was a rare treat in a country where the ordinary bath was a hurried scrub in a washtub in the kitchen.

To prepare crust: In medium bowl, mix first 3 ingredients until well blended. Press into bottom only of 9" springform pan. Set aside.

To prepare filling: In heavy saucepan over low heat, melt butterscotch chips, stirring constantly. Set aside. In a large bowl, beat cream cheese until fluffy. Gradually add sweetened condensed milk and continue beating until well blended. Add melted butterscotch and beat until well blended, scraping sides of bowl frequently. Add eggs and vanilla, and beat until well blended and mixture has uniform color. Pour into pan. Bake at 300° for 1 hour and 5 minutes or until center is set. Cool on wire rack for ½ hour. Refrigerate for at least 3 hours. With sharp knife, dipped in hot water, loosen sides of cheesecake from pan. Remove sides of pan. Garnish with whipped cream and chocolate curls. Can be frozen for up to 2 weeks, if wrapped airtight after chilling.

Pumpkin Cheesecake

Crust:
2 cups crushed cinnamon graham crackers
¼ cup sugar
½ tsp. cinnamon
½ cup melted butter

Filling:
3 - 8 oz. pkgs. cream cheese
¾ cup sugar
¾ cup brown sugar
5 eggs
¼ cup whipping cream
1 lb. plain, solid pack, canned pumpkin
1 tsp. cinnamon
½ tsp. ground cloves
½ tsp. nutmeg

To prepare crust, mix all crust ingredients. Press mixture into bottom and about ¾" up the sides of a buttered 9" springform pan. Chill for 1 hour. For the filling, cream first 3 ingredients. Add eggs, one at a time, beating well after each addition. Add all remaining ingredients and beat 3-5 minutes at medium speed, scraping sides of bowl. Pour filling into chilled crust. Place pan on an edged baking sheet (cake will drip) and bake at 350° for 1 ½-1 ¾ hours. Cool on rack until cake settles. Cover lightly and refrigerate for 6 hours.

"Crowd again. Seventeen for supper… Mrs. Burgess was down from the Little Cabin. She has got a new hat."

From the diary of
Lulie Margie Crawford
Sept. 24, 1881

Chocolate Chip Cheesecake
Sinfully rich but worth every bite!

Crust:
¾ cup butter
1 ¼ cups flour
¼ cup sugar
1 egg yolk

Filling:
5 - 8 oz. pkgs. cream cheese, softened
1 ¾ cups sugar
3 Tbsp. flour
2 egg yolks
5 eggs
¼ cup milk
¼ tsp. salt
1 cup semi-sweet chocolate chips

To prepare crust: Combine all ingredients until well mixed. Form into a ball. Press ½ of the ball onto bottom of 11" springform pan. Bake at 400° for 8 minutes. Cool. Press remaining dough around sides of pan. Do not bake.

To prepare filling: Beat cream cheese at medium speed until smooth. Beat in sugar, flour and egg yolks. Add remaining ingredients, except chocolate chips and beat at medium speed for 5 minutes. Stir in chocolate chips. Pour filling into pan over crust. Bake at 450° for 12 minutes. Reduce heat to 300° and bake 1 hour. Turn oven off and let cheesecake sit in oven for 1 hour. Cool, then refrigerate until well chilled (overnight).

Deer Park Date Pudding
A great Christmasy dessert.

1 cup coarsely chopped walnuts
¼ cup flour
1 tsp. baking powder
1 egg, well beaten
1 cup granulated sugar
⅞ cup milk
1 cup graham cracker crumbs
1 cup chopped dates
maple syrup, warmed
whipping cream

Combine nuts, flour and baking powder and set aside. Beat egg and sugar until light. Add remaining ingredients and the nuts. Mix well. Pour into a greased 11" x 7" pan. Bake at 350° for 45 minutes. Serve cold or warm. Spoon 1 Tbsp. or more hot maple syrup over each serving and top with whipped cream. Steaming is the best method for reheating or warming.

Deer Park was named in the late 1870s by brothers Bill, Ben and John Nichols who hunted deer in the park and sold the meat in a Georgetown market. The Deer Park area was notorious for bootlegging and area ranchers even today find remains of stills. The Deer Park School was built around 1900 and functioned until the early 1950s, although the district was renamed Lower Oak Creek in the 1930s.

Grand Marnier Bread Pudding

⅓ cup raisins
8 slices thin sliced white bread, crusts removed
butter
⅔ cup sugar
3 cups milk
1 cup light cream
1 long lemon peel curl
4 eggs, lightly beaten
cinnamon

Custard Sauce:
1 cup milk
¾ cup heavy cream
4 egg yolks
½ cup sugar
pinch of salt
1 tsp. vanilla
3 Tbsp. Grand Marnier

Plump raisins in boiling water for 3 minutes; drain. Lightly butter bread and cut each slice lengthwise into 3 pieces. Place a layer of bread strips, buttered side up in a 1 ½ quart greased baking dish. Sprinkle with ⅓ of the raisins and 1 Tbsp. sugar. Repeat layers. You should have 3 layers. Heat milk, cream, lemon peel and remaining sugar to boiling. Pour into beaten eggs, while stirring briskly. Strain the mixture around the sides of baking dish, not over the bread. Sprinkle with cinnamon. Let stand for 45 minutes. Put dish in a larger ovenproof pan and pour simmering water around it. Bake at 325° for 1 hour or until custard is set and top is browned.

To prepare the sauce, scald milk and cream. In the top of a double boiler, whisk yolks. Gradually whisk in sugar and salt. Gradually stir in scalded cream. Place over, not in, simmering water. Stir until mixture thickens and coats a spoon, about 10 minutes. Remove from heat and strain into a bowl. Stir in vanilla; cool. Strain again if necessary. Stir in Grand Marnier. Refrigerate until ready to serve. To serve, spoon sauce over individual servings of bread pudding. Serve 6.

English Raspberry Trifle

3 Tbsp. sugar
1 ½ Tbsp. cornstarch
3 egg yolks
2 ½ cups milk
1 tsp. vanilla
1 pound cake, cut into ½" slices
sherry
2 cups fresh raspberries
1 cup whipping cream, whipped

Whisk sugar, cornstarch and yolks together in saucepan. Whisk in milk in a thin, steady stream. Cook over medium heat, stirring constantly, until thickened. Cool completely. Line a glass bowl with the pound cake. Sprinkle, do not soak, with sherry. Top with raspberries. Pour cooled custard over berries and top with whipped cream. Cover with plastic wrap and chill several hours. If time is a factor, substitute a small box of vanilla pudding, prepared as directed, for the custard.

Baker Peak was named for Jim Baker, an early hunter, trapper and guide who had a cabin at the foot of the peak.

Baker Peak Bisquit Tortoni

6 Tbsp. powdered sugar
2 eggs, separated
1 ½ cups macaroon crumbs
2 Tbsp. rum
1 cup heavy cream

Beat egg yolks and 2 Tbsp. powdered sugar until thick. Beat egg whites and 2 Tbsp. sugar until stiff. Beat cream and 2 Tbsp. sugar until thick. Sprinkle 1 cup macaroon crumbs with rum, then beat them into egg yolks. Fold in whipped cream and then egg whites. Divide mixture into 8-10 servings, using either small ramekins or cupcake inserts. Sprinkle remaining crumbs on top. Freeze at least 3 hours, or overnight.

Crème Brûlee

1 quart heavy cream
1 vanilla bean
4 Tbsp. sugar
8 egg yolks
salt
¾-1 cup light brown sugar

In a large saucepan, scald cream with vanilla bean. Add sugar and stir until dissolved. In a large bowl, beat yolks until light. Stir in hot cream mixture. Add a pinch of salt. Strain mixture into a 10" baking dish (or 8 - 4 oz. ramekins). Place dish in a large pan and pour boiling water halfway up sides of dish. Bake 50-60 minutes (35-40 for ramekins). Brûlee is done when knife inserted in center comes out clean. Cool and refrigerate 6-8 hours. An hour before serving, push brown sugar through sieve. Spread smoothly on top of custard. Broil 4-6" from broiler for 2-4 minutes. Turn dish so it caramelizes evenly. Chill until ready to serve. Serves 8.

Chocolate Angel Pie

2 egg whites at room temperature
⅛ tsp. salt
⅛ tsp. cream of tartar
½ cup sifted granulated sugar
½ cup finely chopped pecans
½ tsp. vanilla
4 oz. Baker's German Sweet Chocolate
2 Tbsp. water
1 tsp. vanilla
1 cup whipping cream, whipped

For Meringue Shell:
Beat whites, salt and cream of tartar until foamy. Gradually add sugar (1-2 Tbsp. at a time), beating until glossy, stiff peaks form. Fold in nuts and vanilla. Spread in a greased 8" pie pan and bake at 300° for 55 minutes. Remove from oven and cool completely.

For Filling:
Melt chocolate with water over low heat, stirring constantly. Cool until thickened. Stir in vanilla. Fold into whipped cream and pile into cooled shell. Chill for at least two hours. Serves 8.

French Silk Pie

1 ⅓ cups graham cracker crumbs
⅓ cup butter, melted
1 ¼ cups butter, softened
¾ cups sugar
2 beaten eggs
1 tsp. vanilla
1 ½ ozs. semisweet chocolate, melted

Combine graham cracker crumbs and melted butter in 9" pie pan. Press firmly onto bottom and sides of pan. Refrigerate. With electric mixer, cream softened butter until smooth. Gradually add sugar and continue beating until very fluffy. Add eggs, vanilla and chocolate; blend well. Pour into pie shell and chill until ready to serve. May be served cold or at room temperature, with a dollop of whipped cream if desired. Serves 6.

Chocolate Mocha Torte

Meringue:
6 egg whites
1 cup sugar
1 tsp. almond extract

Filling:
6 oz. pkg. semi-sweet chocolate chips
6 egg yolks
⅓ cup water
2 Tbsp. instant coffee, powder or crystals
½ cup butter, softened

Cream:
2 cups chilled whipping cream
½ cup sugar
1 tsp. vanilla

To prepare meringue: Beat egg whites until foamy. Add sugar, 2 Tbsp. at a time, beating until stiff. Add almond extract. Grease parchment paper or cut grocery bags to fit cookie sheets. Spread meringue into 3-8" circles. Bake at 250° until light brown, about 1 ½ hours. Cool.

To prepare filling: Combine first 4 ingredients in saucepan over very low heat. Stir until smooth. Cool. Add softened butter and beat until fluffy.

Whip cream, sugar and vanilla until stiff.

To assemble: Layer one meringue, ⅓ of the chocolate filling, and ⅓ of the whipped cream. Repeat 2 more times. Refrigerate for at least 4 hours. Serves 8.

Snowdrift Mousse

This presentation and flavor is guaranteed to impress.

Mousse:
1 lb. white chocolate, cut into small pieces
1 cup butter, melted
7 large eggs, separated
½ cup sugar
1 ½ cups heavy cream, chilled

Chocolate Sauce:
4 ozs. semi-sweet chocolate
1 tsp. instant coffee powder
1 Tbsp. water
4 Tbsp. butter
2 Tbsp. heavy cream

Melt white chocolate in a double boiler, stirring frequently. Remove from heat and beat with electric mixer while gradually adding butter. Beat in yolks, 1 at a time and continue to beat for 5 minutes. In a separate bowl, beat egg whites until foamy. Add sugar, 2 Tbsp. at a time and beat to soft peaks. In a chilled bowl, whip cream until stiff. Fold egg whites into cream, then gently fold into cooled white chocolate mixture. Spoon mousse into goblets or bowl coated with chocolate sauce and chill at least 2 hours.

For chocolate sauce, combine all ingredients in double boiler. Melt and stir until smooth. Cool a bit and swirl around goblets or bowl to coat thoroughly. Chill for several hours until set. Serves 6-8.

Jeff Davis grew up within sight of the famed ski jumps of Howelsen Hill and spent his youth skiing with the Winter Sports Club. A tough competitor, Jeff finished 17th in the 70-meter jump at the 1980 Lake Placid Olympics only three weeks after undergoing knee surgery.

Mousse au Chocolate

4 egg yolks
¼ cup sugar
¼ cup orange liqueur
6 ozs. semi-sweet chocolate
4 Tbsp. butter, softened
6 egg whites

In the top of a double boiler off the heat, beat yolks and sugar until thick and pale yellow. Add liqueur and beat over simmering water until foamy and lukewarm. Set aside. Melt chocolate over low heat, stirring constantly, being careful not to burn. Remove from heat. Beat in butter a little at a time. Fold into egg mixture. Beat egg whites until stiff. In 3 additions, carefully fold whites into chocolate and egg mixture. Do not overwork. Spoon into dessert cups or a serving bowl and refrigerate at least 2 hours or overnight for better consistency. Try substituting other liqueurs, such as kahlua, frangelica or amaretto.

Iced Chocolate Mousse
Melt-in-the-mouth magic.

4 eggs, separated
½ cup sugar
4 ozs. semi-sweet chocolate
4 Tbsp. water
1 Tbsp. rum
¼ cup heavy cream
whipped cream (garnish)
grated chocolate (garnish)

Beat egg yolks with sugar until thick. Melt chocolate with water over low heat. Cool a bit, then add rum and stir into egg mixture. Whip cream and fold into chocolate mixture. Beat egg whites to stiff peaks and fold into chocolate mixture. Pour into 4-6 individual ramekins or goblets and freeze for 4 hours. Remove from freezer 10 minutes before serving. Garnish with whipped cream and grated chocolate. Serves 4-6.

Tiramisu
Viva Italia!

6 egg yolks
½ cup sugar
½ cup sweet Marsala
16 ozs. mascarpone cheese
½ cup strong coffee, room temperature
2 Tbsp. Kahlua liqueur
4 ozs. semi-sweet chocolate, grated or shaved

24 ladyfingers

Beat yolks and sugar with an electric mixer until light and fluffy. Gradually mix in Marsala. Add mascarpone and beat until thick and smooth. Combine coffee and Kahlua. In a glass bowl, place a layer of ladyfingers. Sprinkle with half the coffee mixture. Spoon in half the mascarpone mixture and sprinkle with half the chocolate. Repeat layers and chill for at least 2 hours. This may also be made in individual servings. Line 8 goblets or dessert dishes with ladyfingers. Spoon in the cheese mixture and sprinkle with chocolate. Serves 8.

Strawberry Margarita Pie

2 cups graham cracker crumbs
¾ cup sugar
1 cup butter, very soft
14 oz. can sweetened condensed milk
2 ½ cups frozen strawberries, thawed
1 Tbsp. lime juice
4 ozs. tequila
4 ozs. Triple Sec
2 ½ cups whipping cream

Make crust by mixing first 3 ingredients well in processor. Grease springform pan and line with crust. Mix next 5 ingredients in processor. Whip cream until stiff, fold in strawberry mixture. Put into crust and freeze overnight. Garnish with whipped cream and fresh strawberries.

Frozen Fruit Terrine

As delicious to look at as it is to eat.

2 envelopes unflavored gelatin
2 cups milk
1 cup sugar
6 egg yolks
1 tsp. vanilla extract
1 Tbsp. orange liqueur
1 ½ cups heavy cream
5 cups fresh fruit (raspberries, blueberries, strawberries, sliced kiwi,
    halved grapes, etc.)

Raspberry Sauce:
½ pint raspberries
2 -3 Tbsp. sugar
juice of 1 lemon

Soften gelatin in ½ cup milk and set aside. In a saucepan, scald remaining milk. In a bowl, beat yolks and sugar until thick and pale. Gradually whisk hot milk into yolks. Return to saucepan and cook over medium heat, stirring constantly for 10-15 minutes or until mixture coats the back of spoon. Remove from heat and stir in vanilla, liqueur and gelatin mixture. Strain into bowl and refrigerate until thickened, about 30 minutes. Whip cream to soft peaks and fold into custard. Fold in fruits. Spoon into a 7 cup loaf pan which has been lined with plastic wrap and sprayed with a non-stick spray. Cover and freeze.

To make raspberry sauce, combine all ingredients in a processor blender. Strain if desired. Cover and refrigerate.

Remove fruit custard from freezer 10-15 minutes before serving. Unmold, remove plastic and slice. Serve with raspberry sauce.

Bananas in Coffee Cream

3-4 medium bananas
¼ cup coffee flavored liqueur
½ cup whipping cream
1 Tbsp. instant coffee, powder or crystals
½ cup toasted almonds, sliced or slivered

Cut bananas into 1" thick slices. Place in a bowl, add coffee liqueur and toss gently. The bananas can marinate up to 20 minutes, if desired. Remove bananas with slotted spoon and arrange in serving dishes. Beat cream until foamy. Add coffee and beat until soft peaks form. Spoon cream mixture over bananas and top with almonds. Serves 4.

Papaya Vanille

papaya
fresh lime juice
vanilla yogurt
red seedless grapes
mint leaves (opt.)

A sub-chief of the Utes, Yarmony or Yahmonite, was very friendly to the early settlers. He was so well liked that a creek, a mountain, a street, and an addition to Steamboat Springs were all named after him.

Cut papaya in half and scoop out seeds. Cut a thin slice from the bottom of each half so the papaya will sit flat on a plate. Sprinkle with lime juice. Fill middle of papaya with the yogurt. Cut seedless grapes in half lengthwise. Place grapes around the edge of the yogurt. Garnish with mint leaves. Serves 2.

Blueberries with Lemon Mousse

1 cup heavy cream
⅓ cup sugar
juice and grated zest of 2 small lemons
1 pint blueberries
fresh mint leaves

In a chilled bowl, beat together cream, sugar, juice and zest until soft peaks form. Refrigerate up to 2 hours. To serve, place berries in 4 dessert bowls or goblets. Spoon mousse over berries and garnish with mint leaves. Serves 4.

Berry Merry Parfait

1 cup whipping cream
2 Tbsp. powdered sugar
4 Tbsp. sour cream
1 pt. blueberries, strawberries, raspberries or blackberries

Whip cream with powdered sugar. Fold in sour cream. Cover and chill at least 2 hours. Layer berries and cream in 4 goblets or a glass serving bowl. Chill until serving time. Serves 4.

Mixed Berries with Zabaglione Sauce

4 eggs
¾ cups sugar
½ cup dry white wine
1 cup heavy cream
2 pints mixed berries (blueberries, raspberries, blackberries, strawberries)

Whisk eggs, sugar and wine in top of a double boiler until thick and light. Place over simmering water and whisk until thick. Cool. Stir in cream and chill. Serve with berries. Serves 6-8.

Strawberry Sabayon

1 ½ lbs. fresh strawberries, rinsed and hulled
¾ cup sugar
2 Tbsp. Grand Marnier
6 egg yolks
⅓ cup Marsala wine
⅓ cup dry white wine
1 quart vanilla ice cream

Slice strawberries in a large bowl and toss with ¼ cup sugar and Grand Marnier. Cover and refrigerate several hours. In the top of a double boiler, mix egg yolks and ½ cup sugar. Whisk until thick and pale yellow. Pour in the wines. Place pan over very hot, but not boiling water. Beat yolks constantly until they foam, about 5 minutes. Beat another 5 minutes until Sabayon doubles in bulk, becoming thick but light. Serve strawberries over ice cream and top with generous servings of Sabayon.

Chocolate Covered Strawberries

Serve on their own in a pretty basket or use to adorn other desserts.

1 pint strawberries (with stems, if possible)
4 ozs. chocolate (bittersweet, semisweet, or milk chocolate)
1 scant Tbsp. shortening (not butter or margarine)

Wash the berries and dry on paper towels for several hours. They must be completely dry. Melt chocolate and shortening in double boiler over hot water. Stir until smooth. Hold berries by stem or hull and dip in chocolate. Let some red show at top. Place on waxed paper or foil lined tray. Refrigerate a few minutes until chocolate is firm. Remove from tray and store at room temperature. These will keep for 1 day.

Strawberry Park Meringue Torte

A luscious lowfat alternative to shortcake.

⅔ cup sugar
2 tsp. cornstarch
1 tsp. grated lemon rind
⅓ cup water
⅓ cup fresh lemon juice
1 egg, beaten
5 cups fresh strawberry halves
meringue shell (recipe below)
mint sprigs

Combine first 3 ingredients in saucepan. Slowly stir in water and lemon juice. Place over medium heat and bring to a boil, stirring constantly. Cook for 1 minute. Gradually stir about ¼ of mixture into egg. Stir back into saucepan and cook about 4 minutes, until thickened, stirring constantly. Pour into bowl, cover and chill. Combine strawberries with chilled lemon mixture. Spoon into meringue shell and garnish with mint sprigs.

Meringue Shell:
2 egg whites, at room temperature
½ tsp. vinegar
⅛ tsp. salt
½ cup sugar

Combine egg whites, vinegar and salt in bowl. Beat until soft peaks form. Add sugar, 1 Tbsp. at a time, continuing to beat until stiff peaks form. Draw an 8" circle on parchment paper which has been cut to fit a cookie sheet. Spoon meringue onto circle, mounding sides 1 ½"- 2" higher than center. Bake at 275º for 1 hour. Turn oven off and cool meringue in oven 2 hours before opening door. Remove from paper and cool completely on wire rack before filling. Serves 4-6.

Strawberry Park, once named Sheddeger (or Schedger) Park after a Swiss settler, refers to a long, lush meadowland north of Steamboat Springs where strawberries were commercially grown between 1900 and 1916.

Heart Mountain Strawberries Romanoff

A must for Valentine's Day.

Coeur a la Crème:
1 lb. cottage cheese
1 lb. cream cheese, softened
¼ cup powdered sugar
pinch salt
2 cups heavy cream

Strawberries Romanoff:
4 cups strawberries, washed and hulled
½ cup powdered sugar
1 oz. vodka
1 ½ oz. Triple Sec
1 oz. rum

Combine first 4 ingredients in mixer or processor. Gradually add cream, beating constantly until mixture is smooth. Pour mixture into Coeur a la crème mold which has been lined with cheesecloth (cheesecloth should be dampened and wrung out). Place mold on a deep plate and chill. (The mold should have holes in bottom to allow drainage.) Toss berries with sugar. Add vodka, Triple Sec and rum. Chill overnight. When ready to serve, unmold heart and remove cheesecloth. Surround with berries. Serves 6-8.

Heart Mountain was named by the George Rossi family, who have ranched in the area since 1908, because a slide near the top is shaped like a heart. The Heart Mountain School served the region from the early 1920s until 1952 and at one time had as many as 24 students.

Poires a la Reine

(Poached Pears in Brandied Cream Sauce)

½ cup sugar
1 ¼ cups light red wine (i.e., Côtes du Rhone or Côtes de Provence)
1 ¼ cups water
4 cloves
4 peppercorns
1 tsp. vanilla extract
peel of orange, removed with vegetable peeler
4 Tbsp. Armagnac
3 large pears, peeled, cored and halved or, preferably
6 small pears, peeled, left whole with stems
½ cup heavy cream

Place all ingredients except pears in a heavy saucepan which will later hold the pears in one layer. Heat to boiling, reduce heat and simmer, uncovered, for about 10 minutes. Put pears in liquid and simmer, uncovered for 15-25 minutes or until tender. Remove from heat and cool in liquid. Refrigerate until ready to serve (can be kept in liquid for several days). Remove pears to serving dish. Place saucepan over high heat and reduce liquid to about ¾ cup, until it becomes syrupy. Cool. Whip cream to soft peaks. Fold into syrup. Pour over pears and serve. Serves 6.

Gratin de Fruits

This is much like poaching fruit but the Crème Anglaise insures a richer outcome.

Crème Anglaise:
1 cup milk
3 Tbsp. sugar
3 egg yolks
1 tsp. vanilla extract

1 tsp. unsalted butter
2 ozs. kirsch
2 Tbsp. water
2 Tbsp. sugar
1 apple, peeled and sliced
1 pear, peeled and sliced
1 peach, peeled and sliced
12 blueberries
8 raspberries
8 strawberries, quartered

Ansten Samuelstuen, born in 1929, learned to ski in his native Norway and honed his jumping skills during World War II, when he competed in illicit meets outlawed by the Nazis. He dreamed of coming to the United States and immigrated to Steamboat in 1954. While skiing for the Winter Sports Club from 1955-1965, he was the top U.S. finisher in the '60 Olympics in Squaw Valley.

To prepare crème anglaise, scald milk in a small saucepan, stirring constantly. Remove from heat. Whisk sugar and yolks until thick. Slowly, stir in the hot milk. Return mixture to saucepan and cook on low heat, stirring constantly until thickened. Do not let it simmer or boil. Strain the sauce through a sieve and cool. When cool, stir in vanilla and refrigerate until needed.

In a shallow skillet, put butter, kirsch, water and sugar. Bring to a boil and add the apple, pear, and peach slices. Simmer for 2-3 minutes. Add remaining fruits and cook for 1 more minute. Place fruits in a small, deep, ovenproof dish. Cover them with crème anglaise. Bake briefly at 400° until bubbly and barely browned. Serve immediately. Serves 4.

Chocolate Fondue

3 - 4 oz. bars sweet cooking chocolate
    (Bakers German Sweet Chocolate)
6 Tbsp. heavy cream
⅛ tsp. cinnamon
2 Tbsp. brandy
fruit, cut into chunks (apples, pineapple, pears, oranges, bananas)

Heat cream; add chocolate in chunks. Stir until smooth. Stir in cinnamon and brandy. Serve with fruits for dipping. Serves 4.

Lime Ice Cream

A refreshing way to end a meal.

1 cup and 2 Tbsp. fresh lime juice
2 Tbsp + 2 tsp. lime peel, grated (about 2 ½ limes)
4 cups extra fine granulated sugar
pinch salt
4 cups cream
4 cups milk

Mix first 4 ingredients together.   Add cream and milk slowly.
Refrigerate until well chilled. Freeze in ice cream maker according to
directions. Garnish with sliced lime fan. Makes 1 gallon + 2 cups.

Gramma Darling's Lemon Sherbet

2 cups sugar or 1 cup sugar and 1 cup white corn syrup
2 cups milk
grated rind of 1 lemon
juice of 2 lemons
2 egg whites
2 Tbsp. sugar
1 cup whipping cream

Dissolve 2 cups sugar in milk. Add lemon rind. Stir while adding
lemon juice. Freeze until firm. Beat egg whites until frothy. Add 2
Tbsp. sugar, and beat until soft peaks form. Whip the cream and
combine egg whites with cream. Beat in frozen lemon mixture. Cover
and freeze.

Cinnamon Ice Cream

Wonderful with apple pie or fruit cobbler.

2 tsp. ground cinnamon
3 cups milk
6 egg yolks
1 cup sugar
1 cup heavy cream

In a saucepan, combine milk and cinnamon. Bring to a boil. Remove
from heat, cover, and set aside. In a large mixing bowl, beat yolks and
sugar at high speed for 2 minutes, or until thick and lemon colored.
Return milk mixture to a boil and pour ⅓ into the yolk mixture,
beating constantly. Pour this mixture back into saucepan and cook
over medium low heat, stirring constantly with a wooden spoon for
about 5 minutes or until mixture thickens and coats the spoon. Do not
let it boil. Remove from heat and stir in cream. Strain through a sieve
into bowl. Cool completely. Transfer to ice cream freezer and freeze
according to directions.

Mystic Mocha Ice Cream

6 ozs. semi-sweet chocolate
8 egg yolks
1 ½ cups half and half
⅔ cup sugar
pinch salt
6 Tbsp. unsalted butter, chilled and cut in pieces
1 ½ - 2 Tbsp. instant espresso powder
2 cups heavy cream, chilled

In a double boiler over hot water, melt chocolate and set aside. Combine yolks, half and half, sugar and salt in saucepan. Stir constantly over medium low heat until mixture thickens and coats a spoon. DO NOT GET CLOSE TO A BOIL. Remove from heat and add butter, chocolate and espresso powder. Stir until butter melts. Refrigerate until mixture is room temperature, stirring occasionally. Stir in cream and taste. Add more coffee powder if needed. Put custard in ice cream maker and process according to instructions. Yields 1 ½ quarts.

Praline Sauce

1 ½ cup brown sugar
⅔ cup light corn syrup
4 Tbsp. butter
5.3 oz. evaporated milk
pecans

Mix first 3 ingredients in a medium saucepan, Bring to a boil, add milk, and simmer until thickened. Makes 2-3 cups.

Chocolate Sauce

10 ½ ozs. unsweetened chocolate
9 ozs. sweet chocolate
2 ¾ cups water
1 cup + 2 Tbsp. sugar
1 ½ tsp. vanilla

Melt both chocolates in a double boiler. In a small saucepan, dissolve sugar in water and cook syrup, undisturbed for 5 minutes. Add syrup to chocolate, whisking. Add vanilla and beat until smooth.

Incredible Fudge Sauce

2 squares unsweetened chocolate
2 Tbsp. butter
1 cup sugar
7 oz. can evaporated milk

Cook all ingredients in a double boiler until thick, at least 1 hour. Cooking for 2-3 hours improves consistency.

Amaretto Fudge Sauce

1 ½ cups heavy cream
12 ozs. semi-sweet chocolate chips
4 Tbsp. butter
½ tsp. vanilla
3 Tbsp. Amaretto

Combine cream, chocolate and butter in saucepan. Heat until hot, but not boiling. Remove from heat and stir until smooth. Stir in vanilla and Amaretto. Makes 2 ½ cups.

Chocolate Hazelnut Sauce

This lovely sauce makes a quick, easy hostess gift.

3 ozs. semi-sweet chocolate
¼ cup margarine or butter
5 oz. can evaporated milk
½ cup sugar
3 Tbsp. hazelnut liqueur

In a heavy saucepan, melt the chocolate and margarine over low heat, stirring frequently. Stir in the evaporated milk and sugar. Cook and stir over medium heat about 5 minutes or until the mixture is slightly thickened and bubbly. Remove from heat. Add the hazelnut liqueur; stir until mixture is smooth. Cool slightly. Pour into a pint jar. Cover and chill for up to 1 month. Heat through to serve. Makes 1 ½ cups.

Butter Fudge Fingers

2 squares unsweetened chocolate
½ cup butter
2 eggs
1 cup sugar
¾ cup flour

Topping:
¼ cup butter
2 cups powdered sugar, sifted
2 Tbsp. cream
1 tsp. vanilla
1 square unsweetened chocolate
1 Tbsp. butter

Melt chocolate and butter. Beat in sugar and eggs. Mix in flour. Spread in greased 8" square pan. Bake at 350º for 30 minutes. Do not overbake. Cool slightly. For topping, brown butter, blend in sugar and stir in cream and vanilla. Spread over fudge. Melt chocolate and butter and spread a very thin layer over the topping. Cut into 2"x1" fingers. Refrigerate to set topping.

Finger Rock, estimated as nearly 300 feet high, is a basalt spire resembling a pointing index finger. Indian legend holds that a young warrior wrestled with the God Manitou, broke off his finger, and left it as a symbol of the struggle.

King Mountain Caramels

2 cups sugar
1 ¾ cups light corn syrup
1 cup butter
1 cup cream
1 cup evaporated milk
1 cup chopped walnuts, optional

Mix sugar, corn syrup, butter and cream and boil 10 minutes. Add evaporated milk. Boil slowly and stir until fairly hard-ball stage (approximately 235°). Add vanilla and chopped walnuts. Pour into an 8" x 8" buttered pan. When cooled to just warm cut into squares and wrap in wax paper. Do not double this recipe.

King Mountain and King Creek were named for Preston King, a civil engineer from New Jersey who suffered from gold fever and moved west in 1879. King, who surveyed roads from Yampa to Steamboat Springs, was one of the early homesteaders in Egeria Park in the early 1880s. His son, Elmer King, ran one of the first steam threshing machines in south Routt County.

True Love Truffles

6 ozs. semi-sweet chocolate
4 Tbsp. unsalted butter
2 egg yolks
2 Tbsp. Cognac or ½ tsp. vanilla
unsweetened cocoa

In a double boiler over hot water, melt chocolate. Remove from heat and add butter, stirring until smooth. Carefully stir in yolks. Return to double boiler and stir and heat for 2 minutes. Remove from heat and stir in Cognac or vanilla. Chill until firm. Scoop out truffle mixture by rounded teaspoonfuls and roll into balls. Roll in cocoa. Chill. 24 Truffles.

Option #1 - Substitute 2 Tbsp. orange liqueur and 2 tsp. grated orange peel for Cognac.
Option #2 - Substitute 3 tsp. rum and 3 tsp. coffee for Cognac.
Option #3 - Substitute ½ tsp. almond extract for Cognac and roll balls in sliced almonds, toasted and chopped.

Ski Town Toffee
Great for holiday giving.

¼ cup water
1 cup butter
1 cup sugar
½ tsp. lecithin (available at health food stores)
½ cup sliced almonds, toasted
4 Hershey Bars (or 6 oz. chocolate of your choice)
1 cup finely chopped walnuts

In a heavy saucepan, bring first 4 ingredients to a boil. Cover and boil for 7-9 minutes. Add almonds. Turn heat to high and stir rapidly until coffee-colored streaks appear. Immediately, pour onto buttered cookie sheets. The mixture will spread. Break Hershey bars on top and, as they melt, spread to edges. Sprinkle with walnuts and cool completely. Break into pieces using a butter knife.

Cookies & Bars

Cookies & Bars

Cowboy Cookies

1 cup unsalted butter or shortening
1 cup sugar
1 cup brown sugar, firmly packed
2 eggs
1 tsp. vanilla
2 ½ cups flour
1 scant tsp. baking soda
½ tsp. salt
2 cups old fashioned oats
6 oz. pkg. chocolate chips

Cream butter and sugars. Add eggs and vanilla. Beat for 2 minutes.
Gradually add flour, soda and salt. Mix well. Stir in oats and chocolate
chips. Drop by spoonfuls onto ungreased cookie sheet. Bake at 350°
for about 12 minutes. Remove from cookie sheets immediately.
Cookies will be moist and chewy. If desired, ½ cup of wheat germ or
oat bran may be substituted for ½ cup of the oatmeal. Makes 5 dozen
cookies.

Monster Cookies

Your little monsters will love this flourless cookie.

½ cup butter
1 ¼ cup brown sugar
1 cup sugar
3 eggs
1 ⅓ cup peanut butter
2 tsp. baking soda
4 ½ cups oatmeal
⅔ cup M&M's candies
⅔ cup chocolate chips
2 Tbsp. vanilla
½ cup chopped nuts

Cream butter and sugars. Beat in eggs. Stir in remaining ingredients. Drop by teaspoonfuls onto baking sheets. Bake at 350° for 10 minutes. Makes about 8 dozen small cookies.

Aunt Carol's Billygoat Cookies

1 cup brown sugar
1 ¼ cups butter
⅔ cup sour cream
2 eggs
2 heaping cups flour
⅔ tsp. baking soda
2 tsp. cinnamon
¼ tsp. ground cloves
1 cup chopped dates
1 cup raisins
½ cup chopped nuts

Cream butter and sugar. Add sour cream and eggs. Mix dry ingredients and add to creamed mixture. Fold in dates, raisins and nuts. Drop onto cookie sheet. Bake at 375° for 15 minutes. Makes 4 dozen cookies.

Mae Mae's Chocolate Cookies

A fragile, rich chocolate cookie.

1 cup butter
1 ½ cups sugar
3 eggs
3 ozs. unsweetened chocolate, melted and cooled
1 ½ cups flour
1 tsp. vanilla

Cream butter, sugar and eggs. Add chocolate, flour and vanilla and mix well. Drop by teaspoonfuls on ungreased cookie sheet and bake at 350° for 10-12 minutes. Remove from cookie sheets immediately and cool on wire racks. Makes 4 dozen cookies.

Chocolate Coconut Cookies

2 squares unsweetened chocolate
½ cup butter
1 cup sugar
2 eggs
½ tsp. vanilla
1 ¼ cups flour
1 ¾ tsp. baking powder
½ tsp. salt
½ cup chopped nuts
1 cup coconut

Melt chocolate over low heat or in double boiler and cool. Cream butter, sugar, eggs and vanilla. Blend in chocolate. Mix in flour, baking powder and salt. Stir in nuts and coconut. Drop by spoonfuls onto cookie sheet. Bake at 375° for 8 minutes.

Jarle Halsnes, born in Norway, is a recent Steamboat transplant. His 3-year reign as World Professional Ski Champion came after a highly successful amateur career high-lighted by the 1979 Europa Cup title and 11th place in GS in the 1980 Olympics.

Moon Hill Macaroons

2 egg whites
pinch of salt
½ cup sugar
1 cup sweetened shredded coconut
½ tsp. vanilla

Preheat oven to 325°. Lightly grease cookie sheets. Beat egg whites and salt in small bowl until stiff. Gradually beat in sugar and continue beating until stiff, shiny peaks form. Fold in coconut and vanilla. Drop batter by heaping tablespoonfuls 2" apart on greased cookie sheet. Bake at 325° for 20 minutes until light brown around edges. Don't overbake. Cool macaroons on sheets for 5 minutes. Remove to wire racks to cool completely. Store in airtight container. Makes 15 cookies.

Old Fashioned Lace Cookies

Truly, a melt in your mouth cookie.

1 cup Old Fashioned oats (regular or quick)
1 cup sugar
3 Tbsp. flour
½ tsp. salt
¼ tsp. baking powder
½ cup butter, melted
1 egg yolk, beaten

Mix butter and egg yolk together and set aside. Mix dry ingredients together. Combine the 2 mixtures and stir with fork. Refrigerate overnight. Cover cookie sheet with heavy duty aluminum foil (dull side up). Drop cookie dough by tablespoonfuls on cookie sheet. Bake at 350° for 12 minutes or until bubbling stops; remove from oven and let sit 2 minutes. Slide foil onto cool surface for a few minutes. Peel cookies from foil. Makes about 2 dozen cookies.

Oatmeal Snickerdoodles

A crisp and crunchy treat.

2 cups flour
1 tsp. baking soda
½ tsp. salt
1 tsp. cinnamon
1 cup butter
1 tsp. vanilla extract
¾ cup sugar
¾ cup brown sugar, firmly packed
2 eggs
1 ½ cups oatmeal
¼ cup sugar
1 Tbsp. cinnamon

Sift together flour, baking soda, salt and cinnamon; set aside. Cream butter, vanilla and ¾ cup of each sugar. Add eggs, 1 at a time, mixing well. Gradually blend in flour mixture. Stir in oatmeal. Drop by rounded teaspoonfuls on foil-covered cookie sheet. Combine ¼ cup sugar and 1 Tbsp. cinnamon. Sprinkle generously over cookies. Bake at 400° for 10- 12 minutes until browned. Makes 4 ½ dozen cookies.

Gingerbread Cookies
A holiday classic for munching or tree trimming

½ cup butter
1 cup dark brown sugar, loose
¼ cup molasses
1 egg
2 cups flour
½ tsp. cinnamon
2 dashes ground cloves
1 dash cayenne pepper
2 tsp. powdered ginger

Blend butter and brown sugar together. Stir in molasses and egg. Mix and add dry ingredients. Knead dough, adding a bit more flour if necessary. Chill 1 hour or overnight. Roll and cut with cookie cutters, decorate with red hots, raisins etc., if desired, and bake at 350° for 10 minutes. Cookies may be decorated with icing when cooled. Makes about 2 dozen cookies.

The Steamboat Springs Winter Sports Club was formed in 1915 to promote a Winter Carnival as the community had caught the skiing fever from Carl Howelsen.

Ginger Cream Cookies
½ cup butter
1 cup sugar
1 egg
1 cup molasses
4 cups flour
½ tsp. salt
2 tsp. powdered ginger
1 tsp. nutmeg
1 tsp. ground cloves
1 tsp. cinnamon
2 tsp. baking soda, dissolved in 1 cup hot water

Icing:
2 cups powdered sugar
¼ cup butter, softened
1 or more tsp. cream or orange juice

Cream butter and sugar. Beat in egg and molasses. Combine flour, salt and spices and add to butter mixture. Stir in soda and water. Drop by spoonfuls onto cookie sheet. Bake at 400° for 8 minutes. Ice while warm. Makes 6 dozen cookies.

To prepare icing, cream butter and sugar. Add liquid to desired consistency.

Gem Lake Gingersnaps

¼ cup butter
½ cup vegetable shortening
1 cup brown sugar
1 egg
¼ cup molasses
2 ¼ cups flour
2 tsp. baking soda
½ tsp. salt
1 tsp. ginger
1 tsp. cinnamon
1 tsp. cloves
granulated sugar

Cream butter, shortening and sugar. Beat in egg. Add molasses. Sift dry ingredients together and add to butter mixture. Make 1" balls and roll in granulated sugar. Space 2" apart on a cookie sheet. Bake at 375° for 8 minutes. Makes 3 dozen cookies.

Gem Lake is named for the unusually clear water which gives it the appearance of a jewel.

Pallas Pineapple Cookies

½ cup butter
1 cup brown sugar, firmly packed
1 egg, beaten
8 ½ oz. can crushed pineapple, well drained, reserving liquid
2 cups flour
1 tsp. baking powder
1 scant tsp. baking soda
½ tsp. salt
¾ cup chopped pecans

Icing:
3 Tbsp. butter
1 Tbsp. vegetable shortening
2 cups powdered sugar
pinch of salt
reserved pineapple juice

At the junction of the main stage route from Steamboat Springs to Yampa, Pallas (or Conger) served as a freight stop for east-west traffic. In 1895 it obtained a post office and changed its name to Pallas. In 1904 the name was changed to Huggins but in 1922 it was again named Pallas. In 1926 the post office closed and Pallas became a whistle stop on the Moffat Road.

Cream butter and sugar. Beat in egg and pineapple. Combine dry ingredients and add to butter mixture, mixing well. Stir in nuts. Chill dough several hours. Drop by spoonfuls onto cookie sheet. Bake at 375° for 10 minutes. Ice while warm. Makes 3-4 dozen cookies.

To prepare icing, brown butter and shortening slightly in a small saucepan. Add sugar and salt. Stir in enough juice to make a spreadable consistency. If icing should become stiff before all cookies are iced, return to heat and add more juice.

Italian Lady Fingers

6 eggs
juice of ½ orange
⅔ tsp. vanilla
1 cup sugar
⅓ cup corn oil
½ cup melted shortening
⅔ cup milk
5 cups flour
5 tsp. baking powder

Butter Cream Frosting:
½ cup butter, melted
1 lb. powdered sugar
1 ½ tsp. vanilla (substitute orange or almond extract)
¼ cup water

Beat eggs on high speed until fluffy. Add orange juice and vanilla. Slowly blend in sugar. Add oils at slow speed and mix well. Add baking powder to flour and mix well. Add egg mixture to the flour. Mix by hand. Dough should not be sticky (add more flour if necessary). Take handfuls of dough and roll between palms, making long thick ropes the thickness of a finger. Cut in 2-3" lengths and bake at 350° for 10-15 minutes or until lightly browned. Makes 6 dozen cookies.

To prepare frosting, mix all ingredients with mixer until smooth. Cookies may be frosted when warm. Dip cookies into frosting and place on rack to dry. Store in tightly covered containers with wax paper between layers. For festive holiday cookies, color the frosting.

Chinese Almond Cookies

2 cups flour
1 cup sugar
½ tsp. baking powder
½ tsp. salt
⅔ cup butter, softened
2 ½ tsp. almond extract
1 egg, slightly beaten
1-1 ½ cups almonds, finely chopped

Combine dry ingredients and set aside. Beat together butter, egg and extract. Add dry ingredients and stir in almonds. Roll into small balls and place on a greased cookie sheet, flatten slightly. For good luck, dip the end of a chopstick in red food coloring and press into top of cookie. Bake at 350° for about 15 minutes. Makes 4-5 dozen cookies.

Icebox Cookies

½ cup brown sugar
½ cup sugar
1 egg
¼ cup butter
¼ tsp. baking soda
1 ½ cups flour
1 lb. pecan halves

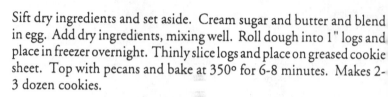

Sift dry ingredients and set aside. Cream sugar and butter and blend in egg. Add dry ingredients, mixing well. Roll dough into 1" logs and place in freezer overnight. Thinly slice logs and place on greased cookie sheet. Top with pecans and bake at 350º for 6-8 minutes. Makes 2-3 dozen cookies.

Country Cupboard Cookies

Filling:
1 cup raisins or currants
1 Tbsp. flour
½ cup sugar
½ cup water
½ cup walnuts (opt.)

Cookie Dough:
1 cup sugar
½ cup butter
1 egg
½ cup milk or cream
1 tsp. vanilla
2 tsp. baking powder
3 ½ cups unbleached white flour

To prepare filling: Combine all ingredients in a small saucepan and cook until thick. Cool. If omitting walnuts, substitute an additional ½ cup of raisins.

To prepare cookie dough: Cream butter and sugar. Add egg, milk and vanilla. Mix well. Add the baking powder and 3 cups of the flour to make a stiff dough, adding additional flour if necessary. Roll out dough to approximately ⅛" in thickness. Cut 2" rounds with a cookie cutter. Place a heaping teaspoonful of the filling onto the center of the rounds and top with another round. Prick top with a fork and place on greased cookie sheets. Bake at 375º for about 12 minutes or until edges turn golden brown. Makes 2 ½-3 dozen cookies.

Walnut Sticks

3 large eggs, well beaten
¾ cup sugar
½ cup vegetable oil
½ tsp. baking soda
½ tsp. salt
1 cup walnuts, chopped
2 tsp. vanilla
2 ½-3 cups unsifted flour
powdered sugar

Combine eggs, sugar, oil, salt and soda and mix well. Blend in vanilla and nuts. Add flour as necessary and knead as for bread dough. Form into 2 long loaves 3-4" wide. Place on a greased cookie sheet and bake at 350° for 30 minutes. Remove and quickly cut into strips while still hot. If a crisper cookie texture is desired, return strips to cookie sheets and toast under broiler, turning once. Watch closely to prevent burning. Cool and sprinkle with powdered sugar. Makes 3-4 dozen.

Twice Baked Walnut Cookies

4 eggs
1 ½ cups sugar
¾ cup butter, melted
2 tsp. vanilla
½ tsp. almond extract
1 tsp. anise flavoring
1 tsp. black walnut flavoring
1 cup chopped walnuts
5 cups flour
4 ½ tsp. baking powder

"It has been a very fine day. Papa put some more straw in the tick on the bed in the front room."

From the diary of
Lulie Margie Crawford
Jan. 19, 1881

Blend eggs and sugar. Stir in butter, vanilla, flavorings and walnuts. Mix flour and baking powder together. Gradually add to creamed mixture, blending well. On floured board, divide into 8 portions. Roll each into 14" rope and place 2" apart on a greased 12" x 15" baking sheet. Bake at 325° about 20 minutes, or until golden. Let cool 2 minutes. Cut diagonally into ½"-¾" slices. Tip slices onto sides and bake again at 375° for 10-15 minutes. Cool on pan. Store in airtight container up to 1 month, or freeze. Makes 12 dozen cookies.

Pecan Dreams

¾ cup shortening
¼ cup butter
½ cup powdered sugar
1 Tbsp. vanilla
1 Tbsp. almond extract
½ cup pecans, minced
2 cups flour
½ tsp. salt
1 cup powdered sugar

Cream shortening, butter and sugar. Add vanilla, almond extract and nuts. Stir in flour and salt. Shape into 1" balls. Place on baking sheet and bake at 325° for 25 minutes. Remove from baking sheets and cool slightly. While still warm, roll in powdered sugar. Makes 4 dozen cookies.

Dutch Creek Date Balls

A great holiday treat.

1 cup dates, chopped
1 cup sugar
¼ tsp. salt
½ cup butter, melted
2 eggs, beaten
2 cups puffed rice cereal
½ cup chopped nuts
½ cup coconut

Dutch Creek was named for Carl Eberhardt, an old German prospector who worked placers on the creek before 1900.

In a medium saucepan, mix dates, sugar, salt and eggs with melted butter. Cook over low heat for 10 minutes. Pour over puffed rice cereal and nuts. Mix and cool to lukewarm. Form into small balls about 1" in diameter. Roll in coconut. Makes 2 ½-3 dozen balls.

Fruit Stand Squares

1 cup butter
1 cup sugar
1 egg yolk
2 cups flour
¾ cup nuts, finely chopped (walnuts, pecans, macadamia, almonds)
10 oz. jar jam (apricot, raspberry, strawberry, peach, etc.)

Cream butter and sugar. Stir in yolk. Mix in flour and nuts. Divide dough in half. Spread half the dough in a 13" x 9" pan. Cover with jam. Drop remaining dough by spoonfuls over jam and spread carefully to edges. Bake at 350° for 40 minutes. Cool slightly and cut into squares.

Apple Annie Bars

½ cup shortening
1 cup sugar
1 egg, beaten
1 tsp. baking soda
1 cup strained applesauce
1 ½ cups flour
¼ tsp. salt
½ tsp. cinnamon
¼ tsp. nutmeg
⅛ tsp. cloves, ground

Cream shortening. Add sugar and egg. Mix well. Add soda and applesauce. Sift remaining ingredients together. Add to applesauce mixture and mix well. Pour into a greased and floured 13" x 9" pan. Bake at 375° for 20-25 minutes. Cool and cut into bars. Sprinkle with powdered sugar.

Raspberry Hazelnut Schnitten

½ cup butter or margarine, room temperature
⅓ cup sugar
1 large egg
2 cups flour
1 egg white, slightly beaten
½ cup raspberry preserves, warmed
½ cup hazelnuts, coarsely chopped
6 ozs. semi-sweet chocolate chips
2 Tbsp. shortening

In a medium sized bowl, beat butter and sugar until fluffy. Beat in egg. Gradually stir in flour until blended. Divide dough in half. Wrap in plastic wrap. Chill 1 hour or until firm enough to roll. Roll out and trim each half of dough to a 12" x 5" rectangle between 2 sheets of waxed paper. Peel top sheet off both rectangles. Invert dough on cookie sheet 2" apart. Peel off paper. Brush a 1" wide border of egg white on each long side. Fold long sides inward ½", keeping borders even. Pat edges to keep sides straight and seal any cracks. Carefully spread half the preserves on each rectangle up to turned in edges. Sprinkle nuts on preserves. Bake 15 minutes at 350° or until edges are golden. While still warm, cut each rectangle into 16 slices. Remove to rack to cool. Melt chocolate and shortening in small saucepan over low heat, stirring until smooth. Dip plain ends of cooled slices into chocolate glaze, scraping off excess from bottom and sides against side of pan. Arrange on waxed paper. Refrigerate to set chocolate. Makes 32 cookies.

Luscious Lemon Bars

1 cup flour
½ cup butter, softened
¼ cup powdered sugar
2 eggs
¼ tsp. salt
1 cup sugar
3 Tbsp. lemon juice
grated rind of 1 lemon
2 Tbsp. flour
½ tsp. baking powder

Cream 1 cup flour, butter and powdered sugar. Press into a greased 9" x 9" pan and bake at 350° for 25 minutes. Beat eggs, salt, sugar, lemon juice and rind. Mix 2 Tbsp. flour and baking powder and fold into egg mixture. Pour over baked crust and return to oven for an additional 25 minutes. Cool and cut into bars.

Cream Cheese Brownies

4 oz. pkg. Baker's German Sweet Chocolate
5 Tbsp. butter
3 oz. pkg. cream cheese
1 cup sugar
3 eggs
1 Tbsp. flour
½ cup flour
¼ tsp. salt
½ tsp. baking powder
½ cup walnuts, chopped
1 ½ tsp. vanilla extract
¼ tsp. almond extract

Melt chocolate and 3 Tbsp. of butter over low heat, stirring constantly. Cool. Cream remaining 2 Tbsp. butter with cream cheese. Gradually add ¼ cup sugar, and cream until fluffy. Blend in 1 egg, 1 Tbsp. flour and ½ tsp. vanilla. Set aside. Beat 2 eggs until light. Gradually add remaining ¾ cup sugar and beat until thickened. Add ½ cup flour, salt and baking powder. Stir in the cooled chocolate, 1 tsp. vanilla, almond extract and nuts. Spread half the chocolate batter in greased 8" or 9" square pan. Top with cheese mixture. Drop spoonfuls of remaining chocolate batter over top. Zigzag a knife through batter to marbleize. Bake at 350° for 35-40 minutes. Cool completely before cutting into squares.

Chocolate Mint Brownies

½ cup unsalted butter
2 squares unsweetened chocolate, finely chopped
2 large eggs, room temperature
1 cup sugar
1 tsp. vanilla
½ cup flour
⅛ tsp. salt
½ cup pecans, coarsely chopped
½ cup finely chopped chocolate mints (Frango, Droste, Bavarian, Andes)

In a saucepan, melt butter over low heat. Remove from heat and add chocolate, stirring until melted. Cool a bit. In a large mixing bowl, beat eggs until light and fluffy, about 2 minutes. Gradually beat in sugar and continue to beat for an additional minute. Beat in chocolate mixture and vanilla. Fold in flour and salt. Then fold in nuts and mints. Spread batter in a greased 8" square baking pan. Bake at 350° for about 25 minutes or until a toothpick inserted halfway between center and edge comes out with moist crumb. Do not overbake. Brownies should be moist. Cool completely before cutting.

"Aunt Nannie has decided to go to Kentucky for a visit the first time Uncle Henry goes out with a wagon."

From the diary of
Lulie Margie Crawford
June 16, 1881

Aunt Nannie's Come Back Coconut Brownies

4 eggs
2 cups sugar
⅔ cup shortening, melted
1 ⅓ cups flour
1 tsp. baking powder
½ tsp. salt
3 squares unsweetened chocolate, melted
2 tsp. vanilla
½ cup slivered or sliced almonds
2 tsp. almond extract
7 ozs. coconut flakes

Beat eggs and sugar. Add shortening. Mix in dry ingredients. Divide into 2 bowls. To one half, add melted chocolate and vanilla. Spread in the bottom of a greased 13" x 9" pan. To the other half, add almonds, almond extract and coconut. Spread on top of chocolate mixture. Bake at 350° for 30-35 minutes. Allow to cool completely and cut into squares.

"Uncle Henry got the horses and took us all to the bath house, but the house had tumbled in. He got a stick and propped it up so we could bathe. Aunt Nannie is here sewing, getting ready to go. I made some little underclothes for Minnie."

From the diary of
Lulie Margie Crawford
June 18, 1881

Aunt Jane's Killer Brownies

½ cup butter
1 cup sugar
3 eggs
2 ozs. unsweetened chocolate, melted
1 tsp. vanilla
½ tsp. salt
½ cup flour
½ cup coarsely chopped pecans

Cream butter and sugar. Add eggs, 1 at a time, beating well after each addition. Add chocolate and vanilla and mix well. Add salt and flour and mix well. Stir in pecans. Pour batter into a greased 8" x 8" pan and bake at 350° for 25-30 minutes, making sure not to overbake. Allow to cool completely and cut into squares.

Silver Bullet Bars

6 ozs. chocolate chips
½ cup evaporated milk
1 Tbsp. sugar
1 Tbsp. butter
½ tsp. salt
½ cup chopped nuts (walnuts, pecans or almonds)
1 tsp. vanilla
1 ¼ cups sifted flour
½ tsp. baking soda
½ tsp. salt
½ cup butter
1 cup brown sugar
1 egg
1 tsp. vanilla
1 ½ cups quick oats

Combine first 7 ingredients, using only ¼ cup of the nuts, in a saucepan and cook over low heat until chocolate is melted. Sift together flour, soda and salt. Cream together butter and brown sugar. Add egg and vanilla. Stir in dry ingredients and oats. Press ⅔ of mixture in a greased 9" x 9" pan. Spread chocolate filling over crust. Crumble remaining ⅓ of mixture over filling. Sprinkle with remaining nuts. Bake at 350° for 25 minutes. Cool and cut into bars.

Peanut Butter Swirl Bars

½ cup crunchy peanut butter
⅓ cup butter, softened
¾ cup brown sugar, firmly packed
¾ cup sugar
2 eggs, beaten
2 tsp. vanilla
1 cup flour
1 tsp. baking powder
¼ tsp. salt
1 cup chocolate chips

Combine the first 6 ingredients and beat until creamy. Blend in flour, baking powder and salt. Spread into a greased 13" x 9" pan. Sprinkle chips over mixture. Bake at 350° for 5 minutes. Remove and run knife through mixture to marbleize. Return to oven and bake for 20-25 minutes. Cool and cut into bars. Makes 4 dozen 2" x 1" bars.

Super Energy Bars

½ cup butter
¾ cup brown sugar
½ cup oats
½ cup unsifted whole wheat flour
½ cup white flour
¼ cup toasted wheat germ
1 Tbsp. grated orange rind
2 eggs
2 cups of your favorite trail mix

Beat butter and ½ cup of the brown sugar until smooth. Add next 5 ingredients. Pat into an ungreased 8" x 8" pan. Mix eggs, trail mix and ¼ cup brown sugar. Pour over crust and spread evenly. Bake at 350° for 30 minutes. Cool, then cut into 16 bars.

The crust may be used by itself as granola bars. Just put a small amount in the bottom of muffin tin pans. Take out of pan while warm. Makes 8-10.

Miracle Bars

½ cup butter
1 ½ cups graham cracker crumbs
15 oz. can sweetened condensed milk
⅓ cup milk
12 oz. pkg. chocolate chips
1 ½ cups flaked coconut
1 ½ cups chopped nuts

Preheat oven to 350º. In a 13" x 9" baking pan, melt butter in oven. Sprinkle crumbs over butter; pour condensed milk and regular milk evenly over crumbs. Top with remaining ingredients, press down firmly. Bake 25-30 minutes or until lightly browned. Cool and cut into bars. Store loosely packed in a covered contained at room temperature or in freezer. Great when served partially frozen.

Kids

Kids

Fun Food Fruit Kabobs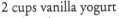

2 cups vanilla yogurt
2 Tbsp. honey
½ tsp. ginger
1 tsp. cinnamon
1 medium cantaloupe
½ large honeydew melon
2 large firm bananas
1 pt. whole strawberries

Combine the first 4 ingredients and chill. Halve and seed melons. Cut into walnut size chunks. Slice bananas into chunks. Rinse, drain, and pull the stems from the strawberries. Thread fruit onto skewers and serve with yogurt mixture or any fruit dip. Serves 6-8.

Apricot Jam Roll Ups

4 flour tortillas (7" diameter)
3 oz. pkg. cream cheese
¼ cup apricot jam
1 Tbsp. milk
1 Tbsp. sugar

Cut tortillas in half. Cut cream cheese into 8 portions; shape each portion into a log about 5" long. Place cream cheese and jam on the cut edge of each tortilla, dividing equally. Roll tortilla around cheese and jam to enclose; place seam side down in a 10"x15" baking pan. Brush rolls with milk, then sprinkle with sugar. Bake at 450° until tortillas are golden, 12-13 minutes. Remove from pan, they will stick if allowed to cool. Serve warm. Serves 4.

Cinnamon Toast Rolls

¼ cup sugar
2 tsp. cinnamon
12- 3/8" thick slices of very fresh homemade white bread, crusts removed
¼ cup unsalted butter, melted

In a bowl, stir together the sugar and cinnamon. Roll out the bread ¼" thick between pieces of wax paper and brush both sides with butter. Sprinkle 1 tsp. cinnamon/sugar on 1 side of each slice, roll the bread tightly jelly-roll fashion, beginning with long side. The rolls may be made up to 1 week in advance at this point and kept wrapped tightly and frozen. Transfer the rolls seam side down to a baking sheet and bake at 350° for 15 minutes, or until browned lightly. Makes 12 rolls.

Fruit Pizza

A good snack, lunch or special birthday party food.

Crust:
¼ cup oil
⅔ cup milk
1 ¼ cups flour
¾ cup oat or whole wheat flour
1 tsp. sugar
½ tsp. salt
1 tsp. baking powder
1 tsp. cinnamon

Filling:
⅓ cup peanut butter
8 oz. pkg. cream cheese
3 Tbsp. honey

Topping:
2 apples, sliced or bananas (dipped in lemon juice)
1 pear, sliced
raisins (garnish)

To prepare crust, combine dry ingredients. Add liquid. Knead 10 times. Press into a 12"x14" pizza pan or a 13"x9" pan. Bake at 425° for 15 minutes. For filling, mix peanut butter and cream cheese and spread on cooled crust. Chill 24 hours. For topping, arrange fruit on filling as desired. Slice and serve. Strawberries, kiwi or mandarin oranges may be used in place of or in addition to apples. Serves 8

Pizza Pocket Sandwiches

pizza sauce
pita bread

Stuffing Variations:
sliced pepperoni
Canadian bacon
grated mozzarella cheese

Vegetable Topping Variations:
tomato slices
halved green pepper rings
sliced pitted black olives
sliced mushrooms
shredded lettuce

Spread pizza sauce inside a pita half. Stuff with your choice of stuffing. Add mozzarella cheese. Next add your choice of vegetable toppings. Top with shredded lettuce for crunch. Dig in right away! If you like 'em hot, just microwave for 30-40 seconds on high. Can be packed in an insulated lunch box along with a frozen pack (or frozen carton of juice) for lunch up to 4 hours later.

Jack Miller has lived in Steamboat since moving here from Boulder at age 3. "Jumpin' Jack" advanced through the ranks of the Winter Sports Club, winning Junior Olympics, Rocky Mountain Trophy Series and Nor-Am events on his way to a berth on the U.S. Ski Team. He competed in the giant slalom and slalom in the '88 Olympics in Calgary.

Fruit Dip

8 ozs. cream cheese
6 ozs. marshmallow cream
¼ cup strawberry juice

Mix all ingredients together and serve with fruit chunks. Use frozen strawberries or mashed fresh berries and sugar for the juice. Fruit juice concentrate of other flavors work too.

Strawberry Fruit Dip

10 oz. pkg. frozen strawberries in light syrup, thawed and drained
3 oz. pkg. cream cheese
½ tsp. cinnamon
⅛ tsp. nutmeg
1 cup whipping cream, whipped
fresh fruit

Blend the first 4 ingredients in a blender. Fold in whipping cream. Serve with fresh fruit. Makes 2 cups.

Chow Down Calzones

Use your imagination with fillings to personalize these!

15 oz. ricotta cheese
1 cup grated Muenster cheese,
3 roma tomatoes, chopped
¼ cup sliced black olives
1 tsp. dried basil
garlic, salt and pepper to taste
2 loaves frozen bread dough, thawed
16 ozs. spaghetti sauce
Parmesan cheese
½ small onion, thinly sliced
1 egg beaten with 1 Tbsp. water

Combine ricotta and Muenster cheese, add tomatoes, olives and seasonings. Divide each loaf of bread into 4 pieces. Roll each piece into a 7" circle. Spoon filling mixture onto ½ of each circle. Brush edges with water and fold over, press edges to seal. Place on greased baking sheet. Slash 1-2 times on the top of each calzone. Brush with an egg wash, sprinkle with Parmesan and top with sliced onion rings. Bake at 400° for 25 minutes or until golden. Serve with hot spaghetti sauce as a dip. If meat is desired, cooked sausage, ham or pepperoni can easily be added to the filling mixture. Serves 8.

Tepee Tamale Pie

1 lb. ground beef
oil for frying
1 large onion, chopped
1 green pepper, chopped
1 15 oz. can kernel corn, drained
1 15 oz. can sliced black olives, drained
green chilies to taste
1 15 oz. can Mexican Style stewed tomatoes
2 Tbsp. flour
Crust (recipe follows)
grated cheese

Brown ground beef, drain and set aside. Brown the onion and green pepper in oil. Add corn, black olives, green chilies, tomatoes, flour and ground beef. Spread crust on an oiled pie plate pressing all edges to form as a pie crust. Fill with ground beef mixture. Bake at 350° for 1 hour. Top with grated cheese and reheat just long enough to melt. Serves 6.

Crust:
1 ½ cups masa harina (corn flour)
1 ½ cups water
1 Tbsp. oil
salt to taste

Combine all ingredients. Mix well. Should be dough-like consistency. Roll out large enough to fill 9" pie plate.

Spaghetti Pie

6 ozs. spaghetti noodles or spinach noodles, cooked and drained
2 Tbsp. margarine, melted
⅓ cup grated Parmesan cheese
⅛ tsp. garlic powder
2 eggs, beaten
1 cup cottage cheese
1 lb. ground beef or sausage, browned and drained
2 cups spaghetti sauce
½ cup grated mozzarella cheese

Stir margarine, Parmesan cheese, garlic and eggs into cooked and drained noodles together. Place mixture into bottom of a 10" buttered pie plate. Spread cottage cheese over noodle mixture. Combine browned meat and spaghetti sauce and pour over noodles and cheese. Bake, uncovered, at 350° for 20 minutes. Sprinkle on mozzarella cheese and bake 5 minutes longer. Serves 6-8.

Mamasita's Lasagne

1 ½ lbs. lean ground beef
1 medium onion, coarsely chopped
½ tsp. cumin
½ tsp. garlic powder
1 tsp. chili powder
salt and pepper
2 ¼ cups salsa
9 flour tortillas
29 oz. can refried beans
1 cup sliced black olives
12 ozs. Monterey Jack cheese, grated
chopped lettuce
chopped tomatoes
sour cream
chopped cilantro

Grease a 13"x9" baking pan. Brown ground beef in skillet with chopped onion until onion is tender. Drain off excess fat. Season with cumin, garlic, chili powder, and salt and pepper to taste. Add salsa. Remove from heat and set aside. Divide 1 can refried beans evenly among flour tortillas. Spread thinly over tortillas. Sprinkle generously with olives and grated cheese. Roll up each tortilla tightly and arrange closely in baking pan. Pour meat sauce over the top, spreading evenly to cover. Sprinkle generously with more cheese. Bake at 400° for 20-30 minutes. Cut in squares and serve garnished with chopped lettuce, tomatoes, sour cream and cilantro. Serves 6-8.

River Runners Rice Dinner

1 lb. hamburger
2 cups cooked rice
16 oz. tomato sauce
2 tsp. sugar
1 tsp. salt
dash garlic powder
½ cup Cheddar cheese, cubed

Brown hamburger and drain. Add cooked rice, tomato sauce and seasonings. Simmer a few minutes. Add cheese and heat until melted. Kids love this.

Keith and Paul Wegeman were born in Denver, and both began skiing as toddlers under the tutelage of their father, Al. The family moved to Steamboat in 1944 when the boys were teenagers. Both brothers represented Steamboat and the U.S. in the Oslo Olympics of 1952.

Rice Pilaf

¼ cup butter
1 cup vermicelli
1 cup rice
1 ½ cups chicken broth
1 cup water
1 tsp. salt
pepper to taste

Melt butter over medium heat. Add vermicelli and cook until lightly browned, stirring constantly. Remove from heat. Stir in rice until well blended, then add chicken broth, water, salt and pepper. Cover and bring to a boil. Reduce heat and simmer 20 minutes or until rice is tender. Stir once and serve. Serves 6.

Arrowhead Rice

1 ½ cup rice
6 Tbsp. butter
1 cup fine egg noodles
2 - 3 Tbsp. salt
3 cups boiling water

Heat butter in a heavy skillet. Add noodles; stir until golden. Add rice and cook five minutes, stirring. Add salt and boiling water. Stir and cover. Cook 20 minutes until water is absorbed. Serves 6.

Paul Wegeman's Macaroni & Cheese

1 ½ cups uncooked elbow macaroni
¾ lb. very sharp natural Cheddar cheese, diced fine
13 oz. can evaporated milk
Lawry's seasoned salt

Cook macaroni in boiling water until barely tender; drain and turn into well greased 1 ½ quart casserole. Stir in cheese and milk. Sprinkle top with seasoned salt. Bake at 350° about an hour, until sauce is consistency desired. Serves 4.

Sandwich Spread

3 cups ham, beef or chicken, cooked
2 hard boiled eggs (opt.)
1 cup grated Cheddar cheese
4 tsp. pickle relish
Miracle Whip salad dressing

Grind meat, eggs, and cheese together into a large bowl. In a separate bowl combine pickle relish and Miracle Whip with a wire whisk. Add to meat mixture and serve spread over favorite bread. Makes 6-8 sandwiches.

Trailbusters Chicken Nuggets

1 lb. boneless chicken breast
2 eggs
1 ¼ cup corn flakes crumbs
½ tsp. garlic salt
½ tsp. season salt

Remove skin and any extra fat from breasts. Cut breasts into chunks about 1 ½ to 2 inch square. Mix corn flakes crumbs, garlic salt and season salt in a medium bowl or large ziploc bag. Beat eggs in a medium bowl. Dip chicken pieces in egg then dip in cornflake mixture, coating well. Kids like to shake these in a ziploc bag. Place on baking sheet sprayed well with vegetable spray. Spray chicken lightly with vegetable spray and bake in 400° oven for 10 minutes. Serve hot with barbecue sauce and honey mustard sauce. Kids go crazy over these! This recipe doubles easily and freezes well. When baking frozen nuggets allow 15 to 20 minutes for baking time. You may also fry them just as you would fried chicken. Fry 5 minutes on each side and drain well. Serves 4.

Banana Boats

1 medium banana, firm but ripe
1 Tbsp. miniature marshmallows
1 Tbsp. chocolate chips

Hold banana as if it were a boat. Cut from one tip to the other, through the peel and halfway through the banana. Press end to open up. Fill with marshmallows and chocolate chips. Place on a plate and cover with wax paper. Microwave on very low heat for 1 minute 15 seconds or until marshmallows and chips have melted. Allow banana to cool slightly before diving in. Serves 1.

Banana Orange Jello

1 envelope unflavored gelatin
2 Tbsp. sugar
⅛ tsp. salt
¾ cup cold water
6 oz. can frozen orange juice
1 Tbsp. lemon juice
3 ice cubes
1 ½ cups fruit, banana and orange sections in chunks

Combine gelatin, sugar and salt in a saucepan. Add water. Cook over low heat, stirring until gelatin dissolves. Remove from heat. Stir in juice concentrate, lemon juice and ice cubes until juice and ice melt. Mixture will be the consistency of unbeaten egg whites. Fold in fruit. Pour into an 8"x8" pan. Chill until firm. Serves 4-6.

Bananas with Raspberry Yogurt Sauce

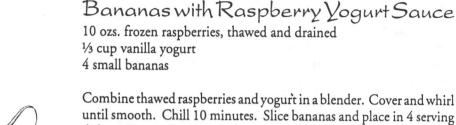

10 ozs. frozen raspberries, thawed and drained
⅓ cup vanilla yogurt
4 small bananas

Combine thawed raspberries and yogurt in a blender. Cover and whirl until smooth. Chill 10 minutes. Slice bananas and place in 4 serving dishes. Top with sauce and serve. Serves 4.

Apple Berry Gurt

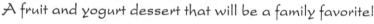

A fruit and yogurt dessert that will be a family favorite!

2 cups unsweetened applesauce
1 cup plain low-fat yogurt
¼ cup honey or to taste
1 cup frozen dry-pack raspberries, thawed

Combine applesauce, yogurt and honey in bowl until blended. Stir in raspberries. Refrigerate until ready to serve. Makes 8 servings.

Gilpin Creek and Gilpin Lake were named after the first territorial governor of Colorado, William Gilpin. Small amounts of gold were found here in the early 1900s at a mine opened by Pony Whitmore some time between his arrival in 1879 and his death in 1884.

Double Crunch Granola Bars

4 cups uncooked quick oats
1 ½ cups chopped nuts
¾ cup melted margarine
½ cup honey or molasses
1 tsp. vanilla
1 tsp. salt (opt.)

Combine all ingredients and mix well. Press firmly into a well greased 15 ½" x 10 ½" jelly roll pan. Bake in preheated very hot 425° degree oven 10-12 minutes or until golden brown and bubbly. Cool slightly and cut into bars while warm.

Gorc

(Good Ol' Raisins and Peanuts, but with Cashews)

2-3 handfuls raw cashews*
2 handfuls golden raisins
1 handful dark chocolate chips
1 handful butterscotch chips

Mix well and put out of sight until arrival in woods. Depending on how big your hand is, this will normally fill 2 medium sized ziploc bags—enough to last about a 25 mile hike. For use as trail food, eat it for breakfast or dessert, and it won't last a day. If it's really hot, substitute the chips with M&M's. Keep away from squirrels. *For young children, replace nuts with Cheerios.

Gilpin Gorp

8 ozs. slivered almonds*
1 cup sunflower seeds
2 cups craisins
1 cup currants
1 cup mini chocolate chips

Pour all ingredients in a container and mix well. A great treat on the trail or at home. Craisins are dried cranberries and are available at most stores. *For young children, substitute Cheerios for slivered almonds.

Fruit Leather

Spiced Apple:
30 oz. jar applesauce
3 Tbsp. honey
1 ½ tsp. cinnamon

Cranberry-Raspberry:
16 oz. can jellied cranberry-raspberry sauce
2 Tbsp. honey

Banana-Peach:
18 oz. can peach halves, drained
1 medium banana

Select your choice for fruit leather. Line 2 - 10"x15" jelly roll pans with plastic wrap. Secure edges with tape or tuck excess under pan. In a blender or food processor, whirl fruit and seasoning until smooth. Spread evenly over bottom of pan. Place pans in an oven set at 150°. When drying more than 1 pan, allow 4" drying space between oven racks. Dry 6-8 hours or until leather is firm and dry to the touch. Remove plastic and leather from pan and roll up while still warm; twist ends to seal. Wrap with additional plastic wrap. Store at room temperature or freeze.

Peanut Butter Chews

1 cup peanut butter
½ cup honey
½ cup powdered milk
coconut

Mix first 3 ingredients together. Roll into 1" balls. Roll in coconut to coat.

Spring Creek Oat Cookies

½ cup oil
¾ cup honey
1 egg
¼ cup water
1 tsp. vanilla
½ cup whole wheat flour
½ cup unbleached flour
½ cup dry milk powder
¼ tsp. salt (opt.)
½ tsp. baking soda
1 tsp. cinnamon
½ tsp. allspice
¼ tsp. cloves
2 cups rolled oats
1 cup wheat germ
½-¾ cup raisins
¼ cup sunflower seeds

Spring Creek was named because the spring that supplied the bathhouse and pool ran along the bed of the stream.

Thoroughly beat oil, honey, egg, water and vanilla. Add flour, dry milk, salt, soda and spices. Beat well. Mix in oats, wheat germ, raisins and seeds. Drop by teaspoonfuls onto a greased cookie sheet. Bake at 350º for 8-12 minutes.

Salt Water Taffy

1 cup sugar
¾ cup light corn syrup
⅔ cup water
1 Tbsp. cornstarch
2 Tbsp. margarine
1 tsp. salt
2 tsp. vanilla

"We went up to Spring Creek on the ice and took a bath."

From the diary of
Lulie Margie Crawford
Dec. 15, 1880

Butter a square 8"x8"x2" pan. In a saucepan, combine all ingredients. Cook over medium heat until hard ball stage (250º on candy thermometer). Pour into pan. When just cool enough to handle, pull taffy until satiny, light in color and stiff, using buttered hands. Pull into strips ½" wide and cut into 1" pieces. Wrap individually. Makes 1 lb.

Strawberry Eggnog

10 oz. pkg. frozen strawberries in syrup, thawed
2 eggs or ½ cup egg substitute
2 ½ cups milk
1 tsp. vanilla
ground nutmeg

Blend all ingredients in a blender. Pour into glasses and sprinkle with nutmeg.

Fudgesicles

1 pkg. instant chocolate pudding
¼ cup sugar
½ cup heavy cream
1 cup milk
1 cup water

Mix all ingredients together until all sugar dissolves. Freeze in popsicle molds or paper cups with popsicle sticks for handles. Enjoy ... and make plenty because they won't last long!

Sparkling Fruit Slushes

2 cups sugar
4 cups water
12 oz. can concentrated orange juice
⅓ cup lemon juice
46 oz. can fruit juice of your choice
ginger ale

Combine sugar and water and heat until sugar is dissolved. Add orange juice concentrate, lemon juice and fruit juice. Fill 6-7 ice cube trays and freeze until firm. When frozen, remove cubes to plastic bags.

For 1 serving: Fill a glass with fruit slush cubes. Add ginger ale to cover. Let stand 10-15 minutes. Stir and serve. Great in the summer.

Designer's Dough

1 cup salt
1 ½ cups hot water
4 cups flour

Dissolve salt in hot water. Let cool. Add flour slowly. Knead until smooth (8-10 minutes). Create ornaments, beads, figures of your own design. Bake at 325° until hard. Dough art can be painted or decorated with beads, yarn and other "glue on's." NOT EDIBLE.

Fingerpaint

½ cup cornstarch
cold water
1 pt. boiling water
¼ cup talcum powder
½ cup mild soap flakes (ivory snow)

Dissolve cornstarch in enough cold water to cover. Add this mixture to boiling water, stirring until it bubbles. Cool. Add soap flakes and talcum powder. When cooled, add food coloring. Store in covered jars. NOT EDIBLE.

Sugar Crystals

1 cup water
2 cups granulated sugar
food coloring
clear, clean widemouthed jars

Heat water to near boiling point. Add sugar and a few drops of food coloring. Cook over medium heat until sugar is completely dissolved and mixture is syrupy. Remove from heat and let cool for 15 minutes. Pour mixture into jar. Place jar in a safe, well lit place where it won't be bumped, moved or disturbed. Before long, crystals will begin to form. Entire process takes about a month. NOT EDIBLE.

Sculptors Soft Pretzels

1 pkg. yeast
1 ½ cups warm water
1 Tbsp. sugar
1 tsp. salt
4 cups flour
1 egg
coarse salt

In bowl, dissolve yeast, sugar and salt in warm water. Stir in flour and knead until smooth. Divide dough and use (like play dough) to form pretzels in the shape of letters, animals, etc. Place on ungreased cookie sheet. Beat egg with 1 Tbsp. water. Brush pretzels with egg glaze. Sprinkle with salt, if desired. Bake at 375° until golden brown. Baking time depends on size/thickness of pretzels.

Kool Playdough

3 cups flour
¾ cup salt
2 Tbsp. cream of tartar
3 Tbsp. cooking oil
3 cups hot water
1-2 pkgs. unsweetened Kool Aid

Blend all ingredients in a non-stick pan. Cook over medium heat until a "glob" is formed. Let cool until comfortable to touch. Knead until smooth. Keep in plastic bag or airtight container. NOT EDIBLE.

Munchable Playdough

1 cup creamy peanut butter
1 ½ cup dry milk solids
½ cup honey
¼ cup cocoa, optional

Mix all ingredients together and let kids have fun. Decorations to use: chocolate chips, raisins, sunflower seeds and nuts.

the Pantry Shelf

the Pantry Shelf

Grandma's Holiday Chutney

Grandma came from England and crossed the Western plains in a covered wagon. This recipe has been handed down through generations.

4 cups cranberries
2 cups raisins
2 ½ cups sugar
1 tsp. cinnamon
⅓ cup vinegar

Combine all ingredients in a heavy pot. Cook over medium heat, until cranberries have popped, approximately 30 minutes. Stir often to prevent burning. Store refrigerated.

Jalapeño Jelly

Tie with a bright red bow—a great holiday gift!

1 cup ground green bell pepper
1 cup ground jalapeño peppers
6 cups sugar
1 ½ cups white wine vinegar
1 box liquid fruit pectin
green food coloring

Mix first four ingredients and boil for 10 minutes. Add pectin and boil for 4 more minutes. Add food coloring as desired. Strain and pour into sterilized jars and seal. Makes about 8 - ½ pint jars. Serve as an appetizer by spreading some over a block of cream cheese accompanied with crackers.

Rose Hip Syrup

Great on pancakes, waffles or French toast.

10 cups rose hip juice (recipe follows)
4 cups cranapple juice
¼ cup lemon juice
2 ½ -3 cups sugar

Place all the ingredients in a large kettle. Bring to a boil, lower heat and simmer 30-45 minute, until reduced and thickened. Pour into sterilized jars and process accordingly. Store in a cool, dark place.

Rose Hip Juice:
Rose hips grow in abundance in Routt County from late August through September. Pick stems off rose hips and wash in cold water. Add 2 cups water to each cup of hips. Boil 15 minutes. Mash hips with a potato masher and simmer 10 minutes more. Set aside for 24 hours in a glass or steel container. Strain juice through cheese cloth.

Lonnie Vanatta began skiing with the Winter Sports Club when he was 4 years old. He was selected to the U.S. Ski Team in 1977 and turned Pro in 1978. He raced on the Pro Circuit from 1978 to 1984 and three of those years he placed in the top 5 and was the top American money winner. He was also the World Pro Skiing Slalom Champion of 1980. Lonny had 20 professional victories in all. He continues to ski and to lead others to victory as a coach for the Steamboat Springs Winter Sports Club.

Plum Jam

3 ½ lbs. plums
¾ cups water
¼ cup lemon juice
1 box pectin
1 ½ cup honey

Combine the chopped plums, water, lemon juice, and pectin in a large kettle. Bring mixture to boil and add the honey. Continue cooking, stirring occasionally for about 20-30 minutes. Mixture should be thickened and reduced. Pour into sterilized jars and process accordingly. Yields 4-5 pints.

Apple Butter

The kitchen smells heavenly when this is cooking!

1 sack of Red Delicious apples
juice from 1 lemon
1 Tbsp. cinnamon
1 tsp. allspice
1 tsp. cloves

Grate or finely chop apples. Put in a crockpot and stir in lemon juice and spices. Cook covered on low heat for 6 hours. Remove cover and cook and additional 12-18 hours on low heat, stirring occasionally. When apple butter is dark brown and thick, pour into sterilized jars and process accordingly. Will keep refrigerated several weeks without processing. Peach butter can be made with this recipe, by substituting peaches for apples. Makes about 4 - 8 oz. jars.

Pumpkin Apricot Butter

A special fall treat.

29 oz. can pumpkin
2 cups honey
1 cup finely chopped dried apricots
1¼ cups water
¾ cup lemon juice
1 tsp. vanilla

In a large kettle, cook pumpkin and honey over medium heat until warm and blended. Add apricots, water, lemon juice and vanilla. Continue cooking to boiling, stirring constantly. Reduce heat and simmer about 20 minutes, stirring frequently, until thickened. Pour into sterilized jars and process in hot water bath. Yields 5 half pints.

Hazie's Honey Butter

Terrific on toast, cornbread or bagels.

Honey
Butter or Margarine

Whip equal parts of honey and butter together until mixture is light and creamy.

Cranapple Butter

6 lbs. apples
1 ½ qts. cranberry juice
2 ¼ cups honey

Quarter apples, remove seeds and stem. Cook in cranberry juice until tender. Press through a food mill and return to kettle with honey. Cook until thick, about 1 hour, stirring frequently. Pour into sterilized jars and process in a water bath for 5 minutes. Yields 5 pints.

Cranberry Applesauce

Great for gift-giving.

3 lbs. Macintosh Apples
12 ozs. cranberries
1 cinnamon stick
1 cup sugar
1 cup water
cinnamon to taste

In a large pot, combine apples, cranberries, cinnamon stick, sugar and 1 cup water. Bring mixture to a boil and simmer, covered, stirring occasionally for 30- 35 minutes, until apples are tender. In a food processor with a steel blade, purée mixture and return to pot. Stir in cinnamon and additional sugar to taste. Cool and pour into quart jars and process accordingly. Yields 6 cups.

"Been awful busy today. The popcorn came and I popped some of it. Made a cake. Went over to Aunt Nannie's. Snowing. Dave gone with the mail. Scrubbed the floor and ironed. Fried doughnuts and did a thousand and one things besides, and am so tired I can hardly sit up."

From the diary of
Lulie Margie Crawford
Dec. 23, 1880

Easy Carmel Corn

½ cup butter or margarine, melted
1 ⅓ cups sugar
½ cup light corn syrup
1 tsp. vanilla
2 quarts of popped popcorn

Add the sugar and corn syrup to the melted butter or margarine. Boil gently to 290° (about 10 minutes). Add vanilla and pour over popcorn. Stir and pour onto a greased cookie sheet and spread quickly. Cook and serve.

Sugar and Spice Pecans
Very festive—great for holiday gift-giving.

¼ cup butter
3 cups pecan halves
½ cup sugar
3 Tbsp. sugar
1 Tbsp. cinnamon
1 ½ tsp. ginger
1 ½ tsp. nutmeg

Melt butter in a skillet. Stir in pecans and ½ cup sugar. Cook over medium heat, stirring occasionally until sugar melts and nuts brown, 8-12 minutes. Combine remaining ingredients in a large bowl. Stir in pecans and coat well. Spread on waxed paper and cool completely.

Easy Peppery Pickles
1 peck small cucumbers
1 gallon vinegar
1 cup sugar
1 scant cup dry mustard
1 cup salt
1 scant cup black pepper

Wash small cucumbers; soak overnight in cold water. Combine remaining ingredients and mix well. Place pickles in quart jars. Pour pickling solution over pickles, making sure the solution is well-blended each time you pour into a jar. Screw tops on tightly and turn upside down. Shake several times each day for a week. These pickles may be processed if desired in boiling water bath. These spicy little pickles are wonderful with sliced sausage or used in sandwiches. Makes 10 quarts.

George's Gulch in Clark is named for George, a stallion who made it his domain in the days of the open range.

Pickled Jalapeño Peppers
1 cup vinegar
¼ cup water
¼ cup olive oil
1 tsp. salt
1 tsp. pickling spice
fresh jalapeños

Mix first 5 ingredients in a pot and heat to boiling. Pack fresh jalapeños into a hot, sterilized pint jar. Pour boiling liquid over peppers. Leave 1 inch at top of jar. Cover with lid and process for 20 minutes. Multiply recipe for larger quantities. Makes 1 pint.

Bucking Chute Chili Sauce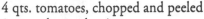

4 qts. tomatoes, chopped and peeled
2 cups chopped onions
1 cup chopped sweet red bell pepper
1 cup chopped green bell pepper
1 small chopped hot red pepper
3 Tbsp. salt
½ cup sugar
1 Tbsp. mustard seed
1 tsp. allspice
1 tsp. cinnamon
2 ½ cup vinegar (red wine or cider)

Combine vegetables, salt, sugar and cook until mixture begins to thicken. Add vinegar and spices. Put mustard seeds in a bag and cook until mixture becomes a thick sauce. Pour into hot, sterilized jars and seal.

Salsa Fresca

This is delicious fresh or canned.

1 medium onion, diced
2 large garlic cloves, diced
3 fresh jalapeños without seeds, diced
3 to 4 tomatoes, diced
1 tsp. salt
1 tsp. sugar
1 tsp. cider vinegar
1 Tbsp. chopped fresh cilantro
2 tsp. lemon juice

Fresh:
Combine first four ingredients and mix. Add remaining ingredients and mix well. Delicious fresh and cans well. Be careful to protect hands when working with fresh jalapeños.

To Can:
For each one cup of salsa, add ½ cup tomato sauce. Bring to a boil, pack into prepared jars. Process in boiling water bath 50 minutes (for pints) or 55 minutes (for quarts). These times are for altitudes at 7,000 feet above sea level.

Spaghetti Sauce

4 onions, finely diced
6 cloves garlic, diced
2 Tbsp. olive oil
30 ripe tomatoes, peeled and chopped
2 - 6 oz. cans tomato paste
4 tsp. oregano
3 tsp. basil
2 tsp. salt
1 tsp. black pepper
¼ tsp. red pepper (cayenne)

Sauté onion and garlic in olive oil. Add tomatoes and tomato paste. Add seasonings and simmer for 15 - 20 minutes. Pour into prepared jars and process in a boiling water bath for 50 minutes (pints) or 55 minutes (quarts). These times are for altitudes at 7,000 feet above sea level. Makes approximately 4 pints.

Nelson Carmichael moved to Steamboat from Niagra Falls in 1977, at the age of 12. He soon began skiing with Park Smalley's Great Western Freestyle Center and the Steamboat Springs Winter Sports Club. Nelson has been winning national and international mogul championships with great regularity since 1984. He competed in the Calgary Olympics in 1988, and became the first Winter Olympic medal winner from Colorado when he won the bronze in 1992 at Albertville.

Sweet and Hot Dill Mustard

1 cup dry mustard
1 cup cider vinegar
1 cup sugar
1 ½ tsp. dill weed
2 eggs, slightly beaten

Whisk all ingredients except eggs in a heavy saucepan. Let stand at room temperature 4 - 6 hours. Stir beaten eggs into mixture and cook over low heat, stirring constantly, until thickened (8-10 minutes). Cool and cover, or pour into sterilized jars. Refrigerate 24 hours before serving. Stores covered in refrigerator for up to 3 months. Yield 1½ pints.

Amaretto Liqueur

Great in coffee or poured over ice cream!

8 cups sugar
6 cups water
1 pint grain alcohol
6 ozs. almond extract
6 tsp. vanilla

Simmer sugar and water for 1 hour. Cool to room temperature. Add alcohol and extracts. Store in airtight jars or bottles. Makes 3-4 qts.

Berry Punch

16 oz. pkg. frozen strawberries in syrup, thawed
12 oz. can frozen concentrated raspberry juice
12 oz. can frozen concentrated limeade
1 liter bottle ginger ale, chilled
2 liter bottle soda water, chilled

Purée strawberries in a blender. Combine all ingredients in a 6 quart bowl and serve.

Banana Punch

4 cups sugar
6 cups water
12 oz. frozen orange juice
1 46 oz. frozen pineapple juice
5 bananas, mashed
2 quarts ginger ale
2 lemons, thinly sliced

Combine sugar and water in a saucepan and bring to a boil. Set aside and allow to cool. When cool, add to orange juice, pineapple juice, and bananas. Mix and freeze in a bowl. This will take about 2 ½ hours. Before serving, mash with potato masher and add ginger ale. Serve with lemon slices. Yields approximately 5-6 qts.

Champagne Punch

½ cup fresh orange juice
¼ cup brandy
½ cup light rum
2 Tbsp. Grand Marnier
1 orange, cut into rounds
½ cup pineapple chunks
1 bottle champagne

Mix together everything except champagne. Refrigerate for a few hours. When ready to serve, pour orange juice mixture over ice in a punch bowl. Pour in champagne.

Cookbook Tea

1 cup dry Tang
½ cup instant lemon flavored tea, sweetened
1 tsp. cinnamon
1 tsp. ground cloves

Mix and store dry in a covered container. To serve, stir powdered mixture into a cup of boiling water.

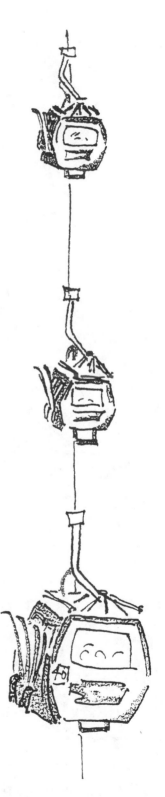

Doak's Margaritas

⅓ tequila
⅓ fresh lime juice
⅓ Triple Sec

Mix equal parts of the 3 ingredients and freeze at least 4 hours. Pour into a blender and spin slightly. Allow only 2 per guest!

Homemade Irish Creme

1 can sweetened condensed milk
1 pint whipping cream
4 Tbsp. chocolate syrup
½ tsp. almond extract
2 cups blended Irish whiskey

Blend first 4 ingredients with an electric mixer or blender. Stir in whiskey. Pour into bottles and keep refrigerated. Shake gently before each use.

Instant Cocoa Mix

2 cups nonfat powdered milk
Dash salt
1/4 cup cocoa
1 cup confectioners sugar
1/3 cup non-dairy powdered creamer
1 Tbsp. malted milk powder (optional)

Mix all ingredients and store in a covered container. To serve, spoon 4 Tbsp. (or to taste) into a cup of boiling water and stir. Enjoy!

Kahlua Under the Kitchen Sink

4 cups water
4 cups sugar
¾ cup instant coffee
1 vanilla bean, cut into small pieces
1 fifth of vodka (cheap works well)

Simmer water and sugar for 25 minutes until clear. Cool completely. Add coffee, vanilla and vodka. Put mixture into a jug and place it under the kitchen sink. Shake it once each day when you do the dishes. (Don't sneak!) After 3 weeks, strain through a paper towel and pour into bottles or jars. Great for Christmas gifts.

Spiced Wassail

6 cups apple juice
2 cups cranberry juice
1 tsp. aromatic bitters
6 sticks of cinnamon
1 tsp. whole allspice
3 oranges, studded with 16 cloves
1 cup rum (if desired)

Simmer 10 minutes, covered.

Kiwi Lime Cooler

2 kiwi fruit, peeled and halved
½ cup white grape juice
2 (4 oz.) lime frozen fruit bars, cut into chunks
2 tsp. lime juice
strawberries for garnish

Purée all ingredients, except strawberries, in blender until thick and frothy. Pour into glasses and top with sliced strawberries. Serves 2.

Mint Chocolate Malt Mix

2 cups chocolate flavored malt milk powder
½ cup butter mints
3 cups dry milk powder
½ cup pre-sweetened cocoa mix

In a blender, combine 1 cup malted milk powder and the mints. Cover and blend 1 minute or until mints are finely chopped. Turn into mixing bowl and add remaining malted milk powder, milk powder, and cocoa mix. Stir well. Store in airtight container. For one serving, stir ¼ cup mixture into cup of boiling water. Top with marshmallows.

Shandy

A British drink—serve on a hot
"Out of Africa" afternoon.

For each serving:
6 ozs. cold beer
6 ozs. tart lemonade or limeade
ice

In a chilled mug, combine the beer and lemonade. Add ice if desired.

Sparkling Harvest Cider

2 quarts apple cider or juice
1 cup lemon juice from concentrate
½ cup sugar
32 oz. bottle ginger ale, chilled

In punch bowl, combine cider, lemon juice and sugar. Stir until sugar dissolves. Chill. Just before serving, add ginger ale. Garnish as desired. Serve over ice. Makes about 3 quarts.

Hot Cranberry Punch

1 cup water
1 cup sugar
1 pkg. whole fresh cranberries
2 qts. water
1 ½ qts. pineapple-orange juice
¼ cup lemon juice

Combine sugar and 1 cup water in a saucepan. Bring to a boil and simmer for 2-3 minutes; set aside. Combine cranberries and 2 qts. water in a large saucepan. Bring to a boil and simmer until they all pop. Cool and strain. Combine sugar, syrup and cranberry juice in a large kettle. Add pineapple-orange juice and lemon juice. Heat until hot. Makes ¾ gallon.

Strawberry Lime Cooler

1 pint strawberries, hulled and sliced
1 ½ cups seltzer
½ cup lime syrup
½ cup fresh lime juice
½ cup ice cubes

In a blender at high speed, blend strawberries, seltzer, lime syrup, lime juice, and ice cubes until mixture is smooth. Pour mixture into chilled glasses. Makes 4 drinks.

Tangerine Tea

2 cups water
1 ½ cups fresh tangerine or orange juice
¼ cup sugar or to taste
¼ tsp. ground cinnamon
⅛ tsp ground cloves
2 tea bags

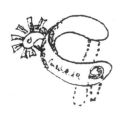

Heat water to boil in large saucepan. Stir in tangerine juice, sugar, cinnamon and cloves. Heat to boil, simmer and stir until sugar dissolves. Add tea bags; remove from heat. Let steep three to four minutes. Serves 4.

Restaurants

Restaurants

Blue Pheasant Restaurant at Steamboat
Sundance Plaza • Steamboat Springs, Colorado
(303) 879-6680

Spinach Crêpes
(Crêpes aux epinards)

1 cup milk
1 cup flour
¼ cup butter
3 eggs
salt
Spinach Filling (recipe follows)

Melt butter. Whisk eggs until light and add all remaining ingredients. Blend well. Let stand refrigerated several hours. Lightly butter an 8" non-stick crêpe or frying pan. Pour a little batter into hot pan. Swirl around until it coats pan. Cook several minutes and flip, cook several minutes more. Fill crêpes with spinach filling. Makes 12 crêpes. Serves 6.

Spinach Filling:
1 - 10 oz. package frozen spinach
½ cup cream
½ cup chicken stock
1 ½ Tbsp. flour
¼ cup minced onion, cooked

Cook spinach and drain very well. Mix in cream, chicken stock, flour and onion.

Cantina
818 Lincoln Avenue • Steamboat Springs, Colorado
(303) 879-0826

Guacamole

6 ripe avocadoes, halved and seeded
1 small tomato, diced
¼ cup mild diced green chilies
1 clove garlic, minced
1 tsp. salt
¼ tsp. cumin
2 Tbsp. lemon juice

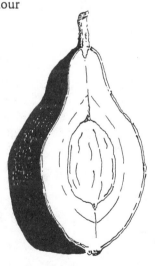

With a large spoon, scoop pulp from skin of avocadoes into bowl. Mash avocadoes with potato masher, leaving slightly chunky; set aside. Combine remaining ingredients and mix well. Fold into avocadoes gently not to mush. Chill until ready to serve. Serve as dip with tortilla chips. Yields 4 cups.

Bluepoint Bakery
1307 E. 6th Avenue • Denver, Colorado
(303) 839-1820

Tomato Chili Cheese Bread

A delicious, spicy loaf.

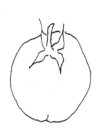

2 cups tomato juice, warmed
2 Tbsp. dry yeast
2 eggs
6 ½ cups flour (bread flour preferred)
1 Tbsp. salt
1 ½ Tbsp. ground chili pepper
2 cups grated Cheddar cheese
1 egg mixed with 1 Tbsp. water

In a large mixing bowl, sprinkle yeast over tomato juice and let stand until yeast is dissolved. Add eggs and mix well. Stir in 4 cups of flour, seasonings, and cheese until well blended. Add enough remaining flour to make a soft dough. Turn out onto a floured surface and knead 5-8 minutes until dough is no longer sticky. Place in a greased bowl and let rise until doubled. Punch down and divide into two pieces. Shape each piece into a round loaf. Place on a greased baking sheet and brush loaves with egg and water mixture. Sprinkle tops with chili pepper. Cover and let rise until doubled. Bake at 350º for 40 - 45 minutes. Makes 2 loaves.

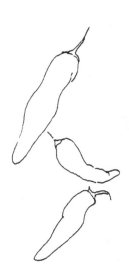

The Chart House
2165 Pine Grove Road • Steamboat Springs, Colorado
(303) 879-6976

Coconut Crunchy Shrimp

2 lbs. large shrimp, shelled, butterflied lengthwise
2 cups rice flour
1 cup dry tempura mix
cold water
2 cups gourmet Oriental bread crumbs
1 cup shredded coconut
oil for frying

Thoroughly coat shrimp with rice flour. Mix Japanese breadcrumbs and coconut together. Mix tempura batter according to package instructions and dip shrimp in tempura batter. Hold shrimp by the tail and coat entire shrimp well. Dip coated shrimp in coconut - breadcrumb mixture. Deep fry in 2 inches of hot oil until entire shrimp is golden brown. Serve with duck sauce, soy-ginger sauce or cocktail sauce. Serves 8. Oriental breadcrumbs are available at specialty food stores.

Café Blue Bayou
701 Yampa Street • Steamboat Springs, Colorado
(303) 879-8282

Herb Crusted Salmon and Greens

4-6 oz. each fresh salmon fillets, skinned and deboned

Lemon Wine Butter:
1 tsp. minced garlic
dash onion powder
juice of 2 lemons
¼-⅓ cup sweet white wine
1 cup butter

Herb Coating:
1 tsp. each, thyme, basil, rosemary and tarragon

Lemon Vinaigrette:
1 Tbsp. minced pimiento
2 Tbsp. minced capers, drained
1 clove garlic, minced
½ small white onion, minced
1 Tbsp. minced green onion tops
¾ cup lite olive oil
½ cup wine vinegar
¼ cup sweet white wine
1 tsp. fresh thyme or ¼ tsp. dried
2 Tbsp. lemon juice
salt to taste

4-6 oz. each fresh salmon fillets, skinned and deboned
warmed salad greens (see recipe below)
1 lemon, thinly sliced (garnish)
fresh herbs (garnish)

Prepare lemon wine butter by melting butter and adding remaining ingredients; set aside. Combine seasonings for herb coating; set aside. Prepare lemon vinaigrette by mixing pimientos, capers, garlic, onion and green onion tops. Combine remaining ingredients in blender and blend for 5-10 seconds. Pour over pimiento caper mixture and stir well. Refrigerate until ready to serve. Baste salmon fillets in lemon wine butter; coat boned side of fillet with herb coating. Place coated side down on hot grill. Cover and grill for 7 minutes. Turn and baste lightly with lemon wine butter. Cover again and grill for 5-6 minutes, making sure not to overcook.

Warmed Salad Greens:
½ head red leaf lettuce   ½ head green leaf lettuce
1 bunch spinach   white wine
Rinse greens thoroughly and pat dry. Tear lettuce, do not cut. Combine all greens and sauté with wine until warm, 2-3 minutes. Remove from pan with tongs.

To serve, place warmed salad greens in center of 4 individual serving plates, leaving space in center for salmon fillet. Place salmon in middle and ladle 2 ozs. of lemon vinaigrette over entire dish. Garnish with lemon slices and sprig of available herbs. Serves 4.

Cipriani's
Thunderhead Lodge • Steamboat Springs, Colorado
(303) 879-8824

Roast Duck with Raspberry Sauce

1 4-6 lb. whole duck
salt and pepper
1 carrot, peeled and diced
½ yellow onion, diced
3 stalks celery, diced
1 tsp. dried thyme
3 bay leaves
½ cup melted butter
½ cup fresh orange juice

Remove giblets from duck cavity. Clip wing joints and trim fat from both ends of duck. Sprinkle duck with salt and pepper inside and out. Combine next 5 ingredients and stuff into cavity. Place duck in roasting pan and prick with a meat fork several times. Roast at 375° for 30 minutes. Drain fat and baste with combined butter and orange juice. Continue roasting for 1 hour and 50 minutes (for a total cooking time of 2 hours and 20 minutes), draining fat and basting every 20 minutes. Let rest for a few minutes. To serve, pour a pool of raspberry sauce (recipe follows) on each dinner plate. Cut duck in half lengthwise and place on top of sauce. Serves 2.

Raspberry Sauce:
½ pint fresh raspberries
5 oz. white wine (or enough to cover berries)
sugar (1 tsp. - 1 Tbsp. depending on sweetness of the berries)
1 tsp. cornstarch mixed with 2 Tbsp. water

In a small saucepan, gently boil first 3 ingredients for 8 minutes. Strain through a stainless steel seive (aluminum will cause the sauce to darken). Return to pan. Heat and thicken with cornstarch. Sauce should coat a spoon. Thin with water if necessary.

Maria Quintana, freestyle aerial World Champion of 1986, is the only woman to successfully execute triple backflips with two twists in competition. She competed in the Calgary Olympics and also finds time to study medicine at Stanford.

The Coral Grill

Sundance Plaza • Steamboat Springs, Colorado
(303) 879-6858

Salmon Frambois

8 to 10 ozs. fresh raspberry preserves
½ cup white wine
½ tin peppercorns, ground (about ¼ cup)
fresh Norwegian salmon, hand filleted into 7-8 oz. portions
fresh raspberries (garnish)

Combine first 3 ingredients for marinade. Marinate salmon fillets for 3 hours. Place fillets in baking dish and bake at 375° for 12 minutes. Garnish with fresh raspberries. Serves 7.

Dos Amigos
Ski Time Square • Steamboat Springs, Colorado
(303) 879-4270

Filet al Chipotle

2 Tbsp. olive oil
1 large yellow onion, peeled and cut into quarters
1 dried passilla pepper, de-stemmed and seeds removed or 1 tsp. passilla
powder
3 chipotle peppers and juice
12 fresh tomatillos, peeled and washed
½ bunch fresh cilantro, washed and de-stemmed
1 cup beef stock
4-8 oz. tenderloins of beef
4 slices Monterey Jack cheese

Heat oil in sauté pan and add onions, passilla peppers, and chipotle
peppers. Cook until onions are brown and tender. In a blender or food
processor, combine tomatillos, cilantro, beef stock, and cooked onions
and peppers. Blend until smooth. Pour into saucepan and simmer for
1 hour. Cook tenderloins to desired doneness. Place 1 slice cheese over
each tenderloin and place under broiler until melted. To serve, pour
sauce onto four serving plates and place tenderloin into center of sauce.
Serves 4.

The Butcher Shop Restaurant
Ski Time Square • Steamboat Springs, Colorado
(303) 879-2484

Patty's Amaretto Cheesecake

Crust:
1 cup crushed chocolate wafers
¼ cup butter, melted

Filling:
2-8 oz. pkgs. cream cheese, softened
½ cup sugar
2 eggs
½ cup sour cream
⅓ cup Amaretto
1 tsp. vanilla

To prepare crust: combine wafers and melted butter. Press into
bottom and sides of a 9" spring form pan. Use another pie pan to press
mixture down.

To prepare filling: combine all ingredients with electric mixer, adding
Amaretto and vanilla last to suit taste. Pour into crust and bake at 300°
for 35-45 minutes. Cool on wire rack. Serves 8.

Giovanni's Ristorante
127 11th Street • Steamboat Springs, Colorado
(303) 879-4141

Calamari Marchigiani

2 lbs. calamari, cleaned and sliced

Sun Dried Tomato Pesto:
16 ozs. good quality sun dried tomatoes
1 cup fresh basil leaves, washed and patted dry
3 large garlic cloves, minced
½ cup pine nuts
½ cup good quality olive oil
¼ cup grated imported Parmesan cheese
¼ cup grated imported Romano cheese
salt and freshly ground black pepper to taste

1 cup sun dried tomato pesto
1 Tbsp. water
¼ cup heavy cream
4 qts. water
1 ½ Tbsp. salt
1 lb. fresh fettuccine
freshly ground black pepper
freshly grated Parmesan or Romano cheese

To prepare pesto: combine sun dried tomatoes, basil, garlic and pine nuts in the bowl of a food processor and chop. Leave the motor running and add the olive oil in a slow, steady stream. Shut off motor, add the cheeses, a few pinches of salt and liberal grinding of pepper. Process briefly to combine, then scrape out into bowl. Reserve 1 cup and refrigerate any left over.

Heat the pesto in a sauté pan with 1 Tbsp. water and cream over medium heat. Bring water to a boil in large pot. Add salt and pasta. Stir pasta. Boil rapidly until done to taste. Add calamari to pesto and cook until calamari is done, about 3 minutes, stirring occasionally. Drain pasta and return to pan and toss with pesto and calamari mixture. Serve immediately on warm plates with freshly ground pepper and grated cheese. Serves 4-6.

Chariot races, also known as cutter races, were first held in the Yampa Valley in 1957, beginning as a winter event using sleighs. Now they are held throughout the year at the rodeo grounds with wheels or runners according to the season.

ZZ

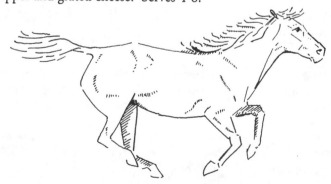

Hazie's
2305 Mt. Werner Circle • Steamboat Springs, Colorado
(303) 879-6111

Sautéed Lamb Loin Pignons

4 - 8 oz. trimmed lamb loins
fresh rosemary
garlic, chopped
crushed juniper berries
salt and pepper
½ cup gold raisins
½ cup pine nuts
¾ cup Madeira wine
½ cup whipping cream

Season lamb loins with rosemary, chopped garlic and juniper berries. Sauté lamb loins in butter until golden brown (2 ½ - 3 minutes per side). Remove from pan and keep warm. Add raisins, pine nuts and Madeira wine to pan with ½ cup whipping cream. Reduce until slightly thickened. Cut loin into thin slices and top with sauce. Serve with fresh green beans, broiled tomato halves and wild rice. Serves 4.

Harwig's Grill
911 Lincoln Avenue • Steamboat Springs, Colorado
(303) 879-1980

Sugar Snap Pea Feta Salad

2 cups fresh sugar snap peas *
¾ cup cubed Feta cheese
2 tsp. finely diced red onion
½ tomato, diced
2 Tbsp. finely chopped walnuts
2 Tbsp. freshly grated Parmesan

½ cup fresh mint
1 tsp. chopped garlic
½ cup white wine vinegar
salt and pepper to taste
1 cup olive oil

Combine first 6 ingredients in a bowl. For the dressing, combine mint, garlic, vinegar and salt and pepper in a food processor. With the machine running, slowly add the olive oil and blend well. Toss dressing with salad and refrigerate until ready to serve. Serves 2.

*Some may prefer to blanch the fresh sugar snap peas for about 30 seconds in boiling water and then rinse in ice water. It's also possible to use thawed frozen sugar snaps if available (don't blanch them).

5th Street Cafe
442 Lincoln Avenue • Steamboat Springs, Colorado
(303) 879-4106

Huevos Verde

Sauce:
¼ onion, chopped
½ lb. cubed pork
½ cup diced green chilies
¼ cup sliced jalapeño peppers
¼ cup white sauce
½ cup crushed tomatoes

Crêpe Batter:
4 eggs
½ cup powdered milk
1 ¼ cups cold water
1 ¼ cups flour

4 cups grated Monterey Jack cheese
sour cream (garnish)
chopped parsley (garnish)

To prepare sauce: sauté first 4 ingredients. Add white sauce; heat just to boiling. Add tomatoes.

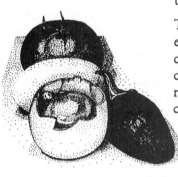

To prepare crêpe batter: combine all ingredients and blend with electric mixer on medium speed until smooth. Pour batter into oiled crêpe pan and cook until bubbly and edges curl slightly. Add ¼ cup cheese per crêpe, fold crêpe in half and remove from pan. Repeat with remaining batter. Serve sauce over cheese crêpes. Garnish with sour cream and parsley. Serves 8.

Old West Steak House
1104 Lincoln Avenue • Steamboat Springs, Colorado
(303) 879-1441

Garlic Dijon Salad Dressing

1 egg
⅓ cup Dijon mustard
⅔ cup red wine vinegar
½ tsp. salt
½ tsp. pepper
6 large cloves garlic, chopped
2 cups olive oil

Combine first 6 ingredients in a blender or food processor. With motor running, add oil in a very slow steady stream. Store in refrigerator until ready to use. Makes about 3 ½ cups.

In Season Bakery and Deli Café
131 11th Street • Steamboat Springs, Colorado
(303) 879-1840

"Cure All" Omelette

Hollandaise Sauce:
2 egg yolks
2 Tbsp. water
1 cup butter, melted
1 tsp. lemon juice
dash of Tabasco and Worcestershire sauce

Spinach Filling:
10 oz. pkg. frozen chopped spinach, thawed and squeezed dry
1 tsp. salt
½ tsp. pepper
¼ tsp. nutmeg

Omelette:
2 Tbsp. butter
1 Tbsp. chopped garlic
2 Tbsp. chopped green onion
8 eggs, beaten with 2 Tbsp. water
salt and pepper to taste

To prepare sauce: whisk egg yolks and water in the top of a double boiler or use a stainless steel mixing bowl. Place bowl over pot of simmering water, continuing to whisk yolks until thickened. Remove bowl from heat. Whisk in butter in a slow steady stream. Add remaining ingredients and mix well. Cover with plastic wrap and keep warm.

To prepare spinach filling: combine all ingredients in a saucepan and gently warm over low heat. Can be microwaved for 1 minute. Cover and keep warm.

To prepare omelette: in a 10" skillet, preferably non-stick, melt the butter. Add garlic and green onion and cook 1 minute. Stir salt and pepper into eggs, then pour into the skillet. When eggs begin to set, scramble a little then let cook about 30 seconds. Turn the omelette over and spread spinach filling over ½ the surface. Fold the omelette over the spinach and slide out of the pan onto a warm serving plate. Spoon some of the sauce over and pass the rest in a bowl. Serve 3-4.

The Inn at Steamboat Lake
61276 County Road 129 • Steamboat Springs, Colorado
(303) 879-3906

Chicken Marsala with Linguine

4 whole chicken breasts, skinned and butterflied
4 eggs
1 cup buttermilk
3 cups plain breadcrumbs
¼ cup grated Parmesan cheese
1 Tbsp. crushed oregano leaves
1 cup finely chopped almonds
2 Tbsp. lemon juice
½ cup Marsala wine
½ cup butter
linguine noodles, cooked

In a large saucepan, melt half the butter. Combine eggs and buttermilk in a small bowl; set aside. Combine breadcrumbs, Parmesan cheese, oregano, and almonds in separate bowl. Dip the chicken breast first in egg mixture, shaking off excess, then dip into breadcrumb mixture, coating well. Place chicken breasts, 1 at a time, in skillet with melted butter. Sauté in butter until cooked, remove and keep warm. Meanwhile, cook linguine according to directions; drain. Combine lemon juice, Marsala and leftover breadcrumbs in skillet and warm slightly. Serve chicken over warm, buttered linguine and dribble sauce over chicken. Serves 4.

Remington's
Sheraton Steamboat Resort • Steamboat Springs, Colorado
(303) 879-2220

Shrimp Scampi

1 lb. large shrimp, peeled and deveined
pinch garlic
pinch parsley
salt and pepper to taste
¾ cup white wine
pinch of demi glace powder mix
½ cup butter

Sauté shrimp in hot pan with garlic, parsley, salt and pepper. When halfway cooked, deglaze with wine. Cook shrimp until light orange, remove from pan and keep warm. Let reduce by ¾ and add demi glace. Slowly whisk in butter. Place shrimp on individual plates and pour butter sauce over. Serves 2-3.
* Demi glace mix can be found in packets at most grocery stores

The Home Ranch
54880 County Road 129 • Steamboat Springs, Colorado
(303) 879-1780

Loin of Venison with Lingonberry Sauce

1 ½ oranges
3 Tbsp. crushed black peppercorns
salt to taste
3 lb. section loin of venison, completely trimmed
2 Tbsp. olive oil
1 Tbsp. butter
1 ½ cups game stock (recipe follows)
¼ cup bottled lingonberries, drained
½ cup cream
3 Tbsp. chives (garnish)

Game Stock:
5 lbs. venison/elk bones, roughly chopped
¼ cup olive or vegetable oil
¼ cup butter
2 medium onions, chopped
2 medium carrots, chopped
2 celery stalks, chopped
1 white part of leek, sliced thinly
12 parsley stems
12 juniper berries
sachet of 1 bay leaf, 1 Tbsp. thyme, 12 peppercorns
½ cup red wine vinegar
2 qts. water
¼ cup currant jelly

"Three gentlemen from Denver came and are going to stay quite a while ... One of the swells killed a nice deer ... Mr. Morgan and Mr. Hulett came in ... Several wagons came in today and several horsemen. One lady and three girls along. They came up after some milk. They are camped down by the river."

From the diary of
Lulie Margie Crawford
July, 1881

Using a citrus zester or a potato peeler, cut off 1" wide swatches of the colored zest of orange. Then cut these into 1/16" wide shreds. In a saucepan, blanch 2 Tbsp. of the shredded orange zest in boiling water to cover for 30 seconds. Immediately rinse with cold running water, drain, and set aside. Preheat oven to 400°. Lay down waxed paper and spread peppercorns on it. Roll venison loin to coat and season with salt. In a large skillet, melt butter with oil over med. high heat. Sear the venison on all sides until deep brown in color, about 7-8 minutes. Place pan in oven and roast 15-20 minutes or until thermometer registers 130°-135° for medium rare. Remove loin and set on platter in a warm spot loosely covered with foil. Add 1 ½ cups stock to pan. As it comes to a boil over med. heat, scrape the pan to dissolve the browned roasting juices. Add the orange zest, lingonberries, and cream. Reduce over med. heat until the sauce thickens slightly. Slice the venison ¼" thick, arrange on plates. Pour sauce over venison and garnish with chives. Serves 8.

To prepare game stock, in a heavy 4 qt. stockpot, brown the bones in oil for 15-20 minutes. Add any trimmings from the loin. Continue browning another 10-15 minutes or until the bones and trimmings have reached a deep brown caramelized color. Pour off the oil. Add the butter, carrots, onions, celery and leeks. Stir. Continue browning all ingredients for another 5-10 minutes. Add the juniper berries, parsley stems and sachet bag. Deglaze with red wine vinegar; add water to cover. Simmer 2-3 hours, add more water as needed. Strain and reduce to 1 qt. Take aside 1 ½ cups, add currant jelly to this until it dissolves. Season with salt. Freeze remaining stock. *If sachet bags are unavailable, tie herbs in a small square of cheesecloth.

La Montaña Mexican Restaurant
2500 Village Drive • Steamboat Springs, Colorado
(303) 879-5800

Tortilla Soup

2 Tbsp. olive oil
⅓ cup diced onion
1 tsp. minced garlic
1 jalapeño pepper, seeds removed and minced
8 cups rich chicken stock, canned or bouillon
1 cup fresh diced tomatoes
½ cup tomato juice
2 Tbsp. chili powder
1 Tbsp. cumin
2 tsp. oregano
2 Tbsp. chopped cilantro
corn tortilla chips, broken
Monterey Jack cheese, grated

Sauté first 4 ingredients in a large saucepan until onions become transparent. Add next 6 ingredients and heat to a boil. Reduce heat and simmer for 30 minutes. Add cilantro and simmer 5 minutes more. To serve: place 2 Tbsp. broken corn tortilla chips in individual serving bowls. Ladle in soup. Add 1 heaping Tbsp. Monterey Jack cheese. Yields 10 cups.

Katy Rodolph (Wyatt), a member of the National Ski Hall of Fame, began skiing in junior high and within six years had finished in the top ten of all three alpine events at the World Championships. Her excellent Olympic performance in Oslo in 1952 was highlighted by a 5th place in giant slalom.

Riggio's Fine Italian Food
705 Lincoln Avenue • Steamboat Springs, Colorado
(303) 879-9010

White Chocolate Mousse

5 egg yolks
¾ cup granulated sugar
¼ cup sherry
1 ½ ozs. dry vermouth
1 ½ ozs. white cream de cocoa
⅓ lb. white chocolate, melted
2 cups heavy cream
⅛ cup sugar

Place first 5 ingredients into a double boiler. Whip vigorously with a wire whisk while cooking, until mixture thickens. When mixture is cooked enough it will lightly ribbon upon itself. Remove from heat and mix in chocolate. With an electric mixer, whip cream and sugar until stiff. Fold into egg chocolate mixture until completely combined. To serve: ladle mousse into serving dishes and refrigerate until set, about 1 hour. Serves 8-10.

The Scandinavian Lodge
2883 Burgess Creek Road • Steamboat Springs, Colorado
(303) 879-0517

Grand Marnier Mousse
3 egg yolks
⅓ cup sugar
1 Tbsp. Knox unflavored gelatin
3 Tbsp. boiling water
⅔ cup whipping cream
3 Tbsp. Grand Marnier liquor

Beat egg yolks until lemon colored and slowly add sugar. Melt the
gelatin in boiling water then add to the egg mixture. Whip the cream
to stiff peaks and fold into the egg mixture. Gently fold in the Grand
Marnier. Pour into serving dishes and chill well. Serves 4.

L'Apogee
911 Lincoln Avenue • Steamboat Springs, Colorado
(303) 879-1919

Sole Grenablaise
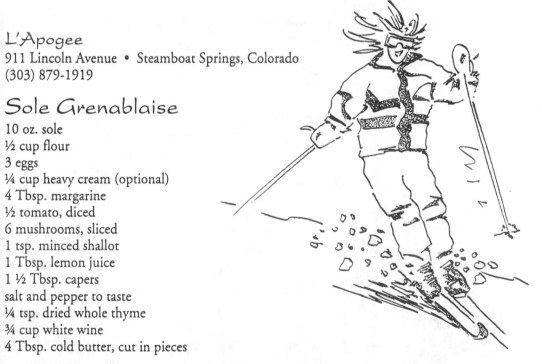

10 oz. sole
½ cup flour
3 eggs
¼ cup heavy cream (optional)
4 Tbsp. margarine
½ tomato, diced
6 mushrooms, sliced
1 tsp. minced shallot
1 Tbsp. lemon juice
1 ½ Tbsp. capers
salt and pepper to taste
¼ tsp. dried whole thyme
¾ cup white wine
4 Tbsp. cold butter, cut in pieces

Beat eggs and cream (if using) together lightly. Dredge sole in flour
and dip in egg batter. Melt margarine in a sauté pan. When it is
medium hot, add sole and cook until golden brown (about 2-3
minutes per side). Remove fish to a serving dish and keep warm. Wipe
out pan, return to heat and add tomato, mushrooms, and shallots.
Sauté briefly. Add remaining ingredients except butter. Bring to boil
and reduce liquid by half. With the pan still on the heat, add butter
in pieces, stirring with each addition. When all the butter is melted,
pour sauce over fish and serve. Serves 2.

Mattie Silks
1890 Mt. Werner Road • Steamboat Springs, Colorado
(303) 879-2448

Lemon Pepper Veal

Lemon Pepper Cognac Sauce:
½ cup butter
2 tsp. cracked pepper
1 tsp. minced garlic
1 Tbsp. chopped shallots or finely diced red onion
½ cup brandy
¼ - ⅓ cup lemon juice
1 tsp. beef bouillon
½ cup heavy cream
1 tsp. Maggi gravy seasoning
1 Tbsp. soy sauce
dash Worcestershire

Veal:
1 lb. milk fed veal, thinly sliced and pounded
½ cup flour
3 eggs, beaten
2 cups breadcrumbs
salad oil

To prepare sauce, melt ¼ cup butter in large sauté pan. Add next 10 ingredients. Cook until reduced to half and add remaining ¼ cup of butter in chunks until melted. Bread veal first with flour, then eggs, then breadcrumbs. Sauté very quickly in oil in separate sauté pan until golden brown on each side. Serve with Lemon Pepper Cognac Sauce.

Ore House at the Pine Grove
1465 Pine Grove Road • Steamboat Springs, Colorado
(303) 879-1190

Blackened Prime Rib / Rib Eye with Roasted Garlic Sauce

prime rib or rib-eye steaks, sliced 1" thick (7-9 ozs. per person)
Cajun seasoning
1 cup onion powder
1 cup garlic powder
½ cup basil
½ cup oregano
1 cup white pepper
½ cup lemon pepper
3 cups paprika
4 cups breadcrumbs
½ cup cayenne pepper
½ cup salt
⅛ cup thyme

Garlic Sauce:
2-3 Tbsp. butter (room temperature)
2 Tbsp. minced garlic
chopped chives
¼ cup Worcestershire sauce
¼ cup beef stock
6-8 ozs. butter

Routt County's hills have been mined since gold was discovered at Hahns Peak in 1866 and have been the leading coal producer in Colorado since the early 1960s.

Trim off most all excess fat from meat. Combine remaining ingredients and coat both sides of the meat completely and evenly. Heat a cast iron skillet until hot. Place meat in skillet and brown, turning once. Turn on fan as smoke from the spices is potent. The spice coating should turn from red to blacken. When the meat is blackened on both sides, remove and keep warm. Repeat with remaining meat.

To prepare garlic sauce: heat butter and garlic in a 8" sauté pan until garlic is browned, but not burned. Add chives and sauté. Remove from heat and add Worcestershire and beef stock. Carefully add butter, a little at a time, whisking until medium dark tan color and the consistency of ranch dressing.

To serve: pour sauce over warm meat and serve with a great bottle of Pinot Noir, Bordeaux or an ice cold beer. Extra Cajun seasonings may be stored for future use.

Ragnar's
2305 Mt. Werner Circle • Steamboat Springs, Colorado
(303) 879-6111

Sea Chowder

¼ lb. butter
1 onion, diced
3 carrots, diced
2 celery stalks, diced
1 cup flour
10 ozs. clam juice
3 bay leafs
¼ tsp. fennel seed
dash cayenne pepper
½ tsp. tarragon
½ tsp. thyme
1 cup fish stock
2 cups chicken stock
½ bottle white wine
½ cup brandy
roux
1 lb. clams
1 lb. shrimp
½ cup cream

Heat butter in a large stock pot. Add vegetables, cover and steam until tender crisp. Add flour and mix with vegetables; add clam juice. Add herbs and spices and mix well. Add fish and chicken stocks, white wine and brandy. Return to a boil. Add roux until soup has reached desired thickness. Simmer for 15 minutes. Add shellfish, simmer gently being careful not to overcook. Stir in cream. Serves 6.

Mazzola's Italian Restaurant
440 South Lincoln Avenue • Steamboat Springs, Colorado
(303) 879-2405

Scampi Calzone

¾ lb. real or imitation crabmeat
¾ lb. tiny salad shrimp
3 Tbsp. butter
1 tsp. garlic powder or 1 Tbsp. minced fresh garlic
15 ozs. ricotta cheese
1 cup grated Romano cheese
1 cup grated mozzarella cheese
pinch of salt
2 tsp. dried basil
dash pepper
2 Tbsp. parsley
1 loaf frozen white bread dough, thawed and divided into 8 portions
32 oz. jar spaghetti sauce

Sauté crab and shrimp in butter and garlic; set aside. Mix cheeses and seasonings; set aside. Roll bread dough portions in thin (⅛" thick) 8" circles. On ½ of dough, put ⅛ each of crab and cheese mixture. Fold over and seal well by pressing edges with fork tines. Cheese will melt out if not sealed well. Place on greased cookie sheet. Repeat with remaining ingredients. Bake at 450° for 20 minutes or until golden brown. Brush with oil for shiny top. Serve with warm spaghetti sauce poured over or as a dip. Excellent cold; can be frozen when assembled and baked later. Serves 8.

The Tugboat
Ski Time Square • Steamboat Springs, Colorado
(303) 879-7070

Bobby's Hamburger Soup

½ cup margarine
½ cup diced onions
1 tsp. black pepper
½ cup white wine
¾ cup minced parsley
1 Tbsp. salt
1 ½ Tbsp. beef base (bouillon)
1 Tbsp. Worcestershire
1 tsp. garlic powder
15 oz. can crushed tomatoes
½ can tomato juice
1 ½ lbs. hamburger, cooked
3 cups water
3 cups cooked elbow macaroni or macaroni shells

In a large pot combine first 11 ingredients. Simmer for 10 minutes. Add remaining ingredients. Cook until heated through, about 15-25 minutes and serve. Serves 6-8.

Vista Verde Guest Ranch
31100 County Road 64 • Clark, Colorado
(303) 879-3858

Classic Chocolate Chip Cookies

2 ¼ cups flour
1 tsp. baking soda
1 cup butter or margarine, softened
¼ cup sugar
¾ cup brown sugar
1 tsp. vanilla
3 ½ oz. pkg. vanilla flavored instant pudding
2 eggs
12 oz. pkg. chocolate chips
1 cup chopped walnuts (opt.)

Combine flour and baking soda and set aside. Combine butter, sugars, vanilla and pudding mix and beat until smooth and creamy. Add eggs. Gradually add in flour mixture. Stir in chocolate chips and walnuts, if desired. Drop by heaping teaspoonfuls 2" apart onto an ungreased cookie sheet. Bake at 375° for 9-10 minutes or until browned. Yields 4 dozen chewy cookies.

Winona's Restaurant
617 Lincoln Avenue • Steamboat Springs, Colorado
(303) 879-2483

Bread Pudding with Whiskey Sauce

Pudding:
6 stale hoagie rolls
1 quart milk
3 eggs
1 ½ cups sugar
2 Tbsp. vanilla
1 cup raisins

Sauce:
8 Tbsp. butter
1 cup sugar
4 Tbsp. whiskey
1 egg

Crumble bread in bowl; pour milk over bread. Let stand for 1 hour. In another bowl, beat eggs, sugar and vanilla. Stir into bread mixture. Stir in raisins. Pour into greased baking dish. Bake 45-55 minutes or until golden brown. Let cool.

To prepare sauce, stir butter and sugar in top of double boiler until sugar is dissolved and mixture is very hot. Remove from heat. Beat in egg with whisk. Beat until sauce has cooled to room temperature. Add whiskey to taste. Pour sauce over pudding. Place on low rack of broiler. Cook until sauce bubbles and becomes thick. Serve hot with whipped cream. Serves 8.

Index

Cookbook Order Form

(If additional order forms are needed, please photocopy this page.)

Steamboat Entertains Cookbook
2155 Resort Drive • Suite 207
Steamboat Springs, CO 80487

*Thank you. Your purchase helps to support
competitive ski racing programs of the
Steamboat Springs Winter Sports Club.*

Name _____

Address _____

City _____ State _____ Zip _____

Mailing Label - Please Print
Steamboat Entertains Cookbook
2155 Resort Drive • Suite 207
Steamboat Springs, CO 80487

TO:

_____

_____

_____

_____

Quantity	Price	Tax 3% (CO residents only)	TOTAL
_____	$17.95	$.54 per book	$_____.___
		Add $1.50 handling per order	$_____.___
		Add $3.00 per book for shipping	$_____.___
		Canadian orders add $5.50 ea. shipping/handling	$_____.___
		Total Enclosed	$_____.___

Make checks payable to:
STEAMBOAT ENTERTAINS COOKBOOK
Please do not send cash. Sorry, no COD's.

Cookbook Order Form

(If additional order forms are needed, please photocopy this page.)

Steamboat Entertains Cookbook
2155 Resort Drive • Suite 207
Steamboat Springs, CO 80487

*Thank you. Your purchase helps to support
competitive ski racing programs of the
Steamboat Springs Winter Sports Club.*

Name _____

Address _____

City _____ State _____ Zip _____

Mailing Label - Please Print
Steamboat Entertains Cookbook
2155 Resort Drive • Suite 207
Steamboat Springs, CO 80487

TO:

_____

_____

_____

_____

Quantity	Price	Tax 3% (CO residents only)	TOTAL
_____	$17.95	$.54 per book	$_____.___
		Add $1.50 handling per order	$_____.___
		Add $3.00 per book for shipping	$_____.___
		Canadian orders add $5.50 ea. shipping/handling	$_____.___
		Total Enclosed	$_____.___

Make checks payable to:
STEAMBOAT ENTERTAINS COOKBOOK
Please do not send cash. Sorry, no COD's.

Save Money On Your Order ...

For a $1.00 discount on your copy of Steamboat Entertains, send us the name, address, and phone number of your favorite store that sells cookbooks. Only $1.00 discount per book, please.

Store _____

Manager _____

Phone ( ) _____

Address _____

City _____

State _____ Zip _____

For a $1.00 discount on your copy of Steamboat Entertains, send us the names and addresses of two friends who like cookbooks. Only $1.00 discount per book, please.

Name _____

Address _____

City _____

State _____ Zip _____

Name _____

Address _____

City _____

State _____ Zip _____

Save Money On Your Order ...

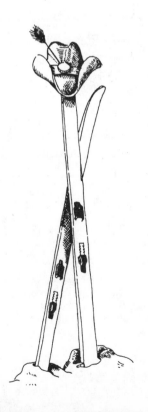

For a $1.00 discount on your copy of Steamboat Entertains, send us the name, address, and phone number of your favorite store that sells cookbooks. Only $1.00 discount per book, please.

Store _____

Manager _____

Phone ( ) _____

Address _____

City _____

State _____ Zip _____

For a $1.00 discount on your copy of Steamboat Entertains, send us the names and addresses of two friends who like cookbooks. Only $1.00 discount per book, please.

Name _____

Address _____

City _____

State _____ Zip _____

Name _____

Address _____

City _____

State _____ Zip _____